GENOCIDE BEFORE THE HOLOCAUST

GENOCIDE BEFORE THE HOLOCAUST

CATHIE CARMICHAEL

YALE UNIVERSITY PRESS
NEW HAVEN AND LONDON

For information about this and other Yale University Press publications, please contact:
U.S. Office: sales.press@yale.edu   www.yalebooks.com
Europe Office: sales @yaleup.co.uk   www.yaleup.co.uk

Set in Minion by IDSUK (DataConnection) Ltd.
Printed in Great Britain by TJ International, Padstow, Cornwall

Library of Congress Cataloging-in-Publication Data
Carmichael, Cathie.
Genocide before the Holocaust / Cathie Carmichael. p. cm.
Includes bibliographical references and index.
ISBN 978-0-300-12117-9 (cloth : alk. paper)
1. Genocide–Europe–History–19th century. 2. Genocide–Europe–History–20th century.
3. Europe–Ethnic relations. 4. Europe–Politics and government. 5. Europe–History–
1871–1918. 6. Europe–History–1918–1945. I. Title.
D395.C276 2009
304.6′63094–dc22
        2009004215

A catalogue record for this book is available from the British Library.
10 9 8 7 6 5 4 3 2 1

Contents

Figures

Acknowledgements

The work for this book began in 2002 when I was a visiting academic at Columbus State University in Georgia. There I had the opportunity to discuss ideas with sympathetic colleagues and students from the very beginning. I would like to thank Kimberley Stokes Pak, Mark Anthony, Neal McCrillis, Jenny Hale and Peter D'Adamo as well as Djordje Stefanović for keeping me company in the United States. Later in 2002 I arrived in a new post teaching European History at the University of East Anglia. Quite a few students took my Master's degree course and their lively input was always much appreciated – thanks to my research students Richard Mills, Dorota Piersa and Andy Willimott in particular. The excellent undergraduates whom this university attracts were also an important source of ideas and encouragement.

In January 2005 I joined the European Network of Genocide Scholars (now INOGS) at the historic first meeting in Berlin. Since then, colleagues from the network and with similar research interests have been supportive of my work. Special thanks go to Donald Bloxham, Mark Levene, Dirk Moses, Brendan Simms, Marko Hoare, Dan Stone, Jürgen Zimmerer and Dominik Schaller. I have also learnt a great deal from Tomislav Dulić, Roland Kostić, Christine Hussenstab, Paul Jackson, Sabrina Ramet and Marcel Stoetzler. In the United States, I have benefited from conversations with Benjamin Lieberman, Brian Glyn Williams and David Curp. Thanks to my 'Slovenian summer' friends Jaka Repič, the late Borut

Brumen, Božidar Jezernik, Rajko Muršič, Bojan Baskar, Peter Vodopivec, Alenka Bartulović, Boštjan Kravanja, Nancy Lindisfarne, Sebina Sivac, Irena Weber, André Gingrich, Henk Driessen and Thomas Schippers for their support. I had the opportunity to present a paper at a workshop on cosmopolitanism at the University of Sydney. Thanks to Glenda Sluga and Julia Horne as well as Patricia Clavin, Sunil Amrith and all the other participants for their comments.

Colleagues at the University of East Anglia have proved to be a great source of inspiration. Jim Casey's knowledge of Islamic and Jewish culture (and many other things beside) is astonishing. Nicholas Vincent suggested new books and found references for me. Edward Acton read an early version of the proposal and has cheered me on ever since. Matthias Neumann's disciplined work habits have set a standard for us all to follow. I have had many opportunities to discuss late Ottoman affairs with John Charmley. Laurence Cole has often discussed Central European history with me. Rob Liddiard, Tom Williamson and Carole Rawcliffe have helped maintain the liveliness of the School of History's research culture. Rowena Burgess and Sarah Burbidge provided excellent research support. Steve Cherry, Stephen Church and Larry Butler have all proved to be stalwart sources of support and good humour. Richard and Marion Wilson as well as Tony and Cathy Howe have also provided good-humoured support and occasional dinners! Stephen Wilson's knowledge of *fin de siècle* France was invaluable. Mark and Emma Knights provided terrific friendship and intelligent discussions. Tim Marshall reignited a love of literature in me after many years on the backburner. Richard Deswarte kept us all cheerful with his tireless optimism and intelligent good sense. Peter Waldron and Francis King have been helpful on all questions Russian. Fiona Nairn, Jane Bryan, Pauline Brown and Ian Farr kept me going through the Saturdays when we opened up the university.

The team at Yale University Press in London have been remarkably accommodating and supportive and I would especially like to thank Elizabeth Bourgoin, Loulou Brown, Rachael Lonsdale and the Senior Commissioning Editor for History, Heather McCallum, for her patience, warmth and good common sense!

My biggest debt of gratitude is to friends and family. Andy Wood has given me unconditional support in all my endeavours for almost two decades. Mike Bowker gave me his loyal support and distracted me in the best possible sense. Richard Maguire and Malcolm McLaughlin were always ready to discuss the 'big ideas' with me. Val, David, Peter, Clare and Olivia dragged me away from my desk to walk in Sheringham. Thanks also to Nebojša Čagorović, Anina Carkeek, Norah Carlin, Daniele Conversi, Cathy Derow, Kate Glass, Helen Graham, Stephanie Lawson, Mark McNay, Laura Riddeck, Mark Thompson, Sanja Thompson, Mary Trimble, Nina Vodopivec and Linda Wild for their encouragement. David, Una, John, Roz and Christina gave me more time, love and indulgence than I probably deserved.

CHAPTER 1

The Violent Demise of the Eastern European Empires

The modernization of Europe was accompanied by enormous suffering and dislocation. Lands far away taken as colonies were ruthlessly plundered for their resources and manpower. Rural populations were forced to leave behind generations of agricultural settlement and traditions to work in overcrowded, squalid and dangerous cities. In these cities illiterate peasants found themselves living beside quite different populations with strange and unfamiliar customs, religions and languages. As factories expanded exponentially and agricultural yields increased spectacularly, existing European states augmented their strengths by attacking and destroying weak neighbours and absorbing them into their own body politic. Furthermore, population growth allowed the new supersized states to take men out of the cities and off the land for civil and military service. The state reached its apogee in Europe at a time of increasing competition in a global economy. State coffers were enriched by taxes from trade and the cities of Europe became more and more cosmopolitan as trade grew.

At the same time modernization led to numerous systemic problems. Strikes, alienation, poor living standards coupled with utopian aspirations about creating a better future dominated the politics of the cities – often with spectacular results, such as the uprisings in Russia in 1905. Increasing rivalry between European states for overseas resources led to militarization and an unprecedented arms race. While this process took a few generations in western Europe, in the east of Europe and Eurasia the rapidity of modernization in the late nineteenth and early twentieth centuries was staggering. Industry began to develop only in the decades immediately before the First World War, as western European and other investors moved into all these regions in search of profits.

It was this process of expansion and then contraction in the eastern European empires that left religious and ethnic minorities vulnerable and led to the pursuit of politics which precipitated their eventual elimination. There is an appalling symmetry about the destruction of religious and ethnic minorities in areas that were once dominated by multiethnic empires. Jews in Imperial Russia (especially on the Black Sea littoral and the Ukraine), Pontic Greeks, Ottoman Assyrians and Armenians and Muslims in the Balkans were the primary victims of this process of modernization in eastern Europe. The expansion and subsequent fracture of these empires had profound consequences for their peoples, and actions designed to homogenize populations developed into genocides in several key cases, especially when rivalry between states developed into competition and war. This is a dramatic and poignant narrative, which involves the disappearance of entire civilizations: Muslims from the Crimea, Caucasus and Balkans; Christians from Anatolia and the Black Sea; and the destruction of European Jewry. During the First World War, Habsburg military actions in the Balkans and a rapid spread of disease also led to mass death amongst the Serbs.[1]

In western Europe, the powerful states of France, Britain and Spain were unified between the sixteenth and eighteenth centuries through expropriation, violence and forced homogenization. The West then experienced increased diversity from the nineteenth century onwards as a result of 'counter-flows to colonialism'[2] and the emancipation of religious minorities, which might ultimately touch upon the security of the state (as the Irish home rule and independence movement were to show in Britain). In central Europe, the states of Italy and Germany were built very rapidly in the nineteenth century and began a process of forced homogenization in the twentieth century. By then central Europe was also experiencing migration, but chiefly from the east of Europe. This eventually led to a crisis of citizenship, albeit one which was overwhelmingly engineered by those in power – often by aspiring nationalists 'alienated' from the large imperial structures.[3] Eastern Europe was a different story; it remained dominated by large dynastic states until the early twentieth century. The Habsburg monarchy had been ruled by the same dynasty since the late Middle Ages. The Ottoman Empire was ruled by a series of sultans for centuries until 1908; for the last fourteen years of its existence it was ruled as a constitutional monarchy. The Russian Empire had come into existence as the result of the expansion of Muscovy in the early modern period and had been ruled by the Romanovs since 1613. The dynastic principle of loyalty (as opposed to the national or ethnic principle) meant that the populations had remained diverse in ethnic and religious terms and the religious homogenization experienced by western Europeans was a phenomenon only known through political traditions and literature. That is not to say that these regions experienced complete harmony between different groups. Both the Ottoman and Russian Empires were effectively *Apartheid* states, which practised heavy forms of discrimination against minority religions. Both also gave privileges to Islam and Orthodoxy respectively. If not fully tolerant, both the Ottoman and Russian Empires had sometimes been *tolerable* for those minorities, particularly before 1870. After this time, the situation deteriorated rapidly.

The volatile nature of state boundaries in the Balkans, Anatolia, Ukraine and the Caucasus – rapid expansion, contraction and the formation of new states – had a profoundly negative impact on previously tolerated subjects. Many simply never made the transition from subjects to citizens. The practice of population elimination in Europe and Eurasia from the nineteenth through to the mid-twentieth century occurred because certain groups were deprived of, or never really granted, full citizenship rights. In many cases these groups had been dynastic subjects for hundreds of years prior to the modern epoch and their right to abode had been taken away. Ernest Gellner argued that both the Habsburg and Ottoman Empires 'were largely indifferent to the national principle . . . faith and dynasty were held to be natural, adequate and appropriate foundations of political order'.[4] In the course of the modern era, subject peoples denied citizenship were excluded sporadically and then more systematically, according to the efficiency of the regime in question, international opinion and whether or not their state was at war. Because large groups were involved, deportation alone could never have been used. Open borders to those who wanted to travel from the eastern parts of Europe to the United

States provided some escape mechanism, particularly for Jews in Imperial Russia until 1924. The Ottoman Empire provided a refuge for Caucasian and Balkan Muslims. Pontic and Anatolian Greeks could find refuge in the Ionian peninsula. Both Armenians in 1915 and Jews in 1941 found themselves trapped and in the hands of regimes which wanted to scapegoat them for their own military failures. In both cases it was possible to stir up extant prejudice at the level of popular culture. Religious belief, so close to the core, or essence, of existence in traditional societies, was an available resource for those who distrusted the loyalty of minorities in strategically vulnerable areas such as borders. Christian theology as practised encouraged the followers of Jesus to blame Jews for his death. *Apartheid* conditions in the Ottoman Empire for centuries had encouraged Muslims to despise non-Muslims or *giaours*. Orientalist or anti-Muslim sentiments grew during the expansion of the Russian Empire in the Caucasus and during the decline of the Ottomans in the Balkans.

The long disintegration of the Ottoman Empire, which had been one of the most durable political structures in history, was marked by violence and insecurity. The last years of the over-extended Romanov Empire before its collapse were also marred by violence. Both empires had failed to modernize sufficiently to withstand reformist forces within the state and the territorial revisions of neighbouring states. In addition to long-term instability, both states also experienced sporadic outbursts of extreme violence against minority religious communities – outbursts which have been variously described as pogroms or massacres. The Habsburg monarchy showed signs of increasing violence in the immediate years before its collapse, with the brutal treatment of its Balkan neighbours during the First World War. The early life of the independent Balkan states which replaced Ottoman authority was volatile and insecure for minorities, particularly for any 'remaining' Muslims. In Serbia two dynasties vied for power until 1903, and the last Obrenović king, Aleksandar I, was killed in such an atrocious manner in a *coup d'état* that many other countries were convinced that violence was a dominant political force in the south-east of Europe.[5] Maria Todorova has argued that in this context the ideologies which replaced the end of Ottoman hegemony were 'essentially defensive' and 'the direct result of problems of unconsolidated nation–states and identities in crisis'.[6]

In this book I argue that these pogroms or massacres of the nineteenth and early twentieth centuries represented a pre-genocidal phase before the clear genocidal crisis of 1912–23. The years between the First Balkan War of 1912 and the treaty of Lausanne of 1923 saw the wholesale destruction of minorities in the Balkans, Black Sea and Anatolia. The events of these years changed the religious map of Europe and the Near East irrevocably and left a general psychological trauma among witnesses and survivors, not only in the countries concerned but across the wider world. Angry diasporas filled European cities and polarized the political landscape still further, at a time when individuals had already taken sides on questions of inclusion and ethnicity in the nation (as demonstrated, for example, in the trial of Alfred Dreyfus in France) – a phenomenon described here as the 'ricochet effect'. Tragically, the idea that questions of nationality and citizenship could be solved by brutal population elimination inspired a generation of the most toxic extremists, or what I have referred to here as 'eliminationists'.[7] Of course, local variants were extremely important, but as a definable political group these shared a belief in the desirability of population homogenization and the removal of targeted minorities. Where they differed, of necessity, was on the precise questions of instrumentalization. Helmut Walser Smith believes that it was the 'wrong adjective for mainstream anti-Semitism in Imperial Germany, but is suggestive when coupled with what Imperial German writers called "lesser peoples", "natural races", or "primitive peoples". Here the elimination of peoples was possible to think and, in the colonial wars, that possibility nearly became a reality . . .'[8] Most eliminationists were opportunistic and craved the chances that chaos and dislocation provided. As Aviel Roshwald put it, 'the trappings of political sovereignty often come within the reach of nationalists suddenly and unexpectedly, under extraordinary and short-lived circumstances arising from a regional and global crisis rather than from strictly internal developments'.[9] In May 1942, a Serb nationalist and Četnik ideologist, Dragiša Vasić, recalled:

I remember very well the situation in which Europe found itself after the last war. The warring countries were so much involved with their own problems, that they so to speak could not follow what the others were doing and which measures they were taking inside their own borders. In the first year after the war, one could have annihilated a considerable amount of one's undesired population, while nobody would care. Consequently, if we are wise, this question of cleansing or resettling and exchanging of populations will not be that difficult.[10]

In 1937 another Serb nationalist, Vaso Čubrilović, articulated a similar point: 'all the Balkan states, since 1912, have solved or are on the point of solving their problems with national minorities through mass population transfers'. He continued: 'If Germany can re-settle tens of thousands of Jews, if Russia can move millions from one end of the continent to another, there will be no world war for the sake of a few hundred thousand re-settled Arnauts' (i.e. Albanians in Kosovo).[11]

The contestation over the nature of citizenship was one of the great battles fought in the nineteenth and twentieth centuries in Europe and Eurasia, and it led directly to genocide and population elimination both 'from below' and as state policy. We might define as 'nationalist' those who wanted to limit citizenship through largely legal means. Nationalists saw their ideal state in simple social and ethnic terms, often in terms of a return to a mythical past of ethnic, racial or religious homogeneity. They should be clearly distinguished from 'eliminationist nationalists', who advocated expulsion or elimination. The removal of ethnic minorities or of any distinct group created opportunities in terms of ownership of property and transfer of deeds, or taking over niches in trade. It also raised the spectre of social chaos, venality and violence, phenomena that these extremists came increasingly to value. One could argue, for example, that the Ittihads would have expelled the Armenians from the Ottoman lands in 1915 without any violence if they could have done so, although clearly they also valued the opportunity to spread criminal guilt and to bind people to them through association. The notion that expelling or even killing minority populations would be politically advantageous to a state had clear roots in pre-1918 Europe. Black Hundreds paramilitaries attacked Jews and other minorities in Russia, claiming for themselves the right to 'solve' the 'national question' by force. The Ittihad regime in the last days of the Ottoman Empire saw itself as the instigator of a final solution to the 'Armenian Question'. Talât

Paşa told the Habsburg ambassador: '*la question arménienne n'existe plus*.'[12] The American Ambassador Henry Morgenthau claimed that Talât said to him: 'I have accomplished more toward solving the Armenian problem in three months than Abdul Hamid accomplished in thirty years.'[13] It was perhaps with this in mind that the Croatian fascist Maks Luburić boasted of the Ustaša fascist government's achievements in October 1942: 'We have slaughtered here at Jasenovac [a death camp] more people than the Ottoman Empire was able to do during its occupation of Europe.'[14]

One of the central tenets of German eliminationism was the notion, entirely fabricated, that Jews had betrayed the fatherland during the war. Was this discourse borrowed from a Russian context via such individuals as Alfred Rosenberg, who promoted a German translation of the notorious *Protocols of the Elders of Zion* – a pamphlet which argued that Jews were conspiring against the old order, spreading discord and placing themselves in a position of world power? Did it develop as part of the German defence of the record of Talât Paşa after his assassination in 1921? Absolutely central to eliminationism was the notion of the moral use of force: that some pressing issue could only be solved in a more direct way than liberals could face. The Procurator of the Russian Holy Synod, Konstantin Pobedonostsev, a highly influential figure under the last two Romanov Tsars, was an individual prepared to articulate the use of violence against Imperial Russia's Jews. In the course of a conversation with Alexander Zederbaum, the editor of the Jewish journal *Hamelitz*, he advocated the expulsion, conversion or death of this population.[15] It was both the ideological and the practical centrality of the use of force that became the most toxic element in this form of extreme nationalism. Although it is true that all states, when pressed, will use force (as the British reluctantly did in 1939 against the threat from Germany), eliminationists believed that force came first and was the most successful way of solving problems.

Facing them was a range of 'pluralist' ideological opponents who came in many varieties: social democrats and other leftists, socialists, liberals, the religious, but above all 'humanist idealists', to adapt Emile Durkheim's phrase,[16] who saw citizenship in less exclusive terms and were concerned with human rights and the preservation of more 'cosmopolitan' identities to indicate those who took an active role in arguing for citizenship rights for religious or other minorities. For the humanists, society was changing with time, but some values such as notions of justice and human rights were seen as universal. For them, citizenship was not an exclusive category but rather belonged to those who enriched the collectivity, whether through culture, education or the economy. Very often patriots, they celebrated the diverse origins of peoples who made up the nation, much in the way that modern Americans recognize *e pluribus unum.* Their vision, influenced by the ideals of the French and American revolutions, was contingent. For them, the nation was a work in progress, not an 'ethnic totality'[17] formed by some version of what Alfred Rosenberg called a community of fate.[18] For the pluralists society was changing with time, but some values such as notions of justice and human rights were seen as a given.

It would be inaccurate to argue that everything in this epoch was defined by a Manichean struggle between pluralism (or humanism) and exclusive nationalism. Individuals are inconsistent, preferring one group, but not another. The plight of Muslims in the Balkans was rarely covered with much sympathy in the liberal press of Europe and the Americas in this period, even though their rights were often flagrantly denied.[19] This was in distinct contrast to the attitude towards the plight of Jews in Imperial Russia, or that of Ottoman Christians.

There was a direct link between the genocidal crisis of 1912–23 and later developments in terms of direct personal involvement. According to T. E. Lawrence in his *Seven Pillars of Wisdom,* which first appeared in 1935 as an account of the break-up of Ottoman authority in the Middle East, 'Fakhri Pasha, the courageous old butcher who had bloodily "purified" Zeitoun and Urfa of Armenians',[20] led the Turkish Twelfth Army Corps in Medina. Lawrence continued: 'Fakhri and his men had served together and had learned the arts of both the slow and fast kill upon the Armenians of the North. This bitter taste of the Turkish mode of war sent a shock across Arabia . . .'[21] Many other individuals were tainted by complicity in genocide. The impact of genocide went beyond those who were directly involved, but also led to a moral deterioration in aspects of European life just at a time when notions of human rights and their preservation were being codified by the League of Nations. When the British writer George Orwell commented in 1942 that 'Tamerlane and Genghis Khan seem credible figures now and Machiavelli seems a serious thinker, as they didn't in 1910',[22] he was acknowledging a shift in consciousness about violence that had occurred during his lifetime. Norman Naimark has rightly commented that the history of ethnically inspired violence is 'interconnected and imbedded in the European twentieth century'.[23]

Even when the notion of wiping a whole people out was repudiated in its entirety as morally repulsive, it was still something that could be *conceptualized*. Without wanting to deprive him of his rightful importance in history, Raphael Lemkin, the lawyer who first coined the word 'genocide' in 1944, was creating a neologism rather than simply forging a juridical concept. He had preoccupied himself with the issue of mass violence against religious and ethnic minorities since his youth.[24] However, even before the Second World War, the notion of genocide was not a remote but rather a living concept, even though the word had yet to be set down. The missionaries Rendel and Helen Harris said that after the attacks on Armenians in the 1890s, they saw children 'playing at massacre' in Malatia.[25] After his travels in the devastated lands of eastern Anatolia in 1930–1, graveyard to Turks, Armenians, Kurds and Russians during the First World War, Edmund Reitlinger concluded that '[t]hese were atrocities which far exceed any we know in history, both in their extent and their appalling cruelty'.[26] In his memoirs, Sergei Witte recalled 'how he once told Alexander III that if one admitted the impossibility of drowning all the Russian Jews in the Black Sea – as one must, according to Witte's obvious, though tacit assumption, then one must recognize their rights to live and create conditions which will enable them to carry on a human existence'.[27] While he was in Baku in 1905 reporting on the fighting between Tatars and Armenians, the Italian historian Luigi Villari recalled: '[o]ne prominent Englishman said to me that he would be glad to see the whole Armenian nation wiped out! He accused them of every conceivable crime, of having been the cause of the whole trouble, of being at the bottom of every revolutionary agitation, and even of having attempted his own life.'[28] In 1914, *The Times* discussed the resettlement policy that the Young Turk government had adopted towards Muslim refugees from the Balkan wars. Assessing the volatility of the situation, the correspondent noted: 'the match once applied to such inflammable stuff as Moslem Macedonian refugees, a conflagration would ensue that would not leave a single Christian alive in Asia Minor'.[29] Adolf Hitler's own rhetorical question: 'Who, after all, speaks today about the annihilation of the Armenians?',[30] designed to harden the spirit of his troops before the invasion of Poland, makes it clear that prior examples do serve as inspirations to those who initiate mass murder.

In his monograph *Terrible Fate* – a tour de force that examines the violent social change in Europe from the Caucasus through to the Balkans and Germany – Benjamin Lieberman has argued that '[t]he first wave of modern European ethnic cleansing emerged along the borders' of the Russian and Ottoman empires.[31] He is right to locate the problem in the systemic decline of the Ottoman state, especially at its periphery. As Mark Mazower has reminded us, it was 'the most successful empire of modern times, lasting from the fourteenth century to the twentieth'.[32] Its collapse and the incessant interference of other European powers in that process, which was known to contemporaries as the 'Eastern Question', had a profound impact on the world. The Ottoman Empire failed to reform for more than one hundred years before its eventual collapse. It lost a series of conflicts with the Russian Empire, which made dramatic gains at the Ottoman's expense in the Crimea and the Caucasus. Systemic instability led to the gradual loss of territory in the Balkans and to the formation of new independent states. The contraction of territory led to a process which has been called 'de-Ottomanization' by the Bosnian historian Safet Bandžović.[33] Ottoman decline had several distinct phases, both in the Balkans and in the Caucasus. Episodes of the killing of minority religious groups are inextricably linked to political crises and to the contraction of Ottoman power. When Serb rebels rose up against the Ottoman local rulers (or *Dahije*) in the first decade of the nineteenth century, their protest started out as a local struggle against injustice. Significantly, this was not just a rebellion against unjust rule, but soon became a repudiation of Ottoman-enforced Islam. Protesting against his imminent execution, Karadjordje ('Black George') Petrović led his men from the city of Orašac and by 1805 had taken control of the province.[34] The rebellion was accompanied by deliberately targeted acts of violence against those individuals who were associated with Ottoman authority, which meant, in effect, Muslims – who soon came to be seen as a group who represented unwelcome foreign authority, although they were Serbian speaking and native to the region. Serb rebels then began a process which eventually ended up with the removal of most of the Islamic architectural heritage in Belgrade, with only one Ottoman mosque now remaining. The Serbian capital now bears little resemblance to its Ottoman predecessor.[35] In January 1815, Tatar regiments often consisting of embittered individuals who had been brutalized fighting the Russians were sent to the Balkans to commit reprisals against the rebels, initiating an often commented upon cycle of violence and revenge.[36]

'De-Ottomanization' was nourished in neighbouring Montenegro, a state which owed its existence to the flight of many Orthodox people from Muslim rule into the barren mountains, which the authorities in Constantinople were never able to conquer.[37] The only part of the Balkans to have remained outside the Ottoman Empire, its ruling dynasty, the Petrovići, were Orthodox bishops. Petar II Petrović Njegoš wrote an epic, *Gorski Vijenac* (*The Mountain Wreath*), in 1847 and dedicated it to the Serb rebel leader Karadjordje Petrović. Vladika Danilo (1700–35), a predecessor of Njegoš, is described as deciding the destiny of local converts to Islam. Vojvoda Batrić replies that 'we will burn down Turkish homes so that no trace of the dwellings of our home-grown faithless devils could be known',[38] clearly drawing on a particular enmity towards Slav Muslims as representatives of the Ottomans, which seems to have been widespread.[39] Retrospectively, it is hard to disentangle the reality of Ottoman rule from a trope which depicted it as universally bad. Banditry had become endemic in the Balkans. Young men who resented the hard taxation and cultural humiliation imposed on Ottoman Christian vassals could join armed groups: the *četa* groups among the Slavs and the *Klephtai* among the Greeks. Bandit traditions clearly do come out of the historical experience of Balkan peasants.[40] Some believed that Marko Kraljević, an important figure in South Slav folklore, would one day return and drive the Turks back across the Bosporus.[41]

Other Balkan populations had similar grievances at this time, grievances inspired by the Serbs. In the 1820s, the Greeks rose up and drove out the Ottomans from the Peloponnese. The Greek fight for independence inspired a generation of Europeans to join the cause. A romantic identification with the liberation from oppression of the descendants of the heroes of the *Iliad* developed. Some years earlier, the French writer François-René Chateaubriand had told a Turk that he had come to the region to see the people, especially the 'Greeks who were dead' (that is, the fictional Greeks of legend rather than the pastoralists and fisherman of his own time).[42] George Gordon, Lord Byron, wrote some of his best poetry that was inspired by the Greeks, before his death on the campaign at Missolonghi. Local Muslims whether or not Greek speaking were subject to violence and atrocities, as they had been in Serbia. In Tripolitsa in October 1821, Muslim women and children were lead to a gap in the mountains and forcibly pushed down to their deaths.[43] Significantly, there was a backlash against Greeks living in the Black Sea and Constantinople.[44] Afterwards, the existence of Anatolian Christians became increasingly precarious, although this depended on political circumstances as well as on the inclinations of individual political leaders.

A series of events in the 1870s continued to weaken the Ottoman hold in the Balkans through reprisals against Muslims, who were deemed to represent the old regime. Bulgarians were subjected to paramilitary violence from Turkish irregulars during the uprising against Ottoman rule.[45] Again, the plight of the Christian subjects of the Ottomans inspired protest across Europe, including passionate interventions from William Gladstone and William Morris. On the subject of Bulgarian atrocities, the novelist Victor Hugo delivered a passionate speech in the *parlement* on 29 August 1876:

> The European governments will be astonished to hear . . . that at this moment, very close by, there, before our eyes they are killing off people, burning, plundering, torturing; fathers and mothers are being slaughtered, young boys and girls are being sold, and the infants, too young to be sold, are being cut into pieces . . . All the world is outraged . . . There are moments when man's conscience begins to speak out and commands to be listened to. Empires that massacre people must be liquidated. Let's put under restraint fanaticism and despotism.[46]

The atrocities committed against the Bulgarians turned the collapse of the Ottoman power into a moral issue and a clash of civilizations as far as the

European public was concerned.[47] In 1876, the historian Thomas Carlyle famously wrote to *The Times* calling for 'the immediate and summary expulsion of the Turk from Europe'.[48] The Ottoman authorities also started to commit revenge attacks against their independence-minded citizens. This process would continue at least until the formation of modern Turkey in 1923. These attacks inspired bloody revenge, initiating a spiral of grotesque violence. In 1877 in Bulgaria, fifty Turkish houses as well as the mosque and local authority buildings were burned down in Yeni Zagra.[49] Shops owned by Jews were also destroyed. In the same year, in Filibe in Bulgaria, mosques were turned into latrines.[50] At the time of the Bulgarian horrors, the Armenians, traditionally the most loyal religious group or 'millet', remained stoically 'impartial', although the American diplomat Eugene Schuyler thought that they believed the Bulgarians rather than the Turkish denials of atrocities – which was perhaps an ominous sign.[51] Insecurity at the periphery of the Ottoman Empire was to ricochet into their heartland of Anatolia.

Despite the ferocity of the Ottoman authorities, other parts of the Balkans began to fall under the control of local Christians. In 1903, the Ilinden Uprising (named after St Ilias Day, when it started) by Macedonian Slavs against Ottoman power was put down with brutality. Macedonia had remained one of the few areas in the Balkans apart from Albania that was still within the empire, but it was subject to agitation by pro-Bulgarian and Serbian activists. The rebellion soon spread to Thrace. Greeks and Muslims were slaughtered by Bulgarian gangs: 'Everywhere they are displaying rage and ferocity and the Mussulman inhabitants are greatly dismayed.'[52] In revenge for the uprising, pro-Ottoman Albanian irregulars burnt down some 150 villages around Bitola.[53] Eventually, the Macedonian crisis culminated in the Balkan Wars of 1912–13, which proved to be the last stand of the Ottoman Empire in the Balkans. The former Ottoman province of Kosovo, which had had a mixed population of Serbs and Albanians since the Middle Ages, was annexed by Serbia in 1912. Ottoman Macedonia became the focus of territorial ambitions of the neighbouring states of Serbia, Bulgaria, Albania and Greece.

Outbreaks of violence against Muslims as representatives of Ottoman power continued in Macedonia in 1912.[54] A commission of seven men – one each from Austria–Hungary, Germany and Great Britain, Russia and the United States and two from France – who travelled in the region in August and September 1913, returned to write an official report later that year in Paris.[55] The *Carnegie Endowment Inquiry*, as it was known, published its findings, which catalogued the atrocities of the conflict, including the second phase of fighting, in which the Balkan powers, having routed the Ottomans, then turned upon each other. The horrors of the Balkan Wars were vividly captured by the young revolutionary Leon Trotsky writing for the newspaper *Kievskaya Mysl,* who spoke to many of the Serb soldiers. Many of his informants spoke about a very direct kind of revenge committed against prisoners of war,[56] a phenomenon also recorded in depth in the Carnegie Report.[57]

If the contraction of Ottoman power in the Balkans was marred by widespread violence, both against 'Turks' (or Muslims) and against other minorities in the new Balkan states, then the expansion of Romanov power in the Caucasus was also extremely violent, and for much the same reasons. Russian expansion in the Caucasus, particularly in the late eighteenth and nineteenth centuries, signalled a profound change in the balance of power and threatened existing communities, many of them Muslim. The forced exodus of Circassians to the Ottoman Empire, who were joined by Muslim Abkhazians, Chechens, Laz, Ajars and Ubykhs in the 1860s, signalled what Brian Glyn Williams has called 'the end of Islam on the northern Black Sea littoral'.[58] The Crimean town of Feodosiya, now populated mostly by Russians, was described by Antole de Demidoff in the 1830s. He saw a Greek Orthodox church, an Armenian church, a mosque and synagogues, as well as hearing sailors from Genoa and Dubrovnik singing folk songs. He reminded his readers that this was the 'Constantinople of the Crimea'.[59] In Georgia in 1837, a French traveller noticed how few Muslim families remained, and that many had left for Turkey. Mosques had been ruined and abandoned.[60] According to Peter Holquist, the conquest of this region involved the deaths of an estimated 500,000 people between 1859 and 1879.[61] Other estimates put the number even higher. Before the nineteenth century there may have been as many as two million Circassians, including the Abkhaz, but only 217,000 were counted by the 1897 Imperial Census. The Circassians, a frontier people like the Cossacks, were often valued by the Russian state for their military prowess and formed some of the elite guards of the Romanov dynasty, being employed as 'tribal soldiers firmly under the control of the state'.[62] Nevertheless, despite some cultural assimilation, Stephen Shenfield has argued that:

[b]y 1864, the north-western Caucasus had been emptied of its indigenous population almost in entirety. About 120–150,000 Circassians were resettled in places elsewhere in the Empire set aside by the Russian government . . . [An estimated] . . . 500,000 were deported to Turkey, in addition, thirty thousand families – perhaps 200,000 people – had emigrated voluntarily in 1858, prior to the deportations. That still leaves well over one-half of the original population unaccounted for, to which must be added those who died at sea or on arrival. The number who died in the Circassian catastrophe of the 1860s could hardly, therefore, have been fewer than one million, and may well have been closer to one-and-a-half million.[63]

This vast population transfer, which is known as *hijra or muhajir* in Turkish (from the Arabic word *muhacir*, meaning 'refugee'), was also known as *makhadzhirstvo* in Russian. For years, travelling bards or *kedays* in the Ottoman lands sang about the sorrow and the panic that had accompanied the migrations.[64] The trauma of the Russian conquest led to religious radicalization, which probably contributed to the eventual fate of the Armenians and Greeks, as expulsion could subsequently be presented in terms of religious duty. Sometimes there was religious pressure put upon Muslims to leave the lands of the Tsar. One Russian landlord remembered that this was the case with the departure of Crimean Tatars in 1860: 'From the start of Spring, Turkish emissaries, mullahs of course, inundated the Crimea and preached among the mosques of all of its cities and villages on the necessity of Muslims to migrate under the banner of the Turkish sultan since, they added, this was declared in the Qur'an. The soil for this propaganda was incredibly fertile. The steppe Tatars were actually horribly oppressed; more than feudal slaves in times past.'[65] As Michael Khodarkovsky has argued, 'This contiguous, extended, and lasting frontier (in the Caucasus) with the world of Islam was perhaps the most distinct feature of Russia's colonial

experience, which set it apart from that of the European colonial powers . . .
The lines of future conflicts were clearly drawn.'[66]

The anger of the displaced Muslims of the Caucasus had a ricochet effect
in Anatolia: 'in exporting some half million starving, traumatized and sick
refugees across the Black Sea to a neighbouring empire not only entirely
lacking in the facilities or long term infrastructure to receive them, but itself
also reeling from its own structural inadequacies',[67] the result was destabilization. In a very real sense one of the ways in which the ricochet effect
worked was through individual and collective anger, passed on through oral
history and community memory. Once suffering has passed from one
generation to another, it becomes even harder to solve conflicts. 'Stories that
are passed down from generation to generation by word of mouth become
part of a group's lore. They often become distorted and exaggerated with
time and treated as received wisdom by group members.'[68] 'Violence . . .
convinced many refugees that they were fundamentally unlike the group
that had caused them to flee.'[69] After such violence, it became harder for
people to live with their former neighbours, a fact which actually increased,
reified and magnified traditional quasi-religious forms of prejudice.

One of the central tenets of Mediterranean ethnology has been the notion
of the existence of social structures that preserved 'honour' and 'shame'.[70]
Revenge as a practice was central to the preservation of this value. In his study
of the Balkans, Božidar Jezernik has looked at the evolution of head-hunting
in Montenegro, which was originally done to dishonour the body of the
slain and to reward the victor with some kind of trophy.[71] Any analysis of
atrocities needs to take into account the element of revenge and dishonour,
which remained crucial values in the southern part of Europe. During the
Russo-Turkish War of 1877–8, the British military attaché Colonel Lennox
noted of the Circassians that 'their actions are almost independent of all
authority and after pillaging, they quietly drive off cattle to their home,
which may be literally hundreds of miles away'.[72] In his memoirs of the
Russo-Turkish War, a Russian soldier recalled that Edirne was 'infested
with bashi-bazouks and Circassians . . . waiting for a propitious moment to
massacre and pillage'.[73]

The Ottomans had allowed religious differentiation through the millet
system, which meant that Christian and Jewish communities had survived

in this Muslim state for centuries. With the loss of the Balkans, the Ottoman Empire became more Islamic. 'Where the Tanzimat had stressed the equality of all subjects, Sultan Abdülhamid realigned . . . the state on a more Islamic basis.'[74] With the Young Turk revolution of 1908, Armenians, often thought of as the most loyal millet, were initially integrated as citizens, but mistrust of that community grew rather than subsided. After the Ottoman catastrophe in Europe of 1912 and the loss of huge amounts of territory and displacement of people, the tendency of Balkan refugees to commit violence against Christians only increased. In 1914, the *Scotsman* reported: '[t]he treatment of Greeks by the Turks is getting daily worse. The principal offenders are Turkish refugees from areas affected by the Balkan Wars.'[75] Many Muslim refugees settled in Anatolia joining the ranks of the disposed, such as the Circassians. Clearly someone had to pay for the humiliation of losing Macedonia. Armenians, with their active revolutionaries, the Dashnaks, and their co-religionists in Russia, were obviously a conspicuous scapegoat. One Turkish nationalist slogan proclaimed 'The Balkan dogs are trampling on Islam',[76] which was a clear call for *jihad*. In the 1890s during the so-called Hamidian massacres, several hundred thousand Armenians were killed. The First World War created an atmosphere of panic, which meant that the Armenians were frequently attacked – either in the army, in areas close to the Russian advance, or universally. Some Armenians went over to the Russians, fuelling further anger about their treachery. The Russian attack on Van lead by Armenian volunteers, including the notorious veteran fighter Andranik Ozanian, led to a Turkish backlash against the Armenian population in Van.[77] Ozanian had joined the Armenian revolutionary Dashnaks after the massacres in Samsun in 1894, and had a long career of guerilla activity against the Ottoman State in the Van region. When he described him in 1912, Leon Trotsky compared him to the vengeful Macedonian anti-Ottoman guerillas, 'akin in their psychology and methods of struggle'.[78]

Armenian Christians, already subject to widespread massacres in the 1890s and 1909, were effectively obliterated as a community in Anatolia during the First World War through the orders of the Ittihad government led by the triumvirate of Djemal, Enver and Talât Paşa. The elimination had several phases. Initially, Armenian soldiers were set upon in the army.

Deportations from different locations, initiated by government telegrams, involved the rounding up and killing of some Armenians on the spot. Many were also subjected to the wrath of their neighbours and put on the open road with no protection. Although they were nominally 'deported', most of the Armenians died of exposure, disease, starvation or violent attack, either from gendarmes or from bands of Kurds in the mountains. In the Black Sea port of Trebizond, the local community was taken out to sea and drowned. Many women were violated and murdered in front of their families. At least two-thirds of the 'deportees' did not survive this treatment; those few who did eked out a precarious existence in refugee camps in Syria or in Russian-controlled areas.

Within a few weeks, an entire community had effectively been destroyed for ever. About one million Armenians died, approximately half of the pre-war population, but their community was never reconstructed within Anatolia itself.[79] Other Christian groups, chiefly Greeks, Nestorians or Assyrians, were also systematically attacked in a general outbreak of vicious state-endorsed communal violence. Europeans had long been used to reports of mistreatment of eastern Christians. Cardinal Newman repeated a typical story of persecution and dislocation in his *Historical Sketches*: '[A] Protestant traveller tells us that he found the Nestorian Christians, who had survived the massacres of their race, living in holes and pits, their pastures and tillage land forfeited, their sheep and cattle driven away, their villages burned, and their ministers and people tortured.'[80] On 9 October 1915, *The Times* of London received a rather lurid account by the Reverend Gabriel Alexander of the slaughter of Assyrians on the Eastern Front, between the Ottoman and Russian empires:

> For three days I went out with the Cossacks to see the country. In all the plain of Urumiah I found the Mahomedan villages full of inhabitants, with much cattle and flocks, but all Syrian Christian villages heaps of ruins, without a single human being, only wild grass grown in their streets. Here and there one could see the bones of human beings left unburied, food for the fowl of heaven and dogs; one could not but feel deep enmity to see the large, fine and old churches burned up. Bibles were stained in the churches with the blood of virgins and sold for a farthing.[81]

Accounts of atrocities not only radicalized the identity of those under attack, but also ricocheted back into the heart of Europe. Rather than creating new cultures and heterogeneity, at this crucial moment the modernization of states led to the narrowing of old identities. The Circassians, who had been subjected to genocide by the Russian state, were frequently named the attackers of the Armenians. According to the Bryce Report presented to British parliamentarians,

[a]t Everek a bomb explosion was the signal for a terrible persecution of the Armenians. The German who narrates this adds that the Governor of Everek was a good man, and was therefore relieved of his duties and replaced by a Circassian of violent character. There had been numerous arrests and atrocities in this district. After that, the wholesale deportations were begun.[82]

Between the beginning of the 1890s and the 1920s, most Christian communities were effectively wiped out in the Near East, which meant that the Turkish Republic was founded without its historic minorities – something that Kemal Atatürk apparently later regretted.[83] The deportations and massacres had effectively used violence to solve what European diplomats had been calling 'the Armenian question' for decades. As Donald Bloxham has argued, the massacres 'enabled the Committee of Union and Progress or Ittihads to secure Anatolia as an ethnically "purified" core area for the development of the Turkish people'.[84]

The vacuum that the collapse of the Ottoman Empire created in the Caucasus led directly to the over-extension of tsarist power and ambition in that region. As the borders changed, peoples caught in the middle of territorial power struggles became suspect in terms of loyalty, which led to a greater number of 'revenge' attacks against them. The Romanov monarchy held on to power until 1917, but its own systemic instability manifested itself in increasing attacks on Jews throughout the Empire. As a state, it had seen huge expansion in the previous years, which coincided with more than three centuries of rule by the Romanov dynasty. As it pushed westwards into what had been the Commonwealth of Poland (1569–1791), it swallowed up the territories of what is now Belarus and most of Ukraine, as well Estonia,

Latvia, Lithuania and large parts of Poland. This was a multi-confessional state, with many different spoken languages and Orthodox, Muslim, Catholic and Uniate peoples as well as the largest Jewish community in the world. Yiddish-speaking central European Jews had moved to Poland and Ukraine because they were tolerated there. The reaction of the tsarist state was to create a 'Pale of Settlement' to contain Jewish habitation legally. With indus-trialization, Jews began to speak Russian and to move outside the Pale, and their traditional shtetls or villages. The Romanovs were notoriously inconsis-tent in their nationalities policies, but they introduced a range of humiliating legal restrictions on Jews and viciously repressed any signs of Polish and other patriotism. In the ember days of the monarchy, Vladimir Lenin infamously referred to the state as a 'prison of peoples', and many of his contemporaries agreed with him.[85]

Russian expansion had been achieved through military prowess but could only be maintained by force. This task became increasingly difficult for a dynasty which had so many subjects who had learnt to loathe them. Jews had been subject to violent attacks from very early times in eastern Europe. In the seventeenth century, Bogdan Khmelnitsky killed thousands of Jews in what is now Ukraine, as his Cossacks attacked all representatives of the Polish *szlachta* or government. Persecution again reached a crisis point after the 1870s, when Jewish life in the Russian Empire was blighted by attacks by nationalists and other gangs,[86] which led to a vast exodus to the Americas, Levant and western Europe. Pogroms, as they were known after 1871,[87] broke out with increasing regularity. The violence in Kishinev in Bessarabia at Easter in 1903 shocked the rest of the world and became a turning point in Jewish national consciousness, the tsarist state being viewed with increasing antipathy by the international community for failing to prevent these attacks.[88] In his autobiography, the American diplomat Andrew Dickson White recorded his opinions of the minister: 'The world stood amazed at the modern cruelties against the Jews at Kishineff, which he might have easily prevented, and nothing more cruel and short-sighted than his dealings with Finland have [sic] been known since Louis XIV revoked the édit of Nantes.'[89] Increasingly the state was weakened by its opponents. In 1904, the Russian Interior Minister Vyacheslav Konstantinovich von Plehve was put on trial *in absentia* by socialist revolutionaries and then assassinated for his role in the pogroms and 'crimes against the people'.[90] In the years between 1905 and 1914, assassination and terrorism became a central feature of Russian political life.

The situation deteriorated further after the Tsar's proclamation of the October Manifesto in 1905. Tsar Nicholas infamously blamed the Jews for the revolution and saw violence against them as a 'natural reaction of loyal citizens to the excesses of the left',[91] which effectively encouraged the 'anticipatory obedience'[92] of paramilitary nationalists. Luigi Villari reported on the violence at the time of the crisis of authority in 1905:

> I saw the effects of the abominable anti-Semitic outrages, and whole streets laid in ruins. From Rostoff onwards it was everywhere the same thing. The train was crowded with Jewish refugees, from Kiev and Odessa chiefly, and ghastly indeed were the tales they told of what Christians had done. One realized the state of mind which made the Saint Barthélemy possible.[93]

Jews and Muslims were effectively excluded from the parliamentary Duma franchise after 1907.[94] Even in the more liberal elections of 1905 and 1906, whole categories of subjects, including Jews, were only nominally represented. Influential ministers such as Sergei Witte envisaged their successful integration into the Russian polity, but the Romanov monarchy remained steadfastly anti-Semitic until 1917. When the Tsarina was killed in 1918, she owned only three books: The Bible, Leo Tolstoy's *War and Peace* and the *Protocols of the Elders of Zion*.[95] As an eye-witness to the fall of the Romanov monarchy in February and March 1917, Nikolaï Sukhanov recorded many scenes from the time. On 25 February, demonstrators outside the *Letopis* offices told him that they wanted 'bread, a negotiated peace with the Germans and equal rights for the Jews'.[96] For him, these demands encapsulated what the anti-Romanov revolution stood for.

The Black Sea region was particularly hit by the conflict. Odessa had been founded in the 1790s as a symbol of Russian expansion in the region. By the late nineteenth century it was a thriving port with a mixed population of Jews, Ukrainians, Russians, Pontic Greeks and Tatars. As Robert Weinberg has remarked, 'no other Russian city in 1905 experienced a pogrom comparable in its destruction and violence to the one unleashed against the Jews of

Odessa'.[97] There were also outbreaks of violence between other religious or ethnic groups living in cities, for instance, Armenians.[98] In 1905, the oil-rich city of Baku in Transcaucasia was also the location of fighting between Tatars and Armenians, as the bitter politics of the Ottoman Empire spilled back over the Russian border from whence it originated. Jews were often attacked by gangs organized by members of the Union of Russian People. Known as the 'Black Hundreds', these were responsible for inciting much of the violence amongst a large *Lumpenproletariat* that survived on poor rations and vodka, in the notorious 'flophouses' where the urban poor in the empire bedded down. Sophie Witte wrote in 1907: 'every member of the union is given a badge and a rubber stick. The badge gives them the strange right to arrest people and to search their houses, while the stick is given to them to beat the "revolutionaries", that is, the Jews.'[99] In 1913, the paramilitary 'double-headed eagles' threatened to lynch Mendel Beilis, who had been wrongly accused of ritual murder, if he were ever released from jail in Kiev.[100] The threat of violence that Jews and revolutionaries of all hues faced from armed paramilitaries only went away after the Bolshevik seizure of power. The Russian Empire in the Black Sea and Caucasus regions saw increasing violence against minority groups, particularly Jews and Muslims, in the years before its final collapse.

Like the Jews of imperial Russia, the Balkan Muslims and Ottoman Christians, Habsburg Serbs in Bosnia and across the border, in the kingdoms of Montenegro and Serbia, faced a huge pressure on their existence as a community between the 1870s and 1918. As the Habsburgs expanded into Bosnia–Hercegovina at Ottoman expense, they faced considerable opposition from the Serb Orthodox and Muslim populations, which amounted to over 80 per cent of the total. There were rebellions in 1878 and 1882, which led to brutal reprisals by the Austro-Hungarian troops.[101] Rebel Bosnians had also been killed after attempting to overthrow Ottoman power a few years earlier.[102] Eventually the Muslims were pacified by the authorities, but the Serbs remained implacably opposed to rule from either Vienna or Budapest (as authority was shared between the two capitals of the empire after the official annexation of the province in 1908). The actions of the Serb nationalist *Mlada Bosna* organization in assassinating the heir to the Habsburg monarchy in Sarajevo in 1914 had led to a huge international diplomatic crisis in which the Serbian people were perceived either as a 'plucky'[103] small nation standing up to tyranny or as the villains of the piece. The long-term antipathy that some Austrians, including Adolf Hitler, felt towards Serbs may have contributed to the second genocide against them by the Nazi-backed *Ustaša* in 1941–3, where it is estimated that between 16 and 17 per cent of Serbs perished.[104]

In his autobiography, Leon Trotsky recalled the anti-Serb sentiment in Vienna at the outbreak of the war. '[T]he inscription *"Alle Serben müssen sterben"* ["all Serbs must die"] appeared on the hoardings and the words became the cry of the street boys.'[105] This formula was subsequently replaced by the more extreme '*Serbien muss sterben*' ('Serbia must die').[106] The liberal politician Ivan Hribar, who was imprisoned between 1914 and 1917 for his opposition to the war, remembered the 'shameful' slogan '*Srbe na vrbe*' ('Hang Serbs on the willows') that appeared in the newspaper *Slovenec* on 27 July 1914,[107] a slogan which was revived and carried out by the Croatian fascist Mile Budak in the 1940s.[108] '[I]n Bosnia . . . a campaign of terror was . . . directed against the Serb population.' The Sarajevo newspaper *Narodna Obrana* compared the destruction in the city after anti-Serbian demonstrations to the Russian pogroms.[109] In Sarajevo, posters were put up, possibly written by the Catholic Bishop Josip Štadler and his assistant Ivan Šarić, which informed the people that there were 'subversive elements' (*prevratih elemenata*) amongst them who should be 'exterminated from their midst' (*iz svoje sredine istrijebe.*)[110] This phrase has a strong biblical resonance with extremely similar words used in the Croatian text of the Book of Maccabees, which demonstrates the infusion of traditional religious language in a modern situation of conflict between states and nations, as well as the role of the religious as agents of eliminationist ideas.

The treatment of Serbs by the Austrians differed markedly from the actions of Wilhelmine Germany in the areas they conquered from the Russian Empire, chiefly in the Baltics. '*Ober Ost* based its economic principles on the 1907 Hague land–war conventions, which made occupiers responsible for maintaining ordered circumstances, but in fact used them as a cover for a severe regime.'[111] Severe was not the same as murderous. Possibly one-quarter of the Serb population, or about 800,000 people[112] perished during the First World War from starvation, disease and war

injuries. Even more daunting is the estimate that 62.5 per cent of
Serb men between 15 and 55 died between 1914 and 1918.[113] Over 150,000
thousand died from typhus, including 30,000 Austrian prisoners of war.[114]
In its march to Corfu, the Serbian army lost over 70,000 men. Although in
strictly numerical terms this was not as significant as the catastrophe that
befell the Armenians *as a whole*, the action to destroy Serbia was part of the
same process of destroying the perceived enemy within and without. Mark
Levene has argued that '[p]lacing the Austrian assault on the Serbs, in 1915,
in the same referential frame as the genocidal killings committed by our
three other retreating empires, in a cognitive sense must represent a departure, at the very least'.[115] But perhaps it is not such a great departure if we
look at the geopolitical circumstances in the Habsburg regions, where south
Slavs lived. Like the Jews, Armenians and Greeks, whose communities strad-
dled international borders, the Serbs lived *within* the Habsburg Monarchy,
but especially in the sensitive border regions of Bosnia and Croatia as well as
in the neighbouring and hostile countries of Serbia and Montenegro. The
Habsburg authorities deported as many as 20,000 Serbs from Srijem and a
similar number from Slavonija, thus removing potentially disloyal individuals from sensitive areas near the border.[116] Mistreatment of Serbs from
within the Habsburg lands was also part of a 'divide-and-rule' strategy
designed to weaken pro-Yugoslav sentiment.[117]

Although it is true, as Levene points out, that Serbs as subjects of
the monarchy killed other Serbs, the level of demoralization amongst
Habsburg south Slavs was notorious.[118] Like many of the Russian 'peasants
in uniform', the south Slavs showed little enthusiasm for war, which made
the Balkan Front a really weak link in the empire's war effort. Mao Tse-
Tung's famous observation that, without the support of the 'ocean' or local
community, 'fish' or a revolutionary army would die,[119] is also true for
the Habsburg army's weak flank in Bosnia and Hercegovina, which was
severely hampered by disloyalty to its regime and sometimes by a clear
preference for Serbia. The Habsburg general Oskar Potiorek, who had
narrowly escaped assassination in Sarajevo in June 1914, complained about
the loyalty of the inhabitants of Višegrad: 'the population worked covertly
against our troops when they were withdrawing successfully and enemy
troops were infiltrating'.[120] The revolutionary Josip Broz Tito, later captured

on the Eastern Front, was initially arrested and imprisoned while he was in the Habsburg army for expressing opposition to the war.[121]

Having entered the war in part to destroy the power of Serbia, the Habsburg monarchy, like the Romanov, found itself totally overextended in 1914. Instability and desperation meant that Austrian military commanders began to attack and degrade Serbs living within the territory they had annexed and beyond the state boundaries. Their inability to win this war and considerable sympathy from other Slavs for the Serbs finally led to the collapse of one of the oldest dynasties in Europe, thus creating a power vacuum. Serb civilians were deliberately killed by General Sarkotić von Lovćen[122] in an attempt to rid them from the crown territories. This was a novel policy for a Habsburg general and clearly reversed Emperor Franz Josef's sentimental vision of a land of many peoples, united by his dynasty. So many brutal deaths deeply disturbed Habsburg citizens. In his diary the writer Fran Milčinski reported mass graves in Dürres (Drač) containing more than 500 people.[123] The Austrian also set up a brutal prison camp at Arad in which about 4,000 Serbs died during the war. Elsewhere witnesses described how Serb prisoners were starved to death in prison camps.[124] In 1915, the American journalist John Reed, who later became very well known for his vivid evocation of the Bolshevik revolution in *Ten Days that Shook the World* (1919), described his utmost horror at Habsburg troop atrocities. He was told by a Mr Samourovitch that 'the Austrians gathered together a hundred citizens of Prnjavor – they could not cram them all into the house, so they made the rest stand close and bound them to it with ropes – and then they set fire to the house, and shot those who tried to escape'.[125] This account is oddly reminiscent of the massacre in Urfa at Christmas in 1895, when 1,200 Armenians were burnt alive in the cathedral,[126] as well as of accounts from the Balkan wars just a couple of years earlier. On 27 July 1917, Serb internees taken from southern Banat to Temesvár (Timişoara) were 'waylaid by enraged mobs who pelted them with stones',[127] actions similar to those of angry Turks attacking Armenians when they were being 'deported'. Certainly the actions of the Austrians were outside the norms of war that were developing in international law at that time, although both the Russians and Ottomans had also committed atrocities against civilians by this stage in the war. Diplomatic apologists of the Arad camp in

The Hague were forced to lie about the concentration camp that had been set up there.[128] Serb suffering during the war was depicted in the *Vreme smrti* (*Time of Death*) by Dobrica Ćosić,[129] which, in the manner of most historical novels, intersperses the actions of fictional characters, chiefly the Katić family, with the real events of the war.[130] It remains one of the most popular works of fiction in contemporary Serbia.

Prior to the First World War, the position of minority religious groups in the Near East deteriorated rapidly. Casualty figures for the First World War were overwhelmingly high across Europe and particularly high on the Eastern Fronts in the Caucasus, Black Sea and Balkans. This should not, however, obscure the fact that many people were not killed as enemy combatants in a strict sense, but were murdered as potentially 'disloyal' citizens by their own states. Indeed, as defection rates amongst Armenians on the Russian Front, Muslims in the Caucasus and south Slavs in the Balkans indicate, many could not be relied on as 'loyal' citizens and those left behind paid severely for the actions of their brethren, being punished collectively. Not only did this phenomenon create a political precedent, but it also meant that thousands of the war's survivors had actively taken part in genocide. Many would spend the next thirty years attempting to revive the spirit of annihilation they had experienced in the war. Others would turn to denial, fatalism, obfuscation, regret or political activism. Adolf Hitler often alluded to these years of crisis in his subsequent writings. Significantly, a small number of individuals came to the conclusion that the fight for universal human rights was more important than ever. Fridtjof Nansen, the human rights activist and winner of the Nobel Prize for Peace, toured the war-torn zones of eastern Anatolia in the 1920s. Remarking on the Treaty of Sèvres, signed between the Allies and the Ottomans in 1920, he thought that it had been conceptualized in a way that implied that the Armenians 'had never existed'.[131] His horror at the conditions of Armenian refugees led him to prompt the League of Nations to help stateless peoples. It is a great paradox that the genocidal crisis occurred at a time when a desire for universal human rights had significantly increased. Unfortunately, the goodwill of activists could only save a small minority and the situation for minorities in the eastern part of Europe deteriorated further after 1918.

CHAPTER 2

The Fatal Quest for 'Loyal Citizens'

During the pre-genocidal period before the First World War, when minority communities were being dispersed, attacked and killed across the Balkans, Anatolia and the Black Sea, contemporaries searched for models to try and understand what had happened and to interpret events in some kind of historical context. The right to belong in Europe, as subject or citizen, was an old question which was often decided by force in different historical epochs or in what Heather Rae has called the 'pathological homogenisation' in state-building in Europe to create 'an ostensibly unified population'.[1] The range of techniques used to achieve this homogenization included legal exclusions, assimilatory practices such as forced conversions, as well as more violent strategies such as expulsion and death. Daniele Conversi has argued that the deliberate process of homogenization 'should be distinguished from the idea of homogeneity per se' and that the French verb *massifier* ('to form into a mass', but with the implication that force has been used) could usefully be adopted.[2]

In England, Jews were expelled in the Middle Ages, and there were riots against foreigners in London at the time of the Peasants' Revolt. After over a century of religious discord, Reformation and persecution of 'old believers' or recusants, Oliver Cromwell allowed Jews to settle in England, where they have prospered ever since. In the nineteenth century the British state emancipated their Catholic and Jewish subjects. With the expansion of the empire, the British also ruled over millions of Muslims whose loyalty to the monarch could usually be relied upon. In historical terms, this emancipation could only have occurred within a context of political security and confidence in identity and in the overwhelming hegemony of Westminster.

In 1492, under the terms of the Decree of the Alhambra, the 'Catholic monarchs' – *los Reyos Catolicos* – that is, Fernando and Isabel, expelled Jews from Spain. Determined to destroy centuries of cohabitation or *convivencia*, they accused Jews of influencing Christians; they were determined to fortify the Inquisition – the religious court of the Catholic church created in the 1480s – in order to prevent further heresy. Perhaps 200,000 people fled Spain at that time and many died en route to the Ottoman lands, as they were vulnerable to attack from bandits. In the same year the Catholic monarchs took Granada, which had a mixed population of Jews and Muslims: they deemed it potentially threatening to the state. Ten years later they banned Muslims from the state or forced them to convert to Catholicism. A ruthless religious persecution of the population which was in effect a form of forced homogenization was then carried out by the Inquisition for more than a century.[3]

In the late sixteenth century France was crippled by religious wars. Some Protestant Huguenot thinkers had even developed potentially treacherous ideas. Jean Bodin justified regicide in the name of 'divine inspiration'.[4] In 1572, the Huguenots of Paris were subjected to a horrific and probably staged pogrom, which spread to the provinces and is now generally known as the St Bartholomew's Day Massacre.[5] Shock at the extent of the violence resonated throughout contemporary Europe, leaving a permanent imprint on the collective imagination. It quickly came to signify the slaughter of unarmed civilians. For Protestants, it became a symbol of 'papal' tyranny.[6] Peace was then restored when the Huguenot leader Henri IV, prince of Navarre, converted to Catholicism, remarking that, for him, 'Paris was well worth a mass'.[7] He then introduced measures of toleration though the Edict of Nantes in 1598. The monarchy or, more particularly, Cardinal Richelieu in the 1620s continued to be highly suspicious of the Huguenots who seemed to represent a state within a state. Only when Louis XIV expelled the Huguenots, under the terms of the Edict of Fontainebleau in 1685, was the state homogenized by force. Their churches were destroyed across France, and as many as 500,000 people left France permanently. The impact was profoundly felt in some areas, such as the Midi, Dauphiné, Poitou and Saintonge.[8] The Huguenots, once expelled from France, could no longer threaten state power or act in concert with the Calvinists in Holland or Geneva. The Jews and Moors could longer challenge the rule of *los Reyos Catolicos* or even the church itself in Spain after 1492.

Mark Levene has argued that the slaughter of the rebels against the French Revolution in the region of la Vendée in 1794 was 'one of the most atrocious single massacres in French history'.[9] But, unlike the killings of earlier centuries, it did not enter the general consciousness as more distinct than the overall terror that accompanied the end of the Bourbon dynasty and the establishment of the Republic. Until the genocidal crisis of the break of the eastern European empires, the violence of St Bartholomew's Day continued to haunt the European mind, almost as a worst case scenario. It was the symbol both of atrocious tyranny and of a formally united but fatally divided community. The American diplomat Andrew Dickson White wrote his memoirs, published in 1905, about the last Romanov tsar. His views were rather prophetic: 'Pity to say it, the European sovereign to whom Nicholas II can be most fully compared is Charles IX of France, under the influence of his family and men and women courtiers and priests, authorizing the massacre of St Bartholomew. The punishment to be meted out to him and his house is sure.'[10] Describing 'indefinite passions of ecclesiatical wrong-headedness' and 'Mahometan fanaticism' in Bosnia in the 1870s, the British writer Arthur Evans spoke about a 'second St Bartholomew's for the Christian minority of Serajevo [*sic*]'.[11] Elsewhere the knowledge of the events on St Bartholomew's Day became a powerful symbol of the indictment of state responsibility. William Pember Reeves wrote in protest about the fate of the Christians of Smyrna in a pamphlet subtitled *Christiani ad Leones!*: 'Poincaré stated "that neither the Turks nor the Greeks can be charged with the conflagration of Smyrna: its origin is veiled in mystery!" Yes, such a mystery as the responsibility for the massacres of Saint Bartholomew . . .!'[12]

The massacre of the Huguenots remained a popular image in political commentary as well as in the arts and culture. In 1829, the popular French writer Prosper Mérimée published his *Chronique du règne de Charles IX*, a strikingly violent piece which reflected the growing taste in Europe for the violent and macabre in fiction, or what Theophil Spoerri called the 'driving urges' and 'the cruel, instinct-driven dramatic element. Primitive passion, the vendetta . . . sadism . . . belief in fatality'[13] which are present in Mérimée's work. In the book, the hero is a Huguenot, Bernard de Mergy, who has a liaison with a Catholic woman, manages to escape the massacre but eventually kills his own Catholic brother. *Les Huguenots*, an opera by Giacomo Meyerbeer, was first performed in Paris in 1836. The libretto was written by Eugène Scribe and Emile Deschamps, but the inspiration for the theme came from Prosper Mérimée.[14] David Llewelyn Wark Griffith's epic silent black and white film *Intolerance*, which came out in 1916, devotes about a third of the screen play to St Bartholomew's Day, with a dramatic lynching of Huguenots by a Parisian mob. The film follows the 'destruction of one Huguenot family, focusing on the daughter and her fiancé on the eve of their wedding'.[15] The massacre in Paris, which began on the evening before St Bartholomew's Feast, also came to symbolize the twilight and the dawn of a terrible new day on which the streets were strewn with bodies. On 29 June 1914, after the assassination of Archduke Franz Ferdinand, the German Consul felt he was witnessing a 'Bartholomew's Day' enacted against the local Serbs by enraged mobs who attacked them on the streets of Sarajevo.[16] The Israeli journal *Ha-aretz* expressed fear of a repetition of St Bartholomew's Day after the elections in Germany in March 1933.[17] Theodor Herzl noted in his diary the pessimism amongst Jews in Vienna in June 1895. After dining with friends, he remembered, '[t]he husband expects a new St Bartholomew's Night. The wife thinks that conditions could hardly be worse.'[18]

For some eliminationist writers, the Parisian massacres were a positive example to be copied. In Karadjordjević Yugoslavia, in the 1930s, one politician, Ivan Bernardić, tried to incite the Croats to 'organize a Bartholomew's Day against the authorities'.[19] The Polish poet Adam Mickiewicz believed that Vladika Njegoš had St Bartholomew's Day massacres in mind when he envisaged the 'cleansing of the land of Muslims' in the poem *Gorski Vijenac*, written in the 1840s.[20] If this is indeed true, it constitutes a direct textual link between the sixteenth and nineteenth centuries. It indicates just how much the practices of violence were part of a 'repertoire'.

One particular image of the crisis in Paris that haunted the European mind was the sound of the bell ringing from the tower of the church of

St Germain l'Auxerrois.[21] Writing thirty years later, Maximilien de Béthune recalled the sounding of the tocsin. Reaching the Collège de Bourgogne in the rue de Reims, the *collège* principal told him that all Huguenots were being killed indiscriminately along 'the model of the Sicilian Vespers[22] against the French'.[23] This refers to the slaughter of the French occupiers in Sicily in 1282. Prior to the storming of the Bastille in Paris in July 1789, the Jacobin Camille Desmoulins announced that the dismissal of Jacques Necker, the finance minister, was like the ringing of a St Bartholomew's bell for patriotic citizens, to alert them to the dangers of foreign invasion and that they should all now wear tricolor cockades to recognize their own side.[24]

Later Europeans were also haunted by the image of the crosses painted on the doors of Catholic homes in order to spare them the wrath of the mob. It remained a chilling image because it captured the particular characteristics of communities which had been so very mixed. Differentiation between those to be attacked and those to be spared became a commonplace form of behaviour *in extremis*; it recalls the marking of the entrance with the blood of a newly slaughtered lamb at Passover by the Israelites in the biblical book of Exodus. Crosses would not have been needed had it been totally clear who was who; as it is, they encapsulate the divisive nature of religious and ethnic violence, which cuts through communities. It is here that the layers of complicity that lead to this type of violence are laid bare and the actions of good men who do nothing, to paraphrase Edmund Burke, are exposed. During the Odessa pogrom of 1871, Christians had placed icons and crosses in their windows, to indicate that no Jews lived there.[25] During the First World War, after widespread attacks by the Russian military on Jewish homes and businesses on the Eastern Front, non-Jews put out visible icons, to spare themselves the fate of their Jewish neighbours.[26] In Neuss in Germany, in 1892, 'large blood red crosses' were painted on the doors of Jews.[27] American missionary Dorothea Chambers, who lived in Cilicia before the First World War, remembered the chalk marks on the doors of Greek and Turkish homes in Adana in 1909, which made her think of St Bartholomew's Day[28]. In Adana, in 1911, Armenian houses were marked with 'red crosses and the inscription "Death" '.[29] When Greek forces advanced on Aidin in 1919, Greeks and Armenians were ordered to place signs on their shops 'to prevent the molestation of non-Turks when the town was pillaged'.[30]

.

The terrible legacy of the Spanish Inquisition also continued to haunt the consciousness of Europeans. A landowner from the Crimea described the exodus of Muslim Tatars in the summer of 1860:

> I am not able to recall this event, which reminded me of the expulsion of the Moors from Spain, without sorrow. Cows, oxen and the best sheep were slaughtered mercilessly, salted in casks and left to dry in the sun; horses and camels that were not preserved were given or sold to close neighbors or *pomeshchiki* for the smallest sum of money . . . Finally they all departed and immediately there was a silence in the village where the day before hundreds of voices had been heard.[31]

Germans witnessing the treatment of Armenians in 1915 also drew a parallel with the 'persecutions of the Jews [*Judenverfolgung*] in Spain and Portugal'. 'Torque Mada [*sic*] and Arbuez are working very hard in the interior collecting the devout' [*Gläubiger*].[32]

The Inquisition also proved to be a popular theme in art and culture. Giuseppe Verdi's opera *Don Carlos*, based on Schiller's eponymous play of 1787 and performed in Paris in 1867 and in Vienna in 1933,[33] contains an *auto da fe* scene during which 'monks appear, dragging their victims to the stake and chanting grimly about the day of wrath'.[34] Tomás de Torquemada frequently appears in nineteenth-century literature as a stock villain.[35] When the novelist Victor Hugo wanted to protest about the violence against Jews in imperial Russia,[36] he chose to publish a play he had first written in 1869 on the life of Torquemada.[37] The Russians were also preoccupied with the Inquisition. A *Life of Torquemada* appeared in Zhizn' zamechatel'nykh liudei (Lives of remarkable people),[38] a series founded by the publisher Florentii Pavlenkov, in 1890. The Savoyard philosopher Joseph de Maistre wrote a curious short treatise in defence of the Spanish Inquisition in 1815 in the form of letters to a hypothetical Russian gentleman. In it, a hypothetical Spaniard argues that through repression of Jews, Muslims, crypto-Jews and heretics the Inquisition saved his country from the violent religious wars seen elsewhere in Europe.[39] In part, de Maistre wished to play devil's advocate by refuting Voltaire and other Enlightenment philosophers who had condemned the Inquisition for its intolerance.

The influence of his ideas in Russia is hard to quantify, but many were quick to compare actual Russian practices with those of the Inquisition. Russian anti-Semitic policy during the reign of Alexander III was formulated by Konstantin Pobedonostsev, who Maurice Paléologue, French ambassador at the time of the Revolution of 1917, had earlier dubbed the 'Russian Torquemada[40] – and this appellation was often used by contemporaries. His influence on Tsar Alexander III was said to resemble that of Torquemada on *los Reyos Catolicos*.[41] The Czech leader Tomaš Masaryk suggested that Pobedonostsev was Dostoevsky's model for the Grand Inquisitor in *Karamazov*.[42] He was also supposed to be the inspiration for Andrei Bely's arch-reactionary senator Apollon Apollonovich Ableukhov in his 1913 novel *Petersburg*.[43] Andrew Dickson White left an intriguing portrait of Pobedonostsev, with whom he became acquainted during his diplomatic career. This piece gives us an honest insight into the mind of a pre-First World War eliminationist from the perspective of an American:

> He seemed to have no harsh feelings against Israelites as such; but his conduct seemed based upon a theory which in various conversations he presented with much force; namely that Russia, having within its borders more Jews than exist in all the world besides and having suffered greatly from these as from an organization really incapable of assimilation within the body politic, must pursue a regressive policy toward them and isolate them in order to protect its rural population.[44]

Robert F. Byrnes believes that Konstantin Pobedonostsev had not read de Maistre and mostly stuck to French *belles lettres*.[45] But a wholesale policy of removing the Jewish people (whatever its inspiration) was not realized before 1914, despite persecution though active discrimination and pogroms and subsequent emigration.

Like the massacre of Huguenots in Paris, the 'model' of the Inquisition was used cynically, to produce some obfuscation in order to justify the atrocities involved in the collapse of the empires in Europe. As a way of deflecting from the present, the past was used by eliminationists to normalize morally dissonant behaviour. In his memories of the period when he was American ambassador in Constantinople, Henry Morgenthau recalled a conversation with a 'responsible Turkish politician' who claimed to have 'delved into the annals of the Spanish Inquisition' and adopted all the suggestions[46] found there.[47] 'Tolerance' was the 'trope that trumped all tropes'[48] used by German apologists of the atrocities committed against Armenians in the Ottoman Empire. In an extraordinary polemic directed against William Gladstone and others who criticized the Ottomans Porte, German Turkophile Hans Barth argued 'that the Empire of the Sultans was the only country [in Europe] without the funeral pyres and witchcraft trials. And the Jews, exiled, persecuted and despised in the Christian world, found sanctuary with the "barbaric" Turks.'[49] In a rhetorical volte-face, Barth called the defender of the Armenians, Pastor Johannes Lepsius, nothing more than a 'pocket-sized Torquemada'.[50] The French orientalist Pierre Loti used the past as a means of diverting moral responsibility away from the Ittihad regime during the First World War. 'We French have had the Saint Bartholomew massacre, for which one could search in vain for a semblance of an excuse . . . and who knows, *hélas*, what tomorrow will reserve for us yet . . . Spain . . . expelled the Jews who thereafter took refuge in Turkey, where they were not done any harm.'[51]

In the 1930s, Max Zweig wrote a play, *Die Marranen*, in which he drew a parallel between the Inquisition and events in the 1930s in Germany, especially the Nuremberg Laws, which excluded Jews from citizenship.[52] He was not alone in drawing such parallels; the militant humanist writer Heinrich Mann also struggled to find similar historical parallels for Nazi brutality.[53] The historian Cecil Roth wrote in a review of a work of Spanish history by the Catholic historian William Thomas Walsh: 'What cannot . . . be passed over in silence is his resuscitation of and implicit belief in those revolting allegations which cost the Jews such untold misery in the Middle Ages and which raise their head, sometimes with ghastly results in the less civilised portions of the world even at the present time.'[54] In his writings on totalitarianism, Carlton Hayes wrote: 'State orthodoxy must be maintained more violently than church orthodoxy ever was, and a Henry VIII or a Torquemada of the sixteenth century would blush at the mass purges of our contemporary totalitarians, Hitler and Stalin.'[55]

One of the most chilling expositions of the Spanish Inquisition in European fiction comes from the French writer Villiers de l'Isle-Adam in his collection *Nouveaux contes cruels*.[56] In the story *La Torture par l'espérance*, the Inquisitor is Pedro Arbuez d'Epila[57] and the story is set in Zaragoza prison. A prisoner escapes through what he thinks is an open door, only to fall into the hands of the Inquisitor. The form of torture that he has to endure is hope itself. That hope is cruelly and sadistically dashed by the Inquisitor, who is a kind of archetypal villain. After the Second World War and terrible fratricidal violence in his native region, the Istrian composer Luigi Dallapiccola produced the opera *Il prigioniero* (*The Prisoner*) – an opera based on Villiers de l'Isle-Adam's short story which Anthony Arblaster has described as 'a direct and manifestly deeply held response to the experience of fascism'.[58] Each generation has reinterpreted the Spanish experience, using it as a trope to describe the use of force over reason as well as the horrific treatment of ethnic minorities by arbitrary states.

As the Ottoman and Russian empires expanded over the centuries, their lands included many different peoples whose diverse religions, languages, business practices and cultures were accommodated with varying levels of success. What Franz Werfel was doing in the initial chapters of his novel *Die vierzig Tage des Musa Dagh*, which was first published in 1933 and conceived after his encounters with Armenian refugees in Damascus in 1929, was to portray the diversity of the Ottoman world that had been lost in the First World War.[59] One of the problems that any individual or government might face if they attempted to homogenize (*massifier*) these lands was that identities usually defied very simple classification.

The boundaries between Islam, Judaism and Christianity are usually deemed to be rather profound and impermeable.[60] Henry Abramson has argued, however, that there was frequent contact between Ukrainians and Jews, particularly women, before the civil war period.[61] And, although '[b]ankers, peddlars, yeshiva students and famous rabbis traded far and wide, well beyond the edges of the peasant imagination',[62] we cannot assume that inter-religious relations were uniformly distant or bad. In the eastern empires of Europe these borders were not always as securely fixed as religious authorities would have liked. Communities often assimilated the customs of their religious neighbours in forms of cultural *convivencia*. On Cyprus, during the Ottoman period, those who were seen to have only nominally converted to Islam (and thus retained their 'essential' Christian characteristics) were

contemptuously known as 'Lardokophtēdes' or 'lard cutters'.[63] Levels of acculturation to elements of Ottoman culture were marked amongst both
Muslims and non-Muslims. Occasionally, Serbs respected the aversion that
their neighbours had to pork by refraining from keeping pigs at all, or at least
by not eating pork in public.[64] In parts of Serbian Sandžak in the early
twentieth century, 'Serbs ... did not keep pigs, nor was there pork in any
of the butchers' shops. During Ramadan, Serbs in the čaršija [market place]
did not eat in public out of respect for Muslims fasting at this period.'[65]
Further south in Albania, in the 1920s, Rose Wilder Lane observed that 'the
Muslim prohibition on eating pork was carefully respected by Christian
neighbours'.[66] Use of certain spices in cooking; styles of food presentation
(such as with yoghurt, dried fruits and kebabs); rituals surrounding the
drinking of coffee,[67] the recreational use of tobacco; as well as the tunes of
folk music have all been linked to the Ottoman legacy. Jovan Cvijić even
argued that the Balkan belief in sudbina or fate was linked to oriental beliefs
about ksmet.[68] It is probable that, when south Slavs say ako bog da ('if
God wills it'), they are translating the Arabic inshallah.[69] In Bosnia, the two
expressions were sometimes uttered simultaneously.[70]

At the beginning of the nineteenth century, the Balkans were covered with
Muslim settlements. Most of these Muslims were not descended from the
Ottomans, but from local converts to Islam. As the poet Vuk Karadžić put it,
'[Muslims] think that they are true Turks and call themselves that, despite
the fact that less than one in a hundred of them knows Turkish.'[71] In these
circumstances, they had adopted Islamic customs, but also retained local
ones. On entering houses, both Christians and Muslims took their shoes
off.[72] Christians sometimes wore similar clothes to those of the Muslims. An
officer in the Bulgarian army reported in 1912 that 'we entered Lozengrad
without a fight ... everywhere on the doors of Christians' homes a cross had
been drawn, sometimes in a very vivid paint that leapt to the eye. It was
obvious that they were still very frightened. Many Christians had previously
worn the fez, but now they threw their fezes away, and as they had no caps,
they went around bareheaded.'[73] In Anatolia, the Armenian father of Veron
Dumehjian escaped detection as a Christian in Adana in 1915 by wearing a
fez.[74] Other survivors of the Armenian genocide also escaped by dressing as
Turks or Kurds,[75] which suggests that ethnic boundaries were relatively easy

to traverse on a basic level, particularly when there was no linguistic boundary to cross. In the Russian empire, Jews were leaving the shtetl or traditional village, taking professional positions, moving outside the Pale of Settlement and speaking Russian in the immediate years before the Revolution, which is clearly a paradoxical situation, given the increase in violence against Jewish people during this era. In the Ottoman Empire, likewise, Armenians were experiencing greater social integration in state institutions just prior to the genocide.

Despite similarities, differences in practices and culture meant that a religious divide could quickly and easily become more fixed and permanent, particularly on economic grounds and owing to endogamous marriage patterns. If there were apparently different standards of living between groups this might arouse a kind of primitive venality, which would help to explain much of the violence at a popular level. Edwin Pears believed that 'traditional feeling' by the Muslims of the Ottoman Empire gave them the right to plunder,[76] although we should also remember that '[i]n some settings, "tradition" is effectively used to justify, excuse and direct violence'.[77] Nikita Khrushchev suggested that enrichment was one motive for the violence against Jews which he witnessed as a child in his home town of Yuzovka. He described the Ukrainian villagers and the Russian industrial workers as desperately poor, but nevertheless emphasized the wanton rather than simply venal nature of the destruction in the pogrom he witnessed. He remembered that '[t]he workers . . . were bragging the next day about how many boots and other trophies they picked up during looting . . . I saw clock repair shops that had been broken into and feathers were flying across the street where the looters were . . . shaking the feathers out of the windows of the Jewish houses.'[78] Even the poorest Jews in Kishinev had feather beds.[79] The feathers flying through the air as a symbol of violence and chaos is powerfully evoked in the poem 'be-'Ir La-Haregah' ('City of Slaughter') by Hayyim Nahman Bialik.[80] Accounts of Kristallnacht in Germany in 1938 also recall wanton but fervent attacks on featherbeds as if this had become archetypal behaviour during pogroms by this time,[81] although it might also be the case that looters thought money was stored there.

Comparisons have been made between the situation of the Jews in the Russian empire and the Christians of the Ottoman Empire before 1914. For

Vahakn Dadrian, the Jews and Armenians were persecuted on a number of different levels. Constant attacks without the possibility of retribution 'compounded their condition of vulnerability'.[82] As both were also barred from certain occupations in *Apartheid* styles of regulation, they achieved in other spheres, which made them vulnerable to their neighbours' envy. This also meant that they were often a distinct element in the national and international economy as traders, 'middlemen'[83] and entrepreneurs. In addition, before the First World War neither group had a 'parent state' to represent their interests.[84] Dadrian has also argued that the position of the Armenians was made yet more vulnerable by legal discrimination and 'the fixed and intractable prescriptions of Islamic canon law as expressed mostly in the Koran and codified in the Sheriat . . . In that system the non-Muslims [were] relegated to a permanently fixed inferior status.'[85] One could also argue that for the Jews in the Russian empire, whose legal status was restricted by the Pale of Settlement, there was a conflation between religious and legal discrimination, which became 'racial' in the late nineteenth century. The situation of the Muslims in the Balkans, in the newly formed national states, was also clearly parallel in terms of their vulnerability.[86]

In the Russian empire, *Apartheid*-style laws prevented Jews in particular from taking part in certain professions. They were given military fines in lieu of service and could have their property confiscated arbitrarily.[87] They could also be told to leave towns and villages at the whim of local officials, a fate vividly conveyed in Sholem Aleichem's short story *Tevye's Daughters*,[88] upon which the famous Broadway musical *Fiddler on the Roof* was based. Barred from certain occupations, Jews filled gaps in the market in the Ukraine and Black Sea regions. Their oppression made them more family-oriented, and the family frequently functioned as an economic unit of production. In the 1970s the French anthropologist Maurice Godelier challenged existing Marxist theory, arguing that, rather than being part of the superstructure of society, religion should be considered as part of the base or infrastructure, a category usually reserved for the material rather than strictly cultural aspects of life.[89] If we take this point of view as regards Pontic Greeks, Armenians and Jews, and even possibly Bosnian Muslims, we see how practices that Yuri Slezkine has called 'corporate kinship'[90] might become important. Religious identity, perpetrated by all kinds of discrimination, in effect meant that Armenians, Jews, Greeks and Balkan Muslims not only became communities of faith, but were also bound together by necessity. Similarly, other religious or linguistic identities became essentially class identities. Ukrainians remained largely peasants. In the Black Sea and Ukraine, Russians were frequently newcomers and industrial workers. In Anatolia, Kurds were frequently pastoralists and Turks farmers. Armenians frequently worked in cities, lent money and traded in carpets. Pontic Greeks were involved in shipping and trade. In the Balkans, Orthodox peoples (Serbs, Bulgarians, Greeks) were frequently pastoralists or farmers, while Muslims lived in the cities.

In Imperial Russia, Jews were barred from many spheres of public life. The May Laws of 1882, which were intended to be temporary regulations, lasted in some cases until 1917. They reinforced the 'exasperating regulations'[91] of the Pale of Settlement, which had confined Jewish movement within the empire since the eighteenth century, and they contributed indirectly to an atmosphere of increased intolerance and violence which then led to the exodus of more than two million Jews in the late imperial period. After 1880, Jews were banned from settling in the Don territory of the Ukraine. During the First World War, Jews were banned even from temporary settlement in Cossack territories.[92] In 1893, Jews were banned from using non-birth names, which did not, of course, stop Leon Trotsky (Lev Davidovich Bronstein) and Julius Martov (Yuli Osipovich Zederbaum) from adopting their well-known *noms de guerre*. Jews had been disenfranchised in local elections in Odessa after 1892, 'when the city government deprived Jews of the right to elect representatives to the city council and limited Jewish representation to six appointed members of the sixty-man council'.[93] Jews (and many other categories of individuals, including Muslims) were effectively excluded from the Duma franchise after 1907, 'rolling back' the limited gains of 1905.[94] In his 1904 study of tsarist Russia, Carl Joubert observed:

> Jews are not allowed to bathe in rivers and lakes, nor are they permitted to go to seaside watering places, sanatoriums or mineral wells. They must reside in the Jewish quarters of the towns, and are not allowed to go to the more salubrious suburbs to live, even if it is necessary for their health.

If a Jew wishes to consult a medical practitioner who lives in some other town, he cannot do so unless he obtains permission from the police.[95]

In the Ottoman Empire a kind of religious *Apartheid* was maintained through the millet system, which divided Ottoman subjects by religion (and perpetuated the power of the clergy). Their status as *dhimmis* 'designated them as members of juridically inferior, but protected, communities'.[96] Non-Muslims were barred from certain (minor) activities such as the wearing of the colour green.[97] The 'hegemonic' practices of the Ottomans in the Balkans and Anatolia were also accompanied by individual and collective cruelties, for instance, forced conversion to Islam, the Janissary system and discrimination in taxation.[98] There was a brief period between the Young Turk Revolution of 1908 and the dissolution of parliament[99] when non-Turks could have been integrated more successfully into the state, but, as in Russia, this opportunity was lost. In the Balkans, even after independence, the local population often maintained a negative memory of the Ottoman period,[100] which the Bulgarian historian Maria Todorova has argued was 'based on more than mere emotional and political conjecture'.[101]

Christians in the Ottoman Empire dominated trade despite their oppression. Greeks and Cilician Armenians developed the business of Smyrna beyond the remit of the empire and travelled to distant places. In Constantinople and elsewhere in Anatolia, elite Armenian families, known as the *amira* class, often lent money and even manufactured the coinage.[102] In the Balkans, Muslims traded and dominated urban spaces before their expulsion. Armenians, Pontic Greeks, Balkan Muslims and Jews of the Russian Pale thus often became, economically as well as culturally, distinctive groups. Because they also had links with wider communities outside the boundaries of their respective states, they were often at the forefront of globalization in the late nineteenth and early twentieth centuries. Furthermore, their religious identity was frequently, in effect, transnational. Greeks could trade with fellow Greeks in other regions and had a wide network of contacts across the Levant. Jews could also move beyond state boundaries with more ease because of their contacts, as could Armenians. This contrasts with the more strongly national identities of Orthodox peoples and Muslims. Destroying religious minorities with a transnational identity therefore had an international dimension. When Tâlât Paşa announced to Henry Morgenthau that his government was now the beneficiary of the insurance policies of dead Armenians, his point was simple. By destroying this religious minority, which had clear contacts with the North American economy, he had increased the potential of the state for autarchy.[103] The origins of genocide in Europe revolved around the question of who could be a citizen. Although neither Vladimir Lenin nor Mustafa Kemal were primary agents in the genocides described here, both Soviet Russia and Atatürk's Turkey moved away from international trade towards a high degree of autarchy and were considerably damaged in the short term. Removing minorities thus created an opportunity for greater economic as well as political autarchy, but damaged the infrastructures of all the regions beyond repair.

If imperial Russian Jews, Ottoman Christians and Balkan Muslims were not just religious minorities, they also formed part of international communities, with contacts with co-religionists in far-flung places outside the states in which they resided. As the regimes changed in Russia, Turkey and the Balkans, so notions about citizenship changed. This did not just happen in these regions, but was a contestation about the nature of modernity itself. In an increasingly globalized system – which would be a fair way to describe the long nineteenth century up to the First World War – a person could be a citizen of one state and have interests in another simultaneously. Loyalty in these circumstances is contigent, elective and up for questioning in a much more existential fashion than it was for the medieval subject, who might have swapped allegiences. When states changed religious affiliation in early modern western Europe, doubt about sides and questions of loyalty to the state were precipitated. Although by 1685 the 'threat' from Huguenots was inconsiderable, Louis XIV clearly did not want to have a fifth column in France. It is in this respect that the analogy between the French and the Spanish experience on the one hand and what happened in the eastern empires of Europe on the other is important, especially if we see the Huguenots, Spanish Jews or Moors as a 'class' in the sense that Godelier intended.

The chief victims of this crisis were religious minorities, who had often been subjected to discriminatory legislation before the modern era. They had also become 'visible embodiments of violence and abuse'.[104] Deprived of their basic security, beaten by centuries of oppression and despised as victims, they had their group identities consolidated by distinctive economic activities. These brought a measure of security and reinforced religion as a kind of ethnic divide, which, according to Maurice Godelier, had a class character. By the nineteenth century, laws were failing to protect the elementary safety of the subjects of the Ottoman and Russian empires. Many contemporary descriptions of both religious minorities suggest that they lived with what Linda Green has called, in another context, 'fear as a way of life'.[105] In Bialik's poem about the aftermath of the Kishinev slaughter, 'it will even seem to you that everyone is scared'.[106] Summarizing a report in a German newspaper about the exodus of Jews from tsarist Russia after the pogroms, the chief rabbi of the British empire, Hermann Adler, wrote:

> A correspondent of the *Berliner Tageblatt*, giving an account of the scenes that are daily to be witnessed at the Charlottenburg railway station, commences with the quotation: 'if you have tears, prepare to shed them now'. And he proceeds to describe the utter wretchedness which the arrival of each train discloses. Haggard men and women are there so weak that they are hardly able to walk, children in scanty raiment, and whole families that have lived in comparative affluence driven at a day's notice from their homesteads and the land which, with all its faults, they still loved.[107]

In a notorious anti-Semitic text written in the 1890s, the Catholic priest Iustinus Pranaïtis, later to be called as an expert witness in the Mendel Beilis case, argued that Jews bowed before Christians not because of civility or deference, but because of religious practice.[108] The term 'cringing' was frequently used both for eastern Christians and for Jews. Sometimes it was used as a generalization about the East and its inhabitants *tout court*. The scholar and translator of the *Arabian Nights*, Richard Burton, described Dragomans he had encountered as 'completely oriental ... [t]he most timid and cringing of men'.[109] 'The beaten Oriental is abject',[110] the British diplomat Valentine Chirol opined in *The Times* in 1923. British travellers Georgina Mackenzie and Adelina Paulina Irby, who visited the Ottoman Balkans in the 1860s, found that '[t]he hereditary insolence of the Mussulman Bosnian is met by the hereditary cringing of the rayah' [Christian peasantry].[111] Describing his experience in Constantinople some years later, William Goodell thought that:

> four centuries of torture, of oppression, and of suspense have stamped its [sic] impress upon an entire community. It is true that the last twenty years have witnessed great improvements in the condition of the native Christians, but constant fear, constant agony, constant humiliation, have so crushed out every trace of manhood, that they are still a cringing, fawning, and abject race.[112]

J. Theodore Bent noted that '[t]he character of the modern Greek has been formed by centuries of ignominious cringing'.[113] He was probably drawing upon Byron's poem *Childe Harold's Pilgrimage* – especially the second canto, which depicts the Greece as the 'sad relic of departed worth' and 'long accustomed' to 'bondage'.[114]

Margaret Lavinia Anderson has argued that this discourse 'essentialized' the Christian in the Near East, who was thus 'the born victim, whose cries for help we have become tired of hearing'.[115] This description of 'cringing' was most frequently reserved for Armenians[116] and Jews, both in imperial Russia and in the Ottoman Empire. On his travels in the Levant, the British novelist William Makepeace Thackeray depicted an Armenian trader in Rhodes 'cringing and wheedling'.[117] In 1910, Captain Townsend remarked: 'If a European were to strike an impertinent Moslem he would be paid back in kind, but an Armenian would become cringing; his spirit is broken by centuries of oppression.'[118] Jean Victor Bates wrote about what he called 'poor, cringing, unmanly Armenians' even after the terrible tragedy that befell the community in 1915, perhaps representing a peculiar orientalist version of the tendency to blame victims for whatever happens to them.[119] Years after the genocide of 1915, Bosworth Goldman noticed that the Soviet Armenians were 'timid', as if fear had become an almost permanent feature in their lives.[120]

The notion of timidity, or fearfulness, also became a common anti-Semitic trope. In Ivan Turgenev's short story 'The Jew', written in 1846, one encounters 'the ordinary timorous alarm peculiar to the Jewish nation'.[121] Even Villiers de L'Isle-Adam's otherwise sympathetic picture in *La Torture par l'espérance* contains a 'trembling rabbi' (*rabbin frémissant*).[122] The French orientalist Pierre Loti described Jews in Constantinople as 'walking with this closed air, devious, humbled like a beaten animal',[123] a sentiment echoed by Richard Burton in his description of Jews in the Ottoman Holy Lands: 'centuries of oppression have necessarily given to many that cringing, deprecating glance, that shifting look which painfully suggests a tame beast expecting a blow'.[124] James Richardson, a British writer, described the 'degrading slavery which [Jews] usually live, their continued habits of cringing servility'.[125] One of the most famous pieces of music in the classical repertoire, Modest Mussorgsky's *Pictures from an Exhibition*, was inspired by Victor Hartmann's paintings, particularly by that of a poor Jew. This has provoked debate about whether the composer's response was simply compassionate. Warren Dwight Allen suggested that Mussorgsky 'revolted against injustice and inequality, as in his sketch "Pictures ...". In this he describes in music the arrogant rich and whining poor.'[126]

According to many writers, servility was only one side of the 'oriental' character. As Margaret Lavinia Anderson reminds us: 'Cringing (yet insolent), the Armenian-as-victim was of course the flip side of the second strand: the Armenian-as-shyster.'[127] Reginald Wyon recorded 'the cringing salaam or imperious insolence which the Turk can change at will',[128] but this was hardly original. In the *Institution of Cyrus*, the ancient Greek historian Xenophon stated: 'It does not appear improbable to me ... I think that of the same man to be insolent in prosperity and when reduced in fortune, to become soon servilely afraid; and yet when freed from apprehension to become insolent again and again to give trouble.'[129] This was a general observation about human character, not intended to denote any particular group. This observation by Xenophon became a trope repeated by later writers. The French philosopher Voltaire was probably paraphrasing him in his *Essai surs les moeurs et l'esprit des nations*, when he characterized Jews as 'grovelling in misfortune, insolent in prosperity'.[130] Michael Marrus has provided a Nazi stereotype of the 'cringing acquiescence' of Jews, who were 'easily manipulated by appeals of individual self-interest'.[131] Did this come from Voltaire, from Xenophon or was it another ricochet from the downfall of the eastern empires and the humiliating descriptions of Armenians that had been current in Germany for years?

Figure 1 Victor Hartmann, *Poor Jew from Sandomir* (1873) (Tretyakov Gallery, Moscow).

Houston Stewart Chamberlain, the British racist philosopher admired by the Nazis, thought that the passage by Voltaire was 'estimable'[132] and he quoted it in full.

Some contemporaries attempted to look at the mistreatment of subject peoples in some historical context. Joseph Jacobs defended the Jews of imperial Russia against their persecutors: 'It is the brutal logic of such intolerance to degrade men by isolating them, by shutting to them the *carrière ouverte*, by marking them out for all men's scorn, and then to complain of the degradation they have themselves produced.'[133] *The Times* considered the plight of eastern Christians in 1921. 'If they are massacred without making any resistance they are called cowards . . . blood for blood, they are called barbarians.'[134] With a rather typically Marxist eye for the power relations underlying oppression, Rosa Luxemburg thought that it was easier to turn nationalities that had been historically mishandled or discriminated against socially into a 'scapegoat' (*Sündenbock*).[135] Writing as she did in 1918 and only a few months before her own violent death, she added that it was likely that this role 'had yet to be played out'.[136]

Some writers thought that new men would emerge after imperial oppression had ended. The poet Hayyim Nahman Bialik condemned the Jews of Kishinev for their passivity towards the perpetrators of violence in his famous Hebrew poem of indignation and resistance 'be-'Ir La-Haregah' ('City of Slaughter'): ' "The Sons of Maccabees" did not defend themselves.'[137] He and other Jewish writers anticipated a time when Jews would take up arms to protect themselves. Maxim Gorky looked to the future after the revolution in Russia and hoped for the end of the *ancien régime* of the oppression of the spirit, to a time when a new type of person would emerge unmarked by oppression.[138] According to Arnold Margolin, a Ukrainian Jew who later defended Mendel Beilis, Americans possessed 'common sense, rapid thinking'. Furthermore, 'absence of servility and inferiority complexes seemed to be a characteristic of most people I met'.[139]

After years of attacks, tradition weighed heavily on Jews and Armenians. The debate on self-defence became even more pertinent in this context. Some observers felt that victims of violence had simply been broken by this experience. A group of intellectuals guided by Ahad Ha'am and Simon Dubnow called upon the Jews of imperial Russia to change: 'Stop weeping and pleading, stop lifting your hands for salvation to those who hate and exclude you! Look to your own hands for rescue!'[140] Serbs in fascist Croatia were initially led to their deaths like so many lambs to slaughter, believing that the worst fate that could happen to them would be mass conversion and trusting the authority of the state to protect them. Because they had not experienced years of oppression (indeed the Orthodox peoples of this region had been given special privileges as 'Grenzer' during the Habsburg period), they had certainly not developed a pogrom mentality and fought back very rapidly, organizing themselves into armed čete (or bands) on a rapid, 'spontaneous and local basis'.[141] Montenegrins, never enslaved by the Ottomans like so many of the other neighbouring peoples, were even considered to have a look of pride and freedom about them.[142] In part, the anger expressed against the Armenians was due to the fact that they might cease to be subservient, especially as political and social systems were evolving. In February 1904, the Turkish newspaper Şura-yi Ümmet expressed dismay at the notion of Ottoman decline: 'Is it not shameful for us! How can Ottomans who once ruled the world become servants to their own shepherds, slaves and servants.'[143] We can assume that the newspaper meant the Christian giaours.

One survival strategy for ethnic minorities was fatalism and increased piety (a phenomenon which was happening amongst Jews, Muslims and Armenians, subjected to frequent missionary work at a time when they were at their most vulnerable[144]). 'The utter failure of all attempts to check the Turk in his purpose of exterminating the Armenians spread far and wide among the Greeks of European and Asiatic Turkey the conviction that they were destined to be next in turn.'[145] Simon Dubnow recalled in his memoirs how the driving out of Jews from Moscow and the reprisals in St Petersburg had led to a fear that the same thing would occur in Odessa in 1881. The Yiddish writer Sholem Abramowitch (who later wrote a pogrom novel, Dos yinsh-fingeril, published in 1889) told Dubnow 'with a bitter smile that his wife had put wheels under her large suitcase so it could be easily rolled out of their home'.[146] Missionary Helen Davenport Gibbons recollected that the fear and fatalism of Armenians was very vivid.

> When we first came to Cilicia and went to church up in the Tarsus Mountains summer place, I remember how queer those people looked to me. They belonged to another world, I was an outsider. I had difficulty in understanding some traits of their character. I was hasty in my judgement of them – hasty through ignorance. I was impatient with their constant fear of 'what might happen any time' to Christians under Moslem rule.[147]

Of course, victims of exclusion had many strategies or 'weapons' for coping with their often parlous situation. Oppression of minority religious populations created 'limits that only the foolhardy would transgress', as James C. Scott has suggested.[148] Another strong mechanism was denial. Some communities, notably Armenians and Jews, anticipated ethnic violence, although not complete and concerted destruction of their communities. Indeed they may have developed a 'pogrom mentality' expecting violence and waiting for it to pass like a storm. Dorothea Chambers Blaisdell recalled in 1909 in Cicilia that 'mother had been through massacres before. She knew one must treat it as an episode and not as a final tragedy.'[149] At his trial for the assassination of Tâlât Paşa, Soghomon Teilirian recalled that his family had talked about the massacres in Erzyngian in 1894 and had feared the repetition of massacres 'for years' before they were murdered in 1915.[150]

In his celebrated study of the *Destruction of the European Jews*, Raul Hilberg suggested that there were identifiable phases through which Jews were physically removed by the Third Reich: definition, expropriation, concentration, and finally annihilation.[151] Much of the focus in genocide scholarship has rightly been on the descent into the last phases; but, as Hilberg observed, a moral Rubicon is already crossed with the definition of who is a citizen and who can be excluded from citizenship. As the foundations of the old empires began to collapse, whole categories of subjects failed to make that transition and their loyalty to the state of residence was constantly questioned. As the collectivity shifts and changes, so too can the groups or individuals accused of treachery. In effect, the inclusive category of 'subject', which can be extended to almost any individual, is replaced by an equally subjective category, that of 'who can belong'. The notion of treachery is not, of course, a new one. In book VII of his *Histories*, the Greek historian Herodotus dealt with the betrayal of the Spartans at the Battle of Thermopylae by Ephialtes of Trachis, a tale which subsequently became one of the most important stories in the construction of European consciousness.[152] The Bible has numerous accounts of treachery and its dire consequences, particularly the betrayal of Jesus Christ by Judas Iscariot. Miroslav Krleža's play *Golgota*,[153] written in 1922 in the early days of Yugoslavia, deals – as the name suggests – with one of the central tropes of Serbian national consciousness: the Serbs' betrayal at the battle of

Kosovo polje in 1389 by one of their own, Vuk Branković, the son of King Lazar.[154]

If individuals are defined as traitors, traditionally they have no right to pity or compassion. They can be eliminated without due process of law and their bodies displayed to serve as an example for those who might contemplate 'treachery'. Describing the massacres of Armenians in Constantinople in 1896, Chalmer Roberts noted:

> One came to expect that venerable Ulemas and ascetic young Softas, on their way from mosque to mosque, would kick the mangled bodies, which block their paths, and curse them for dogs of Armenian traitors. The pools of blood in the streets, in some places actually dripping and trickling downhill, came in time, after you had stepped over and around a hundred of them, to remind you of some early visit to a slaughter house.[155]

Alexander Mavroyéni Bey, Ottoman ambassador to Washington, attempted to explain the atrocities against Armenians in 1896 in terms of loyalty to the state and their own illegitimate presence. 'Suppose for a moment that your Indians were to revolt against your legitimate authority. Suppose that you put down that revolt and suppose that in some country some foreigners were to calumniate publicly your civilization, your race, and your religion . . .'[156]

Missionary Henry Harrison Riggs accused the Turkish authorities of dispensing 'a great deal of fiction to prove that the Armenians were a disloyal element menacing the safety of the Turks'.[157] To underline this potential status as traitors in 1915, 'a number of Armenians were forced to go to the cemetery and destroy the statue which was erected to the memory of martyred Russian soldiers in 1829'.[158] In an article in the *Deutsche Allgemeine Zeitung*, Felix Guse attempted to blame the Armenians for provoking the genocide of 1915: 'The situation of the Turkish army was desperate, and it defended itself. And the behaviour of the Armenians was not that of courageous freedom fighters, but was instead sneaky and perfidious. In order to eliminate the danger in the back of the army, the Turkish government resorted to a decisive measure. It relocated all Armenians.'[159] Punishing treachery gave rise to a peculiarly vicious kind of spite and illustrates the way in which the accusation of betrayal puts individuals or groups beyond consideration of compassion: A refugee named Murad recalled the fate of about 17,000 prisoners of war in Sivas:

> The Russian soldiers of Moslem origin had already been released at Erzeroum, most of the Armenians had been killed, and the Russians were stripped of their clothing. On their way to Sivas they were grossly insulted, spat on by every Moslem passer-by, and whipped by their escort into quicker march. Half their number reached Sivas almost naked, covered with filthy rags, their feet swollen and in some cases with their sheepskin coats glued to their sore bodies. In face of such an outrageous treatment of these Russian prisoners, the Armenians of Sivas provided them with medical help and various comforts. This trivial manifestation of humane feeling displayed by the Armenians, however, caused great resentment among the Moslems. Men belonging to the *Dashnaktzoutioun* and the *Huntchak* parties were subjected to 110 strokes each.[160]

Even 'former Armenians' were persecuted like the *conversos* in Spain, whom the Inquisition believed to have only nominally converted from Judaism to Christianity: 'A few men and women in the service of the Turkish and Kurdish beys were allowed to live until the end of the harvest. The compulsory emigration was even forced upon Armenians who had been converts to Islam since the massacres of 1895. These were deported in October.'[161]

The First World War precipitated a crisis of citizenship across the continent of Europe. Great Britain faced mutiny in the shape of the Easter Uprising in Dublin in 1916. Although this was ruthlessly suppressed, the rebellion revealed the deepening chasm between the British and the nationalist Irish. In 1918, the British state faced open hostility to conscription in Ireland, followed by civil war and full independence for the South in 1922 In imperial Germany, about half the Jewish delegates in the Reichstag had refused to vote for war credits in 1914 – a much higher proportion than amongst the non-Jewish delegates.[162] In 1916, the German army carried out a survey on the participation of Jews in the army – the so-called *Judenzählung* ('Jewcount').[163] Although the survey demonstrated that

German Jews were participating fully in the war as German patriots, it gave a 'no smoke without fire' script to anti-Semites. In his impassioned open letter to Hitler on 11 April 1933, Armin Wegner reminded the Reichskanzler of the sacrifice of 12,000 German Jews who died in the First World War.[164] Despite years of Nazi propaganda, Christopher Browning recorded the reluctance of the Einstatzgruppen to kill Jewish First World War heroes on the Eastern Front in the 1940s.[165]

Armenians in the Ottoman army were accused of all manner of treachery and cowardice in 1915. Volunteer Armenian brigades from outside Anatolia had joined the Russians.[166] The German Ambassador Hans Freiherr von Wangenheim told the German Chancellor Bethmann Hollweg that Turkish officers had accused Armenian soldiers of sympathy towards the Russians and, as a result, the 'old hate' (*alte Hass*) was growing among the Muslim population.[167] In the atmosphere of panic and fear that prevailed, Greeks were also accused of treachery. Wangenheim also became convinced that 'practically all Greeks in the Ottoman Empire were spying for the Entente'.[168] Early in 1915, the *New York Times* reported:

> It is asserted in well-informed circles that the Turks for the present have abandoned their advance against Egypt. In Constantinople anxiety regarding the possible forcing of the Dardanelles continues. It is evident that the situation for Christians is extremely precarious even in the large cities, and Talaat Bey, the Minister of the Interior, has stated to the Councillor of the Greek Patriarchate that in Turkey henceforth there will be room only for Turks. While he was profuse in assurance to the Greek Minister regarding the cessation of anti-Greek persecutions, no real amelioration of the situation is perceptible.[169]

The expulsion or worst punishment of potential 'traitors' was not unique to the Ottoman situation. Jews were moved from European Russia by the tsarist state because it was feared that they would be too friendly to the advancing Germans.[170] When the tsarist army retreated in 1915, they carried out what Aviel Roshwald has referred to as a 'military pogrom', burning Jewish *shtetlach* before they could be taken over by the advancing Germans.[171]

The actions of Balkan governments during the wars of 1912–3, when substantial Muslim communities were expelled from the region, were partly contingent, but also relied on notions of who would not be a reliable citizen in an expanded state. Habsburg south Slavs did question the legitimacy of their war with the Serbs, and both Serbs and Armenians did cross over to the Russians to fight against the Ottomans. In the middle of September in 1914, only a few weeks after the commencement of fighting, the Serbian minister in Petrograd informed his government that many Habsburg Serbs who had been taken prisoner by the Russians wanted to cross over and fight in the Serbian army.[172] In 1915 in Belgrade John Reed saw Austrian prisoners who had been captured by the Serbs. Their captors reprimanded the Serb and Croat 'brothers' for fighting for the Austrians. The Croat responded: 'We asked permission to fight with you, but they wouldn't let us'[173] – at which everyone laughed. Of course, this was irony indeed, as the war had exposed the fragile nature of loyalties across the eastern fronts. In 1918, mutiny broke out on the Adriatic coastline among Dalmatian sailors, followed by rebellion among former prisoners of war from the Russian Front who were released under the terms of the Brest-Litovsk Peace Treaty in 1918.[174] There is no question that Jews in central Europe remained steadfastly loyal to their states, with the possible exception of loyalty to Russia. The British diplomat Robert H. Bruce Lockhart recalled that stories circulating about the loyalty of Jews were 'the stock-in-trade of every gossip and the staple entertainment of every salon' in Russia in 1915. When the Kaiser visited Łodz in the winter of that year, a joke circulated about his (mainly) Jewish audience there.

> As they listened to him, they heard him refer, first to the Almighty and the All-Highest, then to God and himself, and finally to himself and God. When the speech was ended, the leading Jews withdrew into a corner to discuss the situation. 'This man will do for us,' said the Chief Rabbi. 'He's the first Christian I've met who denies the Holy Trinity.'[175]

Vejas Liulevicius described generally good relations between Jews and Germans in the occupied *Ober Ost*.[176] Muslims from Central Asia had remained exempt from conscription to the Russian army until 1916[177] because of questions of loyalty.

One of the most important texts to encourage the notion of disloyalty of a minority religious group in a modern state was the infamous *Protocols of the Elders of Zion*, which was widely known before 1914 but republished and translated after 1918. Although entirely fabricated, either by the Russian Okhrana, as Norman Cohn believed,[178] or by an active anti-Semitic group in Russia between 1902 and 1903,[179] it became an urtext for extremists across the world (and is still regularly reprinted in the Middle East). Its banal simplicity, stating as it did that Jews were involved in a conspiracy to dominate the world, caught the imagination of eliminationists at a time when Jews were clearly rather powerless in the Russian empire and their situation was rapidly deteriorating.[180] In a pamphlet of 1904, Russian anti-Semites referred to the Jews as 'the enemy in our midst'.[181] In 1906, a Black Hundreds election address repeated the insinuation that Jews could not be trusted and did not belong. The Jewish question should be solved by laws and administrative measures separate from other tribal questions, in view of the ongoing spontaneous hostility of Jewry to Christianity and to non-Jewish nationalities, and the Jews' striving for world domination.[182] During the Russian Civil War, White officers read the *Protocols of the Elders of Zion* aloud to their troops.[183]

The lies contained in the *Protocols* were simple enough to feed into earlier currents of anti-Semitism and into already existing prejudices across Europe. Alfred Rosenberg read the *Protocols* and linked them to Bolshevism: 'First subversion, then dictatorship.'[184] In 1927, the daily newspaper *Makedonia* discussed the '*poison of disintegration* with which they [Jews] infect society'.[185] In January 1940, two teenagers selling the British Union newspaper *Action in Shoreditch* were recorded as shouting out to a crowd: 'Why don't you Yids go to the Front and fight, you rotten foreigners.'[186] Prior to his assassination in 1921, the German Foreign Minister Walter Rathenau was dubbed an 'Elder of Zion' – which presumably legitimized his execution in the eyes of eliminationists.[187] Of course there were liberal exceptions to a general acceptance of the accusations contained in the *Protocols*. In Berne in 1935, a Nazi was fined after distributing the *Protocols*, which the Cantonal Court considered to be fraudulent material.[188]

Prejudice and accusation had begun to alienate religious minorities across the Balkans, Black Sea and Anatolia before 1914, creating a growing problem of mutual radicalization. Many Armenians became involved in the revolutionary Dashnaksutiun, which was affiliated to the Second International and was close to the Russian leftist parties. In the Russian empire, Jews organized themselves into a separate political party or Bund (although many were also Narodniks or Marxists). But, as persecution continued, they ceased to see themselves as part of pluralist nations. During the fight for independence, Jews in Ukraine did not think of themselves as 'Ukrainian Jews'.[189] In Salonica in 1926, 46 per cent of the Jewish community voted for Zionist candidates.[190] According to the 1930 census in Romania, 728,115 out of 756,930 Jews claimed Jewish rather than Romanian nationality.[191] In the Balkans and Anatolia, the millet system had created a long-term conflation between religion, ethnicity and social class. In imperial Russia, the confinement of minorities to certain areas went hand in hand with restrictions on their economy (in the Pale of Settlement, for instance, Jews were banned from agriculture). Ironically, 'ethnic groups perceive themselves as independent and autonomous, yet it is precisely their inter-dependence which is the origin of their identities, self-perception and differential plans'.[192] Leon Trotsky remarked in December 1922 that 'all Europe is divided by customs barriers and bayonets – in spite of this, there has never been an epoch in human history when the mutual dependence of nations and classes has been so close, as it is in our times!'[193]

The population eliminations in Spain and France in the early modern period had provided Europeans with a model of destruction and underdevelopment. Nevertheless, many were inspired by the example of previous atrocities, thinking in terms of 'pathological homogeneity' rather than of the long-term damage done through the removal of whole groups from society. It was their interdependence that had allowed the economies of the Russian empires, Anatolia and the Balkans to function before 1914. All experienced a profound decline in productivity in the 1920s after the collapse of imperial governments, confirming Maurice Godelier's argument that, in situations where the division of labour is based on religion, religious groups are part of the infrastructure, rather than the superstructure, of that society. In regions which were changing very rapidly by the nineteenth century and experiencing levels of international trade, the role of the state in religious persecutions and the elimination of minorities was crucial. In a globalizing economy, religious minorities often represented what Walter Zenner referred to as 'middlemen' with transnational identities. When Tâlât Paşa announced to Henry Morgenthau that his government could now cash in the insurance policies of dead Armenians, his point was that he could now control aspects of the economy which had once been in the hands of potentially 'disloyal' minorities[194] and establish national economies. In effect, this was an example of what the economist Alexander Gerschenkron described as the state taking the place of 'missing factors of production'.[195] Although this process gave the state more control in the short term, it wrecked very complex networks of trade and family contacts and destroyed a well-developed division of labour between ethnic groups. As a witness to the Armenian genocide, Dr Martin Niepage put it rather forcefully in 1915:

> The Young Turk has the European ideal of a united national state always floating before his eyes. He hopes to turkify the non-Turkish Mohammedan races – Kurds, Persians, Arabs, and so on – by administrative methods and through Turkish education, reinforced by an appeal to their common interests as Mohammedans. The Christian nations – Armenians, Syrians and Greeks – alarm him by their cultural and economic superiority, and he sees in their religion an obstacle to turkifying them by peaceful means. They have, therefore, to be exterminated or converted to Mohammedanism by force. The Turks do not suspect that, in doing this, they are sawing off the branch on which they are sitting themselves. Who is to bring progress to Turkey if not the Greeks, Armenians and Syrians, who constitute more than a quarter of the population of the Empire?[196]

If globalization implied movement of peoples, religious and political ideas, capital, culture and loyalties, then population elimination represented a full-scale attack on that very process of globalization.

CHAPTER 3

'One of these races has got to go . . .': Colonialism and Genocide

In recent years scholars have begun to focus on the wider context of the Holocaust, examining the 'archaeology of genocide' as a phenomenon.[1] Dan Stone has argued that 'scholars now feel [it] incumbent upon themselves . . . to provide a historical framework for understanding genocide that situates it into the broadest developments of world history and human behaviour'.[2] Approaching these events as part of history makes far clearer what Yehuda Bauer has called the 'dialectic nature between the particularism and universalism of the horror'.[3] To some extent, the moral decline in European politics and the growth of eliminationist ideas was encouraged by imperialism. Hannah Arendt believed that fascism had represented an extreme outgrowth of nineteenth-century imperialist aspirations and racism.[4]

The expansion of the European powers between the early modern period and the nineteenth century cost millions of lives. Mark Levene has emphasized the 'fatal nexus between the Anglo-American drive to rapid state building and genocide'.[5] While some Americans were ethnically cleansed for their land, others were simply attacked or captured and worked until they died. Here the motive for expropriation was central. Evgenii Preobrazhensky and Nikolaï Bukharin attacked colonialism as a practice wherein 'the loathsome and sanguinary aspects of capitalism were . . . displayed with exceptional clearness'.[6] The transatlantic slave trade was genocidal in its consequences: of the 12 million taken from Africa, perhaps 1.5 million died en route. The trade cut the survivors off from their lands of origins and gave them an existence in which many died prematurely from diseases in trading ports or simply from sheer exhaustion. An estimated death rate of 130 per thousand per annum means in effect that slaves were being worked to death.[7] In the decades between the 1880s and the First World War, the 'Scramble for Africa' developed into genocide. In 1924, a young radical, Ho Chi Minh, addressed the Communist International in Moscow, imploring his comrades to develop a theory of colonialism that took into account the mass slaughters which had taken place in the preceding decades:

> In the Belgian Congo the population fell from 25 million in 1891 to 8.5 million by 1911. Densely populated and prosperous regions along rivers were turned into deserts within a mere fifteen years. Ravaged oases and villages were strewn with bleached bones. The plight of the survivors was atrocious. The peasants were robbed of their tiny plots of land, the artisans lost their crafts and the herdsmen their cattle. The Matabeles were cattle-breeders: before the arrival of the British they had 200,000 head of cattle. Two years later only 40,900 were left. The Hereros had 90,000 head of cattle. Within twelve years the German colonists had robbed them of half that number.[8]

Outrage at genocide and other extreme abuses of human rights was one of the intellectual building-blocks that led to the creation of the League of Nations and its successor, the United Nations, as well as such pressure groups as the Congo Reform Association, created in 1906 to combat the abuses of the Belgian King Leopold's regime, or Pro Arménia, a French pressure group which supported the Armenians after the Hamidian massacres. Humanist concerns led to a series of conventions in The Hague and Geneva from the late nineteenth century onwards, all aimed at curtailing violent, abusive behaviour and amending international law accordingly. But, at the same time, in the nineteenth and early twentieth centuries those anxious to protect human rights faced another, stronger adversary namely that of the real-life narrative of struggles between races and the inevitable extermination of the 'weakest'.[9] This narrative was to remain dominant in much of Europe until the late 1940s. It permeated

European life at every level, and thus put whole groups outside of what Christopher Browning has called the 'circle of human obligation and responsibility'[10] or, worse still, it helped to present the removal of certain people in terms of a social necessity or good. The German Admiral Hans Humann justified the Ittihad persecution of the Armenians in terms of nature: 'Armenians and Turks cannot live together in this country. . . . One of these races has got to go. The weaker nation must succumb.'[11]

As with the Hamidian massacres, Dreyfus and the increasingly violent tone of literature, the abuses of imperialism created a human rights consciousness which was an intellectual antithesis to eliminationist discourses. The novelist Mark Twain wrote a condemnation of Belgian abuses in the Congo in the form of a 'soliloquy' by King Leopold, who he held responsible.[12] Forming the Congo Reform Association with Edmund Dene Morel and the Irish writer Roger Casement, the writer Arthur Conan Doyle set down an enraged protest, the *Crime of the Congo* in 1909:

> There are many of us in England who consider the crime which has been wrought in the Congo lands by King Leopold of Belgium and his followers, to be the greatest which has ever been known in human annals. . . . There have been massacres of populations like that of the South Americans by the Spaniard, or of subject nations by the Turks. But never before has there been such a mixture of wholesale expropriation and wholesale massacre all done under an odious guise of philanthropy, and with the lowest commercial motives as a reason. It is this sordid cause and the unctuous hypocrisy which makes this crime unparalleled in its horror.[13]

The aim of the Congo Reform Association was to shame. As Morel later argued in his book *The Black Man's Burden*, 'truth' was the 'stalking horse of oppression and injustice'.[14]

As far as the Marxist left of that time is concerned, it is problematic to present it as formed of wholehearted supporters of human rights. Contemporary scholars are still drawn to the writings of Marxists to conceptualize genocide and the destruction of communities: Mark Levene to the developmental theories of Immanuel Wallerstein[15] and Dirk Moses to Walter Benjamin's notion of 'anamnestic solidarity'[16] with the victims of violence.

Many Marxists of the period under consideration were great humanists, and it is explicit within the theory of dialectical materialism that an end to oppression will emancipate humanity. In Italy, Antonio Gramsci also spoke out against the killing of Armenians in the Ottoman Empire,[17] initiating a debate among his comrades about the moral implications of distance. In Serbia, the Marxists Svetozar Marković and Dimitrije Tucović went against the prevailing nationalist grain and supported Albanian rights.[18] At the age of twenty-five, Rosa Luxemburg had tried to get the German Social Democrats, via their newspaper *Vorwärts*, to support the Armenians after the Hamidian massacres. She was rebuffed by Wilhelm Liebknecht who displayed the characteristic obsession of the German left with tsarist abuses of power[19] (to the detriment of their analysis of other political problems). Liebknecht believed that, as a Jew from Poland, Rosa Luxemburg 'would perhaps find a more fruitful field if she occupied herself with the Russian atrocities in Poland, and in Russia itself'.[20]

Among the left-wing in Germany, there was deep concern for the fate of Africans in colonial Namibia and compassion for the Jewish victims of the pogroms. The First World War and the subsequent Bolshevik revolution divided Marxists and, as Geoff Eley has argued, much that was valuable in socialism was lost during the Soviet domination of the Communist International from 1919 to 1943.[21] When Fitzroy Maclean encountered communists in the 1930s in Russia, he remembered 'their terror of responsibility . . . reluctance to think for themselves [and] blind unquestioning obedience',[22] conformist qualities that became one of the central themes of Alfred Andersch's celebrated novel about communism and the moral compromises involved in Stalinism and popular front politics in the 1930s and 1940s: *Sansibar, oder, Der letze Grund*.[23]

The Bolsheviks in power, with a few notable exceptions, had much less of a humanist approach to social change. They had also absorbed the prevailing *zeitgeist* of an apocalyptic world divided between opposing forces. In December 1917, Vladimir Lenin had written about 'cleansing the Russian land of all vermin, of scoundrel fleas, the bedbug rich and so on'.[24] In a famous civil war poster, he was depicted brushing away an Orthodox priest, two monarchs and a fat capitalist. (Fig. 2). Curiously, the Russian verb 'to cleanse' is etymologically the same as the Croatian and Serbian word (*očistiti*), which

Figure 2 'Comrade Lenin cleanses the earth of the unclean.' Soviet poster designed by Mikhail Cheremnykh and Viktor Deni, November 1920.

Vuk Karadžić used to describe the killing of Muslims in Belgrade in 1806.[25] In a speech made in Nova Gradiška in June 1941, the Ustaša Minister Milovan Žanić stated: 'This must be the land of the Croats and no one else and there are no methods that we Ustaše will not use to make this land truly Croat, and cleanse it (*očistimo*) of the Serbs who have menaced us for centuries.'[26] At the beginning of 1917, Austrian diplomatic papers referred to the cleansing of Christians (*von christlichen Elementen gesäubert*);[27] the term is also found in the Lepsius correspondence, where it describes the plight of the Armenians.[28]

Is the repetitive use of the term 'to cleanse' in relation to the removal of a population just a semantic coincidence? Given that the Bolshevik revolution led to the exodus of many groups from Russia and that their victory in the civil war gave them a licence to kill their few remaining political opponents in Tambov in 1920 and in Kronstadt in 1921, it could be argued that the consequence of their revolution was the 'cleansing' of certain elements from the former Romanov monarchy. During the collectivization drive, many more people, classified somewhat subjectively as rich capitalist peasants or kulaks, were slaughtered by the state if they failed to deliver their property to the collective. The communist regime tried to destroy the traditional farming of most of the Soviet Union and many died as a direct result of government policy, the initiatives of fanatics, local ineptitude and inaccuracies in the command economy. Many Ukrainians believe that this amounted to genocide against them and their way of life. If we look at the United Nations' definition of genocide, which is extremely comprehensive, these events should be included, as Raphael Lemkin himself concluded.[29] Rudi Rummel has called this type of event 'death by government'. He notes: 'Power was nearly absolute . . . classes – bourgeoisie, priests, landlords, the rich and officers and officials of the previous regime – were sinful, enemies of the Good. Capitalists of their offspring were especially evil. The verdict for such class membership was often death.'[30] That the communists after 1917 had become so dislocated from their humanist roots should not in itself obscure the fact that there was an elective affinity between the left and humanism.

Those who protested against the persecution of individuals on the basis of ethnicity, religion or race were a diverse but significant constituency, most marked perhaps by their individualism and education. Sigmund Freud famously remarked to Albert Einstein in 1932 that 'whatever makes for cultural development is working also against war'.[31] The philosopher Richard Rorty concluded that an education which promotes empathy for the 'other', sentiment and relativism would produce a tolerant society as well as the preservation of individual human rights: 'That sort of education gets people of different kinds sufficiently well acquainted with one another that they are less tempted to think of those different from themselves as only quasi-human. The goal of this sort of manipulation of sentiment is to expand the reference of the terms "our kind of people".'[32] What perhaps is also important is a sense of spiritual independence. The remarkable small town of Le Chambon-sur-Lignon in the French Auvergne region sheltered and saved thousands of Jews during the Vichy occupation and elimination. What made this town – and others nearby, which assisted them in the struggle – so remarkable? Perhaps its was the minister André Trocmé, his wife Magda and his assistant Edouard Theis, but perhaps also a Huguenot tradition which had lasted for centuries despite persecution by the French state – which meant, in effect, that a form of spiritual independence had been preserved.[33]

Violence against ethnic minorities often provoked what Rosa Luxemburg called a 'gnawing sense of responsibility for social injustice'[34] or what Lynn Hunt has more recently described as 'feelings, convictions, and actions of multitudes of individuals who demand responses that accord with their inner sense of outrage'.[35] In 1861, Alexander Herzen protested about the persecution (*gonenie*) of Muslim Tatars from the Crimea in the pages of his journal *Kolokol,* one of the earliest newspapers set up with the purpose of raising an alarm,[36] in this case about the status quo in tsarist Russia.[37] Leo Tolstoy wrote to the governor of Kishinev:

> Profoundly shocked by the atrocities committed [in your town] . . . we extend our heartfelt sympathy to the innocent victims of mob savagery and express our horror at acts of cruelty perpetrated by Russians, our scorn and disgust with all who have driven the people to such a pass and have allowed this dreadful crime to be committed.[38]

He had such a huge moral impact on generations of Russians that students wore black arm bands after the announcement of his death. For Vladimir

Lenin, his writing had made a 'remarkably powerful, forthright and sincere protest against social falsehood and hypocrisy'.[39] Tolstoy's daughter tried to help Turkish prisoners of war during the Russian occupation:

> After six weeks of this, Countess Alexandra . . . came to Van and took off our hands the care of our 'guests', though they remained on our premises. She was a young woman, simple, sensible, and lovable. . . . When her funds gave out and no more were forthcoming and her Russian helpers fell ill, she succeeded where we had failed and induced the General to send the Turks out into the country with provision for their safety and sustenance.[40]

In France, horror at the Hamidian massacres of Armenians and at the Dreyfus case brought together a remarkable number of artistic and other personalities. Emile Gallé, one of the most important art nouveau designers in glass, designed *Le Sang d'Arménie* (*The Blood of Armenia*) in 1900. Those who were pro Arménia included Jean Jaurès, Georges Clémenceau and Anatole France,[41] who were also committed Dreyfusards.[42] In April 1916, Anatole France helped to organize a meeting in the Sorbonne in 'homage' to Armenia and to condemn the role of the Turks and their allies, the Germans, during the war.[43] As eliminationism was developing, another philosophical current, which might be called a human rights consciousness, was also growing slowly. 'The term "intellectual" as a description of a distinct group of people enters the French language in the latter half of the 1890s. With the Dreyfus Affair, it achieved common currency, being used immediately as a term of abuse by the Right.'[44] In Britain, the Bulgarian horrors of the 1870s had, according to the politician and biographer of Gladstone, Roy Jenkins, 'left a permanent imprint on the line divide in British politics'.[45]

Eliminationist ideas evolved at a time when the lives of colonial peoples had been sacrificed and squandered. There were, of course, many individuals directly linked to colonial atrocities who were also involved in the politics and practice of genocide in Europe. Eugen Fischer, Hermann Göring and Franz Ritter von Epp have been identified as 'human conduits for the flow of ideas and methods between the colony and Nazi

Germany'.[46] Jürgen Zimmerer has argued that there was a fundamental link between colonial practices, including mass killings of Africans in the first decade of the twentieth century in Namibia by German colonists, and the way in which Jews were treated by the Third Reich.[47] If people could be killed because they were in the way, being regarded as inferior or as an obstacle to German expansion and hegemony in Africa, then why not also in eastern Europe? Dominik Schaller argued that there was a link between the Armenian genocide and the Holocaust in terms of the impact of the events of 1915 on the central European psyche and consciousness.[48] In both cases the link was not only at the level of actual people being implicated in these events, but also in terms of the ideological and moral effect that they had on the times in which these people lived. As the Roman historian Tacitus observed in his *Annals*, 'what is this day supported by precedents will hereafter become a precedent'.[49] Winston Churchill 'repeatedly used the example of the Greek–Turkish transfer of populations mandated by Lausanne as a legitimate precedent for removing the Germans'[50] from eastern Europe; they could then go on to inhabit homes in West Germany vacated by dead soldiers and civilians.

Paul Rohrbach (1869–1956) also stands out as a key figure in the intellectual development of European racist thought and imperialism. Rohrbach's academic and applied interest in regions which were to become zones of conflict and ultimately genocide (German South-West Africa, the Ottoman Empire and the Ukraine) was, to say the very least, unfortunate. Helmut Walser Smith has argued that his writings, particularly *Der Deutsche Gedanke in der Welt*,[51] 'allow us to trace the deeper logic of eliminationist racism in Wilhelmine Germany on the eve of the war'. At the very least he represents, as Dominik Schaller has suggested, an intellectual continuity of the German *Weltpolitik* between the first decade of the twentieth century and the Second World War.[52] To what extent could his imperialist writings have contributed to the creation of these genocidal situations in three parts of the world?

Rohrbach, a Baltic German by origin, was a prolific writer, traveller and political activist. His work was popular and his books were short, polemical and accessible, full of mantras and potential slogans. Munroe Smith observed in 1917 that 'popularizers' (and in this he included Rohrbach) 'do more than "solid" writers to mould opinion. [Before the war] . . . at the beer tables German civilians were annexing little neighbours and dividing great empire.'[53] Rohrbach's early theological training meant that he 'infused the vulgar world of imperialism and economic competition with . . . elevated meaning,'[54] writing in his autobiography that theology could be used as a guide through challenges raised by society.[55] In his 1912 book *Der Deutsche Gedanke in der Welt*, he argued that Germans should set a moral standard in world politics, coining a phrase which is almost Lutheran in its prosaic weight: '*Wie unser Volk, so unsere Regierung*' ('As our people are, so our rule will be' – namely, fair and just).[56] Because Germans had a moral duty to act in a particular way and to set an example to the world, Rohrbach had also publicly disapproved of the Kaiser visiting the harem of the Ottoman sultan in 1895.[57] For him, as for many German idealists before him and for the Russian slavophiles, Anglo-Saxon civilization was morally corrupted by materialism,[58] and he believed that Germans would inject much needed *Kultur* to counteract this tendency.[59]

Rohrbach was already well travelled when he took up a post as commissioner for population in German South-West Africa. Describing his career there, Michael Mann has suggested that, '[i]n the most elevated world historical terms, he endorsed complete expropriation, forcing officials into near-slave-labor conditions'. But, as Mann continues: 'He was not contemplating eliminating them. Nor was any official.'[60] It is true that, in his writings on Africa, Rohrbach does not appear to be as extreme as his colleague, General von Trotha, and he cannot be classified as a simple 'eliminationist', but his standard of 'ethics' left little room for native rights. In common with many of his contemporaries, including the anthropologist Eugen Fischer, he considered miscegenation between Africans and Europeans to be morally undesirable.[61] He considered the preservation of black tribes in South Africa to be a 'false philanthropy' if it happened at the expense of white European peoples, however loosely that might be interpreted.[62] Rohrbach wrote as if the future of Africa 'was evolutionary destiny'[63] and as if white people had the right to determine the future of black Africans.

Paul Rohrbach's most controversial role is probably in the Near East, with his work on the expansion of German influence in Ottoman Turkey. Although not himself an eliminationist, he represents a direct link between imperialism and the break-up of both Ottoman and Romanov power. In his pamphlet *Die Bagdadbahn*, Rohrbach had noted the economic potential of the region which would be enjoined with the railway, particularly with regard to petroleum.[64] He also saw the Ottoman Empire as the place to drive a wedge between Russian, French and British overseas interests.[65] For Rohrbach, Egypt was Britain's colonial weak link. If Britain lost control here, it would loose control of the Suez Canal and thereby the colonies in India and Asia.[66] He envisaged that the economic building up of the region would be necessary in order to settle Armenians (and other suitably hardworking groups) in Mesopotamia along the railway route. Germans would not settle there because of the climate.[67]

As a historian and traveller, Rohrbach knew better than most contemporaries the extent to which Armenians had suffered. He toured the eastern part of Turkey in 1901 and included several sympathetic photographs of Armenian orphans in his account.[68] When the Ittihad government turned on the Armenians in 1915, it drove many of them out to 'Mesopotamia'. Perhaps as many as two-thirds of these Armenians died from disease, starvation, attacks, dehydration and trauma en route to the Euphrates.[69] Some contemporaries thought that Rohrbach was the initiator of the idea of deportation.[70] Hacobian mentioned him directly, believing him to be the first person to suggest the deportation of Armenians in 'agricultural colonies along the Baghdad railway line'.[71] The American Ambassador Henry Morgenthau, whose family originally came from Mannheim in Germany, was even more blunt in his assessment:

> the Armenian proceedings of 1915 and 1916 evidenced an entirely new mentality. This new conception was that of *deportation*. The Turks, in five hundred years, had invented innumerable ways of physically torturing their Christian subjects, yet never before had it occurred to their minds to move them bodily from their homes, where they had lived for many thousands of years, and send them hundreds of miles away into the desert. Where did the Turks get this idea? . . . Admiral Usedom, one of the big German naval experts in Turkey, told me that the Germans had suggested this deportation to the Turks . . . this idea of deporting peoples

en masse is, in modern times, exclusively Germanic. Anyone who reads the literature of Pan-Germany constantly meets it.[72]

To speak of the destiny of a people in such sweeping terms clearly inspired later eliminationists. In the autumn of 1941 Adolf Hitler used the idea of deportation as a euphemism for mass murder when talking about European Jews: 'That race of criminals has on its conscience the two million dead of the First World War, and now already hundreds and thousands more. Let nobody tell me that all the same we can't park them in the marshy parts of Russia!'[73]

More recently, Armenian scholars have pointed the finger at German writers. Vakahn Dadrian wrote that 'Rohrbach is . . . suspected to have been the theoretician who implanted in Turkish minds the idea of the expediency of the evacuation of the Armenians from their ancient territories in eastern Turkey and their relocation in Mesopotamia'.[74] In a public lecture in Berlin in February 1914 attended by members of the Turkish Embassy, General von der Goltz is reported to have argued that it was necessary to remove from the Russo-Turkish border-areas, once and for all, the half a million Armenians who inhabited the provinces of Van, Bitlis and Erzerum, which are contiguous to these areas. They should be transported south and resettled in the areas of Aleppo and Mesopotamia. In return, the Arabs of these areas should be resettled along the Russo-Turkish borders.[75] British historian Donald Bloxham takes a rather more nuanced view of Rohrbach's role:

> Contrary to the innuendo of these scholars [Dadrian and Ohandjanian], Rohrbach's concern that the Armenians stayed within the Ottoman sphere did not equate with acquiescence in anything that the Ottomans chose to do with the Armenians. [He] schemed in the economic interests of Germany as a pre-eminent future force in Asia Minor. His ostensibly fantastic suggestion – though such concepts were commonplace in geopolitical thought at the time – involved moving Muslims into eastern Anatolia and transplanting the Anatolian Armenian population to Mesopotamia, where he predicted that they could work fruitfully with and for Germany, for instance on further construction of the Baghdad railway.[76]

During the war, however, Mesopotamia was to become for the Armenians almost what Madagascar was to become for the Jews in 1940: a euphemism for a mass death penalty. Eliminationists often used sweeping and grandiose rhetoric while rarely dwelling on the detail of what the physical consequences of killing so many people would actually be in terms of the disposal of bodies which might spread disease, or even in terms of the psychological impact of mass killing on the perpetrators. But it is as well to remember that the act of genocide involves physical questions about the mechanics of mass death and the disposal of the remains. Christopher Browning notes that the ill-fated Madagascar plan was 'an important psychological step on the road to the Final Solution'.[77] And the euphemism of 'deportation' for women and children might have provided the Ittihad government with a sufficiently plausible script to the effect that, in circumstances of war, they were obeyed by the army and general non-Armenian populace.

Undoubtedly Rohrbach's suggestion about population relocation was largely aimed at building up German economic influence in the region and at trying to break Britain's influence in the Near East and India. Rohrbach was certainly not an enemy of the Armenians in a cultural sense. He regarded them as 'Aryan'[78] and progressive, and, above all, Christian. Thanks to the influence of Rohrbach, Alfred Rosenberg granted official recognition to an Armenian National Council on 15 December 1942. His writings are filled with sympathy for the Armenians after the massacres. He approved of their education by German pastors such as Johannnes Lepsius,[79] so it might be a little unfair to suggest (as did Arnold Toynbee) that Germans were beneficiaries of the destruction of Armenian businesses in Cilicia in 1909.

> [Rohrbach] prophesies that the whole carpet industry of Western Asia, 'from which English and other foreign firms in Smyrna now draw such enormous profits', will soon be concentrated round Urfa in German hands. From Armenia's evil, apparently, springs Germany's good – but in 1911 Dr Rohrbach did not foresee the catastrophe of 1915.[80]

Nevertheless, like many of his contemporaries writing in their most rhetorical vein, he was never one to underestimate the opportunities that chaos and destruction could create. His writing betrays the fact that his geopolitical projections were lacking in overall human considerations when he speaks in abstract terms about '*Menschenmaterial Anatoliens*' ('the human material of Anatolia').[81]

As a Baltic German, Rohrbach retained a special interest in the Russian empire. He was sent to Ukraine as an envoy during the Brest-Litovsk nego-tiations and argued that Germany should take full advantage of a situation of chaos in the region to take control of the territory.[82] After the war, he helped to found the German–Ukrainian society, which influenced leading Nazi and fellow Baltic German Alfred Rosenberg.[83] Their ideas found little favour in the 1920s, but were adapted by Rosenberg in his plans for a 'New Order' in eastern Europe: Ukraine would be bound to Germany yet quasi-independent, and it would counterbalance Russia and Poland.[84] Rohrbach's writings are full of negative evocations of the Russian spirit.[85] It is from Rohrbach that the Nazis probably derived the theory that, if the Soviet Union were attacked, it would fall into segments (like an orange).[86] Germany turning eastwards had already been considered in the imperial period 'in small circles . . . [developing] under the command of Ludendorff when he created the military state of "Oberost" in the Balticum [*sic*], Poland and later in the Ukraine. It carried clearly racist dimensions against Slavonic people and the Jews . . . This policy was framed around settlement.'[87]

It is rare to find an individual writer who will stand up and advocate mass death as a policy option. Adolf Hitler, Tâlât Paşa and Ion Antonescu – who spoke so rhetorically about mass deaths as if they were as inevitable and natural as plagues or thunders – are the rarities. Self-belief and delusion are clearly part of this equation. Even when the mass destruction of a population is not the point of departure, extremely creative ideas that involve control and then upheaval or massive social change and notions similar to the *Lebensraum* of the Nazis[88] are potentially dangerous when combined with a sense of mission and superiority to other peoples. The states of western Europe had been unified by ruthless ethnic cleansing in the medieval and early modern period. In killing so many Africans, Asians and native Americans in their colonial expansion, Europeans had already crossed a moral Rubicon well before the genocidal crisis of

1912–23. Furthermore, individuals who witnessed or took part in mass killing would have been morally blunted by their experience and found banal exemptions for their behaviour through racist discourse. It is often stated by perpetrators that the first murder is always the hardest one to commit.[89] In this context, the continuity between violent events – not just at the personal level, but as a marker of this epoch – should be re-emphasized.

CHAPTER 4

Bitter Religions Divisions

Religious and ideological murders do not require any imagination, just efficiency[1]

Building states and new national identities also raised the spectre of further extremism and factional divides among those who initiated such policies. When the state expands or contracts, the key question becomes who is, and who can no longer be, a citizen. If racist ideologies allowed Europeans to abuse and expropriate the lands of conquered peoples, it could also be used to exclude or eliminate groups within the territory. The English transferred negative images of colonial people to the subordinate Irish in the nineteenth century. In a similar manner, Balkan Muslims, imperial Russian Jews, Muslims and other minorities, and eventually Christians in the Ottoman lands, were defined as liminal to, or part of, potential fifth columns. To compound the misery of minorities in east European and Eurasian regions, they had suffered for centuries from more traditional forms of religious oppression and, as a result, sometimes they lacked the mental resilience to fight any kind of oppression. This should not be overstated when one thinks of the role of the Dashnaks, Bund, and various Zionist groups in raising consciousness. Martin Shaw reminds us that there was a strong element of contingency in determining those who were to be targeted. The role of the irrational in this kind of process is enormous, particularly as crises unfold.[2] Just as nationalism was emulated, as

Benedict Anderson has argued,[3] so population elimination could be seen as offering a model. Moreover, the experience of solidarity that fighting internal enemies offered in terms of group cohesion created a unique political opportunity.

When we compare these genocides to the Nazi obsession with hunting down every last Jew, actions they carried out in part because of racial beliefs, race seems to be a relatively minor cause in the destruction of the ancient religious communities in the Black Sea, Balkan and Anatolian regions. Nevertheless, racial beliefs disseminated into high culture and literature by writers such as Comte de Gobineau and Houston Stewart Chamberlain had percolated into popular culture. As Robert Redfield famously argued, 'great and little tradition can be thought of as two currents of thought and action, distinguishable, yet ever flowing into and out of each other':[4] the literate worlds of the racial theorist overlapped with the illiterate world of peasants or unskilled workers. In Kishinev in 1903, newspapers repeatedly ran headlines such as 'Beat the Yids!',[5] to appeal to the lowest common denominator by imitating the directness of the language of urban workers. The people who wrote such headlines were educated and would have certainly adopted a more sophisticated sort of language in a different context. In Fastov in Ukraine in 1919, Cossacks ordered women they had raped to shout out 'Beat the Yids, save Russia!'[6] According to Karel Berkhoff, the slogan 'Beat the Yids!' had remained commonplace in Ukraine during the Nazi occupation, almost forty years after the pogrom in Kishinev.[7] Eva Sochin, who was badly wounded in a pogrom in Ukraine in 1919, was told by her attacker: '*gus svine ne tovarishch*' ('a goose and a pig cannot be friends').[8] Although this may look like an old peasant saying, it is more likely to be a popular assimilation of racial ideas about essential differences between people. Racism often gains ground because it mimics an essence or a *doxa*, to borrow Pierre Bourdieu's use of a famous Aristotelian term for 'self-evident', unspoken values.[9] Although scientifically indefensible, racist ideas tapped into popular notions which might appear 'commonsensical'.

Before and during the pre-genocidal period of pogroms and massacres and continuing through the First World War crisis, negative essentialist stereotypes did circulate. Both in Russia and in the Ottoman Empire, Jews were subjected to stereotypes about their putative propensity to trade, to become rich and to remain idle. Here is how the Young Turk Eşref Kuşcubaşi described Hidayet, who had coverted from Judaism to Islam: '[H]e went on the haj, ascended Ararat and prayed at the Prophet's tomb. But even in the Holy Places he was unable to repress his true nature, buying rugs and other goods from needy pilgrims . . .'[10] Fyodor Dostoyevsky's novels are filled with anti-Semitic stereotypes and ideas, including the notion that Jews were rich – and this at a time when he lived in St Petersburg alongside Jews who were exceedingly poor.[11] Anatole Demidoff, one of the richest people in Russia, described the Jews he encountered in the Crimea as 'this immortal race of Pharisees'.[12] In 1903, just prior to the pogrom in Kishinev, the newspaper *Bessarabets* published a ridiculous story according to which the Jews had invented a way to make wine without grapes (and would thus be able to undercut an important local industry).[13] George Orwell believed that 'one of the marks of anti-semitism is an ability to believe stories that could not possibly be true'.[14] Carl Joubert, in his curious study *Russia as It Really Is*, opined: 'All over the world, in whatever country you meet him, the Jew has one marked characteristic: he will never perform manual labour unless he is obliged to do so. His genius is for becoming rich on the labour of others.'[15] This stereotype of Jewish lack of labour was a commonplace in nineteenth-century texts. The Catholic priest Pranaïtis, called as an expert witness against Mendel Beilis, referred to Jews as a 'parasitic plant' and remarked that 'they don't work, but simply exploit others'.[16]

Because of this stereotype, 'revenge' against a group seen as having exploited another's labours sometimes took on bizarre theatrical quality and became a form of staged cruelty. When Armenian property was expropriated, it was often taken in a ghastly imitation of previously legal proceedings. One account of the fate of the exiles between Broussa and Yeni-Shehr stressed this:

> All personal property, such as furniture, clothes, tools, etc., which they could not take with them, had to be left behind, and the Turks quite openly distributed them among themselves, often even in the presence of their owners! As regards the houses evacuated by the Armenians, a little more red tape was gone through, but the effect was the same. The Armenian proprietor was called before a magistrate, made to sign a document that he

had sold the house to a certain individual (of course always a Moslem), and was given a roll of banknotes. No sooner had he left the room than the money was taken from him by the police and returned to the magistrate, to be used in hundreds of similar cases![17]

After the Nazi Anschluss of Austria, Jews were forced to clean the streets with toothbrushes and '[t]he crowds gathered to laugh at respectable citizens so demeaned'.[18] The Nazi Karl Stumpp recorded his reaction to Jews in the Ukraine in August 1941: 'They can finally tackle a job – and how they tackle it! There's a particular Jew who appears at my office door every morning, makes a deep bow and cleans up my room. When he is finished, he bows very low and disappears out the door backwards.'[19] Clearly, the idea of cleaning per se can evoke complex responses and lead to a conflation between humans deemed to be 'out of place'[20] and unclean matter. Vejas Liulevicius has argued of the German occupation of the Baltic States during the First World War:

> [N]ative people could come to be regarded together with vermin, the ever-present lice of the East, which were to be exterminated. In *Ober Ost,* often cleanliness was next to violence. In the program of 'cleaning' the East, a crucial concept was deployed, that of '*Raum*'. *Raum* can be very roughly translated into English as 'space', but in fact the term has in German a complex of allied meanings which carry decisive implications. They suggest concepts of 'clearing' and 'cleaning': '*aufräumen*', '*räumen*'.[21]

He continues that, '[c]laiming that they had found Wilna's city hall full of Russian excrement, officials equated cleaning with possession'.[22]

Essentialist views about Armenians were fairly widespread; they had some similarities with those about Jews, and indeed the two religious groups were frequently compared. In 1939, Fritz Bronsart von Schellendorf repeated this comparison: 'By the unanimous judgment of all Near Easterners, this race is nine times worse as profiteers than the Jews!'[23] For him,

> the Armenian is just like the Jew, a parasite outside the confines of his homeland, sucking off the marrow of the people of the host country . . .

Hence the hatred which, in a medieval form, has unleashed itself against them as an unpleasant people, entailing their murder.[24]

By any standard 'nationalist' criteria, Armenians were an 'autochthonous' people in Anatolia. Furthermore, most of Europe's Jews were also 'autochthons', having lived in Europe since before the time of Christ.[25] In 1935, in an article entitled 'L'Invasion: Les Etrangers en France', the French anti-Semite Lucien Rebatet compared the 'dirty' Armenians with Jews: they shared the same aptitudes and lacked attachment to particular territories, they shared the same 'promiscuity' in ghettos and had been subjected to pogroms. They only differed, as far as Rebatet was concerned, in that the Jews were more 'deceitful' and Armenians did not possess the Jews 'feverish vitality'.[26] As so often with prejudice, it reveals more about the writer and their anxieties than about the subject matter. Otto von Feldmann, former chief of staff at the Turkish general headquarters, used the putative difference between Turks and Armenians to excuse atrocities: 'the Turk is indolent, incapable of handicrafts and engages in business unwillingly. Therefore, he has much left to the very active but also unscrupulous Armenian and greatly exploited by him. If these dispositions burst, they, in a way let off steam for which we, thank God, have no understanding.'[27] Such obfuscatory remarks could only have been made in the context of an increasing German encroachment in Anatolia and in an attempt on the part of Germans to justify their own involvement with the Turkish regime.

Although we largely construct the violent actions against groups such as Jews or Armenians in political and ethnic terms, and clearly there was prejudice and even 'racism', most contemporaries regarded the genocides of 1912–23 as primarily a religious phenomenon. Donald Bloxham has argued that, '[i]n terms of their function for the Ottoman state, the 1894–6 massacres combined political elements of a "cull" of a proto-national element, including terrorization and expropriation, with a neo-conservative religious backlash against an "inferior" upstart religious group'.[28] The idea of the religious symbolism within persecution had already entered poetic consciousness before the breakdown of the eastern European empires, and therefore tapped into already existing fears about the position of minorities, especially under the Ottomans. Johann Wolfgang von Goethe described

Christians impaled on stakes and Jews in the fire in his *Venezianischen Epigrammen*.[29] The massacre of Armenians in the Church of St Stephen was carried out by Turks described as '*sanguinaires et sacrilèges*', their victims being described as '*iconastases*' (the images of dead and martyred saints in Byzantine churches).[30] Undoubtedly, sympathy for Christians and antipathy towards Muslims (and sometimes Jews) affected the manner of reporting these events in western Europe and in the United States. In 1915, the archbishop of Canterbury argued that the Armenian massacres had 'no parallel' in the history of the world and that 'Christian aid should flow out ungrudgingly',[31] therefore distinguishing between the fate of the Armenians and that of the Muslims of the Balkans, who had been killed in vast numbers only three years earlier, or that of the Jewish victims of pogroms.

When it became clear that Christianity was likely to disappear from Anatolia with the burning of Smyrna in September 1922 and the exodus of the remaining Greeks, the situation was generally depicted in rather hagiographic terms in a number of influential accounts. The legendary appearance of Atatürk with his troops at Nif on the outskirts of the city – which was soon to become Izmir – signalled the end of *giaour* Smyrna. George Horton's emotional account of these events, *Blight of Asia*, contains one of the most well-known accounts of the genocide; it concludes that '[t]he Turk roams over the land of the Seven Cities and there is none to say him nay, but the last scene in the final extinction of Christianity was glorified by the heroic death of the last Christian'.[32] The death of Greek Orthodox Bishop Chrysostom was described by one writer as 'glorious, but tragic'.[33] '[T]he evidence is conclusive that he met his end at the hands of the Ottoman populace. He was offered a refuge in the French Consulate and an escort by the French marines, but he refused, saying that it was his duty to remain with his flock. He said to me "I am a shepherd and must stay with my flock" '.[34]

Political crises created opportunities for the removal of targeted populations, often through 'traditional' forms of violence. The diplomat Hohenlohe-Langenburg told Chancellor Bethman Hollweg in August 1915 that the beginning of Bairam had coincided with rumours about further attacks on Armenians.[35] However, Islam, Judaism and Christianity are all monotheistic faiths which emphasize the need to contain and restrain violence. More importantly, they stress the necessity to care about the needs of the other beyond the boundaries of the immediate religious community. Nevertheless, where religious boundaries exist, they often harden, which can lead to acts of extreme callousness, outside the spirit of any of the faiths. Violence frequently had a gendered character, sweeping away traditional restraints towards women. In Bulgaria in 1878, Muslim women were raped and then set on fire by their Christian neighbours.[36] In Macedonia, as the Muslim populations were expelled in 1922–3, women in the village of Guvezna 'were said to have gathered together in the marketplace and publicly ridiculed as they were forced to dance naked at gunpoint'.[37] As the Russians advanced in Turkey during the First World War, they killed and attacked Muslims. An American, Grace Higley Knapp, reported that '[t]he wild Cossacks considered the Turkish women legitimate prey'.[38] Sometimes, as the Bryce Report indicates, this was perceived as a direct form of revenge:

A woman, fleeing with her two children – her husband was abroad – met a Moslem mullah in her flight. He took the children, stripped them of their clothing, and threw them all into a stream, which was on the point of freezing. He then offered to marry the woman. On her refusal he left the woman on the road to her fate . . . Later the sorrowing woman found her way to Urmi, and five months afterwards the Russians caught this inhuman brute and made him suffer for his crime.[39]

During Kristallnacht in Germany in 1938 violence took on a 'sadistic, infantile, sexist [and] aggressive' character. One woman ran from her house but was caught by Nazi party members who 'beat her between the legs with a broom and poured water there'.[40]

The violence of this period violated previous norms of hospitality, which are embedded within Islam. In the village of Sagh Gachad in Turkey in 1909, seven Armenian preachers and their party of five visitors were murdered: 'a party of Mohammedans took these travelers from the houses where they had spent the night, and gathering together other Armenians living [there] . . . until they had 92 in all, butchered all the unfortunates in the streets of the village'.[41] Similarly, the Bryce Report recorded an incident which would appear to be an antithesis of Islamic teaching: 'Several Turks

whom I interviewed told me that the motive of this exile was to extermi-
nate the race, and in no instance did I see any Moslem giving alms to
Armenians, it being considered a criminal offence for anyone to aid them.'[42]
There was also a conflation between Armenians and traitors.

> The Bishop of Erzeroum was . . . murdered at Gumush-Khana. Besides the
> deportation order referred to above an Imperial 'Iradeh' was issued
> ordering that all deserters when caught, should be shot without trial. The
> secret order read 'Armenians' in lieu of 'deserters'. The Sultan's 'Iradeh' was
> accompanied by a 'fatwa' from Sheikh-ul-Islam stating that the Armenians
> had shed Moslem blood and their killing was lawful. At Trebizond the
> Moslems were warned that if they sheltered Armenians they would be
> liable to the death penalty.[43]

Religious personnel were often fanatics, responsible for the fanning the
flames of mistrust between religious groups. In Russia, Holy Synod itself was
responsible for provoking violence in many cases.[44] According to another
statement made to Lord Bryce:

> The Hodja [Turkish priest] of our hospital came in, too, and said to us,
> among other things: 'If God has no pity on them, why must you have
> pity? The Armenians have committed atrocities at Van. That happened
> because their religion is *ekzik* [inferior]. The Moslems should not have
> followed their example, but should have carried out the massacre with
> greater humanity.[45]

Some also claimed to have tried to prevent violence. Platon, archbishop
of Kherson and Odessa, recalled: 'I witnessed a mob of 20,000 in Kiev in
1905 . . . mad, blind people ready to destroy Jewish homes and Jewish
lives. I rose against them, appealed to them and begged with them and
finally persuaded them to go to their homes.'[46] In 1896 in Constantinople,
British Vice-Consul Gerald Fitzmaurice noted:

> The Mussulmans here and elsewhere interpreted them as the Sovereign's
> wish that they should put into execution the prescription of the 'Sheri'

[... Islamic law], and proceeded to take the lives and property of the rebellious Armenian 'rayahs' ... rumours reached here of massacres of Armenians by their [*sic*] co-religionists in other towns in Anatolia; they were told that the Armenians were attacking mosques and using dynamite, while word came from their Mussulman brethren in towns where massacres had occurred inciting them to do their duty by Islam.[47]

One striking thing about accounts of violence is their ludic quality[48] of imitating everyday life in a bizarre way; they were what one contemporary called 'Bacchanalian actrocities'.[49] There was an almost ludic and 'barbaric' quality to the death of Chrysostomos. 'The crowd dragged him down the street until they reached a barber's shop ... Someone pushed the barber aside. Grabbed a white sheet and tied [it] around Chrysostomos's neck, shouting "Give him a shave!"'.[50] Similar scenes were repeated elsewhere. Jews often had their beards or earlocks pulled during pogrom violence.[51] In his memoirs, Milovan Djilas described a similar thing happening to bearded Muslims in Montenegro, who also had crosses carved on their foreheads.[52] Many other incidences of violence had a quasi-religious element to them. Again and again, the violence was in excess of what was actually needed in order to cause death. When the Greeks killed the Ottoman outlaw Çakircali Mehmet Efe in the Smyrna hinterland, his decapitated body was 'hanged from his foot to destroy all myths and rumors about his invincibility'.[53] Charles Yriate remarked, concerning the violence during the uprising in Bosnia in the 1870s, that : 'nowadays, the irregular troops don't regard a victory as complete unless they dishonour the cadavre of the enemy'.[54] According to a Reuters correspondent for the *Scotsman*:

> The Greek Bishop of Ephesus was driving in full state in his carriage, when he was held up by Turks on the open road. They cut the embroidered holy images from off his robe, stole his silver episcopal staff and precious stones from his mitre, kicked him, and made off with his horses and carriage, leaving him dying on the road.[55]

There was a religious element to the way in which Crimean Tatars were persecuted by the Soviet authorities. One survivor of the deportations,

Alim, spoke about what had happened at Bilal Agha: 'They hanged Grandpa Djavit and Kaytaz on a tree by the mosque. They shot fifteen people including Hassan Agha, lining them up against the mosque wall.'[56]

Symbolic violence included dishonouring, dehumanization and quasi-religious abuse and taunts. Often this could be a cruel inversion of what Mikhail Bakhtin defined as *risus paschalis* ('Easter laughter'), a form of transgression permitted by the Christian church in the holiday period.[57] In the Black Sea region and Ukraine, outbreaks of vicious violence against Jews and other religious minorities such as Armenians frequently broke out during Easter week. The 'peoples of the book' were, of course, used to religious stories about suffering, and their holy books are full of scenes of violence which can be interpreted in ambiguous ways – for instance, the preparation for the sacrifice of Isaac by Abraham in Genesis, apocalyptic passages in Ezekiel or the Passion. What Heinrich Heine called the 'torture chamber' ('*Folterkammer*') of weapons used against Jesus, including the scourge, the crown of thorns, the nails and hammer, could surely provoke an imitative or violent response if the biblical verses were read aloud to a congregation at Easter.[58] Helmut Walser Smith has argued that in the Middle Ages:

> the violence was overtly linked to theatre – oftentimes literally following the passion plays . . . In some cases of Holy Week violence . . . the people transgressed the symbolic restraints inherent in ritualized violence . . . Well into the nineteenth century, the force and terror of Holy Week violence drew its power from collective memory of these transgressions, from times when the barely controlled aggression of Christians washed over into unrestrained massacre.[59]

In his memoirs Simon Dubnow described the atmosphere of panic in Odessa around Easter in 1881,[60] and the pogrom in Kishinev in 1903 broke out after Holy Week. In the 1890s in Bousseyid, a priest was decapitated and, 'as a sign of complete contempt, his head was placed between his thighs and the young Turks of the locality amused themselves by resuming their testimony on the minister of Christ by flailing his body'.[61] Robert de Heïmann remembered seeing an old Bulgarian with a long beard killed by Turkish irregulars – a man whose head had been propped upon his chest.[62] It was reported in 1919 that '[i]n the village of Koum the Turks recently cut off the noses and ears of a Greek priest and two Greek notables'.[63] No doubt these actions reflect more traditional notions of honour related to the body,[64] mutilations symbolizing a complete victory over the enemy.

Crucifixion occurred during the Balkan wars in Macedonia; it was apparently committed by the Turks. Officer Penev reported that a soldier of the tenth Rhodope infantry had been crucified on a poplar tree by means of telegraph wires.[65] And it was reported that Muslim women were impaled upon stakes in the Aidan district by the Greeks during the war in 1919.[66] According to the missionary Helen Harris, Armenians were slashed across the breast in the form of a cross and asked: 'Where is your Jesus?' in the 1890s.[67] During the Armenian genocide of 1915, soldiers called out to the victims: 'Now let your Christ help you.'[68] Jews were forced to dance at gunpoint and to shout 'I'm Jesus Christ'.[69] Jews were thrown into the Dneister in 1941, with constant taunts about wanting to see the miracle of the Red Sea re-enacted.[70] In Adana in 1909, a Christian woman was crucified and her body then thrown into the river.[71] In the *Magnum Crimen*, a catalogue of crimes committed by clerical fascists in Croatia, Viktor Novak described how the Catholic priest Miroslav Majsterović, sometimes known as Vjekoslav Filipović, killed Serb women and children in quasi-religious rituals. In Rakovac in Bosnia he was reported to shout out: 'Die that I might release your sins.'[72] After the war, the communists continued the cycle of 'religious' atrocity and revenge by hanging Majsterović, in his clerical robes, near Jasenovac.

Many observers noted the mob nature of the violence. The oriental scholar and traveller Richard Burton offered an intriguing theory on female participation. He opined that 'the principal public amusement allowed to Oriental women'[73] were occasions such as funerals and other religious events, and he depicted the death-wail of these women as an opportunity for participation in the public sphere. During the Armenian massacres in the 1890s, a German missionary, Dr Julius Richter, observed that the violence:

was heralded by the blowing of trumpets and concluded by a procession [and] [a]ccompanied by the prayers of the mollahs and muezzins, who from the minarets implored the blessings of Allah . . . The Turkish woman stimulated their heroes by raising a guttural shriek of their war cry . . .[74]

Of course, as Henry Morgenthau suggested, 'beating drums and blowing whistles' would also drown the screams of sufferers.[75]

Church ceremonies, where the faithful gathered together in large numbers, could compound the vulnerability of targets. Perhaps also it 'resonated with the biblical significance of fire ... from the Book of Deuteronomy ... one of humankind's oldest symbols of purification'.[76] The burning of the congregation of 1,200 in the Armenian cathedral in Urfa in 1895 was a significant event, both in Armenian memory and for the wider world.[77] During the First Balkan War at Kurkut, Bulgarian gangs 'drove men into a mosque, set fire to the building, and shot those who tried to escape'.[78] According to the Reuters correspondent for the New York Times, this also happened to the Armenians near Bitlis in 1915.[79] 'At the village of Tikendjik they burnt about 300 in the house of the priest.'[80] Most contemporary sources written by Europeans and North Americans emphasize the religious element of this violence and the precarious situation of minorities. Many voiced deep disquiet about such violence. The novelist Maxim Gorky condemned the pogroms in Kishinev:

> People who regard themselves as Christians, who claim to believe in God's mercy and sympathy, these people on the day consecrated to the resurrection of their God occupy the time in murdering children and aged people, ravishing the women, and martyring the men of the race which gave them Christ ... Shame upon their wicked heads.[81]

A Christian survivor of the ethnic cleansing of Turkey in 1922 remembered that 'the peasants conceived the diabolical idea that ... victory against the Christians should be celebrated by a *Courban* [sacrifice or holocaust] of one or two Christians in each village ... Many prisoners were put to death in an atrocious manner.'[82] This persecution seems to be a particularly grisly imitation of the Passion of Christ. Theory can explain why society would divide along religious lines and gives possible motives associated with venality, wanton or sexual power, but we should also perhaps ask whether it is religion itself that makes individuals more violent. John Allcock argued that the Croatian fascists in the 1940s treated their Serb or Muslim victims as 'sacrificial animals ... [an] atrocity raised to the level of sacrament'.[83]

The Greek Patriarch of Constantinople, Gregorius, was killed in his sacred vestments after celebrating the Easter Day mass, to the horror of the Christian public of Europe.[84]

Robbing victims of their humanity by equating them with animals is commonplace in the litany of atrocities. Mark Levene has suggested that the sawing of victims imitates the dismembering of animal bodies.[85] During the Balkan Wars, several hundred Muslim men were taken to an abattoir and killed.[86] Isaac Babel recalled that in 1920 Jews in Zhitomir were led away to the cattle slaughterhouse.[87] During the Greek occupation of Smyrna in 1919, one Turk was bayoneted in the face and thrown in the hold of a Greek ship among the cattle.[88] One image of gratuitous violence that recurs in some of the accounts of ethnic cleansing is the use of horseshoes as torture weapons.[89] Peter Balakian recounts a story in which an Armenian victim 'awoke from her mother screaming. She hurried down the stairs and found her mother lying unconscious on the floor. She walked to the door and saw two horseshoes nailed to two human feet.'[90] The American ambassador to the Ottoman Empire in 1915, Henry Morgenthau, recalled in his memoirs a conversation with a 'responsible' Turkish official:

> Common reputation throughout Armenia gave a pre-eminent infamy to Djevdet Bey, the Vali of Van. All through this country Djevdet was generally known as the 'horseshoer of Bashkale' for this connoisseur in torture had invented what was perhaps the masterpiece of all – that of nailing horseshoes to the feet of his Armenian victims.[91]

Clearly, once this practice was initiated, from whatever source, knowledge about it spread and it occurred. Prejudices that surrounded different dietary practices could easily be transposed into wild ideas about ritual slaughter during times of ethnic tension. Pierre Bourdieu has defined *habitus* as 'structured structures predisposed to function as structuring structures',[92] which might explain the particular form of radicalization of religious groups during crises, drawing as it does on earlier occurrences. Rumours circulated after the death of the third 'ripper' victim in London in 1888 that the killer had to be a *shochet*, a kosher butcher.[93] Although this rumour gained little currency in Britain, it was widely believed on the continent of Europe.[94]

When a Czech servant of a Jew disappeared in 1892, the locals, blaming the Jews, penned a song. One line read: 'Then all of a sudden, the Jews ran up to her and tied her up; on the spot the butcher rose up and kosher-slaughtered Josefa.'[95] This accusation echoes a story printed by the *Leipziger Allgemeine Zeitung* in the 1840s about the missing Capuchin Tommaso having been 'ceremonially slaughtered by a Jewish religious butcher'.[96]

It is unlikely that religion provided more than just the form and shape of violence, as human societies have been characterized by brutality across space and time.[97] It is certain that faith helped some individuals to reconcile themselves to violence and dislocation. Survivors of the Armenian genocide told of 'moments of epiphany when they had visions of being visited and comforted by a Jesus figure and were thus able to forgive the Turks and be reconciled with their past'.[98] In his description of the killing of Bosnian Muslims in 1915, William Frederick Bailey acknowledged the importance of religious faith at the hour of death.

> They are endeavoring to keep their faces turned towards the sun; and if they live until it sets, and if Allah lends them aid, they will watch the West turn crimson and the great red orb drop behind the mountains. They like to die at sundown, these people. Perhaps they fancy that the light of the world will bear their souls in a cloud of glory to the rose gardens of Paradise.[99]

Günther Schlee has argued that the sacrificial element in religious belief be interpreted in terms of both good and evil.

> The view that social identification . . . is often situational and comprises a dose of opportunism . . . is commonly accepted . . . Empirically valid as it may be, nevertheless it is hard to combine with an equally valid finding, namely that social identities can mobilize deep emotions, emotions which accompany horrible or noble acts, or acts which can be horrible and noble at the same time.[100]

Each confessional community perpetrated atrocities, which were in some way linked to their religious identity or discovered ethnic boundary marker.

Is the religious symbolism in ethnic violence important, and how conscious are the perpetrators of their actions? Although the symbolic element is fairly constant, we don't yet have a systematic analysis of this aspect of inter-ethnic violence.[101] Clearly also, once violence is initiated, it has its own bizarre momentum.

It has been observed that the killing of one's long-term neighbours, with whom one has previously been on good terms, is an act of cognitive dissonance.[102] The element of dissonance seems to be an almost universal characteristic of religious and ethnic prejudice across texts, and may explain the dissonance of violence in practice. We might therefore want to distinguish between dishonouring, dehumanization and symbolic violence rooted in religious imagery. Whereas an individual might have practised gender-based humiliation or violence and would have certainly witnessed or partaken in gratuitous cruelty against animals[103] as part of everyday life experience, directed violence (as opposed to suspicion and prejudice towards another community) might be entirely novel and its litany might be drawn from half-remembered passages from the Bible or Koran. Religious symbolic violence could be described as a reaction to textual influence *in extremis*, and is thus almost entirely ideological in character.

To understand the historical processes described here, we should perhaps return to Vahakn Dadrian's notion of the 'vulnerability' of religious communities at a time when states were unstable. Henry Morgenthau was sceptical as to whether it was really religion that was at the bottom of the events he witnessed in Turkey in 1915.

> Undoubtedly religious fanaticism was an impelling motive with the Turkish and Kurdish rabble who slew Armenians as a service to Allah, but the men who really conceived the crime had no such motive. Practically all of them were atheists, with no more respect for Mohammedanism than for Christianity, and with them the one motive was cold-blooded, calculating state policy.[104]

The pogroms, genocide, exodus and expulsions of the period 1870–1923 were a sign of the weakness of the state and of its inability to transform into a strong polity with civic rather than ethnic or religious notions of citizenship.

Arjun Appadurai has argued that 'the maiming and mutilation of ethni-cized bodies is a desperate effort to restore the validity of somatic markers of "otherness" in the face of the uncertainties posed by . . . changes',[105] and only with death comes 'dead certainty'. Often violence is in excess of what would actually be required to kill or maim an individual. Furthermore, '[e]thnic violence often occurs when there are few cultural markers accessible to differentiate between groups',[106] and these cases of violence can be inter-preted as an 'experience of solidarity'[107] which reaffirms old boundaries, creates bitter divisions between the victims and victimizers, but crucially forges new bonds between the perpetrators. Although it would be simplistic to present heterodoxy as a social norm, it is clear that, for violence to occur, there must be a social crisis in which ideologies of 'homogeneity' such as nationalism can be presented as a new and attractive norm which will forge links between people, even if this means that they are bound through blood. But we should add a note of caution to this observation. Where there are inequalities or extant boundaries, especially if there are elements of asym-metry in social relations, it is probably easier to create a crisis, or a situation in which the participants in violence appear to enjoy the process of destruc-tion because they appear to be committing a kind of 'revenge'. This is not simply a 'collective ludic experience of transgression';[108] it affirms member-ship of the newly defined group in a very real sense. In other words, the very existence of violence as a phenomenon is a sign that acculturation has already taken place and that society is becoming (potentially) more inte-grated. In the Russian empire, Jews were leaving the shtetl, taking profes-sional positions, moving outside the Pale of Settlement and speaking Russian in the immediate years before the revolution – which is clearly a paradoxical situation, given the increase in violence against Jewish people during this era. In the Ottoman Empire, likewise, Armenians were experiencing greater social integration in state institutions just prior to the genocide.

CHAPTER 5

The Battleground in Print

As the empires of eastern Europe clashed over land and stories of vast atrocities were relayed back to the rest of the continent, often with a lurid religious content, the ricochet effect was discernible in art and culture. Music, art and literature began to reflect an increasing preoccupation with violence. Of course, for centuries Europeans had read and thought about violent clashes between civilizations, and classical sources and terms of reference were hardly pacifist. Johann Wolfgang von Goethe thought that human culture would have been quite different had not Europeans come under the influence of the Bible and retained Homeric values.[1] According to Paul Cartledge, the poet Lord Byron 'was the principal avatar of what may fairly be called the "Age of Leonidas" in the early nineteenth century',[2] but he had rivals. Commissioned by Napoleon Bonaparte, Jacques Louis David's *Leonidas at Thermopylae*, painted in 1814, is one of the most celebrated venerations of war in the nineteenth century. Growing up in the Russian empire, Simon Dubnow claimed not only to have learnt grammar from classical writers but also to have absorbed some of the *Weltânschauung* of antiquity.[3] The Polish poet Adam Mickiewicz thought that Serbian folk poems were 'Homeric fragments', retaining values from a past age.[4] In his well-known study *The Great War and Modern Memory*, Paul Fussell maintained that '[t]he British intercourse with literature ... was instinctive and unapologetic – indeed, shameless ... Intact and generative are the ... values associated with traditional symbols – white blossoms, stars, the moon, the nightingale, the heroes of the *Iliad*, pastoral flowers.'[5] The symbolist poet Valery Briusov, who had translated Victor Hugo and Armenian poetry into Russian, claimed that the description of the Battle of Dubno in Nikolai Gogol's *Taras Bulba* was shaped 'not so much by the Ukrainian past as under the influence of Gnedich's translation of the *Iliad*'.[6]

Glorification of war could easily be transposed into an exaltation of inter-ethnic violence. When Gerald Reitlinger travelled through eastern Anatolia in 1930–1, he noted the devastation caused by the events of the wars of 1914–23 more than a decade earlier. In the inn in Kumerlu in Turkey he recalled that:

> the sleeping room [contained] . . . colour prints of the defeat of the Greeks at Dumlupunar. The Turks looked very European in their khaki uniforms, but the Greeks, in every Delacroix-like attitude of agony, had a wild Albanian appearance, in strict accordance with Byronic legend. These prints are possibly by the same hand as the prints of Smyrna, which I have seen in Greece. In these the Greeks are drowning in the harbour in bowler hats, while the Turks . . . are chopping up the women.[7]

Homer's invocation of Priam's grief for his son Hector helped generations of young men educated in a humanist tradition to accept or even expect war and violent death as they leant to accept illness, famine or the movements of the earth. The poet Henry Longfellow put it in a way that left little room for ambivalence: 'Yet better the excess than the defect; better the more than less; better like Hector in the field to die, Than like a perfumed Paris turn and fly.'[8] Other moments of deep compassion or emotion from both the classical and the Christian canon had the same effect. Re-readings of the destruction of Troy, Carthage or other ancient civilizations also helped to create a model of renewal after destruction. It helped to implant the idea that one civilization necessarily replaces another rather than a more historically nuanced idea that cultures weld together and create new cultures. In a Balkan context, literature clearly inspired anti-Ottoman nationalism: 'The names of Byron and Shelley, Goethe, Schiller and Victor Hugo meant nothing to the Sultan, but these were his real enemies.'[9]

Some contemporary writers drew on the classics for themes and inspirations. In his discussion of the novelist Walter Scott, Bob Chase has argued that '[r]omance ... represented human beings as already-made, undeveloping, static types of human substance, continually undergoing stereotypical tests and adventures in a timeless unlocalized landscape and never growing older in the process'.[10] The novelist Mark Twain, in a chapter on 'The Sir Walter disease' published in 1883, famously blamed his fellow novelist for romanticizing battle and creating a cult of violence.

> Sir Walter Scott with his enchantments and with his single might checks this wave of progress, and even turns it back; sets the world in love with dreams and phantoms; with decayed and swinish forms of religion; with decayed and degraded systems of government, with the silliness and emptiness, sham grandeurs, sham gauds, and the sham chivalries of a brainless and worthless long vanished society.[11]

We know that the Montenegrin writer Njegoš, whose poetry has been described as a 'true breviary of interethnic hatred',[12] had a copy of Scott's well-known novel *Ivanhoe* in his library.[13]

When observers saw mass death beside water, they recalled Virgil's lines: 'Wars, horrid wars, I view – a field of blood, And Tiber rolling with a purple flood',[14] or the water 'reddened with blood' in Homer's *Iliad*.[15] In Dante's *Inferno,* the first part of his *Divina Commedia,* the poet, accompanied by the spirit of Virgil, sees 'the river of blood in which the spirits of those who have done violence to others will boil'.[16] The medieval writer provoked a powerful response in later writers. Viktor Novak thought that 'neither Dante nor Goya' would have been able to convey the horrors of the Ustaša camp of Jasenovac.[17] For the Ukrainian poet Taras Shevchenko, 'rivers of blood' would continue to flow until there was freedom and justice.[18] For those living through catastrophe, the notion of rivers of blood also had renewed importance and resonance. In 1915, eye-witnesses to the mass murder of Armenians actually reported that the Euphrates ran red with blood.[19] In work on genocide in the African Great Lakes region, the anthropologist Chris Taylor has suggested that a flowing river could represent 'canals, arteries and conduits along which persons and substances flow'.[20] A river that flows with blood rather than water is one which represents the end of the movement of people, and indeed their violent demise.

Eliminationist writers celebrated the idea that blood would flow in rivers during provoked ethnic violence. The metaphor of rivers of blood was also frequently used in 1932 by the fascist leader Ante Pavelić, in exile in Italy, in the pages of his newspaper *Ustaša*.[21] The Croatian fascists went on to commit genocide against their Serb and Jewish citizens, essentially fulfilling their own prophecy. If Pavelić had a literary source, it may well have been Homer, Virgil or Dante, but in a more local context he may have also been drawing on the vivid metaphorical language of the Montenegrin poem *Gorski Vijenac*, first published in 1847 and widely known in south-eastern Europe. The poem concerns a mythical showdown between Orthodox Montenegrins and Slavonic converts to Islam. Vojvoda Batrić proclaims: 'I do swear by the faith of Obilić and by these arms in which I put my trust, that both our faiths will be swimming in blood [*u krv će nam vjere zaplivati*]. Better will be the one that does not sink.'[22] Defending himself in court after the Second World War, Četnik leader Draža Mihailović claimed that '[e]ntire regions were destroyed by [Bosnian] Muslims . . . but this had repercussions afterwards', as his men revenged themselves and the Drina became 'a river of blood'.[23] In effect, this was a form of obfuscation, as the Četniks deliberately killed Muslims outdoors, on bridges, which had come to symbolize Bosnian unity, rather than killing them in a 'detached ad hoc' manner in a more private place. They then dumped their bodies, in full view, in rivers, in order to 'destroy the very hope of future coexistence between Serbs, Muslims and Croats'.[24]

Violent literary or historical images also created some kind of urtext for violent behaviour. In September 1940 the Romanian Iron Guard 'dragged more than a hundred Bucharest Jews to the city abattoir. Having slaughtered them with butchers knives in a parody of Jewish dietary practice, they then "took the intestines they had plucked out of their victims' bodies and tied them like neckties around the necks of those murdered".'[25] Edward Gibbon's *Decline and Fall of the Roman Empire*, which first appeared in the 1770s,[26] reports a similar practice, but this time the atrocity was perpetrated by Jews.

In Cyrene, [they] massacred 220,000 Greeks; in Cyprus, 240,000; in Egypt, a very great multitude. Many of these unhappy victims were sawed asunder, according to a precedent to which David had given the sanction of his examples. The victorious Jews devoured the flesh, licked up the blood, and twisted the entrails like a girdle around their bodies.[27]

There are several explanations for the similarities of these practices, or at least the similarities of the texts. One possible interpretation is that 'the human impulse to make fictions had been dramatically unleashed by the novelty, immensity and grotesqueness of the proceedings'.[28] The Romanian Iron Guard was immersed in its Roman heritage and, like many of their contemporaries, its members would have read Gibbon. Their leader Ion Antonescu told his cabinet: 'This is the hour when we are masters of our own territory. We must take advantage of it. I do not mind if history judges us barbarians. The Roman Empire performed a series of barbaric acts against its contemporaries and yet it was the greatest political establishment.'[29] Another explanation comes from everyday practices of killing animals and thus from a familiarity with body parts of mammals such as pigs. This suggests that, in extreme acts of violence, there is a conflation between human and animal victims in the eyes of the perpetrators.

Educated Europeans remained governed by the value of honour, dramatizations of masculinity, aversion to physical shame and heroic military values into the nineteenth century and beyond. Growing access to information in terms of print culture and subsequently of cinema and other visual media gave them a greater chance to lead idealized and stylized lives, a tendency acknowledged by Oscar Wilde in his celebrated formula about nature imitating art. Henry Morgenthau thought that Enver Paşa had a sentimental and poetic side to his character. Some of that sentimentality survived the war. He always carried the Koran with him, and a few days before he was killed by the Bolsheviks in Bukhara in 1922 he gathered up the twig of an elm which he had slept under and sent it to his wife.[30] It would be as well to remember that eliminationists thought of themselves not as mass murderers, but as idealists and servants of a cause. Radical evil and idealism are in many respects two sides of the same coin, particularly if that vaunted 'ideal' cannot possibly be realized without dislocation and death. Eliminationist theorists of the nation were nothing if not fantasists immersed in imaginary worlds before they started to create political repercussions amongst contemporaries.

Ironically, as combat skills became less relevant to the lived experience of Europeans, the cult of heroism, and in effect violence, took hold in terms of 'Romanticism'.[31] In his short poem *On Homer's Poetry*, the eccentric pacifist William Blake felt that 'it is the Classics and not Goths or Monks that desolate Europe with wars'.[32] That militaristic values should survive from earlier epoch is one matter. That they should be revived by extreme nationalists is yet another.

The Roman Emperor Nero (r. AD 54–68) has generally been known to posterity as a sex maniac, glutton and pyromaniac who started the Great Fire of Rome, as well as a sadistic tyrant. The arbitrary cruelties of his reign, including (briefly) his persecution of Christians,[33] were described in sordid detail by the Roman historian Suetonius. Tacitus in his *Annals* informed the reader that 'a rumour had spread that when the city was burning, Nero had gone on his private stage, and comparing modern calamities with ancient, had sung of the Destruction of Troy'.[34] Both these Roman historians were

Figure 3 Henryk Siemiradzki, *Pochodnie Nerona* (1876). Christians depicted as human torches (National Museum Krakow).

widely read in the nineteenth and early twentieth centuries. Their vision of Nero inspired an image of violent tyranny that could be made and remade to suit other circumstances, for instance, the treatment of Ottoman Christians or the suppression of Poles in imperial Russia. Leopold, king of the Belgian Congo during the genocides against the local Africans, denied that he could be compared to the Roman emperor, mocking the very suggestion.[35] St Petersburg trained artists, who 'enjoyed international renown'[36] in the later nineteenth century, and produced graphic and violent canvases including Henryk Siemiradzki's *Pochodnie Nerona* (*Nero's Torches*) (1876) and *Dirce* (1897). The former painting depicts the violent execution of Christians in front of the emperor. In Poland, Nero's persecution of early Christians became a metaphor for the oppression of contemporary Christians under tsarist rule, and *Nero's Torches* was donated by the artists to the Old Cloth Hall in Kraków. In 1895 another Pole, Henryk Sienkiewicz, who later won the Nobel Prize for Literature, wrote a popular novel about the Roman persecution of Christians: *Quo vadis?*, which was widely translated. His depiction of Nero as a killer of his mother and wife helped to create an image of the emperor in the popular imagination.[37] His view of Rome as a morally decaying state and as an oppressor of other nations was taken largely from Tacitus. One of the characters in the novel, Petronius, observes that 'the garlanded trophy-bedecked chariot in which Rome was riding at the head of a train of fettered nations was making straight for the abyss'.[38] The man who coined the term 'genocide', Raphael Lemkin, had read Sienkiewicz's novel as a child, and his mother Bella explained the cruelty of the Romans through a contemporary analogy: 'once the state became determined to wipe out an ethnic or religious group, the police and the citizenry became the accomplices and not the guardians of human life'.[39]

The obliteration of Anatolia's Armenian community and the violent exchange of population after the Greek–Turkish War of 1923 emboldened and inspired further moves. In particular, the burning of Smyrna by Atatürk's troops in 1922 inspired the historical imagination of contemporary writers. For Richard Gondrand, it was a tragedy that reminded him of the immolation of Rome, or '*spectacles Néroniens*'.[40] But it is during these tragedies that the question of whether the model of classical catastrophes was sufficiently tragic in comparison with the present was raised. As Gondrand continued: 'History as they say repeats itself perpetually . . . but the history of the present is not a faithful or cruel parody as today's drama [in Smyrna] has eclipsed the past.'[41] Similarly, when Rendel and Helen Harris described the Hamidian massacres in 1890s, they wrote: 'Monsters like Nero have flooded the world with blood . . . but our suffering has no respite.'[42] German evangelicals saw the persecution of the Armenians in the 1890s in terms of the sorrows of the early church. For them Abdülhamid was a Diocletian or a Nero. For Berliners in particular, 'the incendiary Nero was a vivid figure. During the 1880s a popular panorama depicting the Roman emperor's human torches, wrapped like mummies in pitch, had kept crowds aghast.[43] The immolation of so many Armenians inside their churches made the parallel seem self-evident, as did reports of crucifixions.'[44] Nero continued to be a figure for negative historical comparison. Lion Feuchtwanger published his play Der falsche Nero in 1936, which was clearly meant to be interpreted as a political commentary on the Third Reich.[45] Lieutenant Röser was an 'agresssive young officer of the Wehrmacht nicknamed by his own regiment "the Nero of the 12/98" '.[46] Surely Victor Klemperer had Roman despotism in mind when he called the Nazi's euphemistic language 'lingua Tertii Imperii' ?[47]

The romantic revival of the hero had a deep impact on the public of the Russian empire. Experiencing a 'silver age' in culture in the later nineteenth century, readers endured long, snow-bound winters buying books by weight rather than by individual title. They also bought more books than most other European nations, with the exception of the Germans. These were perfect conditions for nationalism or other forms of idealism to flourish. One of the romantic images that held most allure for Russians and Ukrainians was that of the Cossack, although the role of Cossacks as the Praetorian Guard of the tsarist state was also sharply criticized by the radical left.[48] One of the earliest works to celebrate Cossack values, albeit through a Russian lens, was Nikolai Gogol's short story Taras Bulba, first published in 1835. In the style that he used Gogol drew not only on the classics but also on Walter Scott and Alexander Pushkin.[49] This piece tells the story of an old Cossack, Taras, and his sons, all of whom are eventually killed by the treacherous Poles. Even in death, which comes in the form of 'crucifixion', the captured Taras remains defiant as he dies on a burning tree.

They bound him with iron chains to the trunk of the tree, driving nails through his hands and raising [him] as high as possible that the old kazák might everywhere be visible and immediately they began to build a pile of faggots at the foot of the tree. But Taras did not look at the pyre, nor did he think of the fire with which they were preparing to burn him ... But fire had already risen above the faggots; it was lapping his feet, and the flame spread to the tree ... But can any fire, flames, or power be found on earth, which are capable of overpowering Russian strength?[50]

In death he retains his fighting spirit and the respect of the Cossacks. Gogol's short story enjoyed considerable success in its own time and inspired other works. The French literary critic Charles Augustin Sainte-Beuve compared it to the Homeric poems, calling it a 'Cossack Iliad' (*cette Iliade zaporogue*),[51] endowing it with both national and international status. Thus the work of Gogol became canonical in a way that was never achieved by Jewish writers from the region before 1917, despite their overwhelming literary merits. It is difficult to overestimate the importance of *Taras Bulba* in the imagination of the people of this region. Viktor Vasnetsov's drawings illustrated a version of the story published in 1871. Further illustrations to the story were produced by Sergei Ivanov in 1902 and Ilya Repin, arguably the greatest artistic talent of the silver age, also drew Taras in 1903. Several films were made of the story. A Russian version came out in 1909; this was followed by another, made by exiled Russians, in 1935. Nowadays the most enduring piece inspired by Gogol is Leoš Janáček's composition of the same name, which was written during the First World War but not performed until after the end of the Ukrainian Civil War.

During the pogrom in Kishinev in 1903, spikes were driven through the hands, legs and into the heads of Jews. Shlomo Lambroza argues that this act might be interpreted as 'retribution' for the crucifixion,[52] but the crucified figure of Taras and the anti-Semitic nature of Gogol's work might also provide some kind of urtext. Perhaps an even more violent piece of literature that could have fulfilled this function was the passage in Fyodor Dostoyevsky's *Brothers Karamazov* in which the characters Lise and Aloysha discuss Jewish 'practices'. Lise says: 'I read it in a book about a trial some-where ... that a Jew at first cut off a four-year-old child's fingers on both hands, and then crucified him, nailed him to a wall, and then said at his trial that the boy died soon.'[53] In the Ukrainian *Song of the Oprishki* (*Song of the Robbers*), there is a line as follows: 'The Jew merchant shall give clothing at our orders, Or else he'll be nailed to his door.'[54] We might be sceptical as to whether images in Gogol or Dostoyevsky, or even in folk poetry, could provoke violence rather than the more obvious urtext which is Christ's Passion. Edward Judge has reminded us that the ringleaders in the Easter pogrom of 1903 in Kishinev were educated individuals, and one of the chief sources of agitation, the newspaper *Bessarabets*, was edited by Pavle Krushevan, an intellectual.[55]

In one traditional Ukrainian poem, we see the idea that freedom fighters for the Ukraine were being linked to bandit culture, very much as in the Balkans the *čete* (bandits) were perceived to be in the front line against Ottoman oppression. '*Haidamaky* (bandits) they call us, unrelenting and stern. With the wrongs of our nation for vengeance we burn. Our forebears were tortured; our grandsons shall be. Unless we will show them how men may be free.'[56] Although Taras Shevchenko was not an anti-Semite himself, his poem 'Haidamaky' published in 1841 presented the violence of the Koliivshchyna uprising of 1768 in terms of righteous indignation against the Polish landlords (and against Jews who acted as their intermediaries), linking the violence to a notion of class struggle.[57] At some level, Shevchenko's image had also permeated popular consciousness and provided a 'radical new paradigm' for Ukrainian independence.[58] One Jewish victim of pogroms in Ukraine during the civil war had 'a *haidamaka* carved this' into his chest.[59]

The Khmelnitsky Uprising was also a popular theme for writers. Orest Subtelny has argued that, because they were accessible representatives of the Polish *szlachta* between 1648 and 1656, 'tens of thousands of Jews' were murdered.[60] Some years later, in 1857, the historian Mykola Kostomarov, who had met Shevchenko in 1845, published his study *Bohdan Khmelnytsky*. Kostomarov viewed the Jews as 'arrogant' and portrayed the Khmelnitsky Uprising in terms of class struggle, interpreting the suffering of the Jews as popular retribution.[61] The French writer Prosper Mérimée wrote his own version of the Cossack rebellion, *Les Cosaques d'autrefois*, in Paris.[62] This version includes the play *Bogdan Chmielnicki*, which helped to introduce

Cossack culture to a wider European reading public. As he knew Russian, one of his primary historical sources was Kostomarov's work. Mérimée had long been fascinated by the Ukrainian–Russian borderlands. He had previously published *Les Cosaques d'Ukraine et leurs derniers atamans* in 1854 and *Révolte de Stenka Razine* in 1861.[63] For Russians, the image of the Cossacks was promoted through literature and by the publisher Florentiĭ Pavlenkov, who brought out a volume on Khmelnitsky in his popular series *Zhizn' zamechatel'nykh liudei* (*Lives of Remarkable People*).[64]

Taras Bulba is notable for creating a juxtaposition between 'noble' Ukrainian Cossacks, 'miserable' Jews and 'perfidious' Poles. Léon Poliakov argued that it was the first time that a native Jew had made an appearance in Russian letters, only to be drowned and humiliated as a 'plucked chicken'[65] – a metaphor which later appears in Dostoyevsky, Chekhov and Babel. This painful trope entered Jewish consciousness. Yosef Haim Brenner, who was subsequently killed in the pogrom in Jaffa in 1921,[66] wrote *Hu amar lah* (*He Told Her*) about the pogroms of 1905 in Russia. In this story, the callous landlord's daughter is 'amused by Gogol's description ... of Cossacks tormenting powerless Jews in *Taras Bulba*'.[67] For Yosef Haim Brenner, Jewish self-defence was in the form of a combat between 'Yankl's miserable sons against Chmielnicki's muscular offspring,'[68] thus mixing an allusion to a fictional character (Yankl the Jew in Gogol's short story) with a real historical event. In Isaac Bashevis Singer's first novel, *Satan in Goray*, published in 1933, the author described how 'the rebelling *haidamak* peasants . . . slaughtered on all sides ... violated women and afterward ripped open their bellies and sewed cats inside'.[69] When Hayyim Nahman Bialik published his poem about the Kishinev pogrom of 1903, it appeared under the title 'Masa' Nemirov' ('The Oration at Nemirov'), which alluded to the Khmelnytsky Uprising and was intended to alert readers to the calamity the Jews were facing.[70] The stories they were told about the past had an enormous impact on young Jews. Later in life, Isaac Bashevis Singer told his son: 'These stories about the horrors of Chmielnicki and his Cossack murderer are based on facts. As a child, I remember lying in bed at night, trembling with fear. I was scared of every barking dog, every whinnying horse, scared the Cossacks had come back to make a pogrom against the Jews.'[71] The Menshevik Julius Martov recalled the impact of talking to an old woman from Elizavetgrad about the

Figure 4 Vásily Vereshchagin, *The Apotheosis of War* (1871) (Tretyakov Gallery, Moscow).

pogroms in 1881: 'Would I have become what I became had not Russian reality in that memorable night speedily impressed her coarse fingers into the plastic young soul?'[72] Unfortunately, despite the intentions of some authors, an image of the Cossacks as implacably anti-Semitic entered Ukrainian and Jewish consciousness just as the state was emerging; this made the project of creating a civic nationalism which could inspire all peoples of the region, Ukrainians, Jews, Tatars and Russians, a formidable task. It was one that eluded the founders of the short-lived independent Ukraine, including Hetman Symon Petlura.

In 1847, 'Gorski Vijenac' ('The Mountain Wreath') by Petar II Petrović Njegoš, the prince–bishop of Montenegro, was published. The main theme of the poem is the supposed dilemma faced by his predecessor, Danilo (1700–35), about what to do with Muslim Montenegrins. The poem contains violent threats from the character Vojvoda Batrić, who wants to 'burn down Turkish homes so that no trace of the dwellings of our home-grown faithless devils could be known'.[73] Njegoš had a sizeable library which included the Greek classics,[74] so his writing was not wholly outside wider European conventions and was widely translated. For the Nobel Prize-winning Bosnian novelist Ivo Andrić, Njegoš was 'the complete expression of our basic, deepest collective sentiment'.[75] Nationalist writers created the self-image of a perpetual state of mental struggle against the Turks (who were then partially replaced by the Austrians as the enemy in the latter part of the nineteenth century).[76] The youths who challenged the Habsburgs' right to be in Bosnia and lined up to assassinate Archduke Franz Ferdinand in Sarajevo in 1914 had all memorized 'Gorski Vijenac'.[77] Vladimir Dedijer mentions the poem several times in his war memoirs in referring to 'Montenegrin traditions . . . their struggle for freedom . . . the Mountain Wreath'.[78] It would be impossible to estimate the overall influence of this text on the minds of south Slavs. The verse, which draws on the melodic language of the Montenegrins, has been important in influencing later generations.[79] It is almost intertwined with their subconscious use of language, drawing as it does on the cadences of folk poetry. The anthropologist Zorka Milich questioned a number of centegenarian women in Montenegro in 1990. Jovana, aged 102, stated that '[t]he Turks were evil . . . and the use of cosmetics by the women made them stink'.[80] All these sentiments can found in Njegoš, which would make it rather difficult to assess whether they were drawn from a literary text or were actual prejudices. Milovan Djilas suggested that prejudice against Muslims 'left behind' in Montenegro was far greater than their real presence merited. 'The former Turkish landlords . . . were hardly noticed, but here their adversity filled every little corner of life – their songs and stories, evening gatherings under the old pear trees and desperate night carousing.'[81]

If writers from the Balkan region created a literary trope which revolved around the perpetual oppression of the Ottomans, this literary endeavour was augmented by foreign writers in solidarity with Balkan Christians. As he travelled through the region in the 1890s, Harry Thomson remarked: 'I do not think that we western Christians, who have not undergone their fierce trial, appreciate fully the religious heroism these poor peasants have displayed during all the centuries they have been under the domination of the Turks'.[82] Although they were impressed by this struggle, many could not conceal their horror at brutal spectacles such as the dozens of severed and desiccated Turks' heads surrounding the *Vladika* residence in Cetinje in Montenegro.[83] Edward Said described this discourse of Islamic inferiority and barbarity as 'orientalism',[84] but equally important here was a sense that the Balkans were troubled even after independence by this legacy, a problematic discussed by Maria Todorova.[85] Another commonplace trope was that 'orientals' told elaborate stories. Morgan Philips Price, correspondent for the *Manchester Guardian* and an important witness to some crucial events of this period, noted that his Armenian servant gave him 'full particulars of the torturings, burnings and hangings [in the Van vilayet in 1896] with the added imagery of the East'.[86]

Nations which bordered on the Islamic world often absorbed much of that culture, as Orlando Figes has argued has been the case for Russia.[87] In the 1860s, the great Russian painter Vasily Vereshchagin travelled in Turkestan and captured his experiences on canvas.[88] After volunteering for the Russian army in 1867, he broke military conventions by capturing the atrocities against the Russians in pictures of the mutilated dead, but he also demonstrated the cruelty of his own side. As Figes notes, 'it was not clear who was the more "savage" in his pictures of the war: the Russian troops or their Asiatic opponents'.[89] His picture of the Indian Sepoy mutineers who were blown from a cannon by the British also greatly moved the American public when it was exhibited in the United States, juxtaposed as it was by Christ on Golgotha.[90] One of his most famous pictures, *The Apotheosis of War* (Fig. 4), depicts a pyramid of sculls in a barren desert with a destroyed town in the background, while dark predatory birds encircle the tragedy. He must have moved the viewers of his paintings to experience the true horror of war. Kaiser Wilhelm told Vereshchagin at an exhibition in Berlin in 1897 that his pictures were 'the best insurance against war'.[91] The composer Liszt Ferenc described his picture *Forgotten*, which depicts a dead abandoned Russian soldier, as a 'somber [*lugubre*] and terrifying symphony of vultures and crows. I understand it and enter deeply into his prodigious inspiration'.[92] When the German Consul in Aleppo, Walter Rößler, wrote to Germany's Special Envoy in Constantinople, Ernst Fürst zu Hohenlohe-Langenburg, about the miserable group of Armenian women and children he had seen on the road at Ras ul Ain in 1915, he thought that one would need an artist of the ability of Vereshchagin to capture the tragedy of the scene.[93]

Despite some humanist critical voices, a notion about the particular cruelty of some Asian political leaders, especially Attila, Tamerlane and Genghis Khan, remained an important trope in European writing since the Middle Ages, and one that was often used rhetorically.[94] In particular Tamerlane as the scourge of Christianity in Mesopotamia and his 'trademark ... pyramid of skulls'[95] haunted the European mind. Writing about the 'Tatar nations', John Crawfurd observed in 1861 that '[o]ccasionally they have united under a warlike leader and proved the scourge of civilized nations. Under Attila they ravaged Europe and under Gengis and Timur they ravaged Asia.'[96] When travellers crossed the Balkan peninsula, they were reminded of the Ottoman legacy.[97] In Niš in the 1870s, Humphrey Sandwith described the tower of skulls built after the rebellion led by Karadjordje: 'after the ancient and Asiatic tradition, [the Turks] collected the heads of the slain and built them into a tower to commemorate their victory and to strike terror into the conquered population. An ordinary square tower was first built of stone, with mud cement, and into this was foxed the heads of the slain.'[98] This horrible image was kept alive in the modern era by the poet Vasko Popa.[99]

Injustices committed by Attila the Hun were a favourite theme in literature. Géza Gárdonyi Ziegler's popular novel, *A láthatatlan ember* (*Slave of the Huns*), appeared in 1901. The French poet and dramatist Henri de Bornier, well known as the critic of *Nouvelle Revue*, had his drama *Les Noces d'Attila* first performed in 1880. The German writer Friedrich Werner chose Attila as his theme, inspiring Giuseppe Verdi's opera of the same name; the libretto, based on Werner's book, was penned by Temistocle Solera. As Anthony Arblaster has noted: 'The opera tells of how he was deterred from the Holy City and how he was finally killed by the Italians. Attila's name is still a byword for brutality and barbarism, and this image is partially sustained by the opera, at least in relation to his followers who sing cheerfully about feasting all night on limbs and severed heads.'[100]

During the collapse of the Ottoman Empire, outsiders became obsessed with injuries to the head as a quintessential symbol of 'oriental' brutality. In Adana in 1920 there were 'reports counting more than 300 headless bodies

on the fields near the city'.[101] At the trial of the assassin of the former
Ottoman leader Talât Paşa, it was said that 90 per cent of the Armenians
had died from head wounds, after they had fallen on their knees with their
heads bowed and their arms outstretched to heaven.[102] Many other writers
used references to the historical figures of Tamerlane;[103] these included
Johann Wolfgang von Goethe, who wrote about the 'myriad souls'
Tamerlane had killed.[104] In interpreting the attacks on Assyrian Christians
in the Ottoman Empire, Joel Werda wrote:

> The Governor of Urmia, Ejlal-el-Moolk, a personified demon, sent his
> agents to broadcast into the rural districts, under the pretence of quieting
> the people, but in reality to urge the Mohammedans secretly to sell
> even the garments on their backs, and purchase arms for the day of
> revenge. The Assyrians were, of course, aware of this double-crossing by
> the Moslems, but Mar Shimon persisted in his Christian effort, continued
> to hope against hope, thinking that, while these offspring of Taimur the
> lame might have been absolutely barren of the voice of conscience, they
> might still be in possession of a feeble sense of honour.[105]

At the other extreme or perhaps as an inverse reaction, eliminationist nationalists tended to celebrate the 'achievements' of these infamous despots. Like
those who wanted to create 'rivers of blood', there were writers who thought
that cruelty was justified by historical impulses and the inevitable battle
between nations. During a speech in 1939, Adolf Hitler invoked the 'annihila-
tive spirit'[106] of Genghis Khan, who 'set millions of women and children into
death knowingly and cheerfully . . . Yet history sees in him only the great
founder of states.'[107] Ziya Gökalp, often considered to be one of the most
important Turkish nationalist writers,[108] celebrated: 'My Attila, my Jenghis . . .
these heroic figures, which stand for the proud fame of my race, appear on the
dry pages of the history books as covered with shame and disgrace, while in
reality they are no less than Alexander and Caesar.'[109] In 1908, the Young Turk
writer Halidé Edib Hanum thought that the ideal modern Turk would be 'the
Attila or Ghenghis type, who had evolved into a civilized person'.[110] Writing
during the First World War, the historian Arnold Toynbee was critical of the
notion of a pan-Turkish identity or Turanism, which was 'saturated with

forgotten European moods, and its vein of Romanticism is as antiquated as the Kaiser's. It has taken Attila to its heart, and rehabilitated Jenghis Khan, Timur, Oghuz, and the rest with the erudition of a Turanian Walter Scott.'[111] Many of the most passionate who advocated a pan-Turkish identity were 'Tatar exiles' from the Russian Empire.[112]

In *Dreigroschen Román* (*Threepenny Novel*), which first appeared in 1936, the German writer Bertholt Brecht observed (ironically) that 'the most important thing to learn is to think coarsely (*plumpes Denken*), as that is the way the great think.'[113] The Marxist critic Walter Benjamin realized that Brecht had 'put his finger' on one of the things that allowed extremism to flourish in the twentieth century. Coarse or crude thinking 'belong to the household of dialectical thinking precisely because they represent nothing other than the application of theory to practice . . . a thought must be crude in order to come into its own in action'.[114] Many contemporary writers were scornful of the modest abilities of the eliminationists, who clearly celebrated the value of coarse thinking. In 1940, George Orwell observed of Adolf Hitler: 'When one compares his utterances of a year or so ago with those made fifteen years earlier, a thing that strikes one is the rigidity of his mind, the way in which his world view doesn't develop.'[115] Similarly, Hannah Arendt had little praise for Adolf Eichmann's ability to think, observing that he 'repeated word for word the same stock phrases and self-invented clichés', which she thought were constructed with 'an inability to think . . . from the standpoint of anyone else'.[116]

Formulae about the need for population elimination, or indeed about the need to oppose it, did not always have to be entirely invented. The Bible could provide some of the language, both for those who deplored the attacks on minority communities and for those who supported them. Fishel Lahover thought that Bialik's poem on the Kishinev pogrom, in which he implored Jews to defend themselves against violent attacks, was modelled on the voice of the prophet Ezekiel.[117] The overall theme of the book of Ezekiel is both a condemnation of the Jews and a prophecy of the destruction of Jerusalem. Konstantin Pobedonostsev, tutor of the last Tsar and procurator of the Holy Synod, was a leading anti-Semite during the twilight days of imperial Russia. In the course of a conversation with Alexander Zederbaum, the editor of the Jewish journal *Hamelitz*,[118] he advocated that one third of the Jews would convert, one third would die and one third would migrate. In Chapter 5 of the book of Ezekiel, a similar metaphor is used.[119]

> As for you, son of man, take a sharp sword; take and use it as a barber's razor on your head and beard. Then take scales for weighing and divide the hair. One third you shall burn in the fire at the centre of the city, when the days of the siege are completed. Then you shall take one third and strike it with the sword all around the city, and one third you shall scatter to the wind; and I will unsheathe a sword behind them.

Perhaps this passage from the Bible is what Paul Fussell had in mind when he said that the notion of 'a third' has 'sinister' and 'magical' connotations in literature.[120] In the tragedies of Aeschylus, widely known across Europe in the nineteenth and twentieth centuries, the third time an action occurs it is implicitly the last time, signifying 'performing an act of violence that will bring violence to an end'.[121] The poetics of elimination thus made a literary nod towards finality.

Although the actual proportions involved are not implicit, Vuk Karadžić's poem 'Početak Bune Protivu Dahija' about the expulsion of Turks from Serbia also carries the tripartite notion of conversion, expulsion or migration.[122] 'Then Djordje went to the white city. Turks would be cut down, others would be handed over and the rest sent to be baptized.' Karadžić was a highly influential writer, whose work was very well known outside Serbia,[123] and Pobedonostsev may well have been influenced by these lines. The poem repeats verbs which mean 'to cut' (sjeće, isjeće, and, a few lines earlier, posjeći). In 1917, the Serb nationalist Stojan Protić told Ante Trumbić: 'When our army crosses the Drina, it will give the Turks twenty-four or even forty-eight hours to return to the faith of their ancestors. Those who are unwilling will be cut down [posjeći] as we have done on other occasions in Serbia.'[124] This formula recurs in the plans of the Ustaša government, in a speech delivered on 22 July 1941 by Mile Budak, who often repeated formulae and mantras about ethnic violence: 'We will kill a part of the Serbs. Others we will deport, and the rest we will force to accept the Roman Catholic Religion. Thus the new Croatia will be rid of all Serbs in its midst in order to be 100 per cent Catholic within 10 years.'[125]

The use of historical myths, replete with empirical flaws, demonstrates how subjective, ephemeral and weak ethnic boundaries actually are. The repetition of ideas and practices, trawled from the historical and literary past, indicates not so much that human beings are essentially sadistic as that, in order to exclude individuals and communities, it is necessary to take away their qualification to belong, to be part of a region's heritage and of its past, and to legitimize this through recourse to poetry and other forms of culture. Intriguingly, both those who opposed violence and those who advocated peaceful coexistence often used the same rhetorical devices to justify their points of view.

In 1939, while describing his time in the Ottoman Empire during the First World War to the *Hanseatische Verlagsanstalt*, the German officer Fritz Bronsart von Schellendorf complained that 'whining German consuls who understood nothing about the military necessity for the resettlement, became indignant at the "atrocities" '.[126] Of course von Schellendorf was alluding to the major problematic that eliminationists faced, namely those individuals, such as Vasily Vereshchagin, who did not make a very clear distinction between the 'good' death of an enemy and the regrettable death of someone on one's own side. At the same time as eliminationism was emerging as a distinct set of ideas and practices, other individuals had altogether different thoughts about society and humanity. The most prominent defenders of nation as a tolerant place might best be described by using a term which was developed by the German writer Thomas Mann[127] and which appears in his correspondence with his brother Heinrich in 1936, namely 'militant humanism'.[128] In exile from the Nazis in France, Heinrich Mann wrote one of his most important works, *Die Jugend des Königs Henri Quatre*, published in 1935. He had started writing the chapter on St Bartholomew's Day in June 1934[129] and considered Henri IV as a model because he believed the king to have striven for religious tolerance by ending the wars which had divided France in the late sixteenth century and introducing toleration for the Huguenots through the Edict of Nantes.[130] His views were strongly influenced by reading Voltaire's *Essai sur les moeurs*[131] and possibly also by the song for Henri, *'ce roi vaillant'*, in Leo Tolstoy's *War and Peace*.[132] Mann stated that the idea for the novel came from 'my own private experience in life'.[133] In 1934 he told the First Congress of Soviet Writers: 'If later Germany should one day improve on its past performance, then I hope this literature will show itself to be the spiritual antecedent.'[134] His brother Thomas had earlier discussed a 'spiritual' repudiation of Nazism, as Heinrich's books were banned in 1938; the Nazis considered him a 'Jewish lackey' (*Judenknecht*)[135] and placed him on their *vade mecum* of banned and 'undesirable' authors (*Liste des schädlichen und unerwünschten Schrifttums*), along with his brother Thomas and many others, including Walter Benjamin, Bertolt Brecht, Willi Bredel, Albert Einstein, Lion Feuchtwanger, Sigmund Freud, Franz Kafka, Vladimir Lenin, Karl Liebknecht, Rosa Luxemburg, Leon Trotsky, Franz Werfel and the defender of the Armenians, the poet Armin T. Wegner. Like Heinrich Mann, Feuchtwanger also made literature a central part of his attempt to understand the politics of the present. He published the first chapter of *Der falsche Nero* in *Das Wort*, a journal of 'Germanistik' published in exile which he edited with Brecht and Bredel.[136] By doing this he was not only preserving a particular kind of German literary culture, but also providing a point of refuge where his fellow writers could publish.

Franz Werfel, the Prague-born novelist of Jewish origin, took up the cause of the Armenians in inter-war Europe. While he was in Syria in 1929, he saw the condition of Armenian refugees and took up their cause most notably in his novel *Die vierzig Tage des Musa Dagh* (*The Forty Days of Musa Dagh*), which chronicles the uprising at Van.[137] Chapter five of the novel is an imaginary dialogue between Johannes Lepsius, the Lutheran pastor who witnessed the Hamidian massacres, and the Ittihad leader Enver Paşa. In terms of its literary impact, it could be compared to Dostoyevsky's famous Inquisition scene in Seville in *The Brothers Karamazov*. *Musa Dagh* was translated into Hebrew in 1934. The Hebrew writer Dov Kimhi had read it in German and responded. 'Werfel . . . chose the Armenians for expressing the theme of human tragedy, even though there was an impending tragedy closer to him. And since no man can escape his destiny, the Hebrew reader . . . reads this book as the tragedy of ourselves.'[138] Werfel himself was very aware of the symbolic contemporary relevance (*Aktualität*) of a novel about the 'repression and destruction of minorities through nationalism', writing to his parents after Hitler's ascent to power.[139] In his memoirs, Bruno Bettelheim, a psychologist and pupil of Sigmund Freud, recalled the 1930s:

'As a young man I read a then-popular book by a fellow Viennese Jew, Franz Werfel's *The Forty Days of Musa Dagh*. In it, he described how the Turks exterminated the Armenian people. Werfel . . . knew that the extermination of an entire people was possible in our time.'[140]

Those who actively campaigned through writing, the arts or political organization remained a few voices in an era when so many capitulated to the hegemonic narratives about the nation, its 'enemies' and the need to be violent. The Franco-Russian writer and revolutionary Victor Serge observed in the 1930s:

> The civilized person who sees a crime committed under his window, in full daylight, without allowing himself to intervene or even make an audible shout, will he afterwards retain his own self esteem, his clarity of judgment, critical spirit, the capacity to create, if he is an artist? The writer informed of what passes in the world – and I hold that it is the duty of the writer to be thus informed – is often in the uncomfortable position of this civilized person.[141]

The life of a militant humanist became even more difficult in the 1930s; many became 'hostages to fortune', in Francis Bacon's memorable phrase.[142] Walter Benjamin killed himself before he could be captured by the Nazis at the French border with Spain in 1940. Franz Werfel suffered from severe depression after he fled Europe with Heinrich and Golo Mann.[143] He died in the United States in 1945. Armin Wegner was imprisoned and tortured by the Gestapo.[144] Heinrich Mann died almost penniless in 1950, after his exile to the United States. Rosa Luxemburg was lynched by a mob in 1919. The brilliant barrister Henry Torrès, who had defended anarchists in court in France in the 1920s and 1930s, spent his exile from Nazi-controlled France in New York, with no money and without a command of English.[145]

Perhaps the most difficult thing for the historian to record is the actions of ordinary people who made a choice to protect the rights of other people, rather than grand gestures of artists and writers. It is more difficult to trace the actions of those who did not write down their protests but simply helped other people during times of violence because they considered it their human duty to do so. After the Second World War, the Israelis collected thousands of examples of Gentiles who helped Jews and preserved these tales of the 'Righteous Among the Nations' at the Yad Vashem museum. Among them was the story of Armin Wegner, who lived in exile from Germany after the 1930s because of his passionate opposition to Nazi anti-Semitism. To commemorate such acts was an important decision by the Israelis, because it gives us an insight into the extent to which some people resisted the immoral power of the state and stood out as individuals. Some were saintly individuals, such as the Polish priest Maximilian Kolbe, whose life reads like a medieval parable. Others, such as Oskar Schindler, were far more speckled characters, who simply acted in the way they did because of a basic sense of empathy with the ordinary people around them – in this case, Jews.

What are the sources of popular compassion and sentiment that led individuals to save or protect other people? Some compassion must surely come from the religions of the book, which have in some sense codified centuries of folk poetry and values. We would know far less about the genocide against the Armenians were it not for missionaries, soldiers and diplomats such as Dr Martin Niepage, a German teacher and author of an influential account of the genocide,[146] 'with a courage and humanity to which the highest tribute must be paid'.[147] Many Armenians who were saved owed their survival to the actions of non-Christians. Lord Bryce's report on the Armenian genocide contains the story of Zarouhi, who was thrown into the river, but clung to a rock behind some bushes and remained there until the gendarmes and *chettis* had gone away. Coming out of the river she met a kind Kurdish shepherd, who wrapped her in a blanket and took her to the house of a Turk who knew her. The Turk took her to Erzeroum and kept her in his home.[148] The Armenian assassin Sogomon Teilirian stayed for two months with Kurds who burnt his own blood-stained clothes and gave him Kurdish garments to wear which allowed him to travel on towards the Russian front incognito. At the trial, Teilirian stated that these 'good people', including an elderly woman who had sheltered him, had done so on pain of death.[149]

In 1935–6, in internal exile in Mussolini's Italy, the doctor and painter Carlo Levi described peasant life and culture in Aliano, to the south of the peninsula. He thought that the poor peasantry, many of whom were shepherds, were alienated from the workings of the state and had an innate 'sense of justice'.[150] Other writers shared this view of the peasant as possessing a natural morality, or what the poet Salvatore Quasimodo once called '*questo umanesimo di razza contadina*' ('this humanism of peasants').[151] Elie Wiesel's family was offered a refuge in the mountains by the family servant Maria, which they refused, not knowing the terrible truth behind the journey to Birkenau. He recalled that an 'uneducated woman stood taller than the city's intellectuals, dignitaries and clergy . . . not one of them showed the strength of character of this simple peasant woman'.[152]

Despite more than 20,000 named gentiles at Yad Vashem and numerous unnamed Turks and Kurds who helped Greeks and Armenians, despite Serbs who sheltered Muslims in Bosnia and vice versa and Russians who aided Jews and Tatars, much that would otherwise appear to be innate human values seems to evaporate during crises. For many contemporaries, fantasies of violence and the elimination of populations belonged to the realms of what Hannah Arendt was later to call 'radical evil' – a phenomenon that broke down 'all standards we know'.[153] At the Nuremberg Tribunal, Justice Robert H. Jackson delivered a haunting condemnation of the Nazis: 'What makes this inquest significant is that these prisoners represent sinister influences that will lurk in the world long after their bodies have returned to dust. They are living symbols of racial hatreds, of terrorism and violence and of the arrogance and cruelty of power.'[154] Given the depravity involved in colonial conquest and in the slave trade, phenomena involving mass deaths were recent and involved European agency. Nevertheless, the impact of the genocidal crisis of *c.*1912–23 should not be underestimated as a discrete phenomenon, in terms of its impact on the contemporary psyche.

After the slaughter of the Balkan Wars, the First World War, the Russian Civil War and the final break-up of the Ottoman Empire, the pioneering psychologist Sigmund Freud developed a notion about the almost Manichean forces that exist within the human personality.[155] This theory appeared first in his study *Jenseits des Lustprinzips* (*Beyond the Pleasure Principle*), published in 1920.[156] It was developed further in *Das Ich und das Es* (*The Ego and the Id*) in 1923.[157] Libido (or Eros) was a force that created life, and Mortido (sometimes referred to as Thanatos) was the drive for oblivion or death. Freud also became more aware of the fragility of the liberal experiment.[158]

In 1917, Albert Einstein condemned the 'insanity of nationalism' during the war. For him, 'a victory of Bismarck and Treitschke'[159] would bring 'an endless chain of dreadful acts of violence'.[160] T. S. Eliot's celebrated but highly problematic 1922 poem *The Waste Land* was 'openly read as a lament about the state of culture'[161] after 1918. By the time his verses were well known and repeated, his 'Smyrna merchant'[162] hardly existed as an archetype. The exodus by *giaour* or Levantine traders after the fire of September 1922 and encirclement by Kemal Atatürk's army destroyed the ancient civilization of that city.[163] Perhaps the 'unshaven' Mr Eugenides, whose very name suggests a representative of an entire race, is carrying 'currants' in his pocket, not because he is homosexual[164] or because he represents the 'true vine',[165] but because he has been ethnically cleansed and left the city in a desperate hurry, carrying his dried, portable food with him.

After the destruction on the Eastern Front, Valery Briusov wrote his visionary poem *The Last War*, which 'envisages the "miracle" of "eternal peace" '.[166] The communists Evgenii Preobrazhensky and Nikolai Bukharin wrote their most apocalyptic work, *The ABC of Communism*, in 1919. After the shock of the previous years: 'the war produced terrible devastation . . . every attempt to produce a truly human society upon the old capitalist foundations is foredoomed to absolute failure'.[167] In 1921, Preobrazhensky still thought that 'beggarly, devastated, labouring Russia, flowing with blood, will have a reward for its great suffering'.[168] In circumstances where writers and intellectuals begin to believe in the real presence of extreme and negative forces, their attraction to some as well as their repulsion to others simply become more feasible. Also suffering from the shock of war, Thomas Mann completed what is arguably his most Manichean novel, *Der Zauberberg* (*The Magic Mountain*), in the late 1920s. The novel evokes a struggle between enlightened values and the irrational. He explained the war in terms of total catastrophe: '[T]he demoralization had no limits; it could be seen in the deep and fatal anxiety of a nation that despaired of itself, of its history, of its finest treasures.'[169] This novel also marks the transition from Mann the liberal nationalist to Mann the radical, closer than ever to his 'militant' brother Heinrich. In his introduction to the published transcript of the trial of Sogomon Teilirian, who murdered the Ottoman politician Talât Paşa in 1921, the poet Armin Wegner stated that what was at stake was not, in essence, a political but an ethical question: it involved a conflict between two impulses 'that had been in an unholy opposition since the earliest time on earth, namely the opposition between violent force and justice and criminality and humanity'.[170] Manichean struggles between good and evil further reinforced the idea, sown first by the classics, that violent death is not futile but heroic and therefore something higher than 'cowardly survival'.[171]

CHAPTER 6

Instability and Moral Decline in Inter-War Europe

Times are difficult, unusually difficult. Not just for us in Croatia, but in the whole world.[1]

Europe and the Near East did not quickly recover from the First World War. Creaking structures the empires might have been, but the states which replaced them were prone to extremism and structural instability. Awareness of the problems which minorities were likely to face in the new Europe, led to their rights being protected through a series of treaties after 1918 and to the creation of the new League of Nations to safeguard human rights. But the hole left by the disappearance of ancient structures could not simply be filled with notions of cooperation and human rights – which, ironically, became a model for eliminationists to rebel against, if the reactions of German nationalists were typical.[2] The apparent power vacuum of imperial decline created an opportunity, which was too attractive a prospect to be ignored by extremists. Furthermore, the genocides of the First World War, witnessed by many central Europeans first-hand and experienced by all through newspaper reports, only served to fan the flames of hatred of the Other. The existence of desperate diasporas in cities such as Paris, Berlin and London magnified these voices and made violence more visible in everyday life – if not directly then through numerous reports of atrocities in newspapers and letters home from the various fronts. Many had bitter memories of their own suffering and developed what Alan Kramer has described as a 'mentality of hate that did not bode well for peace'.[3] Even 'people from the least educated classes and the remotest regions realize[d] that their daily existence was bound up in politics.'[4] Violence could beget not only further violence but also trauma, diminished morality, despair, depression and political anger. In a historical context, the moral climate had already been damaged by direct participation in colonial genocide and by notions of the naturalness of the clash of civilizations, bolstered as this was by ideologies of racism such as social Darwinism.

The Holocaust could not have taken place without the collapse of the empires in eastern Europe and the impact of that vacuum, which was to ricochet across the world. Of course, there were many examples where individuals behaved in a similar fashion. As Donald Bloxham has observed, 'Behaettin Şakir would drive around in his car from province to province, exhorting the local authorities to ever more vigorous action against the Armenians, much as Heinrich Himmler did for Germany during 1941–2 on the Russian front'.[5] The connection may not just be functional. As a young man, Himmler (who was born in 1900) would have been well aware of the narrative of the destruction of the Ottoman Armenians, which was headline news during the trial of the assassin of Talât Paşa in 1921. He, like all of his contemporaries, knew what had happened in 1915. The state of affairs in Europe after 1918 did not go unnoticed. As the Germans advanced towards the Caspian, the nationalist Paul Rohrbach reminded his fellow Germans of the opportunity this created and:

> pleaded that Germany be courageous enough to make the most of her possibilities. He castigated his fellow Germans for their narrow point of view and called their attention to the greatest upheaval since the collapse of the Roman Empire. Let Berlin recognize the Don and Kuban Cossacks and unite them with the Georgians, Armenians and Tartars in a great Caucasian federal republic! Here was the second bridge from Mitteleuropa to Asia Minor and Persia, one that was safer and less open to attack than the Berlin–Baghdad line. Potentially Germany might have everything – raw materials, markets, and strategic power – if she brought freedom and organization into these lands. No further obstacles need be overcome – only time and space.[6]

It was not just the German nationalists who saw the opportunities that the collapse of imperial Russia brought. Eliminationists also saw their moment. During General Denikin's occupation of the Ukraine in 1918–19 and the first independent government under Symon Petlura, several thousand Jews were systematically massacred. Some historians have estimated that 120,000 people, or about 8 per cent of the Jewish population of the Ukraine were killed by the Whites.[7] Henry Abramson gives a number of 50,0000–60,000, lower than Nakhum Gergel, though he adds that this estimate could be doubled or tripled.[8] This lower estimate still represents approximately 4 per cent of the total Jewish population. Rather than being a 'tragic byproduct for the struggle of control of the country',[9] the civil war pogroms indicate that a significant number of Ukrainians were eliminationist nationalists and wanted to create a new state, without Jews. Similarly, when Polish troops entered L'viv and Vilnius in 1918–19, they took the opportunity to commit atrocities against Jews.[10]

In 1919, Greece invaded Anatolia and attempted to take large swathes of its territory. Initially the Greeks had some success, but, when the Turks reversed their gains, they drove the Greeks into the sea at Smyrna and put an end to millennia of Hellenic civilization in this region. Smyrna, once dubbed the 'flower of the Levant'[11] for its fortunate harbour and beautiful buildings, was famous for its mix of nations – a diverse population of Orthodox Greeks, Turkish Muslims, Armenians and Italians. As George Rendel from the British Foreign Office commented in a memorandum entitled 'Turkish Massacres and Persecutions' in March 1922, 'it is necessary to refer to these pre-armistice persecutions, since there is now a strong tendency to minimize or overlook them and to regard those which followed the armistice as isolated incidents provoked by Greeks landing at Smyrna and the general Turkish policy of the Allies'.[12] Thereafter, in eastern Europe and in the former Ottoman world, the situation for certain religious and ethnic groups deteriorated even more rapidly. In the aftermath of the war between Greece and Turkey in 1919–22, both Greeks and Turks were expelled en masse from Asia Minor and from the Balkans, an operation which was supervised under the terms of the Treaty of Lausanne in 1923, but led to atrocities on both sides. During this time the capital Istanbul had retained some of its cosmopolitan character, but many of the remaining Greeks left after having been subjected to attacks in the 1950s.[13] By 1923, the newly created state of Turkey had very few Christian citizens (although there had probably been about 3.5 million before the First World War). Most had been expelled, killed or been compelled to convert to Islam in the previous decades, culminating in the genocidal years of 1914–1923. Finality was added by Lord Curzon, whose express aim was 'the unmixing of peoples'[14] through the treaty of Lausanne in 1923. He believed that clear, fixed ethnic and national borders would preserve peace in the Near East; thus many remaining Balkan Muslims made their tragic way from Thrace to Anatolia, while hapless Greeks went in the other direction. Atrocities were committed on both sides. A Greek refugee, fleeing from Turkey in 1922, reported that:

> we were . . . shut up in a garden in which Turkish civilians, women and children were allowed to enter. These pointed out some among us, who, they said, maltreated Turks during the Greek occupation. These unfortunate individuals were without further process conducted to unknown destinations.[15]

Muslims in the Balkans became the focus of local nationalist plans of exclusion.[16] Ottoman Macedonia succumbed to the territorial ambitions of the neighbouring states of Serbia, Bulgaria, Albania and Greece, the so-called 'four wolves'. After particularly vicious fighting and atrocities, the remaining parts of Macedonia were divided in 1918 as spoils of war by Bulgaria, the Kingdom of Serbs, Croats and Slovenes, and Greece. The former Ottoman province of Kosovo was annexed by Serbia in 1912, during the Balkan wars; it had had a mixed population of Serbs and Albanians since the Middle Ages. Albanians were discriminated against in the 1920s and the Kaçak rebels took to the hills to oppose the hegemony of Belgrade. During the Second World War, Albanians led by the nationalist Ballists committed atrocities against Serbs and vice versa. The discussion of 'what to do' about Slav Muslims became radicalized during the First World War. Serb nationalist Borivoje Jevtić stated that 'Masaryk realism, good for the northern country and its inhabitants at a much higher level of civilization, was not applicable to Bosnia, which had no corresponding culture and which for its awakening needed the smell of blood'.[17] During the twentieth century, anti-Islam continued to be a dominant theme of Balkan discourse. In the 1920s some Serb eliminationists supported the 'uniting of Slav Muslims with Kemal-Pasha' (that is, Atatürk).[18] In the 1930s the nationalist newspaper *Vidovdan*[19] repeated some of these sentiments.[20] One Yugoslav government minister Kosta Krstić wanted to send the Albanians of Kosovo to 'Asia' without the possibility of return.[21] In 1937 Vaso Čubrilović told the *Srpski kulturni klub* that the ethnic cleansing of Albanians from Kosovo could be achieved by ruthless methods, including intimidation of their religious personnel.[22] There was a process of settling Muslims away from Yugoslavia in the 1920s and 1930s. The League for Democracy in Greece published the journal *Balkan Herald* from 1935–40. In June 1937 it reported: 'A transfer of population unprecedented in Europe in modern times is now being undertaken in the Balkans ... [I]n Asia, districts and settlements have been prepared for their reception'.[23] Political crises and the breakdown of authority led to further attacks on Muslims. Kosovo and Bosnia were the sites of particularly vicious inter-ethnic fighting from 1941 until 1945. Elsewhere in Yugoslavia during the Second World War, Muslims were targeted on the grounds of their faith and ethnicity.[24] Between 86,000 and 103,000 Slav Muslims were killed in Bosnia and Sandžak. Many perished at the hands of Serb nationalist Četniks.[25] To some extent, the genocide in Bosnia in the 1990s can be attributed to a very crude revival, in some circles, of an eliminationist Serb nationalist or Četnik program of the sort proposed by the lawyer Dr Stevan Moljević in the late 1930s.[26]

The vacuum left by the disappearance of these great powers as well as by the collapse of the Habsburg monarchy was one of the primary causes of the Holocaust, as the National Socialists attempted to reorder the eastern part of Europe into a new 'thousand year Reich'. After the Nazis invaded and dismembered Yugoslavia in 1941, they installed home-grown fascists in power in the so-called Independent State of Croatia (*Nezavisna Država Hrvatska*), although that was an extended version of Croatia, which included Bosnia, and was certainly not independent. The Croatian fascists or Ustaša then embarked on a campaign of exterminating the Serbian Orthodox population.

Fascism or eliminationism developed as an ideology in the Balkans simultaneously with similar developments in the rest of Europe. Native fascist movements in south-eastern Europe included the Zbor movement, found by Dimitrije Ljotić in Serbia; the Iron Guard in Romania; and the Ustaša in Croatia, which became the party of government in 1941, being installed by joint agreement between the Third Reich and Mussolini. Without the sponsorship of the Axis powers, these groups, who had tiny numbers of supporters in the late 1920s, would have been unable to have serious political impact beyond terrorism, which was also financed by the fascist governments. When a lone Macedonian killed the Yugoslavian King Aleksandar Karadjordjević in France in 1934, the chain of responsibility went to the Macedonian IMRO revolutionaries, who were funded by the Ustaša, and then back to their protector Mussolini, and ultimately to the Nazis. Fascists were responsible for some of the worst human rights abuses and for the killing of the majority of Jews in the Balkans and peoples of other nationalities, for instance the Roma and the Serb population of the Dinaric region.

There are few real long-term precedents for antagonistic Serb-Croat relations in the same way that poor Christian-Muslim relations have their origins, to some extent, in the oppressive practices of the Ottoman state; and there is little evidence of inter-ethnic rivalry before the twentieth century. Most antipathy towards Serbs can be traced to the work of Ante Starčević,[27] founder of the Croatian Party of Rights (*Hrvatska Stranka Prava*) after whom the Ustaša named its newspaper in interwar Zagreb.[28] The Serb nationalist newspaper *Srbobran* suggested in 1902 that these communities could not live together and that this must finally lead to the extermination 'of us or you'.[29] Part of the Croatian antipathy for the Serbs must be a direct ricochet from the First World War, when almost all the Croats were subjects of the Habsburgs. They also opposed the hegemony of Belgrade in the 1920s and 1930s. The Croatian fascists decided that Bosnian Muslims belonged in the Croatian nation, taking on board Ante Starčević's belief that the Muslim Slavs 'are of Croatian stock, the most able and purest nobility that Europe has'.[30] Tomislav Dulić has looked at what he calls local 'mass killing' in Bosnia and Hercegovina, examining the Četnik attacks on Muslims, the obliteration of the Jews of Sarajevo and the attacks on Serbs by Ustaša. He has argued, concerning eastern Hercegovina, that 'violence . . . was not the result of state policy, but instead of local initiatives based on a general

distrust between Serbs and Muslims'.[31] Ustaša troops carried out the genocide so rapidly in the early summer of 1941 that some confused Serbs
reported their actions to the authorities, largely because they could not
believe that these actions could be sanctioned by a legitimate government
and must be the work of terrorists.[32] In 1941 Serbs were rounded up in Glina
and executed en masse in the village church which was set on fire, thus
repeating the kind of actions that had been witnessed in Prnjavor during the
First World War. Muslim Ustaša, trained by the SS, carried out atrocities
against Serbs in 1943. 12,000 men volunteered to join the Handžar division
of the SS to cleanse Bosnia ethnically.[33] Between 1941 and 1945 and the final
victory of the Communist partisans, the former Yugoslavia was ravaged by
war and attempts by the belligerent Četniks and Ustaša to use the war as a
cover for genocide.

The settlement of Jews in the former Ottoman lands goes back thousands
of years, but a large number of these Jews were Spanish or Ladino-speaking
Sephardi, who came to the relatively tolerant south-east of Europe after their
expulsion from Spain by the Inquisition in the fifteenth and sixteenth
centuries, rebuilding their lives as weavers, traders or medical practi-
tioners.[34] The Jewish communities of Anatolia and the Balkans numbered
over 300,000 individuals in 1900, with the greatest concentrations in cities
such as Sarajevo, Dubrovnik, Constaninople and, above all, Thessalonica,[35]
which had a majority Jewish population in the city itself until its annihilation in the early 1940s. Although Jewish communities had been fragmented
and dislocated at the collapse of the Ottoman Empire, it was during the
Second World War that they were systematically destroyed, when at least 75
per cent of Yugoslavia's Jews were killed.

In Croatia, in a clear imitation of the racial policies of the Third Reich and
Italy since 1938, the Croatian fascists were quick to wage war on their own
population. Within two months of the Ustaša installation into power in
1941, Jews lost their right to citizenship.[36] A Ustaša priest, Franjo Kralik,
writing in Katolički tjednik in July 1941, noted that Jews, freemasons and
communists were external to European civilization and could be removed
from Croatia with a clean conscience (čiste savjesti).[37] Jews in the
Independent State of Croatia were taken to the Jasenovac camp, where many
of them perished in circumstances of extreme cruelty.[38] Within months of

the collapse of Yugoslavia, more than 20,000 Jews and Roma had been killed in Serbia, a puppet state set up by the Nazis. Some Jews managed to flee to relative safety in Italian-occupied Albania, but many were subsequently deported and murdered by the Gestapo in 1944.[39] In Thessalonica, almost the entire Jewish community, which numbered several thousands, was wiped out during the Nazi occupation of Greece. Jews were made to wear yellow stars with either 'Jude' or the Greek 'Evraios' (written in German or Greek) on their clothes,[40] and most Greek Jews were eventually transported to Auschwitz.

The genocide against Jews in the territories that had once been part of the Romanov or Habsburg monarchy had several distinct phases. In 1935, the Nazis had effectively deprived Jews living in Germany of citizenship with the introduction of the Nuremberg Laws, which had led to the exodus of about half the community. The invasion of Austria in 1938 had precipitated a sharp deterioration in their treatment of Jews, as Austrians were encouraged to humiliate and abuse them on a vast scale. The collapse and partition of Czechoslovakia in 1938–9 and the invasion of Poland in 1939 produced a great increase in the number of Jews in territories controlled by the Nazis. In these territories, the Nazis started to confine Jews to very restricted areas in cities and to make life almost impossible for those who were trapped. Many were shot or died by contracting diseases in increasingly unhealthy ghettos where starvation was rife; others had fled to territories in the East and were to perish some years later. The historian Simon Dubnow left Germany after Hitler came to power and settled in Latvia, only to be mowed down, together with at least 25,000 other local people, in a pine forest in Rumbula near Riga in 1941.[41] They had taken refuge in the east of the continent after they were expelled from German citizenship after the Nuremberg Laws in 1935.

When the Nazis invaded the Soviet Union in June 1941, the genocidal intentions of the regime became even clearer. A third of the world's Jews (and statistically over 90 per cent of the Jews of the region) were killed in the early 1940s, mostly between the summers of 1941 and 1943, by a regime which turned murder into mass industrial killing.[42] Even if they had no defined plans for extermination camps such as Auschwitz until 1941, the Nazis' intentions towards Soviet Jews were never good. The conflation between Bolshevism and Judaism had been central to Nazi propaganda since its foundation, and all Jews were to share in the collective fate. Many perished in the first few months of the invasion, killed by the *Einsatzgruppen*, who fought alongside the *Wehrmacht* as mobile killing units. Jews who were not killed immediately were taken to hastily constructed extermination camps such as Sobibor, Treblinka and Auschwitz. Many were killed outright, others were worked to death, and very few survived, even after the liberation at the end of the war. In Ukraine, the Nazi policy of killing Jews escalated to embrace all categories of 'partisans' and the victims clearly numbered far more defenceless non-combatants than actual fighters.[43] One account of German reprisals against those who had joined the partisans states: 'in the mountainous part of the Crimea all villages were burnt and a "dead zone" was created. . . . More than 70 villages were destroyed. In them dwelt more than 25 per cent of the Tatar population of the Crimea. In these villages, in remote woodlands, in the mountains lived only Tatars.'[44] Other groups were singled out for elimination. Anthropologists from the Kaiser Wilhelm Institute for Anthropology, Human Heredity and Eugenics in Berlin experimented on Gypsies and then had them sent to Auschwitz.[45] The death rate among Soviet prisoners of war was extremely high and an estimated 3.2 million perished as slave labourers – over 60 per cent of the total.[46]

The building of extermination camps is perhaps the most morally shocking part of the Holocaust and separates these events from the earlier genocides in terms of the organizational intent of the regime. By killing almost every living soul they singled out for elimination, the Nazis reduced the chance of ever having to face angry survivors in angry diasporas which might have developed outside the confines of the Third Reich. Such diasporas had plagued both the Ottomans and the Romanovs and had ruined their prestige, especially in the 1890s and 1900s, in terms of the protection of human life. With no chance for exemption, the Nazis killed people like infectious animals; all that was left behind was the dust, which was dumped in the Vistula river.[47] Other mass murders had not been carried out with such efficiency; indeed murderers often left piles of bodies around as a form of contempt of the dead. When Russian troops massacred an entire village of Turkmen in Caucasus in 1870s, they left them unburied, fearing to touch their bodies. It was left to the painter Vasily Vereshchagin, who had accompanied the army as an official artist, to dig their graves himself.[48] In Syria in 1916, Armenians:

> who died from [typhus] were left unburied for days. One reason for this, as given to the writer by a superior Turkish Officer, was to increase infection in order that there should be greater mortality among the living. The Armenians however can claim some revenge, for the plague naturally did not confine itself to Armenians only, and the whole country through which these refugees passed was devastated; the writer saw dozens of villages in Syria empty of all inhabitants.[49]

By the time of the fall of the Nazi regime, an estimated 5.8 million Jews from all parts of Europe had perished. Two thousand years of Jewish civilization in continental Europe had effectively been terminated. The indifference of the perpetrators of this catastrophe has frequently struck commentators. Andrew Charlesworth has studied the 'topography' of the Holocaust, noting that '[a]t Birkenau . . . there was a lawn where the women workers could sunbathe as the captives filed past on their way to the gas chambers'.[50] It appears that, at the Wannsee meeting of January 1942 which was designed to coordinate the different governmental bodies responsible for the genocide, the implementation of the Nuremberg Laws in terms of deciding whether individuals who were classified as part Jewish (or perhaps more accurately part German) was of more concern than the 'final solution' itself. Of course, this may be because the purpose of the meeting altered drastically after the United States had entered the war in the previous December, as Christian Gerlach has argued.[51] Whereas in November the participants were dealing with German Jews, by January they were considering the fate of a greater number. But banal indifference of the sort that Hannah Arendt described in her famous study *Eichmann in Jerusalem* has remained a central aspect of contemporary consciousness about these events, and contrasts heavily with the reported reaction of the Allied troops which liberated prisoners who had not been so morally numbed by the crisis before and after the First World War.[52] Elie Wiesel recalled: 'I will never forget the American soldiers and the horror that could be read in their faces. I will especially remember one black sergeant, a muscled giant, who wept tears of impotent rage and shame, shame for the human species when he saw us.'[53]

After the First World War and the catastrophe of the civil war, the infant Bolshevik regime became more extreme in its use of rhetoric and in its practices against its own citizens. After reporting from the Balkan wars, Leon Trotsky wrote: 'Can mankind really find no other ways of settling the affairs of the planet than methods of extermination, mutilation and destruction?'[54] His years as commissar for war may have hardened his outlook and blunted his sensitivities, as he subsequently became an extremely ruthless leader.[55] In 1922 he told Red Army veterans that 'war and revolution are extremely brutal and destructive methods for solving social problems. But no other methods are available!'[56] Apart from the desired outcome, it would be hard to distinguish his use of language from that of contemporary eliminationists. Transforming the Soviet Union from a rural peasant-based economy to an industrialized, mechanized agricultural economy later in that decade and in the 1930s led to mass deaths from famine and dislocation. The ancient agricultural civilization of that part of Europe was effectively wiped out, which led, directly or indirectly, to the genocide of Soviet citizens. Those who questioned the regime, either within the Communist Party or as owners of hitherto private property, were subjected to horrific and often fatal treatment either at the hands of the secret police or in an expanding prison or Gulag system. Even before the Soviet Union was attacked by Nazi Germany and its population exposed to barbaric violence, the population was weakened by years of oppression. Many scholars have compared the processes at work in the Soviet Union with policies of genocidal regimes. Benjamin Valentino has argued that '[e]thnic cleansing, like communist policies such as agricultural collectivization, is fundamentally a policy of social engineering'.[57] During the Second World War, significant measures were taken against minority communities by the Soviets. While this was justified in terms of loyalty to the state, the real reason may have been Stalin's plan to invade the eastern vilayets of Turkey, which had been taken by the Russians briefly during the First World War. As well as the Crimean Tatars, 'several other small, distrusted nationalities living on the Soviet Union's southern borderlands (the Chechens and related highlanders the Ingush, the Turkic pastoralists known as the Karachai and related Balkars, the Buddhist

Mongol Kalmyks, the Meshketian Turks mountain farmers, and the Volga Germans) were targeted for deportation to Siberia.[58]

In looking for an explanation for the flaw, or flaws, in the Yugoslavian project, some scholars have pointed in particular to the human rights abuses and violence of the immediate post-war period, when 'revenge' was taken on those associated with the fascist regimes either through ethnicity or through political action. Between the defeat of Italy in 1943 and the final capitulation of the Third Reich, the Italian and German speakers of the Balkans lost their protectors and became perceived as 'fifth columnists' themselves, in the way that Muslims were often regarded as disloyal or 'alien'. Some ethnic Germans left for Germany in October 1944 and others were expelled at the end of the war.[59] After the war, the victorious communists drove the German and Italian-speaking populations out of Yugoslavia, although, again, this action was associated with a particular historical 'moment' and it is likely that, without the war, any Yugoslav government would have continued to use assimilatory policies rather than ethnic cleansing to 'deal' with minorities. Others who collaborated with the fascists were deemed to be punishable. Tomislav Dulić has argued that, if Serbs suffered higher casualty rates during the war itself, then Croats were more likely to be the victims of communist violence at the end of the war.[60] The ethnic cleansing carried out by communists at the end of war cannot be linked definitively to long-term trends or patterns as there was no long-term antipathy for either ethnic group within the communist or Marxist movement generally. Indeed Tito's partisans wanted to hold on to territorial gains made in Italy and Austria, notably the port of Trieste, which they liberated in 1945, and the majority German parts of Carinthia which contained a Slovene minority. Communist actions were thus largely motivated by the short-term circumstances at the end of the war, although the tendency of local partisans to settle old scores and the ubiquitous role of sadism were probably important factors in explaining violence against both communities. This is not to say that what occurred was not brutal. Josip Mirnić suggested that 100,000 Germans (about half the total ethnic population) left Vojvodina spontaneously and of their own free will when the Third Reich collapsed, since their fate was so inextricably linked to that of the occupiers and they knew how they would be punished.[61] Of course, this does rather stretch the definition of 'dobrovolno', or free will.

According to John Schindler, 'more than ten per cent were murdered, the rest were displaced or expelled from their homeland'.[62] In Poland, Hungary and Czechoslovakia, the Germans were driven out by the victorious communists – a process that involved significant human rights abuses.[63] Often this process involved a significant collaboration between the communists and local nationalists, as David Curp has argued was the case in Poland.[64]

The Italian communities of the Adriatic littoral were driven north, to Trieste or elsewhere in Italy, to become permanent exiles, *esuli* as they are known in Italian political discourse.[65] Others met a terrible fate when they were pushed down *foibe* or holes in the limestone Karst. An Italian priest from Bassovizza – a village outide Trieste that was to become the focus of post-war Italian anger – 'witnessed 250 to 300 civilians and about forty German soldiers being executed'. It is probable that they were all dead before they were thrown into the limestone ravines.[66] Along the coast of Dalmatia and Istria were the several thousand Italian speakers who found in most cases that they were not welcome in communist Yugoslavia. Many were killed by being pushed into Karstic ravines or expelled from their properties, which were then redistributed to the regime's supporters.

In a strikingly original study, the geographer Dean S. Rugg remarked upon the way different regimes and historical epochs had shaped the landscape in eastern Europe, moving from 'landscapes of multinationalism' before the nineteenth century to 'landscapes of nationalism' in the twentieth century.[67] Everything changed, from the shapes of villages and fields to the languages people spoke and the religions they followed. The collapse of empires from 1912 to 1923, predicted in some respects by the pre-genocidal situation in Ukraine, Anatolia and parts of the Balkans before 1912, led to hitherto unknown levels of chaos and dislocation in the whole of Europe. Not only were the empires wiped off the map, but with them the identities of many religions and ethnicities who had owed their continued existence to Ottoman, Habsburg or Romanov protection. The mental, political and human landscape could hardly have altered more in the space of a few years, and the following generation was to pay the price for the collapse of empires with the rise of eliminationist groups across the continent of Europe.

CHAPTER 7

Conflict in the Courtroom

If ethnically purified territories were an ideal first conceived of in newspapers and other forms of literary discourse, the ideological battleground quickly moved into the juridical arena. Again and again, even in court trials where questions of ethnicity were seemingly marginal, the politics and composition of the nation became a crucial factor. As views on the nation differed, so too did views on the role of the law. Amongst the humanists, a view of the law as universal was emerging that eventually resulted in the United Nations Universal Declaration of Human Rights in 1948. The UN Convention codified what had become developing international norms through The Hague and Geneva Conventions. Between 1899 and the second Hague Convention of 1907, rules were set out which prohibited attacking the undefended and pillaging their properties, and protected the rights of prisoners of war who could expect humane treatment under the terms agreed. Between 1864 and 1929, the Geneva Conventions codified rules governing wounded soldiers who had the right to be treated humanely. In the 1920s the convention sought to ban the use of chemical and biological weapons. To some extent, these international norms provided a model for eliminationist ideologues to rebel against.

In *The Origins of Totalitarianism*, Hannah Arendt argued that the impartiality of the law was the 'greatest achievement' of the nineteenth century: 'the doctrine of equality before the law was still so firmly implanted in the conscience of the civilized world that a single miscarriage of justice could provoke indignation from Moscow to New York'.[1] Even among writers whose views were racist, there was a belief in the importance of legal impartiality. Although no friend of the Jewish communities of the Russian empire, the editor of the conservative nationalist newspaper *Kievlyanin*, Vasily Vitalyevich Shulgin, disliked all forms of pogrom violence and viewed trumped-up accusations, as in the case of Mendel Beilis, as shameful to the Russia.[2] The Austrian philosopher Otto Weininger argued that women, blacks and Jews were inferior in spirit to white men; but he would still refuse anyone the right to attack them (*ihn zu lynchen*).[3] For Weininger, only legal authorities could hold the right to punish individuals. In 1909, the self-styled 'Scottish Dreyfus' Oscar Slater was wrongly imprisoned for the murder of an elderly heiress in Glasgow and only released years later thanks to personally funded and persistent campaigning by Arthur Conan Doyle. Slater's Jewish identity and supposed marginality as a petty criminal were possibly among the causes of his wrongful accusation. Conan Doyle, a writer whose work was infused with the commonplace racist sentiments of Edwardian Britain, was nonetheless convinced of his innocence and initially appealed unsuccessfully to Parliament.[4] The latter appealed again when a Midlands solicitor, George Edalji,[5] the son of an Indian Parsi, was accused of maiming cattle in 1903 – a charge that the writer dubbed an 'incredibly stupid injustice'. A *Times* correspondent noted that 'a certain part of the public, generous, but impulsive, believes that the prisoner was wrongly convicted and that there has been another Dreyfus ... case'.[6] Perhaps the parallel was more appropriate than *The Times* correspondent cared to admit. Conan Doyle took up Edalji's case three years later and helped him to win an acquittal. Dr Chowry Muthu wrote to the author of the Sherlock Holmes stories in the columns of the *Daily Telegraph* and thanked him 'on behalf of England's Indian community'.[7] Consistent when it came to flagrant abuses of human rights, Conan Doyle was also active in the campaign against Belgian abuses in the Congo in 1909.

Eliminationist nationalists took an entirely different view of the law – a view best summarized in Reichsminister Hans Frank's address to the Congress of German Jurists, held at Leipzig in October 1935: 'Justice is whatever the German people requires and injustice is whatever harms them' (*'Recht ist was dem deutschen Volk nützt und Unrecht was ihm schadet'*).[8] For them, the perceived interests of the nation were of higher value than the truth. An SS jurist, Werner Best, argued that the racial state (*völkisch Rechtsstaat*) existed 'if and when . . . the "laws of life", that is, racial doctrine, were followed'.[9] In the Ottoman Empire before the First World War, Christians had come to expect that force would be used randomly against them. Helen Davenport Gibbons perceived the fear of the Armenians in 1909, after the massacres: 'They are terror-stricken, and have reason to be. How would you like to live in a country where you knew your Government not only would not protect you, but would periodically incite your neighbors to rob and kill you *with the help of the army*?'[10] Others noted the use of arbitrary force against Ottoman Christians. In January 1915, the *Scotsman* reported: 'The latest intelligence to hand from Asia Minor points to the plight of the Greek population there as a critical one. Besides all the sufferings brought upon them from forcible recruiting, requisitions, and boycott, the Christians find themselves at the mercy of malefactors on account of the total absence of public security.'[11] Routinely before the First World War, Russian revolutionaries and liberals alike complained that the state behaved in an arbitrary [*proizvol*] fashion.[12] Physical or legal security could not be guaranteed, particularly for non-Orthodox peoples. The Russian liberal philosopher Boris Chicherin observed: 'The preservation of the civil order falls into the hands of the police; reprisal takes the place of justice, arbitrariness replace law' [*zakon*].[13] In nineteenth- and early twentieth-century Germany, rioting crowds had called for death for the Jews; but, unlike in Russia, 'the state's demand for law and order had a restraining effect'.[14]

Both visions of law, citizenship and composition of the nation evolved from within Europe. Rather than a historical aberration or the result of a *Sonderweg*, genocidal regimes were simply those in which eliminationist nationalists had taken power. In imperial Russia, Jews were subject to violence because eliminationist ideas had taken hold amongst representatives of local power such as the police or paramilitaries, who had some tacit support from government. Under Sultan Abdülhamid and during the First World War, Ottoman Christians effectively had no protection from the state. Worse still, they were deemed to have a harmful influence in the state, in the sense that Hans Frank intended. Although this division between legal and arbitrary states may seem too 'Manichean',[15] juridical cases about exclusion, where what was at stake was principle rather than a simple criminal act, divided the public in very simple political and philosophical terms.

There were a number of prominent trials before the First World War in which the ethnicity of the defendants, and in effect their right to live as citizens in the country where they were on trial, was at stake. These trials 'point to deep-seated prejudices against Jews which could be mobilised at opportune moments'.[16] Drawing on older prejudices, which were encouraged frequently by the church in the late medieval and early modern periods, these portrayed the Jew as a predator of children: it was reported that they were murdered and their blood used to make Passover matzos.[17] In 1751 Pope Benedict XIV wrote an anti-Semitic encyclical *A Quo Primum*, which helped to perpetuate a cult of martyrs surrounding those who had supposedly been killed by Jewish ritual murderers.[18] These trials 'point to deep-seated prejudices against Jews which could be mobilised at opportune moments'.[19] Hillel Kieval has argued that the existence of these accusations was a profound negation of the project of modernization and political integration which had occurred across Europe: 'Much of the modern ritual murder discourse led logically to the conclusion that the political emancipation of the Jews – which had been accomplished everywhere in Central Europe by 1871 – had been a mistake, that its resulting cultural and social effects had to be opposed.'[20] If European societies were progressing towards pluralism and inclusion, this momentum could be stopped, or at least sabotaged, at any point through artificially revived intolerance. At the time of the 'not-guilty' verdict for Mendel Beilis, the conservative Catholic Austrian newspaper *Christlich-soziale Arbeiter-Zeitung* still insisted on running an article on its front page with a list of so-called ritual murders by Jews.[21] During the First World War, German Zeppelins were dubbed 'Beilises' by the Russians thus equating Jews with the enemy.[22]

If all the world became a stage in court, then the court became the place in which important ideological principles were contested. A Sardinian Capuchin monk, Tommaso, and his servant, Ibrahim Amara, disappeared in Damascus in 1840. Jews in that city were charged with ritual murder and tortured until they confessed. The case was widely debated outside the Ottoman Empire[23] and initiated a wider debate about Jews and their putative practices that shaped later debates, dividing people sharply for or against them.[24] The Jewish community in the city was subject to horrific treatment during the proceedings, and the chief rabbi was abused and flogged.[25] Moses Montefiore, a prominent Victorian philanthropist, had become active in defending the Jews of Damascus in 1840, and later he defended nine local Jewish men[26] accused of murdering a child, Sarra Modebaste, in Kutais in Georgia in 1879.[27] Avraam Zak, a radical Jewish philanthropist, paid for the Kutais defence.[28] They were defended by Alexander Zederbaum, grandfather of the Menshevik Julius Martov,[29] and again society was divided along the lines of for and against. The Russian newspaper *Novoe vremia*, which had a clear association with pogrom violence,[30] asserted that the Jews were certainly guilty in Kutais, and did so even after their acquittal.[31] Such poisonous views spread quickly even to the illiterate, as newspapers were often read aloud.[32] After the assassination of Alexander II of Russia, his killers were rounded up and publicly tried, and the situation of Jews in the Empire deteriorated further. Only one Jew, Hesia Helfman, was implicated in the conspiracy, but the conservative newspapers *Vilenski vestnik* and indirectly *Novoe vremia* associated the murder with Jews at large.[33] The latter newspaper continued to be anti-Semitic in tone. After reading about Emile Zola's defence of Captain Alfred Dreyfus, the playwright Anton Chekhov remarked that 'French newspapers are extremely interesting', but that *Novoe Vremia* 'is simply disgusting'.[34]

The trial of Alfred Dreyfus in France in the 1890s was a cause célèbre and 'pivotal'[35] in a wider international discussion of the shape of the nation, and it divided the French for and against.[36] Dreyfus was found guilty of espionage in a court martial and sentenced to imprisonment. He was then symbolically stripped of his rank by having his sword broken and the epaulettes and buttons ripped from his jacket. 'Outside the courtyard, while the ceremony of degradation was taking place, a mob chanted "Death to the Jews!" '[37] An American writer John Morse described the atmosphere in France over the Dreyfus case as 'mediaeval', but he thought it would 'stop short of the St Bartholomew which some fanatics have dared to mention'.[38] The injustice of the case, based as it was on the flimsiest of evidence, enraged many of France's most prominent public figures. As an internationally renowned writer, Emile Zola, whose letter '*J'accuse . . .!*' to President Félix Faure[39] had stirred up debate, added credibility to the ranks of the doubters. But many people supported the army and Zola ended up in court accused of libel.[40] Theodor Herzl, a witness to Dreyfus' military humiliation and one of the intellectual founders of the Zionist movement, was deeply moved by these events. He thought that the trials were not simply a miscarriage of justice, but that it was the wish 'of the overwhelming majority in France to damn a Jew, and in this one, all Jews'.[41] If the road to Auschwitz was 'paved with indifference', to use Ian Kershaw's well-known formulation,[42] then the road to Devil's Island, where Dreyfus was sent, divided an inflamed nation in both the public and the private sphere. In the case of Dreyfus there was little indifference. The eliminationist periodical *Action Française* was founded in 1898 in response to Zola by Charles Maurras, who later collaborated with the Vichy regime, which sent Dreyfus' granddaughter, Madeleine Lévy, as well as thousands of other French citizens to their deaths in Nazi Germany.[43] In a strange reversal of fortune, after the defeat of the Vichy regime in France, Maurras was found guilty of treason. At his trial in 1945, he shouted out: 'This is Dreyfus' revenge!'[44]

In 1905, Vienna became the centre of controversy when Professor Theodor Beer, was stripped of his title and imprisoned after having been found guilty of a homosexual act. Although he was a convert to Protestantism, the Austrian press emphasized his former Judaism in their reports. The newspaper *Volksblatt* called the case a 'bright searchlight onto the activities of baptized and unbaptized Jews and Jew-descendants'.[45] Another Jew, Leopold Hilsner, was convicted of ritual murder in Bohemia at the turn of the twentieth century.[46] Like Dreyfus, he also found his supporters amongst those who believed that the composition of the nation should be inclusive as well as amongst those who rejected the notion of blood libel as absurd and primitive.[47] Because of mob fighting and the public passions that the trial unleashed, the trial was moved to Písák. After an appeal by Tomáš Masaryk to the supreme court which Jonathan Frankel has called 'a remarkable act of civil courage',[48] Hilsner was pardoned in 1918. Unlike Zola, who did not live to see Dreyfus pardoned, Masaryk's 'public stance in defense of Leopold Hilsner . . . his . . . rectitude in speaking out for justice, made him a true hero in the eyes of civilized nations and especially of Jewry throughout the world'.[49] Twenty years later, when he visited the United States, he received a standing ovation from an audience which had not forgotten his actions.

In imperial Russia, the manager of a brick factory, Mendel Beilis, was arrested on 21 July 1911, after a lamplighter testified that the murdered boy, Andrei Iushchinskii, had been kidnapped by a 'a man with a black beard',[50] a reference to a stereotypical Jewish man at that time and one which, as we saw earlier, featured heavily in ethnic violence. As the boy was buried, a nationalist group, the Double-Headed Eagle, 'distributed leaflets claiming that the boy had been tortured to death by the Jews who needed his blood in order to make their matzos for Passover'.[51] The local judiciary submitted a report to the Tsar which affirmed their belief that Beilis was the murderer. The case exposed the increasing anti-Semitism of Nicholas II, unburdened as he was in the later years of his reign with intelligent, judicious ministers of state. The Constitutional Democrat Vasily Maklakov claimed that 'when Mendel Beilis was arrested, the authorities capitulated before the right: justice before politics'.[52] The procurator in the Beilis case reminded the jury of the Dreyfus case.[53] As one Berlin newspaper put it shortly after the verdict, 'that was not so much a trial of the Jew Beilis, but a trial against all Jews'.[54]

When the trial finally took place in the autumn of 1913, the stage for a Manichean battle was set. Vladimir Dmitrievich Nabokov, father of the famous novelist, and other journalists from *Riech* had their stories about the case confiscated before publication.[55] The chief prosecutor 'invoked the authority' of Dostoyevsky to warn the court about the destructive influence of the Jews in Russia.[56] Every day the courtroom in Kiev was packed out. Expert witness Iustinas Pranaïtis, notorious as the author of a pamphlet on the Talmud,[57] was mocked in foreign papers as being 'unable to speak correct Russian'.[58] *Die Welt* called him a 'Hanswurst with no humour', and the Orthodox monk Autonom, who also gave evidence, was described as 'senile and unlettered' ('*ein seniler Analphabet*').[59] A correspondent for the Hungarian newspaper *Pester Lloyd* thought the trial of Mendel Beilis had functioned in the same way as the Inquisition in the sixteenth century and condemned the 'medieval' atmosphere in the Kiev courtroom.[60] Vladimir Lenin saw a film about the case, *Tainy Kieva* (*Secrets of Kiev*), in 1913 in Kraków.[61] He thought it demonstrated that there was nothing 'resembling legality in Russia'.[62] Many Marxists found the proceedings ridiculous, or even a distraction from what they regarded as 'real' social issues. Victor Adler's response was revealing: he said that it was as if 'the entire world revolved around the Jewish question!'.[63] The more astute Rosa Luxemburg thought that the Beilis case was comparable to the so-called necklace affair of Marie Antoinette just prior to the French Revolution;[64] she was probably drawing on a popular image of the corruption of the Bourbon *ancien régime* from Alexandre Dumas' play, *Le Collier de la reine* (1849–50). Many of her contemporaries saw the Romanov empire in a similar way, declining rapidly and becoming more desperate and decadent as it collapsed.

The indictment against Beilis, written under the influence of Professor I. A. Sikorskii of Kiev State University, a medical psychologist, testified that the murder was one of 'racial vindictiveness . . . or vendetta of the sons of Jacob'.[65] As Beilis rotted in jail for more than two years awaiting trial (a fate so vividly portrayed by the novelist Bernard Malamud in *The Fixer*), the local and international press debated the blood libel guilt of the Jewish community *in toto*.[66] It has been suggested that this case also influenced the novelist Franz Kafka in his famous depiction of a man on trial in *Das Urteil* (1912).[67] Although there were no Jews on the jury (as this was forbidden even after the 1905 reforms), the jury acquitted Beilis. As in the Dreyfus and Multan cases, the public was clearly divided between eliminationists and humanists.

Beilis remained quiet for much of the trial, but protested his innocence. At the summing up, he reminded the courtroom with considerable dignity that he had not seen his children for two and a half years.[68] A protest movement had gathered in St Petersburg and Warsaw.[69] In the Russian capital, students smashed the windows of a prominent witness in the case, Professor Kosorotoff, with shouts of 'we protest in the name of the civilized world'.[70] Over 2,000 had earlier attended a protest meeting in London[71] and 3,000 demonstrated for Beilis in Pittsburgh.[72] In some respects, they were joining an established practice of demonstrating against tsarist abuses. In 1890 there had been a public protest in the Guildhall London, and a petition to the Tsar was returned unopened by the Russian Embassy.[73]

The short-story writer Vladimir Korolenko had put all his strength into defending Beilis in his passionate pamphlet 'Call to the Russian People'. In the 1890s, he became involved in the case of the Multan Votiaks, who had been accused of ritual murder.[74] Looking back over the events when she was in prison in Breslau in 1918, Rosa Luxemburg compared Korolenko to Jean Jaurès in the Dreyfus case.[75] Antatolii F. Koni remarked on the case that 'a judgement is being pronounced on a whole nationality or a whole social stratum and a precedent is being set, which may for future time have the meaning of a judicial affirmation of the guilt of one group of the population or another'.[76] A great moralist in his work, and one who once proclaimed that 'people are made for happiness as a bird is designed for flight',[77] Korolenko made the rhetorical association of light with justice and darkness with injustice.[78] When he spoke, he broke down in tears after having recited a Votiak prayer in Russian. The jury returned a verdict of not-guilty after fifteen minutes and 'much of the courtroom erupted in jubilation'.[79]

If the composition of the nation was being contested before the First World War, then the intolerance towards those who were identified by a commitment to a mixed heritage nation increased. One of the first ideological actions of 1914 by a nationalist was the assassination of Jean Jaurès, a politician who had been associated with pacifism, but also with the passionate defence of Alfred Dreyfus and the persecuted Armenians of the Ottoman Empire. His assassin, Raoul Villain, was imprisoned during the war, but acquitted after a trial in 1919. Symbolically, after the war, Jaurès's bones were reclaimed for the nation in the 1920s, when he was interred in the Panthéon.[80] During the First World War, the situation for many groups deteriorated beyond recognition. The genocides against Jews in the Ukraine during the civil war of 1918–20 and against Christians in the Ottoman Empire left diaspora communities of bitter survivors and a much more polarized political landscape.

As Germany dealt with humiliating defeat, the eliminationist nationalists dealt with their perceived enemies. The example from the Ottoman, Habsburg and Romanov empires was simply too compelling to be ignored. Violence remained a dominant feature of European political life long after the signing of peace treaties. In the first years of Weimar, 354 prominent liberals or leftists were assassinated. 'The average term of imprisonment per assassination in republican Germany was three months.'[81] The Jewish social democrat Kurt Eisner was shot in Munich in 1919.[82] His murderer, Anton

Arco-Valley, was sentenced to death, but the sentence was commuted to a prison sentence and he had been released by 1925. The murderers of Karl Liebknecht and Rosa Luxemburg were never bought to trial.[83] Matthias Erzberger, who had signed the German Armistice, was shot in 1921. In 1916 he had tried to organize humanitarian aid for expelled Armenian Catholics.[84] The murderers Heinrich Tillesen and Heinrich Schulz did not face trial until after the Second World War.[85] Tillesen had said that, if Bolshevism ever broke out (*losbricht*) in Berlin, the time would be right to shoot the Jewish foreign minister Walter Rathenau.[86] In a form of self-fulfilling prophecy, or, perhaps better, in a staged form of events that eliminationists later became notorious for (that is, a violent threat followed by violent action), the minister was shot in his car by a group while he was en route to his office in 1922. He was not just killed for being a Jewish minister of state or a social visionary,[87] but, as *The Times* of London put it in its report, 'because he was trying to make the German Republic a success'.[88] His assassins were youthful nationalists influenced by the *Freikorps*[89] who had been involved in the struggle against the communists at Wilhelmshaven in 1919 and took part in the Kapp Putsch of 1920. They received derisory sentences amidst an atmosphere of some public support. One of the organizers, Ernst von Salomon, was out of prison by 1928.[90] The driver of the car, Ernst Werder Techow, was released in January 1930, having served only half his sentence. His brother was sentenced to four years, only to be implicated in further terrorism in 1929 after his release.[91] Erwin Behrens, who gave testimony against his nephew Ernst Techow, received anonymous hate mail from a 'brave German national'.[92] It was rumoured at the time of the murder trial that the assassins had been funded by Erich Ludendorff,[93] a leading figure on the right in the 1920s, who in his war memoirs had developed the *Dolchstoßlegende* ('myth of the stab in the back') of Germany's wartime betrayal by strikers, communists and Jews.[94] Ludendorff had links with an anti-Semitic organization, *Aufbau*, which had created an important political fusion between White Russian émigrés and the emerging Nazism.[95]

Over a year earlier, on 15 March 1921, former Ottoman Grand Vizier Talât Paşa was assassinated on a Berlin street. He had been spirited out of Constantinople by a German U-Boat and was living in relative comfort in

leafy Charlottenburg,[96] escaping the tribunals organized by the British at
the end of the First World War.[97] Talât was widely believed to be responsible for the Armenian genocide, and it was his regime that destroyed
much of the multi-confessional culture of Anatolia. He had long been one
of the chief individuals associated with the elimination of the Armenians,
even before 1915. Indeed there had been a plot to kill Talât Paşa in 1913 by
Armenian Hunchak party activists, but it was not carried out.[98] In January
1915, the *New York Times* reported a conversation that Tâlât Paşa had had
with the Greek Patriarchate:'[H]e unequivocally replied that there was no
room for Christians in Turkey, and that the best the Patriarchate could do
for his flock would be to advise them to clear out of the country and make
room for the Moslem refugees.'[99]

A young Armenian, Soghomon Teilirian (or Tehlirian, in later Armenian
sources), admitted in court that he wanted to avenge the slaughter of his
family. He had taken modest rooms in Berlin and prepared himself for the
assassination for some time. At his trial it was said that he was guided by
a compulsion to kill the former Ottoman minister, and he was clearly
showing advanced symptoms of stress. During the proceedings, it was
Talât Paşa and his regime that were 'on trial', and the sympathies of the
courtroom and the German public were clearly with the assassin, as a kind
of representative of the collective Armenian experience. Some were more
critical. Teilirian was called a 'political fanatic' in the Hungarian newspaper
Pester Lloyd.[100] There was also a long history of pro-Turkish discourse
in Germany. In the aftermath of the Hamidian massacres in 1898, Hans
Barth published a book *Tuerke, Wehre Dich!* (*Turk, defend yourself!*) He was
perhaps the individual most responsible for 'a turcophile narrative that
would persist in Germany for at least two decades.'[101]

The Berlin newspaper *Deutsche Allgemeine Zeitung*, linked to the right-
wing *Deutsche Volkspartei* (which in turn was linked to the former naval
attaché to Constantinople, Hans Humann), had tried to protect Talât's
reputation.[102] In an anonymous article, which was possibly written by
Humann, the paper stated that:

> it must be regarded as deeply regrettable that the arguments that permit
> the conduct of the Ottoman government – which was engaged in a war of

life and death – to be seen as understandable were simply pushed aside during the proceedings while the proclaimers of more or less embellished horrors gave free reign to their feelings.[103]

The 'embellished horrors' in this case were the descriptions of the deaths of Teilirian's entire family in front of him.[104] His brother's skull had been split by an axe and his sisters were violated before death. He himself had only escaped death by falling faint and injured among the corpses.[105] He was subsequently helped to escape by friendly Kurds, and he told his story in a quiet and dignified manner. During the trial, other Armenians spoke about what had happened to them. Each one had a moving story of tragedy to tell, which gives us great insight into the diaspora community as it had been built in Berlin and into the support its members gave each other. It seems, according to one witness, Erwand Apélian, that the Armenians rarely talked to each other about their sufferings in Berlin.[106] Another acquaintance of Teilirian claims not to have spoken about the massacres even with his wife[107] (who subsequently told the court that only three from her close family of twenty-one, from Garin, survived).[108] From their testaments, the Armenian survivors appear to have recreated a new, close-knit community in their host country, but with clear limits on the domain of memory, limits perhaps comparable to the self-imposed silence during 'los años oscuros' after the civil war in Spain.[109]

Public sympathy for Teilirian, at home and abroad, was overwhelming. The authenticity of some parts of Teilirian's story has been questioned by recent scholars. Rolf Hosfeld believes that he was 'not the victim that he made [himself] out to be', but rather an Armenian Dashnak (or revolutionary) who had been radicalized by what had happened to his family.[110] For the Germans he became the representative Armenian, and in effect that was their chance to repudiate connections with a genocidal regime. When Christine Tersibaschian told the court that the Armenians had been made to kneel and shout out 'long live the paşa!', the audience in the courtroom reacted in horror.[111] The Lutheran Pastor Johannes Lepsius, who himself had been an eye-witness to the Hamidian massacres, gave passionate evidence that would lend the proceedings more gravitas.[112] He reminded the audience that Dr Nazim and Talât, Enver and

Djemal Paşa had been sentenced to death in Constantinople *in absentia* on 5 July 1919 by a military court.[113] Poignant moments in court included the landlady Frau Dittmann's description of how her tenant sang sad songs at night.[114] She and others conveyed a deep compassion for his fate, recalling how, on the morning when he set out to kill Talât, he drank cognac in his tea, presumably for Dutch courage.[115] Reading the trial, one comes to the conclusion that those involved really attempted to understand the Armenian predicament. Teilirian's teacher, Lola Beilenson, had asked him where he was from. He replied that he had no *Heimat* and that all his close relatives had been killed. 'His sorrow rang out so clearly in this answer that I did not want to ask him any further questions.'[116] Of course this was in Berlin, one of the most tolerant and cosmopolitan cities in the Europe of the 1920s, destination of many Huguenots after the revocation of the Edict of Nantes, but above all a city which the Nazis detested as an example of everything they wanted to destroy.

Professor Richard Cassirer, the distinguished neurologist, one of the early pioneers of the study of multiple sclerosis and the anatomy of the central nervous system, was also an expert witness in the case who argued that Teilirian was suffering from a kind of psychosomatic epilepsy (*Affekt-Epilepsie*).[117] When the judgement was read out to a packed courtroom, there were wild shouts of 'Bravo!'[118] He was dubbed by one German newspaper 'an Armenian Tell',[119] after the Swiss national hero. An hour after the trial, he left the courtroom in a car covered with flowers.[120] An American magazine commented:

> It was expected that the known sympathy of the German Government for the Young Turks would result in the prompt conviction and execution of the Armenian. To the surprise of the world, he was acquitted ... Although the technical defense of Teilirian was temporary insanity brought on by a vision of his murdered mother, the real defense was the terrible record of Talaat Pasha; so that in the eyes of Germany the acquittal of the Armenian of the charge of murder became the condemnation to death of the Turk. That such a trial and such a result occurred in Germany with Germans as jurors is particularly significant.[121]

Teilirian eventually moved to San Francisco, California, a state chosen by many of his fellow Ottoman Christian refugees and now the home of the largest diaspora group outside Armenia. He worked as an office clerk until his death from natural causes in 1960.

This case proved to be an important moment in the history of the punishment of genocide.[122] Raphael Lemkin, still a student at the time, was 'inspired' by the case,[123] noting that the law as it stood did not make a distinction between individual and mass murder (that is, the destruction of an entire community). Only when the Nazis came to power was Talât honoured again. In a curious appendix to the social life of Talât's bones, they were repatriated to Turkey in 1943. Writing in the newspaper *Tasvir-I Efkâr*, the nationalist Orhan Seyfi said: 'Today . . . Germany has expressed its respect towards the martyr Talât paşa and has acquitted itself of their old debt to him . . .'[124]

Talât was not the only prominent late Ottoman leader whose execution was planned. A group descended from the revolutionary Dashnaks organized a 'Nemesis' operation to kill the leading eliminationists. Behboud Khan Jivanshir was killed in 1921 in Constantinople. The British occupation forces found the assassin Misak Torlakian guilty in November of that year, but did not give him a custodial sentence and expelled him to Greece.[125] Most of the time at the trial was spent deciding whether he had been compos mentis at the time, and press coverage was sympathetic, as he had been '(d)riven to insanity by the murder of his family in Baku'.[126] In Rome in December 1921, the former Grand Vizier Said Halim Paşa was shot in the back of the head.[127] His assailant, Arshavir Shirakian, who had tracked him down by stealth, subsequently evaded arrest. In July 1922 Ahmet Djema Paşa was assassinated by Armenians in Tbilisi, although his assailants were, again, unknown at the time.[128] Enver Paşa was killed in East Bukhara in 1922 by communists.[129]

Assassins of the left and right had served lenient sentences or been acquitted in Germany in the 1920s, and this pattern of the court being used as a political battleground deciding on questions of the nation was to be repeated in Austria. On 10 March 1925, the novelist Hugo Bettauer was shot at his office desk in Vienna as he worked. Otto Rothstock, a dental assistant, admitted to the murder, and his trial also turned into a trial of the shot man rather than that of the assassin. When he was apprehended by the police he was carrying a copy of the National Socialist newspaper *Deutsche Arbeiterpresse*, although he claimed to be acting alone.[130] The dead man was well known for a number of reasons. Primarily he was known because he had aroused the enmity of the nationalist far right, with whom Rothstock was associated.[131]

In 1922, Bettauer published *Die Stadt ohne Juden* (*The City without Jews*) – a short, satirical novel that envisaged the expulsion of Jews from an imaginary city modelled on Vienna.[132] A film version of *Stadt ohne Juden* was made in 1924 and the book had sold well since its publication, with 80,000 copies of the German edition printed by 1924 and even more of the translated text. Like Berlin and Paris, Vienna was a cosmopolitan city which had experienced a vibrant *fin de siècle* and a great growth in cultural productivity. Many of its most famous writers and artists were Jewish or had some Jewish heritage, including the philosopher Ludwig Wittgenstein, the composer Arnold Schönberg, the psychoanalysts Sigmund Freud and his pupil Bruno Bettelheim and the novelist Joseph Roth. In 1925 the popular German novelist Artur Landsberger, who eventually committed suicide in 1933 when Hitler became chancellor, wrote his own version of the satire, *Berlin ohne Juden*.[133] Both novels deal with scenarios in which Jews are expelled from cosmopolitan cities in central Europe. Their point was simple: without the Jews, the cities would cease to function, opera and theatres would close down and life would be dull.

Critics have been divided about the merits of *Die Stadt ohne Juden*. In 1928, the film was banned in New York on the grounds that it was 'objectionable'. Michael Mindin, managing director of the Fifth Avenue Playhouse, protested that the film 'was passed by the Chicago Board of Censors without a single deletion ... Certainly if Chicago, which is less cosmopolitan than New York can withstand the shock of seeing the film, New York can.'[134] For Scott Spector, it is 'a light-hearted satire rather than a warning toll of catastrophe that it has been made out to be. *The City without Jews* bases itself on the premise, meant to be somewhat absurd, that in a time of financial crisis, not unlike the mid-1920s, the parliament of Austria passes a measure expelling the country's Jews.'[135] However, Spector has omitted important historical context. Bettauer was the sort of citizen of the world that eliminationists despised. As an American national, he had lived for years in New York, where he wrote for the *Morgen Zhurnal.* There he had had intellectual contact with refugees from the Russian pogroms, so the idea of expulsion would have been less absurd. Not long after publication of the book in 1924, quotas were set on emigration to the USA, trapping many Jews in increasingly hostile European countries. Given that the 'League of Truthful Christians' in the book is probably a satire on the notion of the 'Jewish cabal' and on the *Protocols of the Elders of Zion,* the book is anything but 'light-hearted'. Steven Beller has argued that *Die Stadt ohne Juden* was meant as a polemic rather than as a 'serious prophecy', but, as he wistfully concluded in his discussion of the text, 'for anyone who has been to Vienna . . . there are remarkable similarities between what Bettauer foresaw and what the present city is like'.[136]

At the trial, Otto Rothstock testified that he knew what he was doing when he shot his victim and had done it because he wanted to 'drive Bettauer out of this world and into another one in order to protect his people and cohorts'.[137] For him, the assassination was 'a warning shot to alert all people, above all the German nation to carry on with the brutal and ruthless struggle [*Kampf*] before it is too late. Hugo Bettauer derided everything that was German. I am not guilty.'[138]

Bettauer was also well known for his views on sexual emancipation. Back in Austria in the early 1920s, he published his *Wochenschrift,* which gave advice on personal issues and was regarded as feminist and avant-garde and had recently been cleared of charges of indecent publication.[139] Some weeks before Bettauer's assassination, a nationalist paper, *Grobian,* had urged its readers 'to make his newspaper disappear as this filth was more dangerous than other left wing papers'.[140] Rothstock claimed at his trial to be defending moral values and thus he aroused the sympathy of the judge, who also considered Bettauer to be a degenerate radical. Bruce F. Pauley has noted that the 'murder trial turned out to be . . . politicized . . . the judge and the prosecuting attorney . . . were both *völkisch*'.[141] Other eliminationists welcomed Bettauer's death. SS Obersturmbannführer Robert Körber later described *Stadt ohne Juden* 'as a disgrace that dishonours the German people by presenting them as whores and helots of the Jews'.[142] For Alfred Rosenberg, Bettauer had not so much been shot as destroyed himself, confirming his theory about 'Jewish self-destruction', and he added that the 'Hebrews' had a 'world monopoly' ('*ein Hebraeisches Weltmonopol*') 'in pornography' – a prejudice drawn from the *Protocols of the Elders of Zion*, which he himself had published.[143] Beth Noveck has remarked that 'the language of the newspapers, filled with factual errors and lack of attention to detail, was full of hatred'.[144]

Walter Riehl defended Rothstock and used a plea of insanity to divide the jury, which returned a guilty verdict after one hour. The division of the jury over the question meant that he was given a commuted sentence and spent two and a half years in a mental hospital. Rothstock was active again on the violent Austrian right in the 1930s. He later moved to Germany and was badly wounded serving in the *Wehrmacht* on the Eastern Front during the Second World War.[145] Riehl's own career as a defender of right-wing assassins continued when he achieved an acquittal of *Heimwehr* activists after they shot two politicians in Schattendorf in Burgenland. The outcry over the acquittals lead to riots in Vienna and to the torching of the Ministry of Justice. For many leading intellectuals it symbolized the end of a democratic experiment in Austria.[146]

France was another location where the battle for citizenship and exclusion continued to rage in the 1920s as a direct result of the ricochet from the First World War. In January 1923 in France, the extreme nationalist Marius Plateau was assassinated by Germaine Berton, an anarchist, who was acquitted in the December of that year amid an ovation from the spectators.[147] She claimed that she was avenging the death of Jaurès.[148] In Paris on 25 May 1926, another significant assassination took place. Symon Petlura had been Hetman of the Ukrainian Directorate during the civil war, a title which Bogdan Khmelnitsky had carried and which had been revived in 1918. He was shot while out walking in the street. The following year, Sholom Schwartzbard was acquitted of the murder, even though he freely admitted that he had pulled the trigger. As his chief defence, the assassin of Petlura claimed to be avenging the pogroms against Jews.[149] During the civil war, an estimated 4 to 8 per cent of the Jews of Ukraine were killed, including many from Schwartzbard's family. Schwartzbard blamed Petlura for these events, and the French public duly sympathized.[150] Petlura had also become a 'prominent member of Parisian counter-revolutionary circles'[151] at a time of increasing left–right polarization. *Die Neue Welt* stated that the trial of Schwartzbard had become 'the trial of the pogroms' (*Pogrom-Prozeß*).[152] Some historians such as Henry Abramson have been sceptical about the real role of Petlura in the pogroms, noting that he did send out notices against them.[153] Whatever the judgement of history, Petlura remained an important figure both for eliminationist nationalists and for Ukrainian patriots. In Kiev in 1941 there were rumours on the streets that Petlura would return to head a new government, despite the fact that his death had been reported in Soviet media.[154] In 1942, the nationalist society in Kiev *Prosvita* was decorated with blue and yellow ribbons as well as with portraits of Petlura, Hitler and Taras Shevchenko.[155] Fourteen years after the trial, the Nazis carried out a pogrom in L'viv which they dubbed *Aktion Petliura*, in 'revenge' for the death of the Ukrainian Hetman.[156] As eliminationists, the Nazis had their own genealogies and had not forgotten either Tâlât Paşa or Symon Petlura.

Schwartzbard spoke vividly in court and defended himself against accusations from Campinchi for the prosecution that he was a Soviet agent. For the great historian Simon Dubnow (who was subsequently killed at the age of eighty-one by the SS) writing to the newspaper *L'Univers israélite* on 14 October 1927, the trial was the first time that a Jew was in court not as the accused, but as an accuser.[157] One witness for the defence, Haia Greenberg, gave a dramatic testimony in court.

> I shall never forget the reddened snowsleds, filled with the hacked bodies, going to the cemetery to deposit their sad burden, in a common pit. They brought the wounded to the hospital – armless and legless men, mutilated babies and young women whose screams became faint as their wounds overcame them . . . Oh, no, no! I cannot go on! They are before my eyes![158]

While awaiting trial, Schwartzbard had written a moving letter to his wife Anna. He asked for an inscription to be made on his father's tomb. 'Isaac . . . your son Schalom has avenged the sacred blood of your brother Israël and the martyrdom of the entire people of Israël.'[159]

Schwartzbard was defended by the brilliant barrister Henry Torrès,[160] who later helped to defend the Jewish assassin Herschel Grynszpan, whose actions were the excuse given for the Kristallnacht pogroms in Austria and Germany in November 1938.[161] He also represented Anarchist radicals such as Germaine Berton, Emma Goldman and Buenaventura Durruti.[162] Albert Einstein was impressed by his 'magisterial plea vibrant with humanity and justice'[163] and Torrès offered his services to the defence *pro bono publico*.[164] He was the grandson of Isaïe Levaillant who, as editor of *L'Univers israélite* at the time of the Dreyfus case, had battled against anti-Semitism. During the Second World War he fled an execution order from the Pétain regime and edited *La Voix de France* in New York, which attacked ministers of that regime, including the notorious antidreyfusard the elderly Maxime Weygand. In a kind of genealogy of humanist idealists, Torrès begat, or at least trained, the young Robert Badinter,[165] a life-long opponent of the death penalty and president of the Arbitration Commission of the Peace Conference on the former Yugoslavia. 'Famous for his tremendous voice',[166] Torrès put up a notable rhetorical case for acquittal. As one eye-witness put it, he:

> struck the medals on his chest, for in common with all his colleagues, he wears his decorations on his gown – he himself during the war had seen French soldiers shot after trial by Court-martial for lesser offences than massacre. The pogrom of February 1st 1919 at Proskuroff in which he said over 800 Jews were killed in one day. What action was taken? Not a single soldier was shot, although hundreds must have taken part in the massacre.[167]

The trial got violent at times, with fights on the streets outside the court as well as scuffles in the courtroom.[168] After the jury had deliberated for twenty-four minutes,[169] Schwartzbard was acquitted, to the wild approval of a packed courtroom. When the verdict of not guilty was delivered, someone shouted 'Vive la France!' which was repeated and echoed around the court-room.[170] François-Alphonse Aulard, wrote 'It is imperative that the verdict discourage torturers (*les bourreaux*). As a historian and disciple of the French Revolution which emancipated the Jews, I denounce anti-Semitism and these crimes which deny the true genius of France.'[171] Others, including some prominent Jewish writers, were more sceptical about the whole episode. At the time of the trial, the Ukrainian Jew Arnold Margolin, who had been involved in the early legal defence of Mendel Beilis, wrote to the president of the American Jewish Committee, Louis Marshall, persuading him not to take part in Schwartzbard's defence.[172] Marshall was later to write that 'although we can understand how a man ... whose relatives were victims of pogroms is compelled to commit such as desperate act, there is no excuse to make him a national hero'.[173]

Paris had become the most important place of settlement for displaced Jews from Imperial Russia after 1920,[174] and was a place that they were still free to move to. Like Berlin, it had a special status in so far as it remained a vestige of multiethnicity that had been so badly shaken elsewhere by the end of Empires in Europe. In exile in Paris, Hannah Arendt had developed an interest in these cases.[175] Years later and after the Holocaust, she wrote that 'the point in favour of Schwartzbard and Teilirian was that each was a member of an ethnic group that did not possess its own state and legal system, that there was no tribunal in the world to which either group could have brought its victims'.[176]

Unlike the Dreyfus case, the French public took a rapid and firm stance on the rights of Schwartzbard. The trial created what Boris Czerny has called 'un élan spontané de compassion'.[177] *The Times* duly noted that, '[i]n view of the natural leniency of French juries in the face of a plea of justification, the verdict was not unexpected'.[178] All of these cases initiated a discourse in the press and public sphere about the ethnic and cultural composition of the nation, repeating some of the issues that had been discussed during the trials of Leopold Hilsner and Mendel Beilis some years earlier. These trials were seen by contemporaries as a great moral contest between figures who believed that a tolerant society was superior to one which drove out some of its citizens on the grounds of race, religion or ethnicity and those who created the conditions in which mass murder could occur.

These events also represent an important episode in the development of terrorism as a phenomenon. As the extremists newly in power in the east of Europe had eliminated minority groups, individuals used similar techniques to punish those deemed to represent a gross injustice. Steven G. Marks has argued robustly that Russian terrorism of the Narodnik or, more accurately, Bakuninist variety, influenced a number of movements, including Hamas.[179] Coming in part from the Russian revolutionary tradition, the Armenian Dashnaks were closely linked to the assassinations of prominent Ottoman statesmen. Their 'Operation Nemesis' (as it was called) was in effect an 'Armenian Nuremberg' caused by the fact that Armenians had no other proper legal source of justice, as the Constantinople and Malta trials had been so ineffective. Although this was unknown at the time of the trial, Teilirian had been helped throughout the operation by the Dashnaks. Mike Davis called the actions of Samuel Schwartzbard 'defensive terrorism'.[180] Commenting on this case, Maxim Gorky wrote: 'I am not a partisan of terror, but I would not refuse a man the right to defend himself. It seems to me that a murder has perhaps been committed through fear that the past will repeat itself.'[181] An editorial appeared in the *New York Times* at the time of Teilirian's acquittal: 'to hold, as the German jurors did, that his taking off was "morally right" both reveals a queer view of moral rightness and opens the way to other assassinations less easily excusable than his or not accusable at all. And yet – and yet – what other verdict was possible?'[182] At the time, Raphael Lemkin himself described the murder of Petlura as a 'beautiful crime', stressing the fact that there was no international law for penalizing the destruction of national, ethnic or religious groups.[183]

By the 1920s, the battle to define the nature of inclusion and citizenship became far sharper in many European countries. In Poland in 1922, the newly elected President Gabriel Narutowicz, who was perceived as being too pro-Jewish by the National Democrats, was assassinated.[184] His killer, the artist and former Minister for Culture Eligiusz Niewiadomski, was promptly executed, but became a martyr figure for the right. Four days before the assassination the newspaper *Gazeta Warszawska* condemned the new president, who was supported by Jewish deputies: 'The Jews have made a terrible political mistake and provoked an outburst of anger against them.'[185] In Yugoslavia in 1928, the Croatian politician Stjepan Radić, leader of the Croatian Peasant Party (*Hrvatska seljačka stranka*), was assassinated by Puniša Račić, who was himself shot by the Communist

Partisans in 1944. In 1913, Račić had led the violent 'extirpation' of Albanians around Gusinje.[186] The kind of cultures that existed in some cities came under attack. In 1933 the extreme nationalist Gustave Hervé complained about 'the waves of scheming Eastern metics of all ethnic origins who flocked to Paris and Berlin', isolating them from the rest of an increasingly intolerant Europe.[187] The French president Paul Doumer was assassinated in 1932 by a Russian nationalist, Paul Gorgurov, who called himself a fascist. Two years later, the Austrian chancellor Engelbert Dollfuß was assassinated by Nazis, having survived a Nazi attempt on his life the previous year. After his acquittal, Otto Rothstock joined the SS Standarte 11, which was involved in the Austrian chancellor's death.[188] The Croatian fascist Ante Pavelić was tried *in absentia* in Aix-en-Provence in 1935–6 for the part that the Ustaša, the Croatian fascists which he led, had played in the assassination of Aleksandar Karadjordjević and the French Foreign Minister Louis Barthou in Marseille in 1934.[189] The assassin Vlado Chernozemski was lynched by the police, who also killed several in the crowd by accident (and possibly also Barthou) – such was the chaos that ensued. The cameraman who captured it all on film also died of his wounds some days later. Adolf Hitler watched the newsreel of the assassination repeatedly, compulsively, and came to the conclusion that France was finished as a great power.[190] Fascist success in taking power in Germany and Italy and the destabilization of states elsewhere meant that citizenship was restricted and wholesale categories of people began to be legally excluded. Prominent legal cases in the 1920s proved to be an interlude to the degeneration that came with the Second World War – in other words, a brief prelude before a sustained period of eliminationism in European politics. Liberal states were very volatile ideological battlegrounds in the 1920s and incapable of withstanding sustained attacks upon them in the 1930s.

In early November 1938, when a young Jew, Herschel Grynszpan, murdered the German diplomat Ernst vom Rath, the question of assassination for revenge became prominent again.[191] Grynszpan's parents had been brutally expelled from Germany at the end of October, as the deadline for returning to Poland was about to expire and their citizenship would have expired. Their son was also stateless, having been ordered to leave France that summer. Apparently enraged by the fate of his parents, Grynszpan went into the German embassy and shot vom Rath. He then admitted to the police that he had carried out the crime. The assassination was the pretext upon which enraged Germans and Austrians attacked Jewish homes and businesses – the so-called Kristallnacht of 9 November. On hearing of the widespread destruction, President Herbert Hoover remarked that the rioters were 'taking Germany back 450 years in civilization to Torquemada's expulsion of the Jews from Spain'.[192] The prominent journalist Dorothy Thompson supported Grynszpan[193] and appealed for his acquittal on radio. Hannah Arendt was sceptical about the motive for the killing, but noted that 'the French court took it for granted that it was an act of revenge for the expulsion of some seventeen thousand Polish Jews'.[194] Grynszpan's defence lawyer was preparing to defend him, but Grynszpan was still awaiting trial when the Germans invaded France, and he was killed by the Nazis during the war. If he had been tried, he might have been acquitted on the same grounds as Schwartzbard.

Criminal proceedings had proved to be a political battleground across Europe in the years before the outbreak of the Second World War. In the aftermath of the Dreyfus case, the historian Anatole Leroy-Beaulieu thought that anti-Semitism and other 'doctrines of hate' had acquired a 'new vigour'.[195] The case of Soghomon Teilirian and, to an extent, perhaps that of Sholom Schwartzbard had exposed the weaknesses of international law when it came to punishing atrocities after the First World War. The spectacles created by lawyers such as Torrès and Riehl meant that the political battles between humanists and eliminationists were played out in an international arena. 'Schwartzbard's deed offered the French left a much-needed cause around which it could unite to stem the rightward tide.'[196] After the Second World War, the novelist Elias Canetti tried to look at the history of fascism and at the role that Adolf Hitler had played in the rousing of mob anger in his well-known 1960 study *Masse und Macht* (*Crowds and Power*).[197] He had had a history of protest against injustice and his ideas had been formulated earlier, in response to the lynching of three social democrats in Schattendorf in Burgenland in 1927. He had witnessed the political deterioration of Austria in the inter-war period, particularly the burning down of the Ministry of Justice in Vienna after the defendants at the Schattendorf trial were acquitted following a notable defence by Walter Riehl.[198] The countries in which the judiciary, police and armed services upheld the liberty of the individual and the impartiality of the rule of law were the least likely to experience violent political change and the most likely to resist eliminationism as a political phenomenon.

CHAPTER 8

Shattered Worlds

To some extent, we might expect the societies which lost large numbers of their inhabitants to recover quickly and to bury the past in obfuscation, denial, or narratives of triumph and the inevitability of violence. In the mid-fourteenth century, Europe was devastated by a pestilence we have come to know as the Black Death, which killed up to half the population in some areas. The survivors were far better placed in material terms than many preceding generations. They had more property and land and fewer mouths to feed. But, in terms of mentalities, it took generations for people to recover from the trauma of so many gruesome deaths and the wrath of a seemingly angry God. In the art and culture of the subsequent generation we see not the confidence and plenty of the high Middle Ages, but deep pessimism and increased religious piety, reflected in the common image of *La Danse macabre*. Often in the embrace of skeletons, all types of people, from the very high up in society to the very lowly, process towards the inevitable grave.

The horrors of pestilence were largely not man-made. The forced exodus of Muslims and Jews from Spain was devised, just as the removal of Huguenots from France, to have a long-term impact on its society. Joseph Pérez has argued that the influence of both church and state halted intellectual development: 'research and thought in inquisitorial Spain were eventually sterilized. Only a few great minds, sure of their knowledge and courageous, were capable of taking the risks. The rest preferred to stop using their critical faculties.'[1] The expulsion of Huguenots weakened France and benefited other countries economically.[2] The repercussions of the Edict of Fontainebleau, which led to the exodus of a relatively small but significant community of Huguenots, were 'broad and enduring, permeating every domain, from the religious and cultural to the demographic and economic.'[3] Certainly we cannot doubt the impact of both events on political consciousness and culture. In the twentieth century, some writers maintained that repression of ethnic minorities would have the same stultifying effect on Europe that religious persecutions had in the early modern period. In the preface of his book on Tomàs de Torquemada, Thomas Hope, aware of the historical analogies to the contemporary situation, stated that the Inquisitor:

> was one of the leading creators of the machine with which nationalism secures itself against idealism and any other disruptive force. In the fifteenth century the fight was waged against the Jews. In the twentieth century, the struggle has begun again, but now against Progress, against new and practical ideas – and against the Jews. The weapons are still the same; suppression of all freedom, judicial murders and wholesale proscription. The methods are still the same; espionage on a tremendous scale, utter ruthlessness, for instance . . . there is an exact parallel between the La Guardia trial staged by Torquemada and the Reichstag Fire Trial of 1933.[4]

As I have argued in this book, European society did not recover quickly from the extreme violence that accompanied the break-up of the Ottoman, Habsburg and Romanov monarchies. It is therefore difficult to impose retrospective structure and rationale on these events in terms of any kind of gain for those who survived. Of course, eliminationist nationalists presented the removal of populations as a social good rather than the calamity that it actually proved to be. Many writers justified their actions in terms of social necessity. After a Jewish assassin failed to shoot the eliminationist Pavle Krushevan, who was widely linked to the outbreak of violence in Kishinev in 1903, he justified his actions by appealing to the defence of Russia. He styled himself a 'person who represented the idea of state' ('*chelovekom gosudarstvennoi idei*').[5] Extreme nationalist discourse emphasized agency and action over inaction and passivity. The Croatian Ustaša revived a nationalist slogan, *Za Dom- spremni!* ('Ready for action to defend the homeland'). For them, tolerance and *convivencia* with Serbs, Roma and Jews were to be despised and destroyed. Many created true poetics of destruction, lines that could be repeated by mindless followers to legitimize destruction. Extremists styled their actions as being inevitable. Even more, they stated that this is what was needed for progress. In actual fact, violent attacks on ethnic minorities involved such a great cognitive and physical rejection of existing community relations that they usually resulted in widespread criminality such as rape, theft, and mutilation.[6] The world had literally been turned upside down and wrong became right, in a vicious parody of all previously held values. A violent phase was then frequently followed by widespread self-harm and by a 'culture of lies' from the perpetrators, which means that any kind 'normality' was impossible to restore.

The elimination of minorities often created opportunities for business and trade. Stephan Astourian has argued that the taking of businesses out of the hands of Christians in the Ottoman Empire led to a 'nationalization' of the economy, which had begun during the boycott of Greek and Armenian businesses after the Balkan Wars of 1912–13. Those enriched through war were known as 'the merchants of 1916', and supporters of the Ittihad regime were particularly advantaged.[7] Frédéric Macler suggested that Muslim immigrants were quickly installed in Zeitoun, changing the name to Souleïmanié; '[they] had to take possession of the goods and houses of the Armenians who had been massacred and dispossessed by the Young Turks'.[8] In 1922, the *New York Times* reported:

The Armenians in this district are now in a state of virtual slavery. They are not permitted to travel even within the country, and they are absolutely forbidden to leave the country. Since I have been in Harpoot I have been compelled to return $75,000 to people in America who had forwarded it to pay the traveling expenses of relatives desiring to leave the country. All the property of Armenians who died in the deportations has been confiscated by the Turks . . . The Turkish officials, who are six months behind in their salaries, state frankly that the only way they can get money is by blackmailing Armenians.[9]

According to the Bryce Report,

> On the 3rd or 4th July [1915], the order was issued that the women and children should be ready to leave on the following Wednesday. The people were informed that one ox-cart was to be provided by the Government for each house, and that they could carry only one day's food supply, a few piastres, and a small bundle of clothing. The people made preparation for carrying out these orders by selling whatever household possessions they could in the streets. Articles were sold at less than 10 per cent of their usual value, and Turks from the neighbouring villages filled the streets, hunting for bargains.[10]

Another report states that there was a very direct symmetry between the fate of Muslim refugees in the Balkans and the fate of the Armenians: 'The German and Turkish officers made the Armenians leave all their property behind, so that the *mouhadjirs* [refugees] from Thrace might enter into possession.'[11] The historian Andrej Mitrović argued that the *Drang* or push towards the Balkans by the central European powers had involved detailed financial planning for annexation before the outbreak of war in 1914. Once the war started, goods and material were expropriated from Serbia and Montenegro.[12] All kind of goods could be seized from those who had perished or fled. In 1942, an Ustaša priest, Ivo Brkan, wrote to the authorities asking how the killing of people could now be legitimized by the state and the expropriation of property and women as chattel [*ženidba*].[13]

Many contemporaries saw the expulsions and genocide as economically very costly. In 1901 in Diarbekir, Paul Rohrbach sensed that trade and development had gone into 'fearful decline' ('*furchtbarer Niedergang*') since the recent massacres.[14] Silas Bent wrote in the *New York Times* in 1923:

> The Greeks and Armenians and Jews are the backbone of the Turkish State, and the taxes they pay have been the chief source of its revenue. It is impossible not to suppose that their expulsion will prove costly in the long run ... Turkey's poverty may be gauged from the fact that in 1912 her imports averaged only $9 per capita, as compared with $40 for France and $127 for Belgium. The chief purchasing power of her

population, however, rested with its non-Moslem elements. The burden
upon her subjects will be much heavier because of the excision of the
responsible and industrious Greeks from her population.[15]

Although his purpose was to spread an anti-Semitic interpretation in his
book *The Modern Jew* published in 1899, Arnold White's view that 'the
exodus of the Israelite population en masse ... would involve Russian
insolvency'[16] was probably commonplace. In her memoirs, the American
anarchist Emma Goldman noticed how badly Jewish traders in Odessa
had suffered during the persecution of the civil war.[17] Arnold Toynbee
argued that the persecution of Armenians in Cilicia in 1909 raised the
structure of opportunity in economic terms. They had dominated the
carpet industry, which traded through Smryna before the First World War,
but after persecution their role was significantly weakened[18] and disappeared entirely during the First World War. Many weavers made their way
to Egypt and Greece, and the later country even surpassed the Turkish
Republic in terms of carpet production in the 1920s.[19]

Observers, often outsiders to the original conflict, remarked on the
wanton destruction which accompanied ethnic violence, also frequently
accompanied by malicious spite – or what the Russians, Balkan peoples
and Turks all refer to as *inat*. Travelling in the Crimea in the early nineteenth century, the Reverend Edward Clarke noted with some disapproval
that the Russians were using the cover of war to destroy the Islamic
heritage of the town of Caffa (Kaffa).

> [S]oldiers were allowed to overthrow beautiful mosques, or convert them
> into magazines, or pull down the minarets, tear up the public fountains,
> and to destroy all the public aqueducts, for the sake of a small quantity
> of lead they were thereby enabled to obtain ... While these works of
> destruction were going on, the officers amused themselves in beholding
> the mischief.[20]

In his journey in Eastern Anatolia in 1930–1, Gerald Reitlinger noted
Christian churches which had been boarded up in Kars and 'burnt and
gutted houses ... [in] the high street of dead Kulb'.[21] During the war:

When one stood at the gate called Kars Kapou, the eastern entrance to the city, and looked at the panorama it presented in March, 1916, Erzeroum did not seem to have suffered great changes in its general aspect. But I suffered a rude shock in the interior of the city, when I saw Armenian houses occupied by Turks still gloating over their booty, the city deprived of its Armenian element, and the dome of the Cathedral broken away at its base.[22]

Passing through Serbia in early 1916, Henry Morgenthau noticed abandoned farms 'overgrown with weeds and neglected, and the buildings frequently roofless and sometimes razed to the ground. Whenever we crossed streams, we saw the remains of a dynamited bridge.'[23] Falih Rifki Atay, a journalist from Smyrna, remembered the city during the fire in 1922. 'Izmir was burning and along with its Greekness [Rumluk], the peoples of the first civilizations . . . those who held up . . . all of Western Anatolia's agriculture, trade and the entirety of its economy, those who lived in palaces, konaks and çiftliks . . .'[24] A few years later, travelling in the south-east of Turkey, the Swedish geographer John Frödin stayed in Gevaş, where 'the beautiful mosque was in ruins from the time of the Russian occupation from 1915–17'.[25] Some regions and towns never regained their previous stature and ethnic and religious communities had often disappeared altogether by the 1920s, leaving only rubble and graveyards behind. Germanos, archbishop of Amassia and Samsoun, described his visit to formerly Greek villages in 1919:

Toward the end of the year . . . I was at last able to go out toward the mountains to discover and assemble fragments of evidence as to the catastrophe. I found only ruins and desolation: skeletons lay scattered on the mountain. I found close by a very small number of women and children, who, hidden in the caverns and the forests, had been able to escape the fury of the excited rabble. In the majority of the villages I was unable to discover even the ruins. The places has been burned and were now overgrown with grass. The very small number that had escaped complete destruction were void of inhabitants. Spiders had woven their webs over all, and owls flitted about, mournfully hooting.[26]

For dramatic demographic changes to take place, war or crises are necessary. If the 'natural' state of affairs was not towards 'drift' and toleration, it would not be necessary for those who opposed tolerant states to take the initiative. In 1915, the Russian government undertook a project to remove a vast number of Jews from the western frontier regions of the empire. If they had attempted such an operation at any other time, the outcry from a public raised on tales of Mendel Beilis's suffering and haunted by violent images of pogroms would have been deafening. The break-up of the eastern European empires involved the obliteration of entire civilizations. Ani in the imperial Russian Caucasus was once a centre of Armenian civilization, but in 1901 Paul Rohrbach found only the ruins of the cathedral, one monk and one family of herdsmen.[27] Muslim people now live in a fraction of the territory they one inhabited in the Balkans and the Caucasus, and these regions are covered with the ruins of Islamic material culture. Kishinev, Minsk, Odessa and Białystok were all cities in which a sizeable proportion of the inhabitants were Jews.[28] Now just a few remain. When people are killed, the entire culture and fabric of a place changes, as Mark Mazower has so poignantly charted in his account of the 'city of ghosts', Thessalonica.[29] Instead, perhaps, of 'cleansing', we should think in terms of the toxicity of eliminationism and of the emptiness, desolation and 'silence'[30] it left behind. This was the true 'landscape of nationalism'.[31] Many contemporaries were struck by the insanity and self-destructive nature of state policies which led to population elimination. The Danish militant humanist Georg Brandes noted with some disquiet that Russian Jews were being treated abusively by their regime during the First World War: 'One would think that after the belligerent nations had succeeded in turning Europe into a madhouse and ruin, they would at least maintain a sort of peace within their own boundaries ... but the Russian government have commenced a persecution of Russian Jews which is worse than any other they have endured.'[32] The British diplomat Valentine Chirol described the plight of the former Ottoman Empire in 1923: 'Turkey's own plight was desperate when the war [of 1918] ended. Of an army of over a million, hardly two hundred thousand remained; the Arab provinces of the empire were gone; her people were starving. Enver and Talaat fled from Constantinople.'[33]

Amongst the Serbs there is an expression which conveys the loss of authority that the exit of the Ottomans from the Balkans created. '*Drumovi će poželjeti Turaka, al' Turaka više biti neće* ('The roads will long for the Turks, but there won't be any Turks on them!'). This was refigured ironically as a direct paraphrase by the Croatian fascists in 1941 as '*Drumovi će poželjeti Srbalja, al' Srbalja više ne će biti*'[34] ('The roads will long for the Serbs' etc). Raphael Lemkin did not focus specifically on the quantitative question, simply declaring that genocide means 'the destruction of a nation or of an ethnic group',[35] but he was a good enough historian to know what the long-term impact on regions and peoples could be, especially as he was familiar with the history of classical civilizations.[36] Often the removal of populations could be taken so far that the old economy and society were damaged beyond repair and all that remained were the 'dead' towns which Gerald Reitlinger saw in 1930–1. Mustafa Kemal Atatürk, the first president of Turkey, admitted in an interview with the Swiss journalist Emile Hilderbrand in 1926 that the Young Turk triumvirate who had initiated the Armenian genocide in 1915 had weakened the state:

> These leftovers from the former Young Turk Party . . . should have been made to account for the lives of millions of our Christian subjects who were ruthlessly driven en masse, from their homes and massacred . . . [T]his element, who forced our country into the Great War against the will of the people . . . caused the shedding of rivers of blood of the Turkish youth to satisfy the criminal ambition of Enver Pasha.[37]

Expelled minorities and their descendants, as well as individuals who left their native countries because of ethnically or religiously based oppression, had a strong tradition of enriching the states to which they fled. The Dutch philosopher Baruch Spinoza came from a family who had fled from the Inquisition in Spain. The eighteenth-century American revolutionary Paul Revere, immortalized in the poetry of Henry Wadsworth Longfellow,[38] came from a Huguenot family. The music of the composer Aram Khachaturian synthesized Soviet proletarian culture and Armenian folk music extremely creatively. Another Armenian, the painter Martiros

Sarian, also came to symbolize the link between his people and the Soviet Union through his paintings, which often had Ottoman themes. The painter Marc Chagall spent his early years in Vitebsk in the Russian Empire, but left to go to Paris in 1910 only to return infrequently. When the Nazis invaded France, he was forced to go into exile again. His colourful evocations of Jewish life before the First World War and the trauma of the pogroms are vividly captured on his canvases. In *La Crucifixion blanche*, painted in 1938, he tried to depict the entire suffering of the Jewish people, including the fire, dislocation and destruction of a 'representative' and terrifying pogrom.[39] As in many of his paintings, the background is the domestic architecture and culture of the Jewish shtetl, now irreparably lost. Another Jewish painter, Chaim Soutine, originally came from Smilovichi in the Russian empire, quitting his home as a young man to go to Paris. After a brilliant career as an expressionist, he died as a result of injuries sustained during the Nazi occupation of France. Many Austrian Jews, including the philosopher Karl Popper and the psychologist Bruno Bettelheim, left Vienna in the 1930s because of the threat of National Socialism. The future shipping magnate Aristotle Onassis was forced to flee the burning city of Smyrna in 1921 as a teenager. Pathological homogenization or 'massification' of culture often removes those who are most talented and have most potential.

The use of technology to maximize killing is another aspect of the twentieth-century genocides that has had a lasting effect on human consciousness, suggesting that parts of Europe had reached a moral nadir in which all that was solid had really 'melted into air'.[40] Leo Tolstoy anticipated the problem at the end of the nineteenth century: '[Thomas] Edison declared that he will devise such ammunition that can kill in an hour more people than Attila killed in all his battles'.[41] The moral shock of the international community at the destruction of European Jewry led directly to the codification of the term 'genocide'. In 1948, it became obligatory for signatories of the United Nations treaty to accept the necessity for intervention to prevent genocides from occurring (which has unfortunately led to moral obfuscation in cases where signatories believe that it is not in their interests to intervene). The Jewish lawyer Raphael Lemkin had lived through violence as a child, as the pogroms in his home town of Białystok

Figure 5 Marc Chagall, *La Crucifixion blanche* (1938) (Art Institute of Chicago).

in Poland were particularly horrific.[42] As a student in 1921, Lemkin became interested in the assassination trial of Talât Paşa and in the question of how the mass murder of a people could be dealt with by existing legal frameworks.[43] In 1933 he drafted a paper to be read at a conference in Madrid in which 'he drew attention both to Hitler's ascent and to the Ottoman slaughter of Armenians . . . If it happened once . . . it would happen again.'[44] Ten years later he had the chance to make his point, although clearly he had not persuaded enough contemporaries of this very point in 1933, at a time when it was unfashionable to make direct comparisons between central Europe and the 'orient'. As a result of Lemkin's influence, the definition of genocide adopted by the United Nations was very wide; it was clearly meant to encompass all acts of collective murder or elimination of ethnic groups. As Martin Shaw has remarked, 'only a few major ideas can be traced unequivocally to a single person'.[45] The signing of a Genocide Convention also represented both a significant repudiation of the previous years and the catastrophic impact of eliminationism.

In the present convention, genocide means any of the following: acts committed with the intention to destroy, in whole or in part, a national, ethnic, racial or religious group as such. These acts include 'killing members of the group; causing serious bodily or mental harm to members of the group; deliberately inflicting on the group conditions of life calculated to bring about its physical destruction in whole or in part; imposing measures intended to prevent births within the group and/or forcibly transferring children of the group to another group'.[46] William Schabas has pointed out that in some respects Lemkin's codification was narrow in that it was conceived as a crime against 'national groups rather than groups in general', but also broad in that it included acts 'aimed to destroy culture and livelihood'.[47] Although there was no absolute legal term before 1948, contemporaries were in no doubt that they were witnessing something exceptional, which involved mass death. Arnold Toynbee asserted: '[T]here were less than twenty million people in Turkey before the war, and during it the Government has caused a million or so to perish by massacre, starvation and disease.'[48] In 1897, Benjamin Ide Wheeler had noted that '[t]he utter failure of all attempts to check the Turk in his purpose of exterminating the Armenians spread far and wide among the Greeks of European and Asiatic

Turkey the conviction that they were destined to be next in turn'.[49] In Germany, terms such as *Greuel* ('atrocity') were used to describe both the Jewish pogroms and the massacres of Armenians.[50] Major Yowell warned readers of the *New York Times* that '[u]nless outside interference comes soon the final chapter in the history of Asia Minor minorities will shortly be completed'.[51] The Genocide Convention came very late in the day, but it aimed to prevent all types of mass violence that Lemkin had reflected upon.

In this book I have generally avoided contemporary comparisons, or what is sometimes referred to, somewhat inelegantly, as 'presentism'. We can only really understand these events in their genuine historical context, although universal theories about human behaviour *in extremis* as well as the impact of propaganda and literary ideas are clearly very necessary to develop. Generally, I remain sceptical as to how far we can compare genocides, or, indeed, human suffering. Every Jew, Muslim, atheist or Christian who died at this time as a result of being targeted for his or her faith or ethnicity was an individual with his or her own unique martyrdom. However, a few tentative conclusions might be useful to take away. The idea of defending religious, national or community 'tradition' can be easily mobilized by ideologues because it mimics an essence and can therefore be deemed both 'natural' and 'right'. Personal courage, no matter how insignificant it may seem at the time, is the only guarantee that universal humanistic values are not swept away by cant, propaganda and delusion during times of crisis. Firm structures which guarantee the human rights of individuals, protecting them against potentially arbitrary behaviour by national or local authorities, also improve the chances of avoiding crises. Hannah Arendt's insistence that the impartiality of the law was the 'greatest achievement of the nineteenth century' is probably correct.[52] Nevertheless, any state must also combat violence against minority groups in rhetoric before it develops into a lived experience. A political and legal system that does not punish hate speech cannot fully protect its citizens. It is not tolerant to allow individuals to peddle lies and fabrications.

The greatest achievement of the twentieth century in the realm of politics and international relations was arguably the United Nations Convention on Human Rights and its codification of the concept of genocide in 1948. Lynn Hunt has argued that 'it crystallized 150 years of struggle for rights'.[53] For its authors, it was a direct organizational response to decades of the most toxic eliminationism. The elastic application of the Genocide Convention in subsequent years shames the memory of those who died so tragically. Moreover, widespread obfuscation by governments about past genocides in cases where it is deemed to be politically, strategically or economically expedient is not pragmatism, but the worst kind of moral cowardice. The truth should be a higher political principle than expediency for any individual wanting to put a firm distance between themselves and Hans Frank, the Reichsminister and codifier of Nazi law who could not distinguish between the truth and what was 'good for the German people'.[54] The nadir of the United Nations as a moral force in the first years of the twenty-first century has been accompanied by widespread human rights abuses by countries which were once at the forefront of the struggle for liberty in its widest sense. Not learning from the past does indeed suggest that we are tragically doomed to repeat it.

Notes

Chapter 1: The Violent Demise of the Eastern European Empires

1. John K. Cox, *The History of Serbia*, Westport, CT: Greenwood Press, 2002, pp. 65–6.
2. Michael Fisher, *Counterflows to Colonialism: Indian Travellers and Settlers in Britain, 1600–1857*, Delhi: Permanent Black, 2004.
3. Aviel Roshwald, *Ethnic Nationalism and the Fall of Empires: Central Europe, Russia and the Middle East, 1914–1923*, New York: Routledge, 2001, p. 5.
4. Ernest Gellner, 'Nationalism and Politics in Eastern Europe', *New Left Review*, September–October 1991, p. 127.
5. See, for example, 'Servia's Troubled Century of History; How the Claim of the Murdered King's House Originated. Long List of Scandals, Murders, Revolution and Abdications in the Ninety Years of National Existence', *New York Times*, 12 June 1903, p. 3.
6. Maria Todorova, *Imagining the Balkans*, New York/Oxford: Oxford University Press, 1997, p. 183.
7. The term 'eliminationist' is adapted from a phrase introduced by Daniel Goldhagen in his *Hitler's Willing Executioners. Ordinary Germans and the Holocaust*, London: Little, Brown, 1996, although I would want to distance myself from any interpretation that saw this as an exclusively German practice or phenomenon.
8. Helmut Walser Smith, *The Continuities of German History. Nation, Religion and Race across the Long Nineteenth Century*, Cambridge: Cambridge University Press, 2008, p. 168.
9. Roshwald, *Ethnic Nationalism and the Fall of Empires*, p. 2.
10. Tomislav Dulić, 'Mass Killing in the Independent State of Croatia, 1941–1945: A Case for Comparative Research', *Journal of Genocide Research*, vol. 8, no. 3, 2006, p. 266.
11. Djordje Stefanović, 'Seeing the Albanians through Serbian Eyes: The Inventors of the Tradition of Intolerance and their Critics 1804–1939', *European History Quarterly*, vol. 3, no. 35, 2005, p. 481.
12. Johannes Lepsius, *Deutschland und Armenien, 1914–1918: Sammlung diplomatischer Aktenstücke*, Potsdam: Tempelverlag, 1919, p. 147.
13. Henry Morgenthau, *Ambassador Morgenthau's Story*. London: Hodder & Stoughton, 1918, p. 342.

14. Edmond Paris, *Genocide in Satellite Croatia, 1941–45*, Chicago: American Institute for Balkan Affairs, 1961, p. 132.
15. I. Michael Aronson, 'The Attitudes of Russian Officials in the 1880s towards Jewish Assimilation and Emigration', *Slavic Review*, 34, no. 1, March 1975, pp. 1–2.
16. Andreas Wimmer, *Nationalist Exclusion and Ethnic Conflict: Shadows of Modernity*, Cambridge: Cambridge University Press, 2002, p. 43.
17. Michael Burleigh and Wolfgang Wippermann, *The Racial State: Germany 1933–1945*, Cambridge: Cambridge University Press, 1991, p. 26.
18. That is, *Schicksalsgemeinschaft*. Ironically, this term had originally been popularized by Ludwig Holländer in the late 1920s to mean a community of fate between Germans and Jews. Thomas Pegalow, ' "German Jews", "National Jews", "Jewish Volk" or "Racial Jews"? The Constitution and Contestation of "Jewishness" in Newspapers of Nazi Germany, 1933–1938', *Central European History*, vol. 35, no. 2, 2002, pp. 195–221, p. 205, fn. 41.
19. Edith Durham, *The Burden of the Balkans*, Edward Arnold: London, 1905, p. 104.
20. Thomas Edward Lawrence, *Seven Pillars of Wisdom*, Ware: Wordsworth Editions, 1997, p. 36.
21. Ibid., pp. 78–9.
22. George Orwell, 'The Rediscovery of Europe, Broadcast Talk in the BBC Eastern Service', 10 March, 1942, reprinted in Sonia Orwell and Ian Angus (eds), *The Collected Essays, Journalism and Letters of George Orwell*, Vol. 2: *My Country Right or Left 1940–1943*, Harmondsworth, Penguin, 1971 p. 239.
23. Norman M. Naimark, *Fires of Hatred. Ethnic Cleansing in Twentieth Century Europe*, Cambridge, MA: Harvard University Press, 2001, p. 12.
24. Steven L. Jacobs, 'Raphael Lemkin and the Armenian Genocide', in Richard G. Hovannisian (ed.), *Looking Backward, Moving Forward: Confronting the Armenian Genocide*, New Brunswick, NJ: Transaction, 2003, pp. 125–36.
25. Rendel J. Harris and Helen B. Harris, *Letters from the Scenes of the Recent Massacres in Armenia*, London: James Nisbet, 1897, p. 183.
26. Edmund Reitlinger, *A Tower of Skulls*, London: Duckworth 1932, p. 318.
27. S. I. Witte, *Vospominaniia: Tsarstvovanie Nikolaia II*, Berlin 1922, Vol. 1, 188–9, quoted in I. Michael Aronson, 'The Attitudes of Russian Officials in the 1880s towards Jewish Assimilation and Emigration', *Slavic Review*, 34, no. 1, March 1975, p. 3.
28. Luigi Villari, *Fire and Sword in the Caucasus*, London: Unwin, 1906 p. 190.
29. 'The Greek Exodus. No Satisfaction from Turkey. History of the Crisis', *The Times*, Thursday, 18 June 1914. p. 7.
30. Naimark, *Fires of Hatred*, p. 57.
31. Benjamin Lieberman, *Terrible Fate: Ethnic Cleansing in the Making of Modern Europe*, Chicago: Ivan R. Dee, 2006, p. 4.
32. Mark Mazower, 'The G-Word', *London Review of Books*, 23, no. 3, 8 February, 2001, pp. 1–5.
33. Safet Bandžović, 'Ratovi i demografska deosmanizacija Balkana (1912–1941.)', *Prilozi*, 32, Sarajevo, 2003, pp. 179–229.
34. Wayne S. Vucinich, *The First Serbian Uprising 1804–1813*, New York: Columbia University Press, 1982.
35. Andrei Simić, 'Nationalism as Folk Ideology. The Case of the Former Yugoslavia', in Joel M. Halpern and David A. Kideckel (eds), *Neighbors at War. Anthropological Perspectives on Yugoslav Ethnicity, Culture and History*, Pennsylvania: Penn State Press, 2000, p. 112.
36. 'Frontiers of Servia', *The Times*, 27 February, 1815, p. 2.

37. Christopher Boehm, *Montenegrin Social Organization and Values: Political Ethnography of a Refuge Area Tribal Adaptation*, New York: AMS Press, 1983.

38. Petar Petrović Njegoš, *Gorski Vijenac*, Sarajevo: Svjetlost, 1990, l. 2604–2606, p. 155.

39. Jovan Cvijić, *La Péninsule balkanique. Géographie humaine*, Paris: A. Colin, 1918, p. 353.

40. Traian Stoianovich, *Balkan Worlds: The First and Last Europe*, New York and London: Sharpe, 1994, pp. 167–8.

41. Ibid., p. 169.

42. Maria Todorova, *Imagining the Balkans*, New York/Oxford: Oxford University Press, 1997, p. 78.

43. C. M. Woodhouse, *The Greek War of Independence: Its Historical Setting*, London: Hutchinson, 1952, p. 74.

44. Misha Glenny, *The Balkans 1804–1999. Nationalism, War and the Great Powers*, London: Granta, 1999, p. 28.

45. James Reid, 'Batak 1876: A massacre and its significance', *Journal of Genocide Research*, vol. 2, no. 3, 2000, pp. 375–409.

46. Chavdar Lynbenov Iliev, 'The Bulgarian Nation through the Centuries', *Journal of Muslim Minority Affairs*, vol. 10, no. 1, 1989, pp. 9–10.

47. Simon Goldsworthy, 'English Non-Conformity and the Pioneering of the Modern Newspaper Campaign, Including the Strange Case of W. T. Stead and the Bulgarian Horrors', *Journalism Studies*, vol. 7, no. 3, June 2006, pp. 387–402.

48. Vesna Goldsworthy, *Inventing Ruritania: The Imperialism of the Imagination*, New Haven: Yale University Press, 1998, p. 37.

49. Justin McCarthy, *Death and Exile. The Ethnic Cleansing of Ottoman Muslims 1821–1922*, Princeton, NJ: Darwin Press, 1996, p. 74.

50. Ibid., p. 75.

51. Ronald J. Jensen, 'Eugene Schuyler and the Balkan Crisis', *Diplomatic History*, vol. 5, no. 1, 1981, p. 29.

52. 'The Rising In Macedonia. A Russian Consul Murdered', *The Times*, 10 August 1903, p. 3.

53. Ivo Banac, *The National Question in Yugoslavia: Origins, History, Politics*, Ithaca: Cornell University Press, 1984, p. 316.

54. McCarthy, *Death and Exile*.

55. Richard C. Hall, *The Balkan Wars 1912–13. Prelude to the First World War*, London: Routledge, 2000, p. 138.

56. Leon Trotsky, *The Balkan Wars 1912–13*, New York: Monad Press, 1980, p. 119.

57. George Kennan, *The Other Balkan Wars: A 1913 Carnegie Endowment Inquiry in Retrospect*, Washington DC: Carnegie Endowment for International Peace, 1993, pp. 310–11.

58. Brian Glyn Williams, *The Crimean Tatars: The Diaspora Experience and the Forging of a Nation*, Leiden: Brill, 2001, p. 156.

59. Anatole de Demidoff, *Voyage dans la Russie Méridionale et la Crimée par la Hongrie, la Valachie et la Moldavie exécuté en 1837*, Paris: Ernest Bourdin et Cie. Editeurs, 1854, p. 406.

60. Frédéric Dubois de Montpéreux, *Voyage autour du Caucase, chez les Tcherkesses, et les Abkhases, en Colchide, en Géorgie, en Arménie et en Crimée*, Paris: Librarie de Gide, 1839, p. 267.

61. Peter Holquist, 'To Count, to Extract, to Exterminate: Population Statistics and Population Politics in Late Imperial and Soviet Russia', in Ronald Grigor Suny and Terry Martin (eds), *A State of Nations: Empire and Nation-Making in the Age of Lenin and Stalin*, New York and Oxford: Oxford University Press, p. 119.

62. Mark Levene, *Genocide in the Age of the Nation State: The Rise of the West and the Coming of Genocide*, London: I. B. Tauris, 2005, Vol. 2, p. 301.

63. Stephen Shenfield, 'The Circassians: A Forgotten Genocide?', in Mark Levene and Penny Roberts (eds), *The Massacre in History*, Oxford: Berghahn, 1999, p. 154.

64. Williams, *The Crimean Tatars*, p. 168.

65. Brian Glyn Williams, 'Hijra and forced migration from nineteenth-century Russia to the Ottoman Empire', *Cahiers du monde russe*, vol. 41, no. 1, 2000, p. 103.

66. Michael Khodarkovsky, 'Of Christianity, Enlightenment, and Colonialism: Russia in the North Caucasus, 1550–1800', *Journal of Modern History*, vol. 71, no. 2, 1999, pp. 429–30.

67. Levene, *Genocide in the Age of the Nation State*, Vol. 2, p. 302.

68. Michael E. Brown, 'The Causes of Internal Conflict: an Overview', in Michael E. Brown, Owen R. Cote Jr, Sean M. Lynn-Jones, Steven E. Miller (eds), *Nationalism and Ethnic Conflict*, revised Edn, Cambridge, MA: MIT Press, 2001, p. 13.

69. Lieberman, *Terrible Fate*, p. 34.

70. Jean G. Peristiany (ed.), *Honour and Shame: The Values of Mediterranean Society*, Chicago: University of Chicago Press, 1966.

71. Jezernik, *Dežela, kjer je vse narobe*, pp. 146–6.

72. Maureen P. O'Connor, 'The Vision of Soldiers: Britain, France, Germany and the United States observe the Russo-Turkish Wars', *War in History*, vol. 4, no. 3, 1997, p. 270.

73. Robert de Heimann, *A cheval de Varsovie à Constantinople par un capitaine de hussards de la garde impériale russe, Avec une préface de Pierre Loti*, Paris: Paul Ollendorf, 1893, p. 263.

74. Selim Deringil, 'The Invention of Tradition as Public Image in the Late Ottoman Empire, 1808 to 1908', *Comparative Studies in Society and History*, vol. 35, no. 1, 1993, pp. 3–29.

75. 'Turkish Atrocities against Greeks. Massacres in Asia Minor', *Scotsman*, 19 June 1914, p. 7.

76. Ben Kiernan, *Blood and Soil. A World History of Genocide and Extermination from Sparta to Darfur*, New Haven, CT: Yale University Press, 2007, p. 403.

77. Donald Bloxham, *The Great Game of Genocide*. Oxford: Oxford University Press, 2005, pp. 76–7.

78. Trotsky, *Balkan Wars 1912–13*, pp. 250.

79. Bloxham, *Great Game of Genocide*, p. 1.

80. John Henry Newman, *Historical Sketches, 1. The Turks in Their Relation to Europe, Marcus Tullius Cicero, Apollonius of Tyana, Primitive Christianity*, London: Longman Green, 1889, p. 113.

81. 'Urumiah Massacres. Death Of 12,000 Nestorian Christians', *The Times*, 9 October 1915, p. 5.

82. 'Everek: Statement published in the Armenians Journal "Gotchnag" of New York, 28 August, 1915', in James Viscount Bryce and Arnold Toynbee, *The Treatment of Armenians in the Ottoman Empire, 1915–1916: Documents Presented to Viscount Grey of Falloden*, Reading: Tadaron Press, in association with the Gomidas Institute, 2000, p. 351.

83. Emile Hilderbrand, 'Kemal Promises More Hangings of Political Antagonists in Turkey', *Los Angeles Examiner*, 1 August, 1926, p. 1.

84. Bloxham, *Great Game of Genocide*, p. 4.

85. Vladimir I. Lenin, *Selected Works*, Vol. 5, New York: International Publishers, 1935, p. 288.

86. Anon., 'Opfer der Pogrome in Rußland', *Zeitschrift für Demographie und Statistik der Juden*, vol. 2, no. 12, 1906, p. 191.

87. John Klier, 'The Pogrom Paradigm in Russian History', in John Klier and Shlomo Lambroza (eds), *Pogroms: Anti-Jewish Violence in Modern Russian History*, Cambridge: Cambridge University Press, 1991, p. 35.

88. Monty Naum Penkower, 'The Kishinev Pogrom of 1903: A Turning Point in Jewish History', *Modern Judaism*, vol. 24, no. 3, 2004, pp. 187–225.

89. Andrew Dickson White, *Autobiography of Andrew Dickson White*, Vol. 2, New York: Century, 1905, p. 39.

90. Nikolaï Dimitrievich Erofeev, *Partiya sotsialistov-revolyutsionerov, dokumenty i materialy Vol. 1: 1900–1907*, Moscow: Rosspen, 1996, pp. 153–5. Many thanks to Dr Francis King for this reference.

91. Abraham Ascher, *The Revolution of 1905: A Short History*, Stanford, CA: Stanford University Press, 2004, p. 83.

92. Wendy Lower, 'Anticipatory Obedience' and the Nazi Implementation of the Holocaust in the Ukraine: A Case Study of Central and Peripheral Forces in the Generalbezirk Zhytomyr, 1941–1944, *Holocaust and Genocide Studies*, vol. 16, no. 1, 2002, pp. 1–22.

93. Villari, *Fire and Sword in the Caucasus*, p. 325.

94. Vladimir Levin, 'The Jewish Socialist Parties in Russia in the Period of Reaction', in Stefani Hoffman and Ezra Mendelsohn (eds), *The Revolution of 1905 and Russia's Jews*, Pennsylvania: Penn State Press, 2008, pp. 111–27.

95. Deborah Dwork and Robert Jan van Pelt, *Holocaust: A History*, London: John Murray 2003, p. 46.

96. Nikolaï Nikolaevich Sukhanov, *Zapiski o revoliutsii*, Vol. 1, Moscow: Izdatel'stvo politicheskoï literatury, 1991–2, p. 58.

97. Robert Weinberg, 'Workers, Pogroms, and the 1905 Revolution in Odessa', *Russian Review*, vol. 46, no. 1, 1987, p. 54.

98. Leon Trotsky, *1905*, Harmondsworth: Penguin, 1973, p. 151.

99. Sophie Witte (sister of the Count Witte, late premier of the empire) 'A Year of Terror', *New York Times*, 3 February 1907, p. SM2.

100. 'Ende des Beilis-Prozeß', *Allgemeine Zeitung des Judentums*, Heft 46, 14 November 1913, p. 545.

101. John R. Schindler, 'Defeating Balkan Insurgency: The Austro-Hungarian Army in Bosnia-Hercegovina, 1878–82', *Journal of Strategic Studies*, vol. 27, no. 3, 2004, pp. 528–52.

102. A vivid account of the uprising was set down by Arthur J. Evans, *Through Bosnia and the Herzegovina on Foot during the Insurrection, August and September 1875*, London: Longmans, Green, 1876.

103. Valentine Chirol, 'A Plea for Servia', *The Times*, 15 September 1914, p. 4.

104. Dulić, 'Mass killing in the Independent State of Croatia', p. 273.

105. Leon Trotsky, *My Life. An Attempt at an Autobiography*, Harmondsworth: Penguin, 1975, p. 240.

106. Andrej Mitrović, *Serbia's Great War 1914–1918*, London: Hurst, 2007, p. 52.

107. Ivan Hribar, *Moji Spomini*, Vol. 2: *Osvobojevalna doba*, Ljubljana: Merkur, 1928, p. 69. Hribar committed suicide in 1941 at the age of 90 after the Third Reich's invasion of Yugoslavia.

108. Milan Bašta, *Rat je završen sedam dana kasnije*, Belgrade: OOUR, 1986, p. 151.

109. Rory Yeomans, 'Of "Yugoslav Barbarians" and Croatian Gentlemen Scholars: Nationalist Ideology and Racial Anthropology in Interwar Yugoslavia', in Marius Turda and Paul Weindling (eds), *'Blood And Homeland': Eugenics And Racial Nationalism in Central And Southeast Europe, 1900–1940*, Budapest: Central European University Press, 2006, p. 105.

110. Andrej Mitrović, *Srbija u prvom svetskom ratu*, Belgrade: Srpska književna zadruga, 1984, p. 31.

111. Vejas Gabriel Liulevicius, *War Land on the Eastern Front. Culture, National Identity and German Occupation in World War I*, Cambridge: Cambridge University Press, 2000, p. 65; Roshwald, *Ethnic Nationalism and the Fall of Empires*, p. 125.

112. Mark Levene, *Genocide in the Age of the Nation State*, London: I. B. Tauris, 2005, Vol 2, p. 323.

113. Mark Cornwall, 'Introduction', in Mitrović, *Serbia's Great War 1914–1918*, p. vii.

114. Winfried Süss, *Der 'Völkskörper' im Krieg: Gesundheitspolitik, Gesundheitsverhältnisse und Krankenmord im nationalsozialistischen Deutschland 1939–1945*, Munich/ Oldenbourg: Wissenschaftsverlag, 2003, p. 226.

115. Levene, *Genocide in the Age of the Nation State*, Vol. 2, p. 323.

116. Mitrović, *Serbia's Great War 1914–1918*, p. 78.

117. Roshwald, *Ethnic Nationalism and the Fall of Empires*, pp. 84–5.

118. John Reed, *War in Eastern Europe. Travels through the Balkans in 1915*, London: Orion, 1999, p. 28.

119. Stuart R. Schram, *The Thought of Mao Tse-Tung*, Cambridge: Cambridge University Press, 1989, p. 47.

120. Mitrović, *Serbia's Great War 1914–1918*, p. 75.

121. Vladimir Dedijer, *Josip Broz Tito: prilozi za biografiju*, Belgrade: Kultura, 1953, p. 60.

122. Richard B. Spence, 'General Stephan Freiherr Sarkotić von Lovćen and Croatian Nationalism', *Croatian Review of Studies in Nationalism*, vol. 17, nos 1–2, 1990, pp. 147–55.

123. Diary entry, 8 May 1916. Fran Milčinski, *Dnevnik 1914–1920*, Slovenska malita: Ljubljana, 2000, pp. 175–6.

124. Alan Kramer, *Dynamic of Destruction: Culture and Mass Killing in the First World War*, Oxford: Oxford University Press, 2007, p. 67.

125. Reed, *War in Eastern Europe*, p. 49.

126. Fridtjof Nansen, *Armenia and the Near East*, London: George Allen & Unwin, 1928, p. 288.

127. Mitrović, *Serbia's Great War 1914–1918*, p. 77.

128. Vladimir Ćorović, *Crna knjiga. Patnje Srba Bosne i Hercegovine za vreme svetskog rata 1914–1918. godine*, Belgrade: Biblioteka Jugoslovenski dosìje, 1989, pp. 74–5.

129. Dobrica Ćosić, *Vreme smrti*, Belgrade: Prosveta, 1972.

130. Nick Miller, *The Non-Conformists: Culture, Politics and Nationalism in a Serbian Intellectual Circle, 1944–1991*, Budapest: Central European Press, 2007, p. 216.

131. Nansen, *Armenia and the Near East*, p. 320.

Chapter 2: The Fatal Quest for 'Loyal Citizens'

1. Heather Rae, *State Identities and the Homogenisation of Peoples*, Cambridge: Cambridge University Press, 2002, p. 5.

2. Daniele Conversi, 'Homogenisation, Nationalism and War: Should We Still Read Ernest Gellner?' *Nations and Nationalism*, vol. 13, no. 3, 2007, p. 2.

3. Joseph Pérez, *The Spanish Inquisition: A History*, New Haven, CT: Yale University Press, 2005.

4. Victoria Ann Kahn and Lorna Hutson, *Rhetoric and Law in the Early Modern Europe*, New Haven, CT: Yale University Press, 2001, p. 210.

5. Known as '*le massacre de la Saint-Barthélemy*' in French, '*Bartholomäusnacht*' in German and '*Vartolomejska noc*' (also spelt with a 'b') in Serbian (with very similar variants in other Slavonic languages).

6. David El Kenz, 'La Naissance de la tolérance au 16e siècle: l'"Invention" du massacre', *Revue Sens publique*, September 2006, p. 2.

7. 'Paris vaut bien une messe', in Théophile Sébastien Lavallée, *Histoire des Français*, Paris: Charpentier, 1856, p. 27.
8. Raymond A. Mentzer and Andrew Spicer, *Society and Culture in the Huguenot World, 1559–1685*, Cambridge: Cambridge University Press, 2002, p. 224.
9. Mark Levene, *Genocide in the Age of the Nation State: The Rise of the West and the Coming of Genocide*, Vol. 2, London: I. B. Tauris, 2005, p. 104.
10. Andrew Dickson White, *Autobiography of Andrew Dickson White*, Vol. 2, New York: Century, 1905, p. 31.
11. Arthur J. Evans, *Through Bosnia and the Herzegovina on Foot During the Insurrection, August and September 1875*, London: Longmans, Green, 1876, p. 249.
12. William Pember Reeves, *The Great Powers and the Eastern Christians. Christiani ad Leones! A Protest*, London: Anglo-Hellenic League, 1922, p. 11.
13. Theophil Spoerri, 'Mérimée and the Short Story', *Yale French Studies*, no. 4, 1949, p. 8.
14. Robert Ignatius Le Tellier, *The Diaries of Giacomo Meyerbeer*, Cranbury, NJ: Associated University Presses, 1999, p. 80.
15. Miriam Hansen, *Babel and Babylon: Spectatorship in American Silent Film*, Cambridge, MA: Harvard University Press, 1994, p. 134.
16. Andrej Mitrović, *Srbija u prvom svetskom ratu*, Belgrade: Srpska književna zadruga, 1984, p. 32.
17. 'Yehudei Germanyeh ba-Metsar', *Ha-aretz*, 5 February 1933, cited in Na'ama Sheffi, 'The Jewish Expulsion from Spain and the Rise of National Socialism on the Hebrew Stage', *Jewish Social Studies*, vol. 5, no. 3, 1999, p. 89.
18. Robert S. Wistrich, *Laboratory for World Destruction. Germans and Jews in Central Europe*, Lincoln: Nebraska University Press/Vidal Sassoon International Center for the Study of Antisemitism, 2007, p. 220.
19. Ivana Dobrivojević, 'Policija i žandarmerija u doba šestosiječanjskog režima kralja Aleksandra (1929.–1935.)', *Časopis za suvremenu povijest*, Vol. 1, 2006, p. 115.
20. Krešimir Georgijević, *Srpskohrvatska narodna pesma u poljskoj književnosti. Studija iz uporedne istorije slovenskih književnosti*, Belgrade: Srpska kraljevska akademija, 1936, p. 138.
21. See, for example, Josip Stritar, *Zbrano Delo, Šesta knjiga, Pogovori 1870–1879*, Ljubljana: Državna založba Slovenija, 1955, pp. 93–4.
22. Inspired in part by the paintings of Francesco Hayez, Giuseppe Verdi composed an opera on the theme: *Les Vêpres siciliennes* (or *I vespri siciliani*), first performed in 1855. This in turn had a profound effect on nascent Italian national consciousness. 'As Garibaldi's Thousand made their way to Palermo, they were awakened in the morning by village bands playing the music of Verdi's opera.' Albert Boime, *The Art of the Macchia and the Risorgimento: Representing Culture and Nationalism in Nineteenth-Century Italy*, Chicago: University of Chicago Press, 1993, p. 57.
23. Mark Greengrass, 'Hidden Transcripts: Secret Histories and Personal Testimonies of Religious Violence in the French Wars of Religion', in Mark Levene and Penny Roberts (eds), *The Massacre in History*, New York and Oxford: Berghahn, p. 76.
24. Lucie Simplice Camille Benoist Desmoulins, *Œuvres de Camille Desmoulins avec une étude biographique . . . précédées d'une étude biographique et littéraire par M. Jules Clarétie*, Vol. 2, Paris: Charpentier et Cie, 1874, p. 199.
25. John Klier, 'The Pogrom Paradigm in Russian History', in John Klier and Shlomo Lambroza (eds), *Pogroms: Anti-Jewish Violence in Modern Russian History*, Cambridge: Cambridge University Press, 1991, pp. 26–7.
26. Aviel Roshwald, 'Jewish Cultural Identity in Eastern and Central Europe during the Great War', in Aviel Roshwald and Richard Stites (eds), *European Culture in the Great War: The Arts, Entertainment and Propaganda, 1914–1918*, Cambridge: Cambridge University Press, 1999, p. 96.

27. Helmut Walser Smith, *The Butcher's Tale. Murder and Anti-Semitism in a German Town*, New York and London: Norton, 2002, p. 176.

28. Dorothea Chambers, *Missionary Daughter. Witness to the End of the Ottoman Empire*, Portland, Oregon: 1st Books Library, 2002 p. 70.

29. 'Armenians fear massacre. Red crosses, with the word "death" marked on houses at Adana', *Washington Post*, 24 January 1911, p. 12.

30. Benjamin Lieberman, 'Ethnic Cleansing in the Greek and Turkish Conflicts from the Balkan Wars through the Treaty of Lausanne: Identifying and Defining Ethnic Cleansing', in Steven Vardy and Hunt Tooley (eds), *Ethnic Cleansing in Twentieth Century Europe*, New York: Columbia University Press, 2003, p. 190.

31. Brian Glyn Williams, 'Hijra and Forced Migration from Nineteenth-Century Russia to the Ottoman Empire', *Cahiers du Monde russe*, vol. 41, no. 1, 2000, p. 99.

32. DE/PA-AA/R14086, 4 July 1915, Vice-Consul Kuckhoff to Ambassador Hans von Wangenheim, in Wolfgang Gust, (ed.), *Der Völkermord an den Armeniern 1915/16: Dokumente aus dem politischen Archiv des deutschen Auswärtigen Amts*, Springe: Zu Klampen, 2005, p. 208.

33. Anthony Arblaster, *Viva la libertà! Politics in Opera*, London and New York: Verso, 1992, p. 133.

34. Ibid., p. 138.

35. Marguerite Jouve, *Torquemada. Grand Inquisiteur D'Espagne*, Paris: Editions de France, 1934, p. v.

36. Graham Robb, *Victor Hugo*, London: Macmillan, 1997, p. 432.

37. Victor Hugo, *Torquemada*, Paris: Calmann Lévy, 1882.

38. Stephen Moeller-Sally, 'Parallel Lives: Gogol's Biography and Mass Readership in Late Imperial Russia', *Slavic Review*, vol. 54, no. 1, 1995, p. 66.

39. Joseph de Maistre, *Lettres à un gentilhomme russe sur l'Inquisition espagnole*, Paris: chez Méquignon fils ainé, éditeur 1822, pp. 90ff.

40. Maurice Paléologue, *Journal de l'affaire Dreyfus, 1894–1899: L'affaire Dreyfus et le Quai d'Orsay*, Paris: Librarie Plon, 1955, p. 132.

41. Léo Errera, *Die russischen Juden. Vernichtung oder Befreiung? Mit einem einleitenden Briefe von Th. Mommsen und einem Bericht des Verfassers über die Vorgänge in Kischinew 1903*, Leipzig: Schulze, 1903, p. 19.

42. John D. Basil, 'Konstantin Petrovich Pobedonostsev: An Argument for a Russian State Church', *Church History* 1995, vol. 64, no. 1, pp. 44–61, at 45–6.

43. Marshall Berman, *All That Is Solid Melts Into Air: The Experience of Modernity*, Harmondsworth: Penguin, 1988, p. 257.

44. Dickson White, *Autobiography of Andrew Dickson White*, Vol. 2, pp. 59–60.

45. Robert F. Byrnes, 'Russia and the West: The Views of Pobedonostsev', *Journal of Modern History*, vol. 40, no. 2, 1968, p. 250.

46. It is possible that the official was referring to Henry Charles Lea, *A History of the Inquisition of the Middle Ages*, London: Sampson Low, 1888, which does contain extensive passages on methods of torture used and their outcomes. This well-known book was available in translation, including a French version from 1902 and a German edition of Lea's writings, which appeared in 1908.

47. Henry Morgenthau, *Ambassador Morgenthau's Story*, London: Hodder & Stoughton, 1918, p. 307.

48. Margaret Lavinia Anderson, ' "Down in Turkey, Far Away": Human Rights, the Armenian Massacres, and Orientalism in Wilhelmine Germany', *Journal of Modern History*, vol. 79, March 2007, pp. 80–111, at 97.

49. Hans Barth, *Türke, Wehre Dich!*, Leipzig: Renger, 1898, p. 133.

50. Ibid., p. 14.

51. Pierre Loti, *Les Massacres d'Arménie*, Paris: Calmann Lévy, 1918, pp. 24–5.

52. Na'ama Sheffi, 'The Jewish Expulsion from Spain and the Rise of National Socialism on the Hebrew Stage', *Jewish Social Studies*, vol. 5, no. 3, 1999, pp. 82–103.
53. Heinrich Mann, *Der Pogrom*, Zurich: Verlag für Soziale Literatur, 1939.
54. Cecil Roth, Review of William Thomas Walsh, Isabella of Spain, *Dublin Review*, October 1932, pp. 219–31.
55. Carlton J. H. Hayes, 'The Challenge of Totalitarianism', *Public Opinion Quarterly*, vol. 2, no. 1, Special Supplement: 'Public Opinion in a Democracy', January 1938, p. 22.
56. Auguste Villiers de l'Isle-Adam, *Nouveaux contes cruels*, Paris: Calmann-Lévy, 1893.
57. Inquisitor in Zaragoza, canonized in 1867.
58. Arblaster, *Viva la libertà!*, p. 281.
59. Franz Werfel, *Die vierzig Tage des Musa Dagh*, Berlin: P. Zsolnay, 1933.
60. For a discussion of the boundary between Christianity and Islam in the Balkans, see Cathie Carmichael, 'Violence and Ethnic Boundary Maintenance in Bosnia since 1992', *Journal of Genocide Research*, vol. 8, no. 3, 2006, pp. 283–93.
61. Henry Abramson, *A Prayer for the Government. Ukrainians and Jews in Revolutionary Times, 1917–1920*, Cambridge, MA: Harvard University Press, 1999, p. 9.
62. Yuri Slezkine, *The Jewish Century*. Princeton, NJ: Princeton University Press, 2004, p. 28.
63. Stavro Skendi, 'Crypto-Christianity in the Balkan Area under the Ottomans', *Slavic Review*, vol. 26, no. 2, 1967, p. 230.
64. Charles Yriarte, *Bosnie et Herzégovine: Souvenirs de voyage pendant l'insurrection*, Paris: Plon, 1876, pp. 204–5.
65. Munevera Hadžišehović, *A Muslim Woman in Tito's Yugoslavia*, trans. Thomas J. Butler and Saba Risaluddin, College Station: Texas, Texas A&M Press, 2003, p. 4.
66. Rose Wilder Lane, *The Peaks of Shala: Being a Record of Certain Wanderings among the Hill Tribes of Albania*, London: Chapman & Dodd, 1924, p. 86.
67. Božidar Jezernik, *Dežela, kjer je vse narobe: Prispevki k etnologiji Balkana*, Ljubljana: Znanstveno in publicistično središče, 1998.
68. Jovan Cvijić, *La Péninsule balkanique. Géographie humaine*, Paris: A. Colin, 1918, p. 351.
69. Edwin Herbert Lewis, *Those about Trench*, New York: Macmillan, 1916, p. 248.
70. Tone Bringa, *Being Muslim the Bosnian Way*, Princeton, NJ: Princeton University Press, 1995, p. 68.
71. Vuk Karadžić, 'Serbi sve i svuda', in Mirko Grmek, Marc Gjidara and Neven Simac (eds), *Etničko Čišćenje. Povijesni dokumenti o jednoj srpskoj ideologiji*, Zagreb: Nakladni zavod Globus, 1993, p. 29.
72. Bringa, *Being Muslim*, p. 68.
73. Leon Trotsky, *The Balkan Wars 1912–13*, New York: Monad Press, 1980, p. 209.
74. David Kherdian, *The Road from Home. The Story of an Armenian Girl*, New York: Greenwillow, 1979, p. 66.
75. Armin T. Wegner, *Der Prozeß Talaat Pascha: Stenographischer Prozeßbericht*, Berlin: Deutsche Verlagsgesellschaft für Politik und Geschichte, 1921, p. 10.
76. Akaby Nassibian, *Britain and the Armenian Question 1915–1923*, Beckenham: Croom Helm, 1984, p. 40.
77. Stephanie Schwandner-Sievers, 'The Enactment of "Tradition". Albanian Constructions of Identity, Violence and Power in Times of Crisis', in Bettina E. Schmidt and Ingo W. Schröder (eds), *Anthropology of Violence and Conflict*, London: Routledge, 2001, p. 97.
78. Nikita Khrushchev, *Khrushchev Remembers. With an introduction, commentary and notes by Edward Crankshaw*, trans. and ed. Strobe Talbott, Vol. 1, London: Deutsch, 1971, p. 267.
79. Edward H. Judge, *Easter in Kishinev: Anatomy of a Pogrom*, New York: New York University Press, 1992, p. 57.

80. Meyer Waxman, *A History of Jewish Literature*, New York: Thomas Yoseloff, Vol. 4, part 1, 1960.
81. Gottfried Kössler, Angelika Rieber and Feli Gürsching, . . . *dass wir nicht erwünscht waren: Novemberpogrom 1938 in Frankfurt am Main. Berichte und Dokumente*, Frankfurt: Dipa-Verlag, 1993, p. 95.
82. Vahakn N. Dadrian, 'Comparative Aspects of Armenian and Jewish Cases of Genocide: A Sociohistorical Perspective', in Alan S. Rosenbaum (ed.), *Is the Holocaust Unique? Perspectives on Comparative Genocide*, Boulder, CO: Westview Press, 1996, p. 114.
83. Walter Zenner, 'Middlemen Minorities', in John Hutchinson and Anthony Smith (eds), *Ethnicity*, Oxford: Oxford University Press, 1996, pp. 179–86.
84. Dadrian, 'Comparative Aspects', pp. 113–18.
85. Vakahn N. Dadrian, 'The Armenian Genocide: An Interpretation', in Jay Winter (ed.), *America and the Armenian Genocide*, Cambridge: Cambridge University Press, 2003, p. 57.
86. A case for drawing parallels between the situation of Muslims and other religious groups in Europe in this period has been made by Justin McCarthy in his monograph *Death and Exile, The Ethnic Cleansing of Ottoman Muslims 1821–1922*, Princeton: Darwin Press, 1996.
87. Dickson White, *Autobiography of Andrew Dickson White*, Vol. 2, p.4.
88. Sholem Aleichem, *Tevye's Daughters*, New York: Crown, 1949.
89. Maurice Godelier, 'Infrastructures, Societies and History', *Current Anthropology*, vol. 19, no. 4, 1978, pp. 763–71.
90. Slezkine, *The Jewish Century*, p. 34.
91. Dickson White, *Autobiography of Andrew Dickson White*, Vol. 2, p. 51.
92. Peter Holquist, *Making War, Forging Revolution. Russia's Continuum of Crisis, 1914–1921*, Cambridge, MA: Harvard University Press, 2002, p. 24.
93. Robert Weinberg, 'Workers, Pogroms and the 1905 Revolution in Odessa', *Russian Review*, vol. 46, no. 1, 1987, p. 56.
94. Aviel Roshwald, *Ethnic Nationalism and the Fall of Empires: Central Europe, Russia and the Middle East, 1914–1923*, New York: Routledge, 2001, p. 57.
95. Carl Joubert, *Russia as It Really Is*, London: Eveleigh Nash, 1904 p. 130. Jews were also excluded from some leisure resorts in Germany before the Nazi rise to power. On this phenomenon, see Frank Bajohr, '*Unser Hotel ist judenfrei'. Bäder-Antisemitismus im 19. und 20. Jahrhundert*, Frankfurt am Main: Fischer Verlag, 2003.
96. Roshwald, *Ethnic Nationalism and the Fall of Empires*, p. 29.
97. Mark Mazower, *The Balkans*, London: Weidenfeld & Nicolson, 2000, p. 80.
98. Robert William Fraser, *Turkey Ancient and Modern*, Edinburgh: Adam and Charles Black, 1854, pp. 128–32.
99. Roshwald, *Ethnic Nationalism and the Fall of Empires*, p. 105.
100. Vera Mutafchieva, 'The Notion of the "Other" in Bulgaria: The Turks. A Historical Study', *Anthropological Journal on European Cultures*, vol. 4, no. 2, 1995, 53–74.
101. Maria Todorova, *Imagining the Balkans*, New York/Oxford: Oxford University Press, 1997, pp. 163–4.
102. Hagop Barsoumian, 'Economic Role of the Armenian Amira Class in the Ottoman Empire', *The Armenian Review*, vol. 31, March 1979, pp. 310–16.
103. Morgenthau, *Ambassador Morgenthau's Story*, p. 339.
104. I have adapted the phrase from Arjun Appadurai, 'New Logics of Violence', http://www.india-seminar.com/2001/503/503%20arjun%20apadurai.htm, accessed 3 March 2005.
105. Linda Green, *Fear As a Way of Life: Mayan Widows in Rural Guatemala*, New York: Columbia University Press, 1999.

106. Batsheva Ben-Amos, 'A Tourist in 'Ir ha-Haregah (A Tourist in the City of Slaughter) – Kishinev 1903', *Jewish Quarterly Review*, vol. 96, no. 3 (summer 2006), 359–84, p. 369.

107. Hermann Adler, 'Russian Barbarities and their Apologist', *North American Review*, no. 420, November 1891, p. 513.

108. Iustinus Bonaventura Pranaïtis, *Das Christenthum im Talmud der Juden*, Vienna: Verlag des Sendboten des Hl. Joseph, 1894, pp. 90–1.

109. Richard Burton, *Personal Narrative of a Pilgrimage to Al-Madinah and Meccah*, New York: Dover, Vol. 1, 1893, p. 128.

110. Valentine Chirol, 'The Turk Old and New. Eight Years of War', *The Times*, 16 January 1923, p. 9.

111. Georgina Mary Muir Sebright Mackenzie and Adelina Paulina Irby, *The Turks, Greeks and Slavons. Travels in the Slavonic Provinces of Turkey in Europe*, London: Bell & Daldy, 1867, p. 20.

112. William Goodell, 'The Bedlams of Stamboul', *Atlantic Monthly*, vol. 28, no. 169, November 1871, pp. 543–4.

113. J. Theodore Bent, 'The Lords of Chios', *English Historical Review*, vol. 4, no. 15, July 1889, p. 475.

114. 'Fair Greece! sad relic of departed worth! Immortal, though no more; though fallen, great! Who now shall lead thy scatter'd children forth, And long accustom'd bondage uncreate?', George Gordon, Lord Byron, *Childe Harold's Pilgrimage: A Romaunt and Other Poems*, London: John Murray, 1812, p. 101.

115. Margaret Lavinia Anderson, ' "Down in Turkey, Far Away": Human Rights, the Armenian Massacres, and Orientalism in Wilhelmine Germany', *Journal of Modern History*, vol. 79, March 2007, pp. 80–111, at 99.

116. Noel Buxton and the Reverend Harold Buxton, 'Travel and Politics in Armenia', *Times Literary Supplement*, 11 June 1914, p. 279.

117. M. A. Titmarsh (William Makepeace Thackeray), *Notes of a Journey from Cornhill to Grand Cairo, by way of Lisbon, Athens, Constantinople and Jerusalem*, London: Chapman & Hall, 1846, p. 138.

118. Captain A. F. Townsend, *A Military Consul in Turkey. The Experience and Impression of a British Representative in Asia Minor*, London: Seeley, 1910, p. 92.

119. Jean Victor Bates, *Our Allies and Enemies in the Near East*, London: Chapman & Hall, 1918, p. 15.

120. Bosworth Goldman, *Red Road Through Asia*, London: Methuen, 1934, p. 239.

121. Ivan Turgenev, trans. Constance Black Garnett, *The Jew and Other Stories*, London: Heinemann, 1899, p. 22.

122. Villiers de l'Isle-Adam, *Nouveaux contes cruels*, p. 21.

123. 'Ils marchaient avec cet air renfermé, sournois, cette mine humble de bête battue', Pierre Loti, *Fleurs d'ennui, Pasquala Ivanovitch, voyage au Montenegro, Suleima*, Paris: Calmann Lévy, 1891, p. 124.

124. Richard Burton, *The Jew, the Gypsy and El-Islam*, London: Hutchinson, 1898, p. 59.

125. James Richardson, *Travels in Morocco*, London: Charles Skeet, 1860, Vol. 2, p. 15.

126. Warren Dwight Allen, 'Music in Russia and the West', *Russian Review*, vol. 8, no. 2, 1949, p. 108.

127. Margaret Lavinia Anderson, ' "Down in Turkey, Far Away" ', p. 100.

128. Reginald Wyon, *The Balkans From Within*, London: J. Finch, 1904, p. 160.

129. J. S. Watson and Henry Dale (eds), *Xenophon's Cyropaedia or the Institution of Cyrus and the Hellenics or Grecian Historys*, London: Henry G. Bohn, 1855, p. 78.

130. 'Rampante dans le malheur et insolente dans la prospérité', Voltaire, *Essai surs les moeurs et l'esprit des nations*, Paris: chez Werdet et LeQuien fils, 1829, p. 191.

131. Michael Marrus, 'The History of the Holocaust: A Survey of Recent Literature', *Journal of Modern History*, vol. 59, no. 1, 1987, p. 151.

132. '*Beachtenswert*': Houston Stewart Chamberlain, *Die Grundlagen des Neunzehnten Jahrhunderts*, I Hälfte, Munich: F. Bruckmann, 1904, p. 337.

133. Joseph Jacobs, 'The Official Defense of Russian Persecution. A Reply to a "Voice for Russia", *The Century, A Popular Quarterly*, vol. 46, no. 3, July 1893, p. 362.

134. 'Turks and the Christian Populations', *The Times*, 22 December 1921, p. 6.

135. Rosa Luxemburg, 'Einleitung (geschrieben im Strafgefaengnis Breslau im Juli 1918)', in Wladimir Korolenko, *Die Geschichte meines Zeitgenossen*, Berlin: Paul Cassirer, 1919, p. vii.

136. Ibid., p. vl.

137. Anita Shapira, ' "In the City of Slaughter" versus "He Told Her" ', *Prooftexts*, vol. 25, 2005, p. 89; see also David Aberbach, 'The Poetry of Nationalism', *Nations and Nationalism*, vol. 9, no. 2, 2003, p. 261.

138. Maxim Gorky, 'The Barbarians', in Theodor Shanin (ed.), *Peasants and Peasant Societies*, Penguin: Harmondsworth, 1971, p. 371.

139. Victoria Khiterer, 'Arnold Davidovich Margolin: Ukrainian–Jewish Jurist, Statesman and Diplomat', *Revolutionary Russia*, vol. 18, no. 2, 2005, p. 158.

140. Shapira, ' "In the City of Slaughter" ', p. 89.

141. Matteo Milazzo, *The Chetnik Movement and Yugoslav Resistance*, Baltimore and London: Johns Hopkins University Press, 1975, p. 49.

142. Jean-Marie Chopin, *Provinces Danubiènnes et Roumaines: Bosnie, Servie, Herzegovine, Bulgarie, Slavonie, Illyrie, Croatie, Montenegro, Albanie, Valachie, Moldavie et Bucovine*, Paris: Firmin Didot Frères Editeurs, 1856, p. 137.

143. Nader Sohrabi, 'Global Waves, Local Actors: What the Young Turks Knew about Other Revolutions and Why It Mattered', *Comparative Studies in Society and History*, vol. 44, 2002, p. 64.

144. It is for this reason that missionaries are among the most important eye-witnesses to the fate of the Christians in the Near East.

145. Benjamin Ide Wheeler, 'Greece and the Eastern Question', *Atlantic Monthly*, vol. 79, no. 476, June 1897, pp. 721–2.

146. Simon Dubnow, *Mein Leben*, Berlin: Jüdischer Buchvereinigung, 1937, p. 94.

147. Helen Davenport Gibbons, *Red Rugs of Tarsus. A Woman's Record of the Armenian Massacre of 1909*, New York: Century, 1917, pp. 109–10.

148. James C. Scott, *Weapons of the Weak. Everyday Forms of Peasant Resistance*, New Haven, CT/London: Yale University Press, 1985, p. 247.

149. Blaisdell, *Missionary Daughter*, p. 61.

150. Armin T. Wegner, *Der Prozeß Talaat Pascha: Stenographischer Prozeßbericht*, Berlin: Deutsche Verlagsgesellschaft für Politik und Geschichte, 1921, p. 6.

151. Raul Hilberg, *The Destruction of the European Jews*, New Haven, CT/London: Yale University Press, 2003, vol. 1, 3rd edn, pp. 50–1.

152. Herodotus, *The Histories*, trans. Robin Waterfield with an introduction by Carolyn Dewald, Oxford: Oxford University Press, 1998, p. 480.

153. Miroslav Krleža, *Golgota*, Belgrade: Biblioteka savremene i klasične drame, 1959, p. 78.

154. Ivan Čolović, *Dubina: članci i intervjui, 1991–2001*, Belgrade: Samizdat B92, 2001, p. 16.

155. Chalmer Roberts, 'A Mother of Martyrs', *Atlantic Monthly*, vol. 83, no. 495, January 1899, pp. 90–6.

156. 'Miss Barton Wavers. Red Cross Mission to Armenia at Least Delayed. Mavroyeni Bey defends Turkey. His Country, He Insists, Has No Animosity Whatever Against the Armenians, and Only Wishes to See Them Prosper Under Rightful Authority', *Washington Post*, 15 January 1896, p. 2.

157. Suzanne E. Moranian, 'The Armenian Genocide and American Missionary Relief Efforts', in Jay Winter (ed.), *America and the Armenian Genocide*, Cambridge: Cambridge University Press, 2003, p. 191.

158. 'Erzeroum: Abstract of a Report by Mr B. H. Khounountz, representative of the "All-Russian Union" on a Visit to Erzeroum after the Russian Occupation, Published in the Armenian Journal "Horizon" of Tiflis, 25th February 1916', in James Viscount Bryce and Arnold Toynbee, *The Treatment of Armenians in the Ottoman Empire, 1915–1916: Documents Presented to Viscount Grey of Falloden*, Reading: Tadaron Press, in association with the Gormidas Institute, 2000, p. 263.

159. Christoph Dinkel, 'German Officers and the Armenian Genocide', *Armenian Review*, vol. 44, no. 1, 1991, p. 96.

160. 'Sivas. Record of an Interview Given by the Refugee Murad to a Mr A. S. Safrastian at Tiflis', in Bryce and Toynbee, *The Treatment of Armenians in the Ottoman Empire, 1915–1916*, p. 345.

161. 'Narrative of an Armenian Refugee from H, Communicated to Lord Bryce by the Correspondent of the London "Times" at Bukarest', ibid., p. 297.

162. Sarah Gordon, *Hitler, Germans and the Jewish Question*, Princeton: Princeton University Press, 1984, p. 51.

163. Werner T. Angress, 'The German Army's "Judenzählung" of 1916: Genesis – Consequences – Significance', in *Leo Baeck Institute Year Book*, vol. 23, 1978, pp. 117–135; Werner E. Mosse and Arnold Paucker (eds), *Deutsches Judentum in Krieg und Revolution 1916–1923*, Tübingen: Schriftenreihewissenschaftlicher Abhandlungen des Leo Baeck Instituts, 1971, p. 25.

164. Kurt Schnöring, *Auschwitz begann in Wuppertal: Jüdisches Schicksal unter dem Hakenkreuz*, Wuppertal: Hammer Verlag, 1981, p. 77.

165. Christopher Browning, *Ordinary Men. Reserve Police Battalion 101 and the Final Solution in Poland*, London: Penguin, 2001, p. 67.

166. 1915-04-15-DE-002 From the Ambassador in Constantinople Wangenheim to the Reichskanzler Bethmann Hollweg, 15 April 1914, in Gust (ed.), *Der Völkermord an den Armeniern*, p. 135.

167. 1914-12-30-DE-001 From the Ambassador in Constantinople Wangenheim to the Reichskanzler Bethmann Hollweg, 30 December 1914, in Gust (ed.), *Der Völkermord an den Armeniern*, pp. 118–19.

168. Dinkel, 'German Officers and the Armenian Genocide', p. 104.

169. 'Christians in Great Peril. Talaat Bey Declares That There is Room Only for Turks in Turkey, *New York Times*, 13 January 1915, p. 3.

170. Eric Lohr, 'The Russian Army and the Jews: Mass Deportation, Hostages, and Violence during World War I', *Russian Review*, vol. 60, no. 3, 2001, pp. 404–19.

171. Aviel Roshwald, 'Jewish Cultural Identity in Eastern and Central Europe during the Great War', in Aviel Roshwald and Richard Stites (eds), *European Culture in the Great War: The Arts, Entertainment and Propaganda, 1914–1918*, Cambridge: Cambridge University Press, 1999, p. 92.

172. Andrej Mitrović, *Serbia's Great War 1914–1918*, London: Hurst, 2007, p. 84.

173. John Reed, *War in Eastern Europe. Travels through the Balkans in 1915*, London: Orion, 1999, p. 28.

174. Roshwald, *Ethnic Nationalism and the Fall of Empires*, p. 75.

175. Robert H. Bruce Lockhart, *Memoirs of a British Agent. Being an Account of the Author's Life in Many Lands and of his Official Mission to Moscow in 1918*, London and New York, Putnam, 1932, p. 105.

176. Vejas Gabriel Liulevicius, *War Land on the Eastern Front. Culture, National Identity and German Occupation in World War I*, Cambridge: Cambridge University Press, 2000, pp. 119–20.

177. Roshwald, *Ethnic Nationalism and the Fall of Empires*, p. 20.

178. Norman Cohn, *Warrant for Genocide: The Myth of the Jewish World-Conspiracy and the Protocols of the Elders of Zion*, Harmondsworth: Penguin, 1967.

179. Cesare G. De Michelis, *Il manoscritto inesistente: I 'Protocolli dei Savi di Sion': un apocrifo del XX secolo*, Venice: Marsilio, 1998.
180. Abramson, *A Prayer for the Government*, p. 110.
181. Shlomo Lambroza, 'The Pogroms of 1903–1906', in John Klier and Shlomo Lambroza (eds), *Pogroms: Anti-Jewish Violence in Modern Russian History*, Cambridge: Cambridge University Press, 1991, p. 214.
182. Yu. I Kir'yanov (ed.), *Pravye partii, dokumenty i materialy 1905–1910*, Moscow: Rosspen, 1998, pp. 277–9. (Thanks to Francis King both for this reference and for his thought on the term '*pleme*' in this context.)
183. Robert Gellately, *Lenin, Stalin and Hitler: The Age of Social Catastrophe*, New York: Alfred A. Knopf/London: Jonathan Cape, 2007, p. 68.
184. Michael Kellogg, *The Russian Roots of Nazism: White Emigrés and the Making of National Socialism*, Cambridge: Cambridge University Press, 2005, p. 75.
185. Aristotle A. Kallis, 'The Jewish Community of Salonica Under Siege: The Antisemitic Violence of the Summer of 1931', *Holocaust and Genocide Studies*, vol. 20, no. 1, spring 2006, 34–56, p. 36.
186. Miriam Gottlieb, ' "Motherly Hate": Gendering Anti-Semitism in the British Union of Fascists', in *Gender and History*, vol. 14, no. 2, 2002, p. 304.
187. Hans-Joachim Bieber, 'Anti-Semitism as a Reflection of Social, Economic and Political Tension in Germany 1880–1933', in David Bronsen (ed.), *Jews and Germans from 1860–1933: The Problematic Symbiosis*, Heidelberg: Carl Winter Universitätsverlag, 1979, p. 63.
188. Catherine Nicault, 'Le Procès des "Protocoles des Sages de Sion". Une tentative de riposte juive à l'antisémitisme dans les années 1930', *Vingtième Siècle. Revue d'histoire*, no. 53, January–March, 1997, pp. 68–84.
189. Abramson, *A Prayer for the Government*, p. 40.
190. Kallis, 'The Jewish Community of Salonica under Siege', p. 39.
191. William I. Brustein and Ryan D. King, 'Balkan Anti-Semitism: The Cases of Bulgaria and Romania before the Holocaust', *East European Politics and Society*, vol. 18, no. 3, 2004, pp. 430–54.
192. Daniele Conversi, 'Violence as an Ethnic Border: The Consequences of a Lack of Distinctive Elements in Croatian, Kurdish and Basque Nationalism', in Justo G. Beramendi, Ramón Máiz and Xosé M. Núñez (eds), *Nationalism in Europe Past and Present*, Vol. 1, Santiago de Compostela: Universidade de Santiago de Compostela, 1994, p. 169.
193. Leon Trotsky, *How the Revolution Armed. The Military Writings and Speeches of Leon Trotsky*, Vol. 5, 1921–3, trans. Brian Pearse, London: New Park, 1981, p. 124.
194. Slezkine, *The Jewish Century*, pp. 38–9.
195. Alexander Gerschenkron, *Economic Backwardness in Historical Perspective*, Cambridge, MA, Harvard University Press, 1962. The factors of production are usually defined as land/natural resources, capital, enterprise and labour.
196. Martin Niepage, *The Horrors of Aleppo . . Seen by a German Eyewitness*, London: T. Fisher Unwin, 1916, p. 20.

Chapter 3: 'One of these races has got to go . . .': Colonialism and Genocide

1. Jürgen Zimmerer, 'Colonialism and the Holocaust. Towards an Archaeology of Genocide', in A. Dirk Moses (ed.), *Genocide and Settler Society: Frontier Violence and Stolen Indigenous Children in Australian History*, New York/Oxford: Berghahn, 2004, p. 64.
2. Dan Stone, 'The Historiography of Genocide: Beyond "Uniqueness" and Ethnic Competition', *Rethinking History*, vol. 8, no. 1, spring 2004, pp. 134–5.

3. Yehuda Bauer, 'Comparisons with other genocides', in *idem, Rethinking the Holocaust,* New Haven, CT: Yale University Press, 2002, p. 67.

4. Hannah Arendt, *The Origins of Totalitarianism,* London: Andre Deutsch, 1986.

5. Mark Levene, *Genocide in the Age of the Nation State: The Rise of the West and the Coming of Genocide,* Vol. 2, London: I. B. Tauris, 2005, p. 84.

6. Evgenii Preobrazhensky and Nikolai Bukharin, with an introduction by Edward Hallett Carr, *The ABC of Communism,* Harmondsworth: Penguin, 1969, p. 189.

7. Philip D. Curtin, 'Epidemiology and the Slave Trade', in Gad J. Heuman and James Walvin (eds), *The Slavery Reader,* London: Routledge, 2003, p. 21.

8. Ho Chi Minh, 'Report on the National and Colonial Questions at the Fifth Congress of the Communist International', in *Selected Writings 1920–1969,* Hanoi: Foreign Languages Publishing House 1977, pp. 35–6

9. Mike Hawkins, *Social Darwinism in European and American Thought, 1860–1945,* Cambridge: Cambridge University Press, 1997.

10. Christopher Browning, *Ordinary men: Reserve Police Battalion 101 and the Final Solution in Poland,* London: Penguin, 2001, p. 73.

11. Henry Morgenthau, *Ambassador Morgenthau's Story,* London: Hodder and Stoughton, 1918, p. 375.

12. Mark Twain, *King Leopold's Soliloquy. A Defense of his Congo Rule,* Boston, MA: P. R. Warren, 1905.

13. Arthur Conan Doyle, The *Crime of the Congo,* New York: Doubleday, Page, 1909, p. iii.

14. Edmund Dene Morel, *The Black Man's Burden,* London: National Labour Press, 1920, p. 194.

15. Mark Levene, *Genocide in the Age of the Nation State: The Rise of the West and the Coming of Genocide,* Vol. 1, London: I. B. Tauris, 2005, pp. 178–9.

16. A. Dirk Moses, 'Conceptual Blockages and Definitional Dilemmas in the Racial Century: Genocides of Indigenous Peoples and the Holocaust', *Patterns of Prejudice,* vol. 36, no. 4, 2002, p. 8.

17. Antonio Gramsci, *Cronache Torinesi 1913–1917,* ed. and sel. Sergio Caprioglio, Turin: Einaudi, 1980, pp. 184–6.

18. Djordje Stefanović, 'Seeing the Albanians through Serbian Eyes: The Inventors of the Tradition of Intolerance and their Critics 1804–1939', *European History Quarterly,* vol. 35, no. 3, 2005, pp. 472–3.

19. Aviel Roshwald, *Ethnic Nationalism and the Fall of Empires: Central Europe, Russia and the Middle East, 1914–1923,* New York: Routledge, 2001, p. 49.

20. M. L. Anderson, ' "Down in Turkey, far away": Human Rights, the Armenian Massacres, and Orientalism in Wilhelmine Germany', *Journal of Modern History,* vol. 79, no. 1, 2007, p. 86.

21. Geoff Eley, 'Reviewing the Socialist Tradition', in Christina Lemke and Gary Marks (eds), *The Crisis of Socialism in Europe,* Durham, NC: Duke University Press, 1992, pp. 21–60.

22. Fitzroy Maclean, *Eastern Approaches,* London: Reprint Society, 1951, p. 238.

23. Alfred Andersch, *Sansibar, oder Der letze Grund,* Olten: Walter Verlag, 1957.

24. Orlando Figes and Boris Kolonitskii, *Interpreting the Russian Revolution. The Language and Symbols of 1917,* New Haven, CT: Yale University Press, 1999, p. 185.

25. Tim Judah, *The Serbs. History, Myth and Destruction of Yugoslavia,* New Haven, CT and London: Yale University Press, 1997, p. 75.

26. Viktor Novak, *Magnum Crimen: pola vijeka klerikalizma u Hrvatskoj,* Zagreb: Nakladni Zavod Hrvatske, p. 606.

27. Konfidentenbericht an k.u.k. Ministerium des Äußeren, 27.12.17, quoted in Hosfeld, *Operation Nemesis,* p. 261.

28. Johannes Lepsius, *Deutschland und Armenien, 1914–1918: Sammlung diplomatischer Aktenstücke*, Potsdam: Tempelverlag, 1919, pp. 25 and 483.

29. Robert Conquest, *The Harvest of Sorrows: Soviet Collectivization and the Terror-Famine*, Oxford: Oxford University Press, 1986, p. 272.

30. Rudi. J. Rummel, *Death by Government: Genocide and Mass Murder since 1900*, New Brunswick, NJ: Transaction Publishers, 1994, p. 101.

31. 'Preface', in Joseph P. Merlino, Marilyn S. Jacobs, Judy Ann Kaplan and K. Lynne Moritz (eds), *Freud at 150: 21st-Century Essays on a Man of Genius*, Plymouth: Rowman & Littlefield, 2008, p. ix.

32. Richard Rorty, 'Human Rights, Rationality and Sentimentality', in *Truth and Progress. Philosophical Papers*, Cambridge: Cambridge University Press, 1998, p. 176.

33. Patrick Henry, 'Banishing the Coercion of Despair: Le Chambon-sur-Lignon and the Holocaust Today', *Shofar: An Interdisciplinary Journal of Jewish Studies*, vol. 20. no. 2, 2002, pp. 74–5.

34. Rosa Luxemburg, 'Einleitung (geschrieben im Strafgefaengnis Breslau im Juli 1918)', in Wladimir Korolenko, *Die Geschichte meines Zeitgenossen*, Berlin: Paul Cassirer, 1919, p. xiii.

35. Lynn Hunt, *Inventing Human Rights: A History*, New York: W. W. Norton, 2007, p. 213.

36. *Kolokol* means 'tocsin' or 'warning bell'.

37. Brian Glyn Williams, 'Hijra and Forced Migration from Nineteenth-Century Russia to the Ottoman Empire', *Cahiers du monde russe*, vol. 41, no. 1, 2000, p. 81.

38. Henri Troyat, *Tolstoy*, Harmondsworth: Penguin, 1970, p. 807.

39. Vladimir I. Lenin, 'Leo Tolstoy as the Mirror of the Russian Revolution', in David Craig (ed.), *Marxists on Literature*, Harmondsworth: Penguin, 1977, p. 347.

40. 'The American Mission at Van: Narrative printed privately in the United States by Miss Grace Higley Knapp (1915)', in James Viscount Bryce and Arnold Toynbee, *The Treatment of Armenians in the Ottoman Empire, 1915–1916: Documents Presented to Viscount Grey of Falloden*, Reading: Tadaron Press, in association with the Gormidas Institute, 2000, p. 83.

41. Claire Demesmay and Eddy Fougier, 'Die französische Malaise im Spiegel der Türkei-Debatte', in Angelos Giannakopoulos and Konstadinos Maras (eds), *Die Türkei-Debatte in Europa. Ein Vergleich*, Wiesbaden, VS Verlag für Sozialwissenschaften, 2005, pp. 49–62.

42. Anderson, ' "Down in Turkey, Far Away" ', pp. 84–5.

43. Maud Mandel, *In the Aftermath of Genocide: Armenians and Jews in Twentieth Century France*, Durham, NC: Duke University Press, 2003, p. 26.

44. Jeremy Jennings, 'Of Treason, Blindness and Silence. Dilemmas of the Intellectual in Modern France', in Jeremy Jennings and Anthony Kemp-Welch (eds), *Intellectuals in Politics*, London: Routledge, 1997, p. 69.

45. Simon Goldsworthy, 'English Non-Conformity and the Pioneering of the Modern Newspaper Campaign, Including the Strange Case of W. T. Stead and the Bulgarian Horrors', *Journalism Studies*, vol. 7, no. 3, June 2006, p. 388.

46. Benjamin Madley, 'From Africa to Auschwitz: How German South West Africa Incubated Ideas and Methods Adopted by the Nazis in Eastern Europe', *European History Quarterly*, no. 3, vol. 35, 2005, p. 430.

47. Jürgen Zimmerer, 'Geburt des "Ostlandes" aus dem Geiste des Kolonialismus, die nationalsozialistische Eroberungs- und Beherrschungspolitik in (post-)kolonialer Perspektive', *Sozialgeschichte*, vol. 19, no. 1, 2004, pp. 10–43; Jürgen Zimmerer, *Von Windhuk nach Auschwitz. Beiträge zum Verhältnis von Kolonialismus und Holocaust*, Münster: LIT Verlag, 2007.

48. Dominik Schaller, 'Die Rezeption des Völkermordes an den Armeniern in Deutschland', in Hans-Lukas Kieser and Dominik J. Schaller (eds), *Der Völkermord an den Armeniern und die Shoah*, Zürich: Chronos Verlag, 2002, pp. 517–55.

49. Tacitus, quoted in Marjorie Housepian, *Smyrna 1922: The Destruction of a City*. London: Faber, 1972, p. 39.

50. N. M. Naimark, *Fires of Hatred: Ethnic Cleansing in Twentieth Century Europe*, Cambridge, MA: Harvard University Press, 2001, p. 110.

51. Helmut Walser Smith, *The Continuities of German History. Nation, Religion and Race Across the Long Nineteenth Century*, Cambridge: Cambridge University Press, 2008, p. 201.

52. Schaller, 'Die Rezeption des Völkermordes', p. 520.

53. Munroe Smith, 'German Land Hunger', *Political Science Quarterly*, vol. 32, no. 3, September 1917, p. 462.

54. Gertjan Dijtink, 'Geopolitics as a Social Movement?', *Geopolitics*, vol. 9, no. 2, 2004, p. 466.

55. 'Die Theologie . . . erschein sie mir als eine Führerin durch die Welt der sozialen Probleme', Paul Rohrbach, *Um des Teufels Handschrift. Zwei Menschenalter erlebter Weltgeschichte*, Hamburg: Hans Dulk, 1953, pp. 15–18.

56. Paul Rohrbach, *Der Deutsche Gedanke in der Welt*, Düsseldorf and Leipzig: Karl Robert Langewiesche, 1912, p. 60.

57. Gottfried Hagan, 'German Heralds of Holy War: Orientalists and Applied Oriental Studies', *Comparative Studies of South Asia, Africa and the Middle East*, vol. 24, no. 2, 2004, p. 147.

58. 'Der Deutsche Gedanke, nicht im Sinne politischer Vorherrschaft oder materieller Kolonisation, sondern rein als Weltkulturfaktor', in Rohrbach, *Der Deutsche Gedanke in der Welt*, p. 235.

59. Schaller, 'Die Rezeption des Völkermordes an den Armeniern in Deutschland', p. 520.

60. Michael Mann, *The Dark Side of Democracy. Explaining Ethnic Cleansing*, Cambridge: Cambridge University Press, 2005, pp. 101–2.

61. Paul Rohrbach, 'Koloniale Rassen- und Ehefragen', in *Die Hilfe*, no. 19, from 9/5/1912; p. 291 in Schaller, 'Die Rezeption des Völkermordes an den Armeniern in Deutschland', p. 547, n. 30.

62. Rohrbach, *Der Deutsche Gedanke*, p. 143.

63. Philipp Prein, 'Guns and Top Hats: African Resistance in German South West Africa 1907–1915', *Journal of South African Studies*, vol. 20, no. 1, 1992, p. 107.

64. Paul Rohrbach, *Die Bagdadbahn*, Berlin: Verlag von Wiegandt und Grieben, 1902, pp. 23–47, esp. 26–30.

65. Rohrbach, *Der Deutsche Gedanke*, p. 36.

66. Rohrbach, *Die Bagdadbahn*, p. 18; Rohrbach, *Der Deutsche Gedanke*, p. 166.

67. Rohrbach, *Die Bagdadbahn*, p.35.

68. Paul Rohrbach, *Vom Kaukasus zum Mittelmeer. Eine Hochzeits- und Studienreise durch Armenien*, Leipzig and Berlin: B. G. Teubner, 1903, pp. 152, 194, 218.

69. Donald Bloxham, *The Great Game of Genocide*, Oxford: Oxford University Press, 2005, p. 1.

70. 1915-08-05-DE-002, Scheubner-Richter to Hohenlohe-Langenburg, Erserum, 5 August 1915, in Wolfgang Gust (ed.), *Der Völkermord an den Armeniern 1915/16: Dokumente aus dem Politischen Archiv des deutschen Auswärtigen Amts*, Springe: Zu Klampen, 2005, p. 226.

71. A. P. Hacobian, *L'Arménie et la guerre. Le Point de vue d'un Arménien avec un appel à la Grande-Bretagne et à la prochaine Conférence de paix*, Paris: Hagop Turabian, 1918, p. 67.

72. Henry Morgenthau, *Ambassador Morgenthau's Story*, London: Hodder & Stoughton, 1918, pp. 365–6.

73. Sarah Gordon, *Hitler, Germans and the Jewish Question*, Princeton, NJ: Princeton University Press, 1984, p. 131.

74. Vahakn Dadrian, *The History of the Armenian Genocide. Ethnic Conflict from the Balkans to Anatolia to the Caucasus*, Oxford: Berghahn, 2003, p. 254.
75. Ibid. p. 255.
76. Bloxham, *The Great Game of Genocide*, p. 120.
77. Christopher Browning, with contributions by Jürgen Matthäus, *The Origins of the Final Solution*, Lincoln, NE: University of Nebraska Press, 2004, p. 81.
78. Christopher J. Walker, *Armenia. The Survival of a Nation*, New York: St Martin's Press, 1980, p. 357.
79. Rohrbach, *Die Bagdadbahn*, p. 54.
80. Arnold Joseph Toynbee, *Turkey: A Past and a Future*, New York: George H. Doran, 1917, p. 55.
81. Rohrbach, *Die Bagdadbahn*, p. 19.
82. Henry C. Meyer, 'Rohrbach and his Osteuropa', *Russian Review*, vol. 2, no. 1, autumn 1942, p. 68.
83. Peter Borowsky, 'Paul Rohrbach und die Ukraine: Ein Beitrag zum Kontinuitätsproblem', in Immanuel Geiss and Bernd Jürgen Wendt (eds), *Deutschland in der Weltpolitik des 19. und 20. Jahrhunderts. Fritz Fischer zum 65. Geburtstag*, Düsseldorf: Bertelsmann, 1973, pp. 437–62.
84. Andreas Kappeler, 'Ukrainian History from a German Perspective', *Slavic Review*, vol. 54, no. 3, autumn 1995, pp. 691–701, at 694.
85. Gregory Moore, 'From Buddhism to Bolshevism: Some Orientalist Themes in German Thought', *German Life and Letters*, vol. 56, no. 1, January 2003, p. 38.
86. Paul Rohrbach, cited in Oleksyj Kuraev, 'Der Verband "Freie Ukraine" im Kontext der deutschen Ukraine-Politik des Ersten Weltkriegs', Osteuropa-Institut München: *Mitteilungen*, no. 35, August 2000, pp. 1–47, at 8, n. 10.
87. Helmut Bley, 'Continuities and German Colonialism: Colonial Experience and Metropolitan Developments 1890–1955', paper presented at the Nineteenth International Conference of the Vereinigung von Afrikanisten in Deutschland, Hannover University, 2–5 June 2004.
88. Schaller, 'Die Rezeption des Völkermordes an den Armeniern in Deutschland', pp. 520–1.
89. George Kassimeris, *Warrior's Dishonour: Barbarity, Morality and Torture in Modern Warfare*, Dartmouth: Ashgate, 2006 p. 8.

Chapter 4: Bitter Religions Divisions

1. Milovan Djilas, *Wartime: With Tito and the Partisans*, New York: Harcourt, Brace, Jovanovich, 1977, p. 13.
2. Martin Shaw, *What Is Genocide?*, Cambridge: Polity, 2007, p. 34.
3. Benedict Anderson, *Imagined Communities: Reflections on the Origin and Spread of Nationalism*, New York: Verso, 1991, pp. 80–2.
4. Robert Redfield, *Peasant Culture and Society*, Chicago: University of Chicago Press, 1965, p. 43.
5. Edward H. Judge, *Easter in Kishinev. Anatomy of a Pogrom*, New York: New York University Press, 1992. The phrase 'we've got to get rid of the Yids' was crudely recycled in inter-war Britain by fascists, in an attempt to imitate 'model' anti-Semitic behaviour. See Miriam Gottlieb, ' "Motherly Hate": Gendering Anti-Semitism in the British Union of Fascists', *Gender and History*, vol. 14, no. 2, 2002, p. 297.
6. Robert Gellately, *Lenin, Stalin and Hitler: The Age of Social Catastrophe*, New York: Alfred A. Knopf/London: Jonathan Cape, 2007, p. 69.
7. Karel Berkhoff, *Harvest of Despair. Life and Death in Ukraine under Nazi Rule*, Cambridge, MA: Belknap/Harvard University Press, 2004, p. 80.

8. Henry Abramson, *A Prayer for the Government. Ukrainians and Jews in Revolutionary Times, 1917–1920*, Cambridge, MA: Harvard University Press, 1999, p. 128.
9. Pierre Bourdieu, *Outline of a Theory of Practice*, Cambridge: Cambridge University Press, 1977, p. 164.
10. Selim Deringil, ' "There Is No Compulsion in Religion": On Conversion and Apostasy in the Late Ottoman Empire: 1839–1856', *Comparative Studies in Society and History*, vol. 42, no. 3, July, 2000, p. 564.
11. Aleksandr Senderovich, 'How Dostoyevsky's "Jew" Is Made: Judeophobia and the Problems of National Identity', Paper presented at the American Association for the Advancement of Slavic Studies, Boston, 5 December 2004. I am also indebted to remarks made by Harriet Lisa Murav in discussions on the subject of Dostoyevsky's anti-Semitism.
12. '*Cette race immortelle de pharisiens*': Anatole de Demidoff, *Voyage dans la Russie Méridionale et la Crimée par la Hongrie, la Valachie et la Moldavie exécuté en 1837*, Paris: Ernest Bourdin et Cie. Editeurs, 1854, p. 387.
13. Judge, *Easter in Kishinev*, p. 40.
14. George Orwell, 'Antisemitism in Britain', originally published in the *Contemporary Jewish Record* in April 1945 and reprinted in Sonia Orwell and Ian Angus (eds), *The Collected Essays, Journalism and Letters of George Orwell*, Vol. 3: *As I Please 1943–1945*, Harmondsworth: Penguin, 1970, p. 381.
15. Carl Joubert, *Russia as It Really Is*, London: Eveleigh Nash, 1904, p. 101.
16. The first phrase was a paraphrase of Johann Gottfried von Herder and the second of Constantin Frantz: Iustinus Bonaventura Pranaitis, *Das Christenthum im Talmud der Juden*, Vienna: Verlag des Sendboten des Hl. Joseph, 1894, p. 110.
17. 'Broussa. Report by a Foreign Visitor to the City, dated 24th September 1915, communicated by the American Committee for Armenian and Syrian Relief', in James Viscount Bryce and Arnold Toynbee, *The Treatment of Armenians in the Ottoman Empire, 1915–1916: Documents Presented to Viscount Grey of Falloden*, Reading: Tadaron Press, in association with the Gormidas Institute, 2000, p. 414.
18. Michael Billig, *Laughter and Ridicule: Towards a Social Critique of Humour*, London: Sage, 2005, p. 172.
19. Eric J. Schmaltz and Samuel D. Sinner, 'The Nazi Ethnographic Research of Georg Leibbrandt and Karl Stumpp, in Ukraine, and Its North American Legacy', in Ingo Haar and Michael Fahlbusch (eds), *German Scholars and Ethnic Cleansing, 1920–1945*, New York and Oxford, Berghahn, 2005, p. 62.
20. Mary Douglas, *Purity and Danger: An Analysis of the Concepts of Pollution and Taboo*, London: Routledge & Kegan Paul, 1966, pp. 35–7.
21. Vejas Gabriel Liulevicius, *War Land on the Eastern Front. Culture, National Identity and German Occupation in World War One*, Cambridge: Cambridge University Press, 2000, p. 106.
22. Ibid., p. 160. Wilna is Vilnius or Vilna.
23. Christoph Dinkel, 'German Officers and the Armenian Genocide', *Armenian Review*, vol. 44, no. 1, 1991, p. 103.
24. Vahakn Dadrian, *The History of the Armenian Genocide. Ethnic Conflict from the Balkans to Anatolia to the Caucasus*, Providence, RI and Oxford: Berghahn, 1995, p. 259.
25. It is frequently said in Rome that the oldest Romans are the Jews, as they have lived in the city for so many centuries.
26. Maud Mandel, *In the Aftermath of Genocide: Armenians and Jews in Twentieth Century France*, Durham, NC: Duke University Press, 2003, p. 44.
27. Dinkel, 'German Officers and the Armenian Genocide', p. 97.
28. Donald Bloxham, *The Great Game of Genocide*, Oxford: Oxford University Press, 2005, p. 55.

29. 'Mit den Christen an Spieß und den Juden ins Feuer': Johann Wolfgang von Goethe, 'Venezianischen Epigrammen', in *Selected Verse*, introduced by David Luke, Harmondsworth: Penguin, 1986, p. 120.

30. Richard Gondrand, *La Tragédie de l'Asie Mineure et l'anéantissement de Smyrne 1914–1922*, Marseille: Y Armen, 1935, p. 115.

31. Akaby Nassibian, *Britain and the Armenian Question 1915–1923*, Beckenham: Croom Helm, 1984, p. 64.

32. Horton, George, *The Blight of Asia: An Account of the Systematic Extermination of Christian Populations by Mohammedans and the Culpability of Certain Great Powers. With the True Story of the Burning of Smyrna*, Indianapolis: Bobbs-Merrill, 1926, pp. 136–7.

33. E. Dourmoussis, *La Verité sur un drame historique. La Catastrophe de Smyrne, September 1922*, Paris: Librarie Caffin, 1928, p. 80A.

34. Horton, *Blight of Asia*, pp. 136–7.

35. 1915-08-12-DE-001, Ernst Fürst zu Hohenlohe-Langenburg to Theobald von Bethmann-Hollweg, 12th August 1915, in Wolfgang Gust (ed.), *Der Völkermord an den Armeniern 1915/16: Dokumente aus dem Politischen Archiv des deutschen Auswärtigen Amts*, Springe: Zu Klampen, 2005, p. 242.

36. Justin McCarthy, *Death and Exile: The Ethnic Cleansing of Ottoman Muslims 1821–1922*, Princeton, NJ: Darwin Press, 1996, p. 72.

37. Anastasia N. Karakasidou, *Fields of Wheat, Hills of Blood. Passages to Nationhood in Greek Macedonia 1870–1990*, Chicago: University of Chicago Press, 1997, pp. 151–2.

38. 'The American Mission at Van: Narrative printed privately in the United States by Miss Grace Higley Knapp (1915)', in Bryce and Toynbee, *The Treatment of Armenians in the Ottoman Empire, 1915–1916 documents presented to Viscount Grey of Falloden*, Reading: Tadaron Press in association with the Gomidas Institute, 2000, p. 82.

39. 'Urmia, Salmas and Hakkiari: Fuller Statement by Mr Paul Shimmon, edited as a pamphlet by the Reverend F. N. Heazell, organizing secretary of the Archbishop of Canterbury's Assyrian Mission', ibid., p. 585.

40. Wolfgang Benz, 'The November Pogrom of 1938: Participation, Applause, Disapproval', in Christian Hoffmann, Werner Bergmann and Helmut Walser Smith (eds), *Exclusionary Violence. Antisemitic Riots in Modern German History*, Ann Arbor: University of Michigan Press, 2002, p. 151.

41. 'Village murdered guests. Oriental tradition violated in the massacre at Sis. Wife of the local governor looked down while Moslems put Christian Travelers to Death', *Washington Post*, 15 May 1909, p. 4.

42. 'Smyrna–Aleppo–Damascus–Aleppo–Smryna: Itinerary of a Foreign Traveller in Asiatic Turkey, Communicated by the American Committee for Armenian and Syrian Relief', in Bryce and Toynbee, *The Treatment of Armenians in the Ottoman Empire*, pp. 474–5.

43. Armenian Massacres. Report by an Eye-Witness, Lieutenant Sayied Ahmed Moukhtar Baas, 26 December 1916, Public Record Office, London. FO 371/2768/1455/folios 454–8.

44. Edward H. Judge, *Easter in Kishinev. Anatomy of a Pogrom*, New York: New York University Press, 1992, pp. 30–2.

45. 'Erzindian. Statement by Two Red Cross Nurses of Danish Nationality, Formerly in the Service of the German Military Mission at Erzeroum, Communicated by a Swiss Gentleman of Geneva', in Bryce and Toynbee, *The Treatment of Armenians in the Ottoman Empire*, p. 280.

46. Platon, Archbishop of Kherson and Odessa, 'Prelate Explains Speech on Jews', *New York Times*, 17 July 1919, p. 3.

47. Robert F. Melson, *Revolution and Genocide: On the Origins of the Armenian Genocide and the Holocaust*, Chicago: University of Chicago Press, 1992, pp. 47–8.
48. Dan Stone, 'Genocide as Transgression', *European Journal of Social Theory*, vol. 7, no. 1, 2004, pp. 45–65.
49. M. A Andréadès, *La Destruction de Smyrne et les dernières atrocités turques en Asie Mineure*, Athens: P. D. Sakellerios, 1923, p. 9.
50. Marjorie Housepian, *Smyrna 1922: The Destruction of a City*, London: Faber, 1972, p. 133.
51. Robert Blobaum, *Antisemitism and its Opponents in Modern Poland*, Ithaca, NY: Cornell University Press, 2005, p. 137.
52. Milovan Djilas, *Land without Justice. An Autobiography of Youth*, with an introduction by William Jovanovich, New York: Harcourt, Brace, 1958, p. 208.
53. Reşat Kasaba, 'Izmir 1922; A Port City Unravels', in Leila Fawaz and C. A. Bayly, with the collaboration of Robert Ilbert (eds), *Modernity and Culture from the Mediterranean to the Indian Ocean, 1890–1920*, New York: Columbia University Press, 2002, p. 220.
54. Charles Yriarte, *Bosnie et Herzégovine: Souvenirs de voyage pendant l'insurrection*, Paris: Plon, 1876, p. 151.
55. 'Turkish Atrocities against Greeks. Massacres in Asia Minor', *Scotsman*, 19 June 1914, p. 7.
56. Brian Glyn Williams, *The Crimean Tatars: The Diaspora Experience and the Forging of a Nation*, Amsterdam: Brill, 2001, p. 389.
57. Mikhail Bakhtin, *The Dialogic Imagination: Four Essays*, ed. Michael Holquist, trans. Caryl Emerson, Austin: University of Texas Press, 1981, p. 72.
58. Heinrich Heine, *Gedichte*, London: Duckworth, 1948, p. 142.
59. Helmut Walser Smith, *The Butcher's Tale. Murder and Anti-Semitism in a German Town*, New York and London: Norton 2002, pp. 172–3.
60. Simon Dubnow, *Mein Leben*, Berlin: Jüdischer Buchvereinigung, 1937, p. 94.
61. Félix Charmetant, *Tableau Officiel des Massacres d'Arménie*, Paris: Burcan des Oeuvres d'Orient, p. 60. A similar outrage was perpetrated against a Greek in Istanbul in the 1820s. See Misha Glenny, *The Balkans 1804–1999. Nationalism, War and the Great Powers*, London: Granta, 1999, p. 28.
62. Robert de Heïmann, *A Cheval de Varsovie à Constantinople par un capitain de hussards de la garde impériale russe. Avec une préface de Pierre Loti*, Paris: Paul Ollendorf, 1893, p. 236.
63. 'Reported Turkish Atrocities in Asia Minor', *Scotsman*, 22 September 1919, p. 5.
64. Pieter Spierenburg, 'Masculinity, Violence and Honor: An Introduction', in idem (ed), *Men and Violence. Gender, Honor and Rituals in Modern Europe and America*, Ohio: Ohio State University Press, 1998, p. 4.
65. Walter Harrington Crawfurd Price, *The Balkan Cockpit: The Political and Military Story of the Balkan Wars in Macedonia*, London: T. Werner Laurie, 1914, p. 355.
66. Anon., *An Authentic Account of the Occurrences in Smyrna and the Aidan District (On the Occupation by the Greeks)*, London: Cole, 1919, p. 5.
67. Rendel J. Harris and Helen B. Harris, *Letters From the Scenes of the Recent Massacres in Armenia*, London: James Nisbet, 1897. pp. 32–3.
68. Edward Frederick Benson, *Crescent and Iron Cross*, London: Hodder & Stoughton, 1918, p. 77; Henry Morgenthau, *Ambassador Morgenthau's Story*, London: Hodder & Stoughton, 1918, p. 306.
69. Ben Shepherd, *War in the Wild East. The German Army and Soviet Partisans*, Cambridge, MA: Harvard University Press, 2004, p. 67.
70. Mark Levene, 'The Experience of Genocide: Armenia 1915–1916 and Romania 1941–1942', in Hans-Lukas Kieser and Dominik J. Schaller (eds), *Der Völkermord an den Armenien und die Shoah*, Zürich: Chronos Verlag, 2002, p. 450.

71. 'Massacres Inspired. Armenians convinced that orders were sent to kill. Crucified woman in river. Missionaries in districts of uprisings are safe. They call for funds to feed and case for thousands of refugees. Ambassador Leishman says worst is over', *Washington Post*, 1 May 1909, p. 4.

72. Viktor Novak, *Magnum Crimen: pola vijeka klerikalizma u Hrvatskoj*, Zagreb: Nakladni Zavod Hrvatske, 1948, p. 648.

73. Richard Burton, *Personal Narrative of a Pilgrimage to Al-Madinah and Meccah*, New York: Dover, Vol. 1, 1893, p. 181.

74. Housepian, *Smyrna 1922*, p. 35.

75. Morgenthau, *Ambassador Morgenthau's Story*, p. 36.

76. Walser Smith, *The Butcher's Tale*, p. 175.

77. Johannes Lepsius, *Deutschland und Armenien, 1914–1918: Sammlung diplomatischer Aktenstücke*, Potsdam: Tempelverlag, 1919, p. lvi.

78. Benjamin Lieberman, *Terrible Fate: Ethnic Cleansing in the Making of Modern Europe*, Chicago: Ivan R. Dee, 2006, p. 61.

79. 'Burn 1,000 Armenians. Turks Lock Them in a Wooden Building and Then Apply the Torch', *New York Times*, 20 August, 1915, p. 7.

80. 'Condition of Greeks of Pontus', Head of British Naval Mission of Athens, FO 286/833.

81. 'Gorki [*sic*] denounces the "cultivated" Russians', *New York Times*, 23 May 1903, p. 3.

82. International Commission of Inquiry appointed at the Request of the Greek Red Cross, *Treatment of Greek Prisoners in Turkey*, London: Anglo-Hellenic League, 1923, p. 27. The word 'courban' or 'churban' 'alludes to the destruction of the second Temple and the subsequent diaspora of the Jews'. Frangiski Abadzopolou, 'The Holocaust: Questions of Literary Representations', in Ioannes K. Chasiotes et al. (eds), *The Jewish Communities of Southeastern Europe: From the Fifteenth Century to the End of World War II*, Thessalonica: Institute for Balkan Studies, 1997, pp. 2–3.

83. John B. Allcock, *Explaining Yugoslavia*, London: Hurst, 2000 p. 398.

84. A. R. Marriott, *The Eastern Question: An Historical Study in European Diplomacy*, Oxford: Clarendon Press, 1940, 4th edn, p. 205.

85. Levene, 'The Experience of Genocide', p. 431.

86. Crawfurd Price, *Balkan Cockpit*, p. 179.

87. Efraim Sicher, ' "The Jewish Cossack". Isaac Babel in the First Red Calvary', in Jonathan Framkel (ed.), *The Jews and the European Crisis, 1914–1921*, Studies in Contemporary Jewry IV, Oxford: Oxford University Press, 1988, p. 115.

88. Anon., *An Authentic Account of the Occurrences in Smyrna and the Aidan District*, p. 3.

89. In George Orwell's *Animal Farm*, first published in 1945, the animals are accused of polygamy, cannibalism and torture with red-hot horseshoes by Mr Pilkington and Mr Frederick, the owners of the adjoining farms. Here Orwell clearly saw these types of rumour as part of a litany of terror.

90. Peter Balakian, *Black Dog of Fate: A Memoir*, New York, Broadway Books; reprint 1998, p. 212.

91. Morgenthau, *Ambassador Morgenthau's Story*, p. 307.

92. Bourdieu, *Outline of a Theory of Practice*, p. 72.

93. Paul Knepper, 'British Jews and the Racialisation of Crime in the Age of Empire', *British Journal of Criminology*, vol. 47, no. 1, 2007, p. 63.

94. Walser Smith, *The Butcher's Tale*, p. 127.

95. Hillel Kieval, 'Death and the Nation: Jewish Ritual Murder as Political Discourse in the Czech Lands', *Jewish History*, vol. 10, no. 1, 1996, pp. 75–91, at 84.

96. Jonathan Frankel, *The Damascus Affair: "Ritual Murder", Politics, and the Jews in 1840*, Cambridge: Cambridge University Press, 1997, p. 74.

97. This point has been argued with some force in William D. Rubinstein, *Genocide*, London: Longman, 2004, especially pp. 11–44.

98. Donald E. Miller and Lorna Touryan Miller, 'The Armenian and Rwandan Genocides: Some Preliminary Reflections on Two Oral History Projects with Survivors', *Journal of Genocide Research*, vol. 6, no. 1, March 2004, p. 137.

99. William Frederick Bailey, *The Slavs of the War Zone*, New York: E. P. Dutton, 1916, p. 256.

100. Preface by the editor in Günther Schlee (ed.), *Imagined Differences. Hatred and the Construction of Identity*, New York: Palgrave, 2004, p. v.

101. Mark Levene, 'The Changing Face of Mass Murder: Massacre, Genocide and Post-Genocide', *International Social Science Journal*, vol. 54, no. 174, 2002, pp. 446, 451 n. 6.

102. Rubinstein, *Genocide*, p. 261; Ben Lieberman, 'Nationalist Narratives, Violence between Neighbors and Ethnic Cleansing: A Case of Cognitive Dissonance?', *Journal of Genocide Research*, vol. 8, no. 3, 2006, pp. 295–10.

103. It has been argued that violence against animals can develop into violence against humans. For a discussion of this view, see John Passmore, 'The Treatment of Animals', *Journal of the History of Ideas*, vol. 36, no. 2 (April–June, 1975), p. 201.

104. Morgenthau, *Ambassador Morgenthau's Story*, pp. 322–3.

105. Arjun Appadurai, 'Dead Certainty: Ethnic Violence in the Era of Globalization', *Development and Change*, vol. 29, no. 4, October 1998, p. 920.

106. Daniele Conversi, 'Nationalism, Boundaries and Violence', *Millennium: Journal of International Studies*, vol. 28, no. 3, 1999, p. 583.

107. Oskar Verkaaik, 'Fun and Violence. Ethnocide and the Effervescence of Collective Aggression', *Social Anthropology*, vol. 11, no. 1, 2003, p. 21.

108. Oskar Verkaaik, *Migrants and Militants: Fun and Urban Violence in Pakistan*, Princeton, NJ: Princeton University Press, 2004, p. 12.

Chapter 5: The Battleground in Print

1. 'Hätten wir die orientalischen Grillen nie kennen gelernt und wäre Homer unsere Bibel geblieben, welch eine ganz andere Gestalt würde die Menschheit dadurch gewonnen haben!': Karl Löwith, *Von Hegel zu Nietzsche. Der revolutionäre Bruch im Denken des 19. Jahrhunderts*, Hamburg: Meiner Verlag, 1995, p. 36.

2. Paul Cartledge, *Thermopylae. The Battle that Changed the World*, London: Pan/Macmillan, 2006, p. 186.

3. Simon Dubnow, *Mein Leben*, Berlin: Jüdischer Buchvereinigung, 1937, p. 50.

4. Krešimir Georgijević, *Srpskohrvatska narodna pesma u poljskoj književnosti. Studija iz uporedne istorije slovenskih književnosti*, Belgrade: Srpska kraljevska akademija, 1936, p. 122.

5. Paul Fussell, *The Great War and Modern Memory*, Oxford: Oxford University Press, 1975, p. 161.

6. Carl R. Proffer, 'Gogol's *Taras Bulba* and the *Iliad*', *Comparative Literature*, vol. 17, no. 2, 1965, p. 143.

7. Edmund Reitlinger, *A Tower of Skulls*, Duckworth: London 1932, p. 272.

8. Henry Wadsworth Longfellow, 'Morituri Salutamus: Poem for the Fiftieth Anniversary of the Class of 1825 in Bowdoin College', in *The Complete Poetical Works*, Boston and New York: Houghton, Mifflin, 1903, p. 312.

9. David Aberbach, 'The Poetry of Nationalism', *Nations and Nationalism*, vol. 9, no. 2, 2003, pp. 255–75, at 261.

10. Bob Chase, 'Walter Scott: A New Historical Paradigm', in Bill Schwarz (ed.), *The Expansion of England*, London: Routledge, 1996 p. 116.

11. Mark Twain, 'Life on the Mississippi', in idem, *Mississippi Writings*, New York: Library of America, 1982, p. 500. For other critiques of Scott's influence, see Bruce Beiderwell, *Power and Punishment in Scott's Novels*, Athens, GA: University of Georgia Press, 1992.

12. Mirko Grmek, Marc Gjidara and Neven Šimac (eds), *Etničko Čišćenje. Povijesni dokumenti o jednoj srpskoj ideologiji*, Zagreb: Nakladni zavod Globus, 1993, p. 25.

13. Vladeta Popović 'Introduction', in idem, *The Mountain Wreath of P. P. Nyegosh, Prince Bishop of Montenegro, 1830–1851*, trans. James William Wyles, London: George Allen & Unwin, 1930, p. 17.

14. Virgil, *The Eclogues translated by Wrangham, the Georgics by Sotheby and the Aeneid by Dryden*, Vol. 2, London: Henry Colburn and Richard Bentley, 1830, p. 97.

15. Homer, *The Iliad*, translated by E. V. Rieu, Penguin: Harmondsworth, 1953, Book 21, p. 380.

16. (*'Ma ficca li occhi a valle, ché s'approccia la riviera del sangue in la qual bolle, qual che per violenza in altrui noccia'*), Dante Alighieri, *Commedia di Dante Alighieri*, with notes by Gregorio Di Siena, Naples: Perotti, 1870, ll. 46–8, p. 171.

17. Viktor Novak, *Magnum Crimen: pola vijeka klerikalizma u Hrvatskoj*, Zagreb: Nakladni Zavod Hrvatske, 1948, p. 649.

18. Rory Finnin, 'Mountains, Masks, Metre, Meaning: Taras Shevchenko's "Kavkaz"', *Slavonic and East European Review*, vol. 83, no. 3, July 2005, p. 411.

19. Richard G. Hovannisian, 'Bitter-Sweet memories. The Last Generation of Ottoman Armenians', in idem (ed.), *Looking Backward, Moving Forward: Confronting the Armenian Genocide*, New Brunswick, NJ: Transaction Publishers, 2003, pp. 113–24, at 120.

20. Christopher C. Taylor, *Sacrifice as Terror. The Rwandan Genocide of 1994*, Oxford: Berg, 1999, p. 128.

21. The phrase appears in the February, July, October and November issues of *Ustaša* for 1932.

22. Petar Petrović Njegoš, *Gorski Vijenac*, Sarajevo: Svjetlost, 1990, ll. 864–7, p. 58.

23. Benjamin Lieberman, *Terrible Fate: Ethnic Cleansing in the Making of Modern Europe*, Chicago: Ivan R. Dee, 2006, p. 191.

24. Tomislav Dulić, *Utopias of Nation: Local Mass Killing in Bosnia and Herzegovina, 1941–42*, Uppsala: Acta Universitatis Upsaliensis, Studia Historica Upsaliensia, 2005, pp. 206–7.

25. Mark Levene, 'The Experience of Genocide: Armenia 1915–1916 and Romania 1941–1942', in Hans-Lukas Kieser and Dominik J. Schaller (eds), *Der Völkermord an den Armeniern und die Shoah*, Zürich: Chronos Verlag, 2002, p. 439.

26. This book was translated widely: translations included an Italian version, *Istoria della decadenza e rovina dell' Impero Romano . . .*, which appeared in Pisa in 1779; a Hungarian edition, *A Római Birodalom hanyatlásának és bukásának története*, which appeared in Pest in 1868; a German edition, *Geschichte der Abnahme und des Falls des Römischen Reiches*, published in Vienna in 1791; and a French version, *Histoire de la décadence et la chute de l'Empire romain*, published in Paris in 1805.

27. Edward Gibbon, *The History of the Decline and Fall* of the Roman Empire, ed. David Womersley, London: Allen Lane, 1994, Vol. 1, ch. XVI, p. 516.

28. Paul Fussell, *The Great War and Modern Memory*, Oxford: Oxford University Press, 1975, p. 115.

29. Mark Levene, 'The Experience of Genocide', p. 440.

30. Rolf Hosfeld, *Operation Nemesis: Die Türkei, Deutschland und der Völkermord an den Armeniern*, Köln: Kiepenheuer und Witsch, 2005, pp. 298–9.

31. Mika LaVaque-Manty, 'Dueling for Equality: Masculine Honor and the Modern Politics of Dignity', *Political Theory*, vol. 34, no. 6, 2006, pp. 715–40.

32. David V. Erdman (ed.), *The Complete Poetry and Prose of William Blake*, new and revised edition with a commentary by Harold Bloom, Berkeley, CA: University of California Press, 1982, pp. 269–70.

33. Gaius Suetonius Tranquillus, *The Twelve Caesars*, trans. Robert Graves, Harmondsworth: Penguin, 1957, p. 271.

34. Cornelius Tacitus, *The Annals of Imperial Rome*, trans. and with an introduction by Michael Grant, London: Penguin, revised edition, 1996, p. 363.

35. A. M. Delathuy, *E. D. Morel tegen Leopold II en de Kongostaat*, Antwerp: EPO, 1985, p. 492.

36. Patrice M. Dabrowski, *Commemorations and the Shaping of Modern Poland*, Bloomington: Indiana University Press, 2004, p. 42.

37. Hansgerd Delbrück, 'Antiker und moderner Helden-Mythos in Dürrenmatts "ungeschichtlicher historischer Komödie" Romulus der Große', *German Quarterly*, vol. 66, no. 3, 1993, pp. 291–317, p. 305.

38. Michael E. Hoenicke Moore, 'Reading Livy against Livy: The Dream and Nightmare of (American) Empire', *The European Legacy. Toward New Paradigms*, vol. 10, no. 3, 2005, pp. 149–59, at 155.

39. Samantha Power, '*A Problem from Hell*': *America and the Age of Genocide*, New York: Perennial, 2003, p. 20.

40. Richard Gondrand, *La Tragédie de l'Asie Mineure et l'anéantissement de Smyrne 1914–1922*, Marseille: Y Armen, 1935, p. 119–20.

41. Gondrand, *La Tragédie de l'Asie Mineure*, p. 119.

42. Rendel J. and Helen B. Harris, *Letters From the Scenes of the Recent Massacres in Armenia*, London: James Nisbet, 1897, p. 9.

43. That is, Henryk Siemiradzki's *Pochodnie Nerona* (*Nero's Torches*), 1876.

44. Margaret Lavinia Anderson, ' "Down in Turkey, Far Away": Human Rights, the Armenian Massacres, and Orientalism in Wilhelmine Germany', *Journal of Modern History*, vol. 79, March 2007, pp. 80–111, at 93.

45. Christa Heine Teixeira, 'Lion Feuchtwanger: *Der falsche Nero* Zeitgenössische Kritik im Gewand des historischen Romans: Erwägungen zur Entstehung und Rezeption', *Amsterdamer Beiträge zur neueren Germanistik*, vol. 51, 2001, pp. 79–89.

46. Mark Mazower, *Inside Hitler's Greece*, New Haven, CT: Yale University Press, new edn, 2001, p. 199.

47. That is, the language of the Third Reich; Victor Klemperer, *Lingua Tertii Imperii: Notizbuch eines Philologen*, Berlin: Aufbau-Verlag, 1947.

48. See, for example, Leon Trotsky, *The History of the Russian Revolution*, trans. Max Eastman, Chicago: University of Michigan Press, 1957, p. 258.

49. Biagio D'Angelo, 'Epique et parodie dans *Taras Boulba* de Gogol en rapport avec le roman historique de son temps', *Interlitteraria*, vol. 6, 2001, p. 275.

50. Nikolai Gogol, *Taras Bulba*, trans. Isabel Florence Hapgood, New York: Lovell, 1888, pp. 281–4.

51. Carl R. Proffer, 'Gogol's *Taras Bulba* and the *Iliad*', *Comparative Literature*, vol. 17, no. 2 (spring, 1965), p. 142.

52. Shlomo Lambroza, 'The pogroms of 1903–1906', in John Klier and Shlomo Lambroza (eds), *Pogroms: Anti-Jewish Violence in Modern Russian History*, Cambridge: Cambridge University Press, 1991, p. 205.

53. Fyodor Dostoyevsky, *The Brothers Karamazov*, trans. and introduction by David Magarshack, Harmondsworth: Penguin, 1969, v. 12, p. 685.

54. Florence Randal Livesay, *Songs of Ukraina with Ruthenian Poems*, London, Paris and Toronto: Dent/ New York: Dutton, 1916, pp. 74–5.

55. Edward H. Judge, *Easter in Kishinev. Anatomy of a Pogrom*, New York: New York University Press, 1992, pp. 30–2.

56. 'Haidamaky', in Livesay, *Songs of Ukraina*, pp. 75–6.
57. Barbara Skinner, 'Borderlands of Faith: Reconsidering the Origins of a Ukrainian Tragedy', *Slavic Review*, vol. 64, no. 1, spring 2005, pp. 88–116; Paul Magocsi, *A History of Ukraine*, Toronto: University of Toronto Press, 1996, p. 295.
58. Andrew Wilson, *The Ukrainians: Unexpected Nation*, New Haven, CT: Yale University Press, 2000, p. 90.
59. Henry Abramson, *A Prayer for the Government. Ukrainians and Jews in Revolutionary Times, 1917–1920* Cambridge, MA: Harvard University Press, 1999, p. 105.
60. Orest Subtelny, *A History of the Ukraine*, Toronto: University of Toronto Press, 2000, pp. 127–8.
61. Zenon E. Kohut, 'The Khmelnytsky Uprising, the Image of Jews, and the Shaping of Ukrainian Historical Memory', *Jewish History*, vol. 17, no. 2, May 2003, pp. 141–63, at 157.
62. Prosper Mérimée, *Les Cosaques d'autrefois*, Paris: Calmann Levy, 1865.
63. Corry Cropper, 'Prosper Merimée and the Subversive "Historical" Short Story', *Nineteenth Century French Studies*, vol. 33, nos 1 and 2, fall–winter 2004–2005, pp. 57–74.
64. Stephen Moeller-Sally, 'Parallel Lives: Gogol's Biography and Mass Readership in Late Imperial Russia', *Slavic Review*, vol. 54, no. 1, 1995, p. 66.
65. Léon Poliakov, *The History of Anti-Semitism*, Philadelphia: University of Pennsylvania Press, Vol. IV, 2003, pp. 75–6.
66. Ehud Luz, 'The Moral Price of Sovereignty: The Dispute about the Use of Military Power within Zionism', *Modern Judaism*, vol. 7, no. 1, 1987, pp. 51–98, at 61.
67. Anita Shapira, ' "In the City of Slaughter" versus "He Told Her" ', *Prooftexts*, vol. 25, 2005, p. 93.
68. Ibid., p. 99.
69. Isaac Bashevis Singer, *Satan in Goray*, quoted in Israel Zamir, *Journey to My Father, Isaac Bashevis Singer*, New York: Arcade Publishing, 1995, p. 108.
70. Sara Feinstein, *Sunshine, Blossoms and Blood: H. N. Bialik in His Time, a Literary Biography*, Lanham, MO: University Press of America, 2005, p. 108.
71. Israel Zamir, *Journey to My Father, Isaac Bashevis Singer*, New York: Arcade Publishing, 1995, pp. 108–9.
72. Israël Getzler, *Martov. A Political Biography of a Russian Social Democrat*, Cambridge: Cambridge University Press, 2003, p. 4.
73. Petar Petrović Njegoš, *Gorski Vijenac*, Sarajevo: Svjetlost, 1990, p. 155, ll. 2, 604–6.
74. Vladeta Popović (ed.), *The Mountain Wreath of P. P. Nyegosh, Prince Bishop of Montenegro, 1830–1851*, trans. James William Wyles, London: George Allen & Unwin, 1930, p. 17.
75. Omer Ibrahimagić, *Srpsko osporavanje Bosne i Bošnjaka*, Sarajevo: Magistrat, 2001, pp. 209–10.
76. T. G. Jackson, *Dalmatia, the Quarnero and Istria with Cettigne in Montenegro and the Island of Grado*, Oxford: Clarendon Press, 1887, p. 67.
77. Branimir Anzulović, *Heavenly Serbia: From Myth to Genocide*, London: Hurst, 1999, p. 92.
78. Vladimir Dedijer, *The War Diaries of Vladimir Dedijer*, Ann Arbor: University of Michigan Press, Vol. 1, 1990, p. 62.
79. Andrew B. Wachtel, 'How to Use a Classic. Petar Petrović Njegoš in the Twentieth Century', in John R. Lampe and Mark Mazower (eds), *Ideologies and National Identities: The Case of the Twentieth Century*, Budapest: Central European University Press, 2004, pp. 131–53, at 135.

80. Zorka Milich, *A Stranger's Supper: An Oral History of Centegenarian Women in Montenegro*, New York/London Twayne Publishers: Prentice Hall International, 1995, pp. 100–2.
81. Milovan Djilas, *Land without Justice. An Autobiography of Youth*, with an introduction by William Jovanovich, New York: Harcourt, Brace, 1958, pp. 356–7.
82. Harry Craufuird Thomson, *The Outgoing Turk; Impressions of a Journey through the Western Balkans*, New York: D. Appleton and Company, 1897, p. 139.
83. Xavier Marmier, *Lettres sur L'Adriatique et le Monténégro*, vol. 2, Paris: Imprimerie Ch. Lahure, Société de Géographie, 1853, p. 120.
84. Edward W. Said, *Orientalism. Western Conceptions of the Orient*, Harmondsworth: Penguin, 2nd edn, 1995 (originally published in 1978).
85. This concept of Balkanism is explored by Maria Todorova, *Imagining the Balkans*, New York/Oxford: Oxford University Press, 1997.
86. Morgan Philips Price, *War and Revolution in Asiatic Russia*, London: George Allen & Unwin, 1918, p. 128.
87. Orlando Figes, *Natasha's Dance. A Cultural History of Russia*, London: Penguin, 2002, pp. 358–429.
88. Basile Vereschagine, 'Voyage dans les provinces du Caucase (1864–65)', *Le Tour du Monde*, vol. 17, 1868, pp. 161–208.
89. Figes, *Natasha's Dance*, p. 411.
90. Joseph O. Baylen and Jane G. Weyant, 'Vasili Vereshchagin in the United States', *Russian Review*, vol. 30, no. 3, 1971, p. 251.
91. Figes, *Natasha's Dance*, p. 412.
92. Franz Liszt, *Briefe*, edited by La Mara, Leipzig: Breitkopf & Härtel, 1893, Vol. 2, p. 320.
93. '*Nur durch den Pinsel eines Wereschtschagin*': 'Der Konsul in Aleppo Rößler an den Botschafter in außerordentlicher Mission in Konstantinopel', 10/17/1915: *DE/PA-AA/ BoKon/170* at armenocide.de, accessed 10 December 2007.
94. W. R. Jones, 'The Image of the Barbarian in Medieval Europe (in Perception of Ethnic and Cultural Differences)', *Comparative Studies in Society and History*, vol. 13, no. 4, October, 1971, pp. 376–407.
95. William D. Rubinstein, *Genocide*, London: Longman, 2004, p. 5.
96. John Crawfurd, 'On the Conditions which Favour, Retard or Obstruct the Early Civilization of Man', *Transactions of the Ethnological Society of London*, vol. 1, 1861, pp. 154–77.
97. Božidar Jezernik, *Dežela, kjer je vse narobe. Prispevki k etnologiji Balkana*, Ljubljana: Znanstveno in publicistično središče, 1998.
98. Humphrey Sandwith, 'From Belgrade to Constantinople Overland', *Living Age*, vol. 130, no. 1684, 16 September 1876, p. 747.
99. Vasko Popa, *Pesme: Izbor*, Belgrade: Rad, 1985, p. 133.
100. Anthony Arblaster, *Viva la libertà! Politics in Opera*, London and New York: Verso, 1992, p. 106.
101. 'Cut Off the Heads of the Fallen. Turks and Senegalese at Adana Make Sure that Foes are Dead', *Washington Post*, 22 September 1920, p. 5.
102. Armin T. Wegner, *Der Prozeß Talaat Pascha: Stenographischer Prozeßbericht*, Berlin: Deutsche Verlagsgesellschaft für Politik und Geschichte, 1921, p. 55.
103. M. A Andréadès, *La Destruction de Smyrne et les dernières atrocités turques en Asie Mineure*, Athens: P. D. Sakellerios, 1923; Guillaume Capus, *A Travers le royaume de Tamerlan – (Asie centrale)* . . ., Paris: A. Hennuyer, 1892.
104. Said, *Orientalism*, p. 154.
105. Joel Werda, *The Flickering Light of Asia or The Assyrian Nation and Church*, New York: published by the author, 1924, p. 35.

106. Vahakn Dadrian, *The History of the Armenian Genocide. Ethnic Conflict from the Balkans to Anatolia to the Caucasus*, Providence, RI and Oxford: Berghahn, 1995, p. 406.
107. Dadrian, *History of the Armenian Genocide*, p. 404.
108. Gotthard Jäschke, 'Der Turanismus der Jungtürken. Zur osmanischen Außenpolitik im Weltkriege', *Die Welt des Islams*, vol. 23, nos 1 and 2, 1941, pp. 1–54.
109. Arnold Joseph Toynbee, *Turkey: A Past and a Future*, New York: George H. Doran, 1917, p. 19.
110. Hosfeld, *Operation Nemesis*, p. 104.
111. Toynbee, *Turkey. A Past and a Future*, p. 19.
112. Aviel Roshwald, *Ethnic Nationalism and the Fall of Empires: Central Europe, Russia and the Middle East, 1914–1923*, New York: Routledge. 2001, p. 62.
113. Bertholt Brecht, *Dreigroschen Roman*, Munich: Verlag K. Desch 1949, p. 206.
114. Walter Benjamin, *Understanding Brecht*, London: New Left Books, 1977, p. 81.
115. George Orwell, 'Review of *Mein Kampf* by Adolf Hitler', *New English Weekly*, 21 March, 1940, reprinted in Sonia Orwell and Ian Angus (eds), *The Collected Essays . . . of George Orwell*, Harmondsworth: Penguin, 1971, Vol. 2, p. 27.
116. Hannah Arendt, *Eichmann in Jerusalem: A Report on the Banality of Evil*, London: Penguin, 1994, p. 49.
117. Batsheva Ben-Amos, 'A Tourist in 'Ir ha-Haregah (A Tourist in the City of Slaughter) – Kishinev 1903', *Jewish Quarterly Review*, vol. 96, no. 3, 2006, p. 361.
118. I. Michael Aronson, 'The Attitudes of Russian Officials in the 1880s Towards Jewish Assimilation and Emigration', *Slavic Review*, vol. 34, no. 1, March 1975, pp. 1–2, n. 1.
119. Shmarya Levin, *Jugend in Aufruhr*, Berlin: Jüdischer Buchvereinigung, 1935, p. 142.
120. Fussell, *The Great War and Modern Memory*, p. 128.
121. Aeschylus, *The Oresteia*, trans. Alan Shapiro and Peter Burian, Oxford: Oxford University Press, 2003, p. 36.
122. 'Onda Djordje u gradove udje; Što bi Turak' po gradov'ma b'jelim, Što bi Turak za sjeće, isjeće; Za predaje sto bi, to predade; Za krštenja sto bi, to iskrsti', in Tvrtko Čubelić, *Epske narodne pjesme: Izbor tekstova s komentarima i objašnjenjima i rasprava o epskim narodnim pjesmama*, Zagreb: Školska knjiga, 1970, p. 303.
123. Vilmos Voigt, '*Primus inter pares*. Why was Vuk Karadžić the Most Influential Folklore Scholar in South Eastern Europe in the Nineteenth Century?', in Michael Branch and Celia Hawkesworth (eds), *The Uses of Tradition: A Comparative Enquiry into the Nature, Uses and Functions of Oral Poetry in the Balkans, the Baltic and Africa*, London: School of Slavonic and East European Studies, 1994, pp. 179–93.
124. Mirko Grmek et al. (eds), *Etničko Čišćenje*, p. 82.
125. Vladimir Dedijer, *The Yugoslav Auschwitz and the Vatican: The Croatian Massacre of Serbs during World War II*, Buffalo, NY: Prometheus Books, 1988, p. 141.
126. Christoph Dinkel, 'German Officers and the Armenian Genocide', *Armenian Review*, vol. 44, no. 1, 1991, p. 105.
127. Thomas Klugkist, *Der pessimistische Humanismus: Thomas Manns lebensphilosophische Adaption der Schopenhauerschen Mitleidsethik*, Würzburg: Verlag Königshausen und Neumann, 2002, pp. 70–91.
128. Hans Wysling (ed.), *Letters of Heinrich and Thomas Mann, 1900–1949*, Berkeley: University of California Press, 1998, pp. 199–200.
129. Sean Ireton, 'Heinrich Manns Auseinandersetzung mit dem Haß: Eine Analyse der Henri Quatre-Romane im Rahmen der exilbedingten Haßliteratur', *Orbis litterarum: International Review of Literary Studies*, vol. 57, 2002, p. 207.
130. Not all writers agreed with Voltaire and Mann. For Robert Southey, Henri IV 'reconciled himself to an idolatrous, faithless and persecuting Church, before the martyrs of St Bartholomew had mouldered in their graves', *Essays Moral and Political*, London: Murray, 1832, pp. 60–1.

131. Klaus Schroter, *Heinrich Mann*, Hamburg: Revohlt, 1967, p. 119.
132. Leo Tolstoy, *War and Peace*, London: Pan, 1972, p. 1,184.
133. Ireton, 'Heinrich Manns Auseinandersetzung mit dem Haß', p. 205.
134. Karin Verena Gunnemann, *Heinrich Mann's Novels and Essays: The Artist as Political Educator*, Rochester, NY/Woodbridge, Suffolk: Boydell & Brewer, 2002, p. 183.
135. Schröter, *Heinrich Mann*, p. 132.
136. Lion Feuchtwanger, 'Neros Tod', *Das Wort*, no. 6, December 1936, pp. 33–41.
137. Franz Werfel, *Die vierzig Tage des Musa Dagh*, Berlin: P. Zsolnay, 1933, in part as a warning to European Jewry about the dangers they were facing.
138. Yair Auron, '*The Forty Days of Musa Dagh*. Its Impact on Jewish Youth in Palestine and Europe', in Richard G. Hovannisian (ed.), *Remembrance and Denial: The Case of the Armenian Genocide*, Detroit, Michigan: Wayne State University Press, 1999, p. 150.
139. Stefan Karsten, *Der Völkermord an den Armeniern in Romanen von Werfel, Hilsenrath, Mangelsen und Balakian*, Munich/Ravensburg: Grin Verlag, 2007, p. 47.
140. Bruno Bettelheim, 'Freedom from Ghetto Thinking', in *Recollections and Reflections*, London: Penguin, 1992, p. 259.
141. Victor Serge, 'The Writer's Conscience', in David Craig (ed.), *Marxists on Literature*, Harmondsworth: Penguin, 1977, p. 441.
142. Jean-Michel Palmier, *Weimar in Exile: The Antifascist Emigration in Europe and America*, London: Verso, 2006, pp. 100–01.
143. Karsten, *Der Völkermord an den Armeniern in Romanen von Werfel*, p. 44.
144. Palmier, *Weimar in Exile*, p. 39.
145. Henry Torrès, *Accusés hors série*, Paris: Gallimard, 1957, p. 20.
146. Martin Niepage, *The Horrors of Aleppo . . . Seen by a German Eyewitness*, London: T. Fisher Unwin, 1916.
147. Edward Frederick Benson, *Crescent and Iron Cross*, London: Hodder & Stoughton, 1918, p. 97.
148. 'Erzeroum: Abstract of a Report by a Dr Y. Minassian, who Accompanied Mr Khounountz to Erzeroum as Representative of the Caucasian Section of the "All-Russian Urban Union", published in the Armenian Journal "Mschak" of Tiflis, 8th March, 1916', in James Viscount Bryce and Arnold Toynbee, *The Treatment of Armenians in the Ottoman Empire, 1915–1916: Documents Presented to Viscount Grey of Falloden*, Reading: Tadaron Press, in association with the Gomidas Institute, 2000, pp. 265–6.
149. Wegner, *Der Prozeß Talaat*, pp. 9–10.
150. Carlo Levi, *Cristo si è fermato a Eboli*, Turin: Einaudi, 1990, p. 201.
151. Salvatore Quasimodo, 'Ai Fratelli Cervi, alla loro Italia', in *Il falso e vero verde: Con un discorso sulla poesia*, Milan: Mondadori, 1956, p. 34.
152. Elie Wiesel, *All Rivers Run to the Sea. Memoirs Volume One 1928–1969*, London: HarperCollins, 1995, pp. 69–70.
153. Hannah Arendt, *The Origins of Totalitarianism*, London: Andre Deutsch, 1986, p. 459.
154. Paul R. Carlson, *Christianity after Auschwitz: Evangelicals Encounter Judaism in the New Millenium*, Philadelphia, PA: Xlibris, 2000, p. 242.
155. Niall Ferguson, *The Pity of War. Explaining World War I*, London: Basic Books, 1999, p. 359.
156. Sigmund Freud, *Jenseits des Lustprinzips*, Leipzig: Internationaler psychoanalytischer Verlag, 1920.
157. Sigmund Freud, *Das Ich und das Es*, Leipzig: Internationaler psychoanalytischer Verlag, 1923.
158. Jacques Le Rider, *Modernité viennoise et crises de l'identité*, Paris: Presses Universitaires de France, 1990, pp. 197–222.
159. Heinrich von Treitschke, the historian widely credited with making anti-Semitism *salonsfähig* ('respectable') in Wilhelmine Germany.

160. Alan Kramer, *Dynamic of Destruction: Culture and Mass Killing in the First World War*, Oxford: Oxford University Press, 2007, pp. 193–4.
161. Marianna Torgovnick, *The War Complex: World War II in Our Time*, Chicago: University of Chicago Press, 2005, p. 136.
162. Thomas Stearns Eliot, *The Annotated Waste Land with Eliot's contemporary prose*, edited with annotations and introduction by Lawrence Rainey, New Haven, CT: Yale University Press, 2nd edn, 2006, p. 63.
163. Ibid., p. 106.
164. David Bradshaw and Kevin J. H. Dettmar, *A Companion to Modernist Literature and Culture*, Oxford: Blackwell, 2006, p. 128.
165. David Ward, *T. S. Eliot Between Two Worlds: A Reading of T. S. Eliot's Poetry and Plays*, London: Routledge, 1973, p. 106.
166. Orlando Figes and Boris Kolonitskii, *Interpreting the Russian Revolution. The Language and Symbols of 1917*, New Haven, CT: Yale University Press, 1999, p. 161.
167. Evgenii Preobrazhensky and Nikolai Bukharin, with an introduction by Edward Hallett Carr, *The ABC of Communism*, Harmondsworth: Penguin, 1969, pp. 184–5.
168. Lars T. Lih, 'The Mystery of the ABC', *Slavic Review*, vol. 56, no. 1, spring 1997, p. 56.
169. Deborah Dwork and Robert Jan van Pelt, *Holocaust: A History*, London: John Murray, 2003, p. 49.
170. 'Gewalt und Recht, Verbrechen und Menschlichkeit', in Wegner, *Der Prozeß Talaat*, p. x.
171. Milica Bakić-Hayden, 'National Memory as Narrative Memory: The Case of Kosovo', in Maria Todorova (ed.), *Balkan Identities: Nation and Memory*, London: Hurst, 2004, p. 37.

Chapter 6: Instability and Moral Decline in Inter-War Europe

1. Viktor Novak, *Magnum Crimen: pola vijeka klerikalizma u Hrvatskoj*, Zagreb: Nakladni Zavod Hrvatske, 1948, p. 611.
2. 'Die Genfer Konvension', *Prager Tagblatt*, 6 October 1922, p. 1.
3. Alan Kramer, *Dynamic of Destruction: Culture and Mass Killing in the First World War*, Oxford: Oxford University Press, 2007, p. 67.
4. Aviel Roshwald. *Ethnic Nationalism and the Fall of Empires: Central Europe, Russia and the Middle East, 1914–1923*, New York: Routledge, 2001, p. 70.
5. Donald Bloxham, *The Great Game of Genocide*, Oxford: Oxford University Press, 2005, p. 79.
6. Henry C. Meyer, 'Rohrbach and his Osteuropa', *Russian Review*, vol. 2, no. 1, autumn 1942, p. 68.
7. Deborah Dwork and Robert Jan van Pelt, *Holocaust: A History*, London: John Murray, 2003, p. 46.
8. Henry Abramson, *A Prayer for the Government: Ukrainians and Jews in Revolutionary Times, 1917–1920*, Cambridge, MA: Harvard University Press, 1999, p. 110.
9. David Engel, 'Being Lawful in a Lawless World: The Trial of Scholem Schwarzbard and the Defence of East European Jews', *Jahrbuch des Simon-Dubnow-Instituts*, Vol. 5, 2006, p. 83.
10. Roshwald, *Ethnic Nationalism and the Fall of Empires*, p. 165.
11. M. l'abbé Jean-Constant-François Delaplanche with Joseph-Norbert Duquet, *Le Pèlerin de Terre sainte: Voyage en Egypte, en Palestine, en Syrie, à Smyrne et à Constantinople*, Québec: Hardy, 1887, p. 235.
12. 'Turkish Massacres and Persecutions', Memorandum by Mr Rendel on Turkish Massacres and persecution of Minorities since the Armistice, 20 March 1922, FO 371/7876, X/P09/94, Public Record Office, London.

13. Henry Giniger, 'Anti-Greek Riots Studied by NATO Council', *New York Times*, 9 September 1955, p. 1.
14. Rogers Brubaker, *Nationalism Reframed. Nationhood and the National Question in Europe*, Cambridge: Cambridge University Press, 1996, p. 148.
15. International Commission of Inquiry appointed at the Request of the Greek Red Cross, *Treatment of Greek Prisoners in Turkey*, London: Anglo-Hellenic League, 1923, p. 27.
16. Djordje Stefanović, 'Seeing the Albanians through Serbian Eyes: The Inventors of the Tradition of Intolerance and their Critics 1804–1939', *European History Quarterly*, vol. 3, no. 35, 2005, pp. 465–92.
17. Borivoje Jevtić, in Vladimir Dedijer, *The Road to Sarajevo*, London: MacGibbon and Kee, 1967, p. 238.
18. *Srbadija*, vol. 29, no. 2, November 1924, quoted in Nusret Šehić, *Četništvo u Bosni i Hercegovini (1918–1941). Politička uloga i oblici djelatnosti Četničkih udruženja*, Sarajevo: Akademija nauka i umjetnosti Bosne i Hercegovine, 1971, p. 109.
19. Named after St Vitus Day (Vidovdan), the date of the legendary defeat of the Serbs in the battle of Kosovo Polje in 1389.
20. Šehić, *Četništvo u Bosni*, p. 120.
21. Branko Horvat, *Kosovsko Pitanje*, Zagreb: Globus, 1989, p. 35.
22. Vasa Čubrilović, 'Iseljavanje Arnauta', in Bože Čović (ed.), *Izvori velikosrpske agresije*, Zagreb: August Cesarec and Školska knjiga, 1991, pp. 106–24.
23. Safet Bandžović, 'Ratovi i demografska deosmanizacija Balkana (1912.–1941.)', *Prilozi*, vol. 32, Sarajevo, 2003, p. 219.
24. Vladimir Dedijer, *Genocid nad muslimanima 1941–45, Zbornik documenta i svjedočenja*, Sarajevo: Svjetlost, 1990.
25. Šehić, *Četništvo u Bosni*, p. 10.
26. Safet Bandžović, 'Koncepcije Srpskog kulturnog kluba o preuredenju Jugoslavije 1937–1941', *Prilozi*, vol. 30, Sarajevo, 2001, pp.163–93.
27. Ivo Banac, *The National Question in Yugoslavia: Origins, History, Politics*, Ithaca, NY: Cornell University Press, 1984, p. 87.
28. Miron Krešimir Begić, *Ustaški Pokret 1929–1941: pregled njegove poviesti*, Buenos Aires: Naklada Smotre Ustaša, 1986, p. 94.
29. Nikola Stojanović, quoted in Marc Biondich, *Stjepan Radić, the Croat Peasant Party and the Politics of Mass Mobilization, 1904–1928*, Toronto: University of Toronto Press, 2000, p. 20.
30. Hrvoje Matković, *Povijest Nezavisne Države Hrvatske*, Zagreb: Nakalda Pavičić, 1994, p. 119.
31. Tomislav Dulić, *Utopias of Nation: Local Mass Killing in Bosnia and Herzegovina, 1941–42*, Uppsala: Acta Universitatis Upsaliensis, Studia Historica Upsaliensia, 2005, p. 181.
32. Aleksa Djilas, *The Contested Country: Yugoslav Unity and Communist Revolution 1919–1953*, Cambridge, MA: Harvard University Press, 1991, p. 121.
33. Francine Friedman, *The Bosnian Muslims. Denial of a Nation*, Boulder, CO: Westview Press, 1996, p. 124.
34. Esther Benbassa, *Juifs des Balkans: Espaces judéo-ibériques, XIVe–XXe siècles*, Paris: La Découverte, 1993.
35. Mark Mazower, *Salonica, City of Ghosts: Christians, Muslims and Jews*, London: HarperCollins, 2005.
36. Ivo Goldstein, *Croatia: A History*, London: Hurst, 1999, p. 136.
37. Novak, *Magnum Crimen*, Zagreb, p. 610.
38. Vladimir Dedijer, *The Yugoslav Auschwitz and the Vatican*, Buffalo, NY: Prometheus Books, 1992, pp. 225–312.

39. Artan Peto, 'La Communauté juive en Albanie avant et durant la seconde guerre mondiale', in Ioannes K. Chasiotes et al. (eds), *The Jewish Communities of Southeastern Europe: From the Fifteenth Century to the End of World War II*, Thessalonica: Institute for Balkan Studies, 1997, pp. 427–31.

40. Mark Mazower, *Inside Hitler's Greece*, New Haven, CT: Yale University Press, new edn, 2001, p. 240.

41. Barry Trachtenberg, 'Di Algemeyne Entsiklopedye, the Holocaust and the Changing Mission of Yiddish Scholarship', *Journal of Modern Jewish Studies*, vol. 5, no. 3, 2006, pp. 285–300, at 293.

42. Yehuda Bauer, 'Comparisons with other genocides', in idem, *Rethinking the Holocaust*, New Haven, CT and London: Yale University Press, 2002, p. 59.

43. Ben Shepherd, *War in the Wild East. The German Army and Soviet Partisans*, Cambridge, MA: Harvard University Press, 2004.

44. Svetlana Alieva, *Tak Eto Bylo. Natsional'noe Repressii v SSSR*, Vol. 3, Moscow: Pisan, 1993, p 99, cited in Brian Glyn Williams, 'Hidden Ethnocide in the Soviet Muslim Borderlands: The Ethnic Cleansing of the Crimean Tatars', *Journal of Genocide Research*, vol. 4, no. 3 pp. 357–73, 2002, p. 359.

45. Benjamin Madley. 'From Africa to Auschwitz: How German South West Africa Incubated Ideas and Methods Adopted and Developed by the Nazis in Eastern Europe', *European History Quarterly*, vol. 35, no. 3 (July 2005), pp. 429–64, at 455–6.

46. Alan Kramer, *Dynamic of Destruction: Culture and Mass Killing in the First World War*, Oxford: Oxford University Press, 2007, p. 337.

47. Andrew Charlesworth, 'The Topography of Genocide', in Dan Stone (ed.) *The Historiography of the Holocaust*, London: Palgrave, 2004, pp. 216–52, at 221.

48. Orlando Figes, *Natasha's Dance. A Cultural History of Russia*, London: Penguin, 2002, p. 412.

49. 'Report by a Resident of Syria on the Condition of Armenian Deportees', 27 November 1916, Public Record Office, London. FO 371/2783/24258.

50. Charlesworth, 'The Topography of Genocide', p. 223.

51. Christian Gerlach, 'The Wannsee Conference, the Fate of the German Jews, and Hitler's Decision in Principle to Exterminate All European Jews', *Journal of Modern History*, vol. 70, no. 4, 1998, pp. 759–812.

52. Hannah Arendt, *Eichmann in Jerusalem: A Report on the Banality of Evil*, London: Penguin, 2002, p. 1,994.

53. Elie Wiesel, *All Rivers Run to the Sea. Memoirs Volume One 1928–1969*, London: HarperCollins, 1995, p. 97.

54. Leon Trotsky, *The Balkan Wars 1912–13*, New York: Monad Press, 1980, p. 316.

55. See, for example, Alexander Rabinowitch, 'The Shchastny File: Trotsky and the Case of the Hero of the Baltic Fleet', *Russian Review*, vol. 58, no. 4, 1999, pp. 615–34.

56. Leon Trotsky, *How the Revolution Armed. The Military Writings and Speeches of Leon Trotsky*, Vol. 5, 1921–1923, trans. Brian Pearse, London: New Park, 1981, pp. 121–2.

57. Benjamin A. Valentino, *Final Solutions: Mass Killing and Genocide in the Twentieth Century*, Ithaca, NY: Cornell University Press, 2004, p. 155.

58. Williams, 'Hidden Ethnocide', p. 358–9.

59. Goldstein, *Croatia*, p. 158.

60. Tomislav Dulić, 'Mass Killing in the Independent State of Croatia, 1941–1945: A Case for Comparative Research', *Journal of Genocide Research*, vol. 8, no. 3, 2006, pp. 272–3.

61. Josip Mirnić, *Nemci u Bačkoj u drugom svetskom ratu*, Novi Sad: Institut za izučavanje istorije Vojvodine, 1974, p. 341.

62. John R. Schindler, 'Yugoslavia's First Ethnic Cleansing. The Expulsion of the Danubian Germans 1944–46', in Steven Béla Várdy and T. Hunt Tooley (eds), *Ethnic*

Cleansing in 20th-Century Europe, Boulder, CO: Social Science Monographs, Columbia University Press, 2003, p. 359.

63. Alfred de Zayas, *A Terrible Revenge. The Ethnic Cleansing of the East European Germans*, London: Palgrave Macmillan, 2nd edn, 2006.

64. T. David Curp, ' "Roman Dmowski Understood": Ethnic Cleansing as Permanent Revolution', *European History Quarterly*, vol. 35, no. 3, July 2005, pp. 405–27.

65. The question of the fate of the Italians is discussed in Pamela Ballinger, *History in Exile. Memory and Identity at the Borders of the Balkans*, Princeton, NJ and Oxford: Princeton University Press, 2003.

66. Glenda Sluga, *The Problem of Trieste and the Italo-Yugoslav Border. Difference, Identity and Sovereignty in Twentieth Century Europe*, New York: State University of New York Press, 2000, pp. 90–1.

67. Dean S. Rugg, *Eastern Europe*, London: Longman, 1985, especially pp. 118–254.

Chapter 7: Conflict in the Courtroom

1. Hannah Arendt, *The Origins of Totalitarianism*, London: Andre Deutsch, 1986, p. 91.

2. Albert S. Lindemann, *The Jew Accused: Three Anti-Semitic Affairs (Dreyfus, Beilis, Frank) 1894–1915*, Cambridge: Cambridge University Press, 1991, pp. 188–9.

3. Otto Weininger, *Geschlecht und Charakter: Eine prinzipielle Untersuchung*, Vienna: Braumüller, 1908, pp. 460–1.

4. Ben Braber, 'The Trial of Oscar Slater (1909) and Anti-Jewish Prejudices in Edwardian Glasgow', *History*, vol. 88, no. 290, 2003, p. 267.

5. The story became the subject of Julian Barnes' 2005 novel *Arthur and George*.

6. 'The Edalji Case', *The Times*, 29 January 1907, p. 13.

7. Shompa Lahiri, *Indians in Britain: Anglo-Indian Encounters, Race and Identity, 1880–1930*, London: Frank Cass, 1999, p. 87.

8. Rudolf Samper, *Die neuen Jakobiner: Der Aufbruch der Radikalen*, Munich: Herbig Verlag, 1981, p. 110.

9. Michael Stolleis, *A History of Public Law in Germany, 1914–1945*, Oxford: Oxford University Press, 2004, p. 358.

10. Helen Davenport Gibbons, *The Red Rugs of Tarsus. A Woman's Record of the Armenian Massacre of 1909*, New York: Century, 1917, p. 106.

11. 'Greeks in Asia Minor. Fresh Campaign of Persecution', *Scotsman*, 11 January 1915, p. 8.

12. For a discussion of the arbitrary nature of Russian bureaucracy, see Thomas C. Owen, *The Corporation Under Russian Law, 1800–1917: A Study in Tsarist Economic Policy*, Cambridge: Cambridge University Press, 2002, pp. 116–54.

13. Kevin M. F. Platt, *History in a Grotesque Key: Russian Literature and the Idea of Revolution*, Stanford, CA: Stanford University Press, 1997, p. 72.

14. Werner Bergman, 'Exclusionary Riots. Some Theoretical Considerations', in Christian Hoffmann, Werner Bergmann and Helmut Walser Smith (eds), *Exclusionary Violence. Antisemitic Riots in Modern German History*, Ann Arbor: University of Michigan Press, 2002, pp. 179–80.

15. Boris Czerny, 'Paroles et silences. L'Affaire Schwartzbard et la presse juive parisienne (1926–27)', *Archives Juives*, vol. 34, 2001/2, p. 62.

16. Daniel Vyleta, 'Jewish Crimes and Misdemeanours: In Search of Jewish Criminality (Germany and Austria, 1890–1914)', *European History Quarterly*, vol. 35, no. 2, 2005, pp. 299–325, at 300.

17. Yehuda Bauer, *A History of the Holocaust*, New York: Franklin Watts, 1982, p. 10.

18. Laurence Cole, *Für Gott, Kaiser und Vaterland: Nationale Identität der deutschsprachigen Bevölkerung Tirols, 1860–1914*, Studien zur Historischen Sozialwissenschaft 28, Frankfurt: Campus Verlag, 2000, p. 200.

19. Vyleta, 'Jewish Crimes and Misdemeanours', p. 300.
20. Hillel J. Kieval, 'Death and the Nation: Jewish Ritual Murder as Political Discourse in the Czech Lands,' *Jewish History*, vol. 10, no. 1, 1996, pp. 75–91, at 76.
21. 'Jüdische Ritual- oder Blutmorder', *Christlich-soziale Arbeiter-Zeitung*, 15 November, 1913, pp. 1–2.
22. Aviel Roshwald, 'Jewish Cultural Identity in Eastern and Central Europe during the Great War', in Aviel Roshwald and Richard Stites (eds), *European Culture in the Great War: The Arts, Entertainment and Propaganda, 1914–1918*, Cambridge: Cambridge University Press, 1999, p. 96.
23. 'Der große Prozeß gegen die Juden in Damaskus, *Der Orient*, vol. 2, no. 11, 1841, pp. 151–3.
24. Jonathan Frankel, *The Damascus Affair: 'Ritual Murder', Politics, and the Jews in 1840*, Cambridge: Cambridge University Press, 1997, p. 12.
25. Ibid., p. 42.
26. Alexander Orbach, *New Voices of Russian Jewry: A Study of the Russian–Jewish Press of Odessa*, Leiden: Brill, 1980, p. 68.
27. Alexander Eliasberg, 'Der Ritualmord-Prozeß zu Kutais im Jahre 1879', *Im deutschen Reich*, vol. 16, no. 7, 1910, pp. 543–64.
28. Harriet Murav, *Identity Theft: The Jew in Imperial Russia and the Case of Avraam Uri Kovner*, Stamford, CA: Stamford University Press, 2003, p. 124.
29. Israël Getzler, *Martov. A Political Biography of a Russian Social Democrat*, Cambridge: Cambridge University Press, 2003, p. 1.
30. John Klier, 'Russian Jewry on the Eve of the Pogroms', in John Klier and Shlomo Lambroza (eds), *Pogroms: Anti-Jewish Violence in Modern Russian History*, Cambridge: Cambridge University Press, 1991, p. 10.
31. Effie Ambler, *Russian Journalism and Politics, 1861–1881: The Career of Aleksei S. Suvorin*, Detroit: Wayne State University Press, 1972, p. 172.
32. Michael I. Aronson, 'The Anti-Jewish Pogroms in Russia in 1881', in Klier and Lambroza (eds), *Pogroms: Anti-Jewish Violence in Modern Russian History*, p. 49.
33. John Klier and Shlomo Lambroza, 'The Pogroms of 1881–1884', in idem, p. 39.
34. Simon Karlinsky (ed.), *Anton Chekhov's Life and Thought: Selected Letters and Commentary*, trans. Michael Henry Heim, Evanston, Illinois: Northwestern University Press, 1997, p. 313.
35. Aviel Roshwald, *Ethnic Nationalism and the Fall of Empires: Central Europe, Russia and the Middle East, 1914–1923*, New York: Routledge, 2001, p. 35.
36. Stephen Wilson, *Ideology and Experience: Antisemitism in France at the Time of the Dreyfus Affair*, Rutherford, NJ: Fairleigh Dickinson University Press, 1982; Walter Goetz, 'Der Dreyfuß-Prozeß', *Der Morgen*, vol. 6, no. 5, 1898, pp. 501–6.
37. Lindemann, *The Jew Accused: Three Anti-Semitic Affairs*, p. 106.
38. John T. Morse, Jr, 'The Dreyfus and Zola Trials', *Atlantic Monthly*, vol. 81, no. 487, May 1898, p. 598.
39. Emile Zola, 'J'accuse . . .! Lettre au Président de la République', *L'Aurore*, 13 January, 1898, pp. 1–2.
40. 'Proceß Zola', *Die Welt*, vol. 2, no. 8, 1898, pp. 11–13; 'Zola verurtheilt', *Die Welt*, vol. 2, no. 8, 1898, p. 10; 'Das Urtheil gegen Zola', *Die Welt*, vol. 2, no. 14, 1898, p. 7; 'Eine Parallele zum Dreyfus-Prozeß', *Im deutschen Reich*, vol. 4, no. 3, 1898, pp. 134–41.
41. Robert S. Wistrich, *Laboratory for World Destruction. Germans and Jews in Central Europe*, Lincoln, NE: Nebraska University Press/Vidal Sassoon International Center for the Study of Antisemitism, 2007, p. 222.
42. Ian Kershaw, *Popular Opinion and Political Dissent in the Third Reich: Bavaria 1933–1945*, Oxford: Oxford University Press, 2002, p. xxi.

43. Michael Curtis, *Verdict on Vichy: Power and Prejudice in the Vichy France Regime*, London: Weidenfeld & Nicolson, 2002, p. 46.
44. Henry Rousso, 'The Dreyfus Affair in Vichy France: Past and Present in French Political Culture', in Jonathan Frankel (ed.), *The Fate of the European Jews, 1939–1945. Continuity or Contingency?*, Oxford: Oxford University Press, 1997, p. 153.
45. Vyleta, 'Jewish Crimes and Misdemeanours, pp. 299–325, at 314.
46. František Cervinka, 'The Hilsner Affair', *Leo Baeck Institute Year Book*, vol. 13, 1968, pp. 142–157; 'Prozess Leopold Hilsner', *Im deutschen Reich*, vol. 20, no. 1, 1914, pp. 6–15.
47. Hillel J. Kieval, 'Antisémitisme ou savoir social? Sur la genèse du procès moderne pour meurtre rituel', *Annales: Histoire, Sciences Sociales*, vol. 49, 1994, pp. 1,091–1,105.
48. Frankel, *The Damascus Affair*, p. 442.
49. Livia Rothkirchen, *The Jews of Bohemia and Moravia: Facing the Holocaust*, Lincoln, NB: University of Nebraska Press, 2005, p. 4.
50. Harriet Murav, 'The Beilis Ritual Murder Trial and the Culture of Apocalypse', *Cardozo Studies in Law and Literature*, vol. 12, no. 2, autumn–winter, 2000, p. 243.
51. John Klier, 'Cry Bloody Murder', *East European Jewish Affairs*, vol. 36, no. 2, December 2006, p. 213.
52. Hans Rogger, 'The Beilis Case: Anti-Semitism and Politics in the Reign of Nicholas II', *American Slavic and East European Review*, vol. 25, no. 4, 1964, p. 619.
53. 'Twenty-Ninth Day of the Kieff Trial', *The Times*, 6 November 1913, p. 7.
54. *Die Welt. Zentralorgan der Zionistischen Bewegung*, no. 46, 14 November 1913, p. 2.
55. Thomas Riha, '*Riech*: A Portrait of a Russian Newspaper', *Slavic Review*, vol. 22, no. 4, December 1963, p. 670. Nabokov was assassinated by an anti-Semite in 1992.
56. David I. Goldstein, *Dostoïevski et les juifs*, Paris: Gallimard, 1976, p. 271.
57. Iustinus Bonaventura Pranaïtis, *Das Christenthum im Talmud der Juden*, Vienna: Verlag des Sendboten des Hl. Joseph, 1894.
58. 'Der Beilis-Prozeß', *Allgemeine Zeitung des Judentums*, vol. 46, 14 November 1913, p. 543.
59. 'Die Lehren des Beilis-Prozesses: Rückblick und Aufgaben', *Die Welt. Zentralorgan der Zionistischen Bewegung*, no. 46, 14 November, 1913, p. 2.
60. 'Beilis dankt . . .', *Pester Lloyd*, 13 November, 1913, pp. 7–8.
61. Joel Berkowitz, 'The "Mendel Beilis Epidemic" on the Yiddish Stage', *Jewish Social Studies*, vol. 8, no. 1 2001, pp. 199–225, at 221.
62. Arno J. Mayer, *The Furies: Violence and Terror in the French and Russian Revolutions*, Princeton, NJ: Princeton University Press, 2000, p. 509.
63. Wistrich, *Laboratory for World Destruction*, p. 82.
64. Rosa Luxemburg, 'Einleitung (geschrieben im Strafgefängnis Breslau im Juli 1918)', in *Wladimir Korolenko, Die Geschichte meines Zeitgenossen*, Berlin: Paul Cassirer, 1919, p. ivl.
65. John Klier, 'Cry Bloody Murder', p. 215.
66. Raimund Elfering, 'Die "Bejlis-Affäre" im Spiegel der liberalen russischen Tageszeitung Reč'', Digitale Osteuropa-Bibliothek Geschichte, no. 7, 2004, www.vifaost.de.
67. Arnold J. Band, 'Kafka and the Beiliss Affair', *Comparative Literature*, vol. 32, no. 2, spring, 1980, pp. 168–83, at 177.
68. 'Der Prozeß in Kiew. Die Urteilsfällung hinausgeschoben', *Prager Tagblatt*, 10 November 1913, p. 1.
69. 'All Russia Roused Over Beiliss Case: Sympathy Strike Starts in Industrial Centres – Students Signing Protests', *New York Times*, 19 October, 1913, p. C1.
70. 'Closing Speeches in Kieff Trial', *The Times*, 8 November 1913, p. 7.

71. 'Express Horror at Beiliss Trial; Leading Englishmen Join in a Protest at Great Mass Meeting in London', *New York Times*, 29 October 1913, p. 6.

72. '3,000 Protest in Pittsburgh. Minister Checks a Panic in Theatre When Lights Go Out', *New York Times*, 10 November 1913, p. 4.

73. 'An Appeal to the Tsar. English Public Opinion on the Condition of Jews in Russia', *Washington Post*, 11 December 1890.

74. Robert P. Geraci, *Window on the East: National and Imperial Identities in Late Tsarist Russia*, Ithaca, NY: Cornell University Press, pp. 210–17.

75. Luxemburg, 'Einleitung', in Korolenko, *Geschichte*, p. xiii.

76. Geraci, *Window on the East*, pp. 214–5.

77. Luxemburg, 'Einleitung', in Korolenko, *Geschichte*, p. ix.

78. Natalia M. Kolb-Seletski, 'Elements of Light in the Fiction of Korolenko', *Slavic and East European Journal*, vol. 16, no. 2, 1972, p. 174.

79. Geraci, *Window on the East*, p. 217.

80. Avner Ben-Amos, 'La "panthéonisation" de Jean Jaurès. Rituel et politique pendant la IIIe République', *Terrain: Revue d'ethnologie de l'Europe*, no. 15, 1990, pp. 49–64.

81. Saul K. Padover, 'Patterns of Assassination in Occupied Territory', *Public Opinion Quarterly*, vol. 7, no. 4, *The Occupation of Enemy Territory*, winter 1943, p. 691.

82. Martin H. Geyer, 'Munich in Turmoil. Social Protest and the Revolutionary Movement 1918–19', in Chris Wrigley (ed.), *The Challenges of Labour: Central and Western Europe, 1917–1920*, London: Routledge, 1993, pp. 51–71, at 59.

83. 'Das Ende Liebknechts und der Luxemburg', *Prager Tagblatt*, 17 January, 1919, p. 1.

84. 1916–03–03-DE-001, 'Matthias Erzberger an der Legationsrat im Auswartigen Amt Rosenberg, Berlin 3rd March, 1916', in Wolfgang Gust (ed.), *Der Völkermord an den Armeniern 1915/16: Dokumente aus dem Politischen Archiv des deutschen Auswärtigen Amts*, Springe: Zu Klampen, 2005, pp. 451–53.

85. 'Murderer of Erzberger Sentenced', *The Times*, 20 July 1950, p. 5.

86. 'Die Vergiftungs-Erscheinungen im Staatsgerichthof', *Prager Tagblatt*, 10 October 1922, p. 2.

87. Carole Fink, 'The Murder of Walter Rathenau', *Judaism*, vol. 44, no. 175, 1995, pp. 259–71.

88. 'Dr. Rathenau Murdered. Monarchist Crime, Berlin Tension', *The Times*, Monday, 26 June 1922, p. 8.

89. 'Der Mord an Rathenau. Die Aussage des Onkels', *Prager Tagblatt*, 7 October 1922, p. 2.

90. 'News in Brief', *The Times*, 10 January 1930, p. 11.

91. 'German Bomb Outrages Reactionaries at Work, Many Arrests', *The Times*, Thursday 12 September 1929, p. 12.

92. 'Rathenau Murder Trial. Techow's Uncle's Story', *The Times*, Saturday, 7 October 1922, p. 9.

93. 'How Dr. Rathenau Was Murdered. Crime Rehearsed', *The Times*, Friday, 6 October 1922, p. 9.

94. Erich Ludendorff, *Meine Kriegserinnerungen, 1914–1918 mit zahlreichen Skizzen und Plänen*, 4 Vols, Berlin 1919.

95. Michael Kellogg, *The Russian Roots of Nazism: White Emigrés and the Making of National Socialism*, Cambridge: Cambridge University Press, 2005, p. 15.

96. Dominik Schaller, 'Die Rezeption des Völkermordes an den Armeniern in Deutschland', in Hans-Lukas Kieser and Dominik J. Schaller (eds), *Der Völkermord an den Armeniern und die Shoah*, Zürich: Chronos Verlag, 2002, p. 531.

97. Taner Akçam, *Armenien und der Völkermord: Die Istanbuler Prozesse und die Türkische Nationalbewegung*, Hamburg: Hamburger Edition, 1996.

98. Vahakn N. Dadrian, 'The Secret Young Turk-Ittihadist Conference and the Decision for the World War I Genocide of the Armenians', *Holocaust and Genocide Studies*, vol. 7, no. 2, 1993, pp. 173–201, at 190.

99. 'Says Turks Advise Christians to Flee. Fear of General Massacre in Constantinople if Allied Fleet Passes Dardanelles', Special Cable, Athens, 9 January, *New York Times*, 11 January 1915, p. 2.

100. 'Der Prozeß gegen den Mörder Talaat Paschas', *Pester Lloyd*, 3 June, 1921, p. 5.

101. Margaret Lavinia Anderson, ' "Down in Turkey, Far Away": Human Rights, the Armenian Massacres, and Orientalism in Wilhelmine Germany', *Journal of Modern History*, vol. 79, March 2007, p. 94.

102. Christoph Dinkel, 'German Officers and the Armenian Genocide', *Armenian Review*, vol. 44, no. 1, 1991, pp. 77–133, at 94.

103. Ibid., p. 95.

104. This tragedy is sensitively retold by Samantha Power in *'A Problem from Hell': America and the Age of Genocide*, New York: Perennial, 2003.

105. Armin T. Wegner, Introduction to *Der Prozeß Talaat Pascha: Stenographischer Prozeßbericht*, Berlin: Deutsche Verlagsgesellschaft für Politik und Geschichte, 1921, p. 8.

106. Ibid., pp. 39–40.

107. Ibid., p. 51.

108. Ibid., p. 53.

109. Michael Richards, *A Time of Silence: Civil War and the Culture of Repression in Franco's Spain 1936–1945*, Cambridge: Cambridge University Press, 1998, p. 10.

110. Rolf Hosfeld, *Operation Nemesis: Die Türkei, Deutschland und der Völkermord an den Armeniern*, Köln: Kiepenheuer und Witsch, 2005, p. 23.

111. Wegner, *Prozeß Talaat Pascha*, p. 55.

112. 'Die Armenischen Greuel. Der moerder Talaat Paschas freigesprochen', *Wiener Morgenzeitung*, 4 June 1921, p. 21.

113. Wegner, *Prozeß Talaat Pascha*, p. 57.

114. Ibid., p. 34.

115. Ibid., p. 33.

116. Ibid., p. 36.

117. Ibid., pp. 78ff.

118. Reuters, 'Talaat's Assailant Acquitted. Armenians Suffering', *The Times*, 4 June 1921, p. 9.

119. Schaller, 'Die Rezeption des Völkermordes an den Armeniern in Deutschland', p. 532.

120. Jacques Derogy, *Resistance and Revenge: The Armenian Assassination of the Turkish Leaders Responsible for the 1915 Massacres and Deportations*, New Brunswick, NJ: Transaction, 1990, p. xxiv.

121. 'Why Talaat's Assassin Was Acquitted', *Current History*, vol. 7, July 1921.

122. Power, *'A Problem from Hell*, pp. 17–20.

123. Steven L. Jacobs, 'Raphael Lemkin and the Armenian Genocide', in Richard G. Hovannisian (ed.), *Looking Backward, Moving Forward. Confronting the Armenian Genocide*, New Brunswick, NJ: Transaction, 2003, p. 127.

124. Robert W. Olson, 'The Remains of Talat: A Dialectic between Republic and Empire', *Die Welt des Islams*, New Series, vol. 26, nos 1–2, 1986, p. 46.

125. Derogy, *Resistance and Revenge*, p. xxv.

126. 'Turks Enraged. British Court Martial Acquits Armenian', *The Times*, 12 November 1921, p. 9.

127. 'Ex-Grand Vizier Murdered. Prince Said Halim's Career', *The Times*, Wednesday, 7 December 1921, p. 9.

128. 'Jemal Pasha Dead. Shot In Tiflis, Tyrant Of Syria', *The Times*, Wednesday, 26 July 1922, p. 10.

129. Vahakn N. Dadrian, *The History of the Armenian Genocide. Ethnic Conflict from the Balkans to Anatolia to the Caucasus*, Providence, RI and Oxford: Berghahn, 1995, p. 341.

130. 'Das Attentat auf Bettauer. Im Arbeitszimmer überfallen', *Wiener Morgenzeitung*, 11 March 1925, p. 1.

131. Murray G. Hall, *Der Fall Bettauer*, Vienna: Löcker, 1978, p. 24.

132. Hugo Bettauer, *Die Stadt ohne Juden. Ein Roman von Übermorgen*, Vienna: Gloriette, 1922.

133. Ruth Ellen Gruber, *Virtually Jewish: Reinventing Jewish Culture in Europe*, Berkeley: University of California Press, 2002, p. 4.

134. 'Bans German Film on Jewish Theme; State Board Refuses to Permit "City Without Jews" to Be Shown by 5th Av. Playhouse. Holds it Objectionable. Theatre Director to Go to Albany to Fight Bar – Chief Complaint Is Over Short Notice', *New York Times*, 1 July 1928, p. 10.

135. Scott Spector, 'Modernism without Jews: A Counter-Historical Argument', *Modernism/modernity*, 2006, vol. 13, no. 4, p. 617.

136. Steven Beller, *Vienna and the Jews, 1867–1938: A Cultural History*, Cambridge: Cambridge University Press, 1990, p. 6.

137. Bruce F. Pauley, *From Prejudice to Persecution. A History of Austrian Anti-Semitism*, Chapel Hill: University of North Carolina Press, 1998, p. 105.

138. Hall, *Der Fall Bettauer*, p. 117.

139. 'New Yorker is Shot by Vienna Dentist; Bettauer, Once on Morgen Journal, Was Recently Cleared on Charge of Indecent Publication', *New York Times*, 11 March 1925, p. 4.

140. The force of the original text is difficult to render into appropriate English, as is much eliminationist language. 'Bettauers Wochenschrift muß verschwinden! Dieses Saublatt ist ja gefährlicher als die *Arbeiter-Zeitung* und *Der Abend* zusammen genommen', quoted in Hall, *Der Fall Bettauer*, p. 79.

141. Pauley, *From Prejudice to Persecution*, p. 105.

142. Hall, *Der Fall Bettauer*, p. 25.

143. Alfred Rosenberg, 'Der Fall Bettauer. Ein Musterbespiel jüdischer Zersetzungstätigkeit', *Der Weltkampf. Halbmonatsschrift für die Jüdenfrage aller Länder*, vol. 2, no. 8, 15 April 1925, pp. 337–51, quoted in Hall, *Der Fall Bettauer*, p. 105.

144. Beth Noveck, 'Hugo Bettauer and the Political Culture of the First Republic', in Günter Bischof, Anton Pelinka and Rolf Steininger (eds), *Austria in the Nineteen Fifties*, Edison, NJ: Transaction Publishers, 1995; *Contemporary Austrian Studies*, Vol. 3, p. 149.

145. Hall, *Der Fall Bettauer*, p. 183.

146. Thomas Köhler and Christian Mertens (eds), *Justizpalast in Flammen. Ein brennender Dornbusch. Das Werk von Manès Sperber, Heimito von Doderer und Elias Canetti angesichts des 15. Juli 1927*, Wien/München: Verlag für Geschichte und Politik/Oldenbourg Wissenschaftsverlag, 2006.

147. Henry Torrès, *Accusés hors série*, Paris: Gallimard, 1957, p. 35.

148. Torrès, *Accusés*, p. 41.

149. Czerny, 'Paroles et silences', p. 59.

150. Ibid., pp. 57–71.

151. David Engel, 'Being Lawful in a Lawless World: The Trial of Scholem Schwarzbard and the Defence of East European Jews', *Jahrbuch des Simon-Dubnow-Instituts*, vol. 5, 2006, p. 85.

152. 'Schwartzbart freigesprochen', *Die Neue Welt*, Friday 28 October 1926, p. 1.

153. Henry Abramson, *A Prayer for the Government. Ukrainians and Jews in Revolutionary Times, 1917–1920*, Cambridge, MA: Harvard University Press, 1999, pp. 80–5. Saul S. Friedman, author of the monograph *Pogromchik. The Assassination of Simon Petlura*, New York: Hart, 1976, is more critical of Petlura's role in the pogroms.

154. Karel Berkhoff, *Harvest of Despair. Life and Death in Ukraine under Nazi Rule*, Cambridge, MA: Belknap/Harvard University Press, 2004, p. 207.

155. Ibid., p. 199.

156. Abramson, *Prayer for the Government*, p. 172.

157. Czerny, 'Paroles et silences', p. 65.

158. 'Petlura Trial', *Time Magazine*, 7 November 1927.

159. Torrès, *Accusés*, p. 94.

160. Bernhard Blumenkranz et al., *Histoire des juifs en France*, Toulouse: Edouard Privat, 1972, p. 381.

161. Torrès, *Accusés*, pp. 291–9.

162. Ibid., pp. 215–21.

163. Ibid., pp. 98–9.

164. Engel, 'Being Lawful in a Lawless World, p. 84.

165. Rober Badinter, 'Une victoire de l'humanité sur elle-même', http://www.ecpm-.org/french/getinformed_featurednews_badinter_interview_fr.shtml, accessed on 22 July 2007.

166. 'Petlura Murder Case. Trial Opened in Paris', *The Times*, 19 October 1927, p. 13.

167. 'Petlura Trial. Question of Pogroms', *The Times*, 20 October 1927, p. 13.

168. 'Spectators Fight at Petlura Trial; Passion Sways Entire Court as Lawyer and Defendant Scream Defiance', *New York Times*, 22 October 1927, p. 6.

169. Abramson, *Prayer for the Government*, p. 172.

170. 'Petlura Trial', *Time Magazine*, Monday, 7 November 1927.

171. Torrès, *Accusés*, p. 94.

172. Victoria Khiterer, 'Arnold Davidovich Margolin: Ukrainian–Jewish Jurist, Statesman and Diplomat', *Revolutionary Russia*, vol. 18, no. 2, 2005, p. 155.

173. Engel, 'Being Lawful in a Lawless World', p. 95.

174. Czerny, 'Paroles et silences', p. 58.

175. Michael R. Marrus, 'Hannah Arendt and the Dreyfus Affair', *New German Critique*, no. 66, 1995, pp. 147–63, at 150.

176. Hannah Arendt, *Eichmann in Jerusalem: A Report on the Banality of Evil*, London: Penguin, 1994, p. 266.

177. Czerny, 'Paroles et silences', p. 67.

178. 'Samuel Schwartzbart', *The Times*, 27 October 1927, p. 11.

179. Steven G. Marks, *How Russia Shaped the Modern World: From Art to Anti-Semitism, Ballet to Bolshevism*, Princeton, NJ: Princeton University Press, 2004, p. 37.

180. 'Mike Davis Talks about "Heroes of Hell" ', Interview with Jon Wiener, *Radical History Review*, no. 85, winter 2003, 227–37, p. 234.

181. Torrès, *Accusés*, p. 95.

182. 'They Simply Had to Let Him Go', *New York Times*, 6 June 1921.

183. Raphael Lemkin, *Totally Unofficial: The Autobiography of Raphael Lemkin*, p. 372, cited in Lutz Fiedler, 'From the Minority Question to the Genocide Convention. The Case of Raphael Lemkin', Paper presented at Bern University Workshop on Genocide Denial, June 2007.

184. Roshwald, *Ethnic Nationalism and the Fall of Empires*, p. 168.

185. Joanna Beata Michlic, *Poland's Threatening Other. The Image of the Jew from 1880 to the Present*, Lincoln, NE: University of Nebraska Press, 2006, p. 125.

186. Mary Edith Durham, *My Balkan Notebook: Drawings, Photographs and Notes made Between 1900–1914*, Royal Anthropological Institute, London, MS 41, vol. 3.

187. Michael B. Loughlin, 'Gustave Herve's Transition from Socialism to National Socialism: Continuity and Ambivalence', *Journal of Contemporary History*, vol. 38, no. 4, 2003, pp. 515–38.
188. Pauley, *From Prejudice to Persecution*, p. 105.
189. '1,000 Police Guard 3 Croat Suspects. Plot Feared to Kidnap or Kill Trio Accused of Complicity in Alexander Assassination', *New York Times*, 18 November 1935, p. 11.
190. Keith Brown, ' "The King is Dead, Long live the Balkans!" Watching the Marseilles Murders of 1934', Paper presented at the Sixth Annual Convention of the Association for the Study of Nationalities, New York, April 2001.
191. Ron Roizen, 'Herschel Grynszpan: The Fate of A Forgotten Assassin', *Holocaust and Genocide Studies*, vol. 1, no. 2, 1986, pp. 217–28.
192. 'These Individuals!', *Time*, 21 November 1938.
193. Karol Jonca, *Noc krysztalowa i casus Herschela Grynszpana*, Wrocław: Wydawn, 1998, p. 247.
194. Arendt, *Eichmann in Jerusalem*, p. 227.
195. Anatole Leroy-Beaulieu, *Les Doctrines de haine: L'Antisémitisme, l'antiprotestantisme, l'anticléricalisme*, Paris: Calmann Lévy, 1902, p. 276.
196. Engel, 'Being Lawful in a Lawless World', p. 85.
197. Elias Canetti, *Masse und Macht*, Hamburg: Claassen, 1960.
198. Gerald Stieg, *Frucht des Feuers: Canetti, Doderer, Kraus und der Justizpalastbrand*, Vienna: Edition Falter im ÖBV, 1990.

Chapter 8: Shattered Worlds

1. Joseph Pérez, *The Spanish Inquisition: A History*, New Haven, CT: Yale University Press, 2005, p. 194.
2. John A. Hall, 'Towards a Theory of Social Evolution: On State Systems and Ideological Shells', in Daniel Miller, Michael Rowlands and Christopher Y. Tilley (eds), *Domination and Resistance*, London: Routledge, 1989, pp. 96–107, at 105.
3. Raymond A. Mentzer and Andrew Spicer, *Society and Culture in the Huguenot World, 1559–1685*, Cambridge: Cambridge University Press, 2002, p. 224.
4. Thomas Hope, *Torquemada. Scourge of the Jews*, London: George Allen and Unwin, 1939, pp. 15–16.
5. Vladimir Korolenko, *Dom no. 13*, Petrograd (n. p.) 1919, p. 1.
6. Benjamin Lieberman, 'Nationalist Narratives, Violence between Neighbours and Ethnic Cleansing in Bosnia–Hercegovina: A Case of Cognitive Dissonance?', *Journal of Genocide Research*, vol. 8, no. 3, 2006, pp. 295–310.
7. Stephan Astourian, 'The Armenian Genocide: An Interpretation', *History Teacher*, vol. 23, no. 2, February 1990, p. 135.
8. Frédéric Macler, *Autour de la Cilicie*, Paris: Imprimerie Nationale, 1916, p. 31.
9. 'Killing by Turks has been Renewed. American Says They Plan to Exterminate the Christians in Asia Minor. Expel Near East Workers. They Have Deported Major Yowell and Associates From Harpoot. Thousands of Greeks Killed', *New York Times*, 6 May 1922, p. 2.
10. 'Narrative of the Principal of the College at X, Communicated by the American Committee for Armenian and Syrian Relief', in James Viscount Bryce and Arnold Toynbee, *The Treatment of Armenians in the Ottoman Empire, 1915–1916: Documents Presented to Viscount Grey of Falloden*, Reading: Tadaron Press, in association with the Gormidas Institute, 2000, p. 355.
11. 'Exiles of Zeitoun. Diary of a Foreign Resident in the Town of B. on the Cilician Plain, Communicated by a Swiss Gentleman of Geneva', in Bryce and Toynbee, *The Treatment of Armenians in the Ottoman Empire*, p. 498.

12. Andrej Mitrović, *Prodor na Balkan. Srbija u planovima Austro-Ugarske i Nemačke 1908–1918*, Belgrade: Nolit, 1981, pp. 156–74.

13. Viktor Novak, *Magnum Crimen: pola vijeka klerikalizma u Hrvatskoj*, Zagreb: Nakladni Zavod Hrvatske, pp. 677–8.

14. Paul Rohrbach, *Vom Kaukasus zum Mittelmeer. Eine Hochzeits- und Studienreise durch Armenien*, Leipzig and Berlin: B. G. Teubner, 1903, pp. 222–3.

15. Silas Bent, 'Uprooting of Greeks in Turkey. Modern Exodus of Outcasts. People Who Have Lived All Their Lives in One Village to Be Driven Forth – No Money, No Destination, No Prospects – Disease and Hunger Already at Work, What It Will Cost Turkey', *New York Times*, 21 January 1923, p. XX5.

16. Sam Johnson, ' "Confronting the East". Darkest Russia, British Opinion and Tsarism's "Jewish question" ', *East European Jewish Affairs*, vol. 36, no. 2, 2006, p. 203.

17. Emma Goldman, *My Disillusionment in Russia*, New York: Doubleday, 1923, pp. 153–5.

18. Arnold Joseph Toynbee, *Turkey: A Past and a Future*, New York: George H. Doran, 1917, p. 55.

19. Donald Quartaert, 'Machine Breaking and the Changing Carpet Industry of Western Anatolia, 1860–1908', *Journal of Social History*, vol. 19, no. 3, 1986, pp. 473–500, at 479.

20. Edward Daniel Clarke, *Travels in Various Countries of Europe, Asia and Africa. I: Russia, Tartary and Turkey*, Vol. 2, London: Cadell & Davies, 1816, p. 144.

21. Gerald Reitlinger, *A Tower of Skulls*, London: Duckworth, 1932, p. 269; p. 275.

22. 'Erzeroum. Statement by Mr A. S. Safrastian, dated Tiflis, 15th March, 1916', in Bryce and Toynbee, *The Treatment of Armenians in the Ottoman Empire*, p. 270.

23. Henry Morgenthau, *Ambassador Morgenthau's Story*, London: Hodder & Stoughton, 1918, pp. 395–6.

24. Biray Kolluoğlu Kirli, 'Forgetting the Smyrna Fire', in *History Workshop Journal*, no. 60, 2005, pp. 25–44, at 38. On the damage to Smryna and its infrastructure, see also Eugène Pittard, *A travers l'Asie-Mineure: Le Visage nouveau de la Turquie*, Paris: Société d'Editions Géographiques Maritimes et Coloniales, 1931.

25. John Frödin, 'La Morphologie de la Turquie sud-est', *Geografiska Annaler*, vol. 19, 1937, pp. 1–29.

26. 'Prelate's Letter Describes Atrocities in Hellenic Territories of Black Sea. Population is Scattered. Declares Deportations Into Snow-Covered Lands Replace Openly Brutal Outrages. Atrocities Perpetrated by the Turks Against the Greeks in the Black Sea Territories Are Described in a Letter of His Grace Germanos, Lord Archbishop of Amassia and Samsoun, in a Letter Sent from Constantinople to M. Constantinides, President of the Pont-Euxine Unredeemed Greeks Committee: 'Into the Valley of Death', *New York Times*, 5 July 1919, p. 8.

27. Rohrbach, *Vom Kaukasus zum Mittelmeer*, pp. 35–6.

28. Many Odessa Jews took part in the filming of Sergei Eisenstein's epic 1925 film *Battleship Potemkin*. Less than twenty years later, this community was annihilated by the Nazis. As Eisenstein favoured using local non-professionals in his films, one can only presume that many of the actors perished.

29. Mark Mazower, *Salonica, City of Ghosts: Christians, Muslims and Jews*, London: Harper, 2005.

30. Brian Glyn Williams, 'Hijra and Forced Migration from Nineteenth-Century Russia to the Ottoman Empire', *Cahiers du monde russe*, vol. 41, no. 1, 2000, p. 99.

31. Dean S. Rugg, *Eastern Europe*, London: Longman, 1985, pp. 118–254.

32. 'With 250,000 Jews Fighting in Russian Armies, the Cruelties Still Continue', *New York Times*, 20 March 1915, p. 9.

33. Valentine Chirol, 'The Turk Old and New. Eight Years of War', *The Times*, 16 January 1923, p. 9.

34. Milan Bašta, *Rat je završen sedam dana kasnije*, Belgrade: OOUR, 1986, p. 202.
35. William A. Schabas, *Genocide in International Law: The Crimes of Crimes*, Cambridge: Cambridge University Press, 2000, p. 230.
36. Samantha Power, *'A Problem from Hell'. America and the Age of Genocide*, New York: Perennial, 2003, p. 20.
37. Emile Hilderbrand, 'Kemal Promises More Hangings of Political Antagonists in Turkey', *Los Angeles Examiner*, 1 August 1926, p. 1.
38. Henry Wadsworth Longfellow, *The Complete Poetical Works*, Boston and New York: Houghton, Mifflin, 1903, p. 209.
39. Rainer and Rose-Marie Hagen, 'The Vitebsk Man of Sorrow', in idem, *What the Great Paintings Say*, Vol. 1, Cologne: Taschen, 2003, p. 477.
40. Marshall Berman, *All That Is Solid Melts into Air: The Experience of Modernity*, Harmondsworth: Penguin, 1988. The quotation in the title is taken from Karl Marx.
41. Takayuki Yokota-Murakami, 'Tolstoy, Attila, Edison: The Triangular Construction of "Peace-Loving". Russian Identity across Borders', *Slavic and East European Journal*, vol. 45, no. 2, 2001, p. 220.
42. Julius Brutzkus: 'Das Blutbad von Bialystok', *Ost und West*, vols 5–6, May 1906, pp. 399–402.
43. Steven L. Jacobs, 'Raphael Lemkin and the Armenian Genocide', in Richard G. Hovannisian (ed.), *Looking Backward, Moving Forward. Confronting the Armenian Genocide*, New Brunswick, NJ: Transaction Publishers, 2003, p. 127.
44. Power, *'A Problem from Hell'*, p. 19.
45. Martin Shaw, *What Is Genocide?*, Cambridge: Polity, 2007, p. 17.
46. Convention on the Prevention and Punishment of Genocide http://www.unhchr.ch/html/menu3/b/p_genoci:htm, accessed 30 November 2008.
47. Schabas, *Genocide in International Law*, p. 25.
48. Toynbee, *Turkey: A Past and a Future*, p. 3.
49. Benjamin Ide Wheeler, 'Greece and the Eastern Question', *Atlantic Monthly*, vol. 79, no. 476, June 1897, pp. 721–2.
50. 'Die Armenischen Greuel. Der moerder Talaat Paschas freigesprochen', *Wiener Morgenzeitung*, 4 June, 1921, p. 21.
51. 'Killing by Turks Has Been Renewed. American Says They Plan to Exterminate the Christians in Asia Minor. They Have Deported Major Yowell and Associates From Harpoot. Thousands of Greeks Killed', *New York Times*, 6 May 1922, p. 2.
52. Hannah Arendt, *The Origins of Totalitarianism*, London: Andre Deutsch, 1986, p. 91.
53. Lynn Hunt, *Inventing Human Rights: A History*, New York: W. W. Norton, 2007, p. 205.
54. Rudolf Samper, *Die neuen Jakobiner: Der Aufbruch der Radikalen*, Munich: Herbig Verlag, 1981, p. 110.

Bibliography

Newspapers and Journals

Allgemeine Zeitung des Judentums
Atlantic Monthly
L'Aurore
Balkan Review
Century: A Popular Quarterly
Christlich-soziale Arbeiter-Zeitung
Current History Magazine
Dublin Review
English Historical Review
Geografiska Annaler
Harper's New Monthly Magazine
Im deutschen Reich
Jewish Quarterly Review
Judge
Kikeriki
Living Age
Literary Digest
Los Angeles Examiner
Menorah
Missionary Review
Neue jüdische Monatshefte
Der Morgen
Der Orient
Die Neue Welt
New York Times
North American Review
Ost und West
Pester Lloyd
Prager Tagblatt
Public Opinion Quarterly
Reichspost

Revue de Paris
La Revue des Balkans
Scotsman
The Times
Times Literary Supplement
Time Magazine
Transactions of the Ethnological Society of London
Ustaša
Washington Post
Die Welt. Zentralorgan der Zionistischen Bewegung
Die Welt des Islams
Wiener Morgenzeitung
Das Wort
Zeitschrift für Demographie und Statistik der Juden

Collections of Documents

Bryce, James Viscount and Arnold Toynbee, *The treatment of Armenians in the Ottoman Empire, 1915–1916: documents presented to Viscount Grey of Falloden*, Reading: Tadaron Press, in association with the Gomidas Institute, 2000

Convention on the Prevention and Punishment of Genocide http://www.uhhchr.ch/html/menu3/b/p_genoci.htm

Čović, Bože (ed.), *Izvori velikosrpske agresije*, Zagreb: August Cesarec and Skolska knjiga, 1991

Dedijer, Vladimir, *Genocid nad muslimanima 1941–45: Zbornik documenta i svjedocenja*, Sarajevo: Svjetlost, 1990

Durham, Mary Edith, 'My Balkan Notebook: Drawings, Photographs and Notes, Made Between 1900 and 1914', MS 41, vol. 3, Royal Anthropological Institute, London

Erofeev Nikolaï Dimitrievich, *Partiya sotsialistov-revolyutsionerov, dokumenty i materialy, Vol. 1, 1900–1907*, Moscow: Rosspen, 1996

Goltz, Hermann und Axel Meissner (eds), *Deutschland, Armenien und die Türkei, 1895–1925: Dokumente und Zeitschriften aus dem Dr. Johannes-Lepsius-Archiv an der Martin-Luther-Universität Halle-Wittenberg*, Munich: K. G. Saur, 1998

Grmek, Mirko, Marc Gjidara and Neven Šimac (eds), *Etničko Čišćenje, Povijesni dokumenti o jednoj srpskoj ideologiji*, Zagreb: Nakladni zavod Globus, 1993

Gust, Wolfgang (ed.), *Der Völkermord an den Armeniern 1915/16: Dokumente aus dem Politischen Archiv des deutschen Auswärtigen Amts*, Springe: Zu Klampen, 2005

Kennan, George F., *The Other Balkan Wars: A 1913 Carnegie Endowment Inquiry in Retrospect, with a New Introduction and Reflections on the Present Conflict*. Washington, DC: Carnegie Endowment for International Peace, 1993

Lepsius, Johannes, *Deutschland und Armenien, 1914–1918: Sammlung diplomatischer Aktenstücke*, Potsdam: Tempelverlag, 1919

Novak, Viktor, *Magnum Crimen: pola vijeka klerikalizma u Hrvatskoj*, Zagreb: Nakladni Zavod Hrvatske, 1948

Public Record Office, London

Primary Sources

Aeschylus, *The Oresteia*, trans. Alan Shapiro and Peter Burian, Oxford: Oxford University Press, 2003

Alaux, Louis-Paul and Rene Puaux, *Le Déclin de l'hellénisme*, Paris: Payot & Cie, 1916

Aleichem, Sholem, *Tevye's Daughters*, New York: Crown, 1949

Andersch, Alfred, *Sansibar oder, Der letze Grund*, Olten: Walter Verlag, 1957

Andréadès, M.A, *La Destruction de Smyrne et les dernières atrocités Turques en Asie Mineure*, Athens: P. D. Sakellerios, 1923

Anon, *An Authentic Account of the Occurrences in Smyrna and the Aidan District (on the Occupation by the Greeks)*. London: Cole, 1919

Bailey, William Frederick, *The Slavs of the War Zone*, New York: E. P. Dutton, 1916

Barth, Hans, *Türke, Wehre Dich!*, Leipzig: Renger, 1898

Bašta, Milan, *Rat je završen sedam dana kasnije*, Belgrade: OOUR, 1986

Bates, Jean Victor, *Our Allies and Enemies in the Near East*, London: Chapman & Hall, 1918

Benson, Edward Frederick, *Crescent and Iron Cross*, London: Hodder & Stoughton, 1918

Bettauer, Hugo, *Die Stadt ohne Juden. Ein Roman von Übermorgen*, Vienna: Gloriette, 1922

Bettelheim, Bruno, *Recollections and Reflections*, Harmondsworth: Penguin, 1992

Bierstadt, Edward H., *The Great Betrayal: A Survey of the Near East Problem*, New York: Robert M. McBride, 1924

Blaisdell, Dorothea Chambers, *Missionary Daughter. Witness to the End of the Ottoman Empire*, Portland, OR: 1st Books Library, 2002

Brecht, Bertholt, *Dreigroschen Roman*, Munich: Verlag K. Desch, 1949

Bruce Lockhart, Robert H., *Memoirs of a British Agent. Being an Account of the Author's Life in Many Lands and of his Official Mission to Moscow in 1918*, London and New York: Putnam, 1932

Burton, Richard, *Personal Narrative of a Pilgrimage to Al-Madinah and Meccah*, New York: Dover, Vols 1–2, 1893

————— *The Jew, the Gypsy and El-Islam*, London: Hutchinson, 1898

Canetti, Elias, *Masse und Macht*, Hamburg: Claassen, 1960

————— *Die gerettete Zunge: Geschichte einer Jugend*, Frankfurt am Main: Fischer, 1979

Capus, Guillaume, *A travers le royaume de Tamerlan – (Asie Centrale) . . .*, Paris, A. Hennuyer, 1892

Chamberlain, Houston Stewart, *Die Grundlagen des Neunzehnten Jahrhunderts*, I Hälfte, Munich: F. Bruckmann, 1904

Charmetant, Félix, *Martyrologe arménien. Tableau officiel des massacres d'Arménie dressé après enquêtes par les six ambassades de Constantinople*, Paris: Bureau des Oeuvres d'Orient, 1896

Chopin, Jean-Marie, *Provinces Danubiènnes et Roumaines: Bosnie, Servie, Herzegovine, Bulgarie, Slavonie, Illyrie, Croatie, Monténégro, Albanie, Valachie, Moldavie et Bucovine*, Paris: Firmin Didot Frères Editeurs, 1856, Vols 1–2

Christowe, Stoyan, *Heroes and Assassins*, New York: McBride, 1935

Ciliga, Ante, *Sam kroz Europu u ratu*, Rome: Na pragu sutranšnjice, 1978

Clarke, Edward Daniel, *Travels in Various Countries of Europe, Asia and Africa*, Vol. 2, London: Cadell & Davies, 1816

Conan Doyle, Arthur, *The Crime of the Congo*, New York: Doubleday, Page, 1909

Ćorović, Vladimir, *Crna knjiga. Patnje Srba Bosne i Hercegovine za vreme svetskog rata 1914–1918. godine*, Belgrade: Biblioteka Jugoslovenski dosìje, 1989

Ćosić, Dobrica, *Vreme smrti*, Belgrade: Prosveta, 1972

Crawfurd, John, 'On the Conditions which Favour, Retard or Obstruct the Early Civilization of Man', *Transactions of the Ethnological Society of London*, Vol. 1, 1861, pp. 154–77.

Cvijić, Jovan, *La Péninsule balkanique. Géographie humaine*, Paris: A. Colin, 1918

Dante Alighieri, *Commedia di Dante Alighieri*, with notes by Gregorio Di Siena, Naples: Perotti, 1870

Davitt, Michael, *Within the Pale: The True Story of Anti-Semitic Persecution in Russia*, London: Hurst & Blakett, 1903

Dedijer, Vladimir, *Josip Broz Tito: prilozi za biografiju*, Belgrade: Kultura, 1953

————— *The War Diaries of Vladimir Dedijer*, Vol. 1, Ann Arbor: University of Michigan Press, 1990

Delaplanche, M. l'abbé Jean-Constant-François, with Joseph-Norbert Duquet, *Le Pèlerin de Terre sainte: Voyage en Egypte, en Palestine, en Syrie, à Smyrne et à Constantinople*, Québec: Hardy, 1887

Demidoff, Anatole de, *Voyage dans la Russie Méridionale et la Crimée par la Hongrie, la Valachie et la Moldavie exécuté en 1837*, Paris: Ernest Bourdin et Cie. Editeurs, 1854

Desmoulins, Lucie Simplice Camille Benoist, *Œuvres de Camille Desmoulins, avec une étude biographique . . . précédées d'une étude biographique et littéraire par M. Jules Clarétie*, Vol. 2, Paris: Charpentier et Cie. Editeurs, 1874

Dickson White, Andrew, *Autobiography of Andrew Dickson White*, Vol. 2, New York: Century, 1905

Djilas, Milovan, *Land without Justice. An Autobiography of Youth*, with an introduction by William Jovanovich, New York: Harcourt, Brace, 1958

———— *Wartime: With Tito and the Partisans*, New York: Harcourt, Brace, Jovanovich, 1977

Dobson, Charles, 'Appendix: The Smyrna Holocaust', in Lysimachos Oeconomos (ed.), *The Tragedy of the Christian Near East*, London: Anglo-Hellenic League, 1923, pp. 21–9

Dostoyevsky, Fyodor, translated with an introduction by David Magarshack, *The Brothers Karamazov*, Vol. 2, Harmondsworth: Penguin, 1969

Dourmoussis, Evdokimos, *La Verité sur un drame historique: La Catastrophe de Smyrne*, Paris: Librarie Caffin, 1922

Dressler, Adolf, *Kroatien*, Essen: Essenerverlagsastalt, 1942

Dubnow, Simon, *Mein Leben*, Berlin: Jüdischer Buchvereinigung, 1937

Durham, Mary Edith, *The Burden of the Balkans*, Edward Arnold: London, 1905

Eliot, Thomas Stearns, *The Annotated Waste Land with Eliot's Contemporary Prose*, edited with annotations and introduction by Lawrence Rainey, New Haven, CT/London: Yale University Press, 2nd edn, 2006

Erdman, David V. (ed.), *The Complete Poetry and Prose of William Blake*, new and revised edn, with a commentary by Harold Bloom, Berkeley, CA: University of California Press, 1982

Errera, Léo, *Die russischen Juden. Vernichtung oder Befreiung? Mit einem einleitenden Briefe von Th. Mommsen und einem Bericht des Verfassers über die Vorgänge in Kischinew 1903*, Leipzig: Schulze, 1903

Evans, Arthur J., *Through Bosnia and the Herzegovina on Foot during the Insurrection, August and September 1875*, London: Longmans, Green, 1876

Feuer, Lewis S. (ed.), *Marx and Engels. Basic Writings on Politics and Philosophy*, Glasgow: Collins, 1969

Fraser, Robert William, *Turkey Ancient and Modern*, Edinburgh: Adam and Charles Black, 1854

Freud, Sigmund, *Jenseits des Lustprinzips*, Leipzig: Internationaler psychoanalytischer Verlag, 1920

———— *Das Ich und das Es*, Leipzig: Internationaler psychoanalytischer Verlag, 1923

Georgijević, Krešimir, *Srpskohrvatska narodna pesma u poljskoj književnosti Studija iz uporedne istorije slovenskih književnosti*, Belgrade: Srpska kraljevska akademija, 1936

Gibbon, Edward, David Womersley (ed.), *The History of the Decline and Fall of the Roman Empire*, London: Allen Lane, 1994, Vol. 1

Gibbons, Helen Davenport, *The Red Rugs of Tarsus. A Woman's Record of the Armenian Massacre of 1909*, New York: Century, 1917

Goethe, Johann Wolfgang von, *Selected Verse*, introduced by David Luke, Harmondsworth: Penguin, 1986

Gogol, Nikolai, *Taras Bulba*, trans. Isabel F. Hapgood, New York: Lovell, 1888

Goldman, Bosworth, *Red Road through Asia; A Journey by the Arctic Ocean to Siberia, Central Asia and Armenia; With an Account of the Peoples Now Living in those Countries under the Hammer and Sickle*, London: Methuen, 1934

Gondrand, Richard, *La Tragédie de l'Asie Mineure et l'anéantissement de Smyrne 1914–1922*, Marseille: Y Armen, 1935

Gorky, Maxim, 'The Barbarians', in Theodor Shanin (ed.), *Peasants and Peasant Societies*, Penguin: Harmondsworth, 1971, pp. 369–71

Hacobian, A. P., *L'Arménie et la guerre. Le Point de vue d'un Arménien avec un appel à la Grande-Bretagne et à la prochaine Conférence de paix*, Paris: Hagop Turabian, 1918

Hadžišehović, Munevera, *A Muslim Woman in Tito's Yugoslavia*, trans. Thomas J. Butler and Saba Risaluddin, College Station: Texas, Texas A&M Press, 2003

Harris, Rendel J. and Helen B. Harris, *Letters from the Scenes of the Recent Massacres in Armenia*, London: James Nisbet, 1897

de Heimann, Robert, *A Cheval de Varsovie à Constantinople par un capitaine de hussards de la Garde impériale russe. Avec une préface de Pierre Loti*, Paris: Paul Ollendorf, 1893

Heine, Heinrich, *Gedichte*, London: Duckworth, 1948

Herodotus, *The Histories*, trans. Robin Waterfield, with an introduction by Carolyn Dewald, Oxford: Oxford University Press, 1998

Ho Chi Minh, *Selected Writings 1920–1969*, Hanoi: Foreign Languages Publishers, 1977

Homer, *The Iliad*, trans. by E. V. Rieu, Penguin: Harmondsworth, 1953

Hope, Thomas, *Torquemada. Scourge of the Jews*, London: George Allen & Unwin, 1939

Horton, George, *The Blight of Asia: An Account of the Systematic Extermination of Christian Populations by Mohammedans and the Culpability of Certain Great Powers. With the True Story of the Burning of Smyrna*, Indianapolis: Bobbs-Merrill, 1926

Hugo, Victor, *Torquemada*, Paris: Calmann Lévy, 1888

International Commission of Inquiry Appointed at the Request of the Greek Red Cross, *Treatment of Greek Prisoners in Turkey*, London: Anglo-Hellenic League, 1923

Jackson, T. G., *Dalmatia, the Quarnero and Istria with Cettigne in Montenegro and the Island of Grado*, Oxford: Clarendon Press, 1887

Joubert, Carl, *Russia as It Really Is*, London: Eveleigh Nash, 1904

Jouve, Marguerite, *Torquemada. Grand Inquisiteur D'Espagne*, Paris: Editions de France, 1934

Karadžić, Vuk, 'Početak Bune Protivu Dahija', in Tvrtko Čubelić, *Epske narodne pjesme: Izbor tekstova s komentarima i objašnjenjima i rasprava o epskim narodnim pjesmama*, Zagreb: Školska knjiga, 1970

Kherdian, David, *The Road from Home. The Story of an Armenian Girl*, New York: Greenwillow, 1979

Khrushchev, Nikita, *Khrushchev Remembers*, with an introduction, commentary and notes by Edward Crankshaw, trans. and ed. Strobe Talbott, Vol. 1, London: Andre Deutsch, 1971

Klemperer, Victor, *Lingua Tertii Imperii: Notizbuch eines Philologen*, Berlin: Aufbau-Verlag, 1947

Korolenko, Wladimir, *Die Geschichte meines Zeitgenossen*, trans. with an introduction by Rosa Luxemburg, Berlin: Paul Cassirer, 1919

———— *Dom no. 13*, Petrograd, n.p., 1919

Krleža, Miroslav, *Golgota*, Belgrade: Biblioteka savremene i klasične drame, 1959

Lane, Rose Wilder, *The Peaks of Shala: Being a Record of Certain Wanderings among the Hill Tribes of Albania*, London: Chapman & Dodd, 1924

Launay, Louis de, *In het Balkanbergland van Bulgarije. De Aarde en haar Volken*, Harlem: Tjeenk Willink, 1906

Lavallée, Théophile Sébastien, *Histoire des français*, Paris: Charpentier, 1856

Lawrence, Thomas Edward, *Seven Pillars of Wisdom*, Ware: Wordsworth Editions, 1997

Lea, Henry Charles, *A History of the Inquisition of the Middle Ages*, London: Sampson Low, 1888

Lemkin, Raphael, *Axis Rule in Occupied Europe*, Washington, DC: Carnegie Endowment for International Peace, 1944

Lenin, Vladimir I., *Selected Works*, Vol. 5, New York: International Publishers, 1935

———— 'Leo Tolstoy as the Mirror of the Russian Revolution', in David Craig (ed.), *Marxists on Literature*, Harmondsworth: Penguin, 1977, pp. 346–51

Leroy-Beaulieu, Anatole, *Les Doctrines de haine: L'Antisémitisme, l'antiprotestantisme, l'anticléricalisme*, Paris: Calmann Lévy, 1902

Levi, Carlo, *Cristo si è fermato a Eboli*, Turin: Einaudi, 1990

Levin, Shmarya, *Jugend in Aufrurhr*, Berlin: Jüdischer Buchvereinigung, 1935

Lewis, Edwin Herbert, *Those about Trench*, New York: Macmillan, 1916

Livesay, Florence Randal, *Songs of Ukraina with Ruthenian Poems*, London, Paris and Toronto: Dent/ New York: Dutton, 1916

Longfellow, Henry Wadsworth, *The Complete Poetical Works*, Boston and New York: Houghton, Mifflin, 1903

Loti, Pierre, *Fleurs d'ennui, Pasquala Ivanovitch, voyage au Monténégro, Suleima*, Paris: Calmann Lévy, 1891

———— *Les Massacres d'Arménie*, Paris: Calmann Lévy, 1918

Mackenzie, Georgina Mary Muir Sebright and Adelina Paulina Irby, *The Turks, Greeks and Slavons. Travels in the Slavonic Provinces of Turkey-in-Europe*, London: Bell & Daldy, 1867

Maclean, Fitzroy, *Eastern Approaches*, London: Reprint Society, 1951

Macler, Frédéric, *Autour de la Cilicie*, Paris: Imprimerie Nationale, 1916

Maistre, Joseph de, *Lettres à un gentilhomme russe sur l'Inquisition espagnole*, Paris: chez Méquignon, 1822

Mann, Heinrich, *Die Jugend des Königs Henri Quatre*, Amsterdam: Querido, 1935

———— *Der Pogrom*, Zürich: Verlag für Soziale Literatur, 1939

Mann, Thomas, *Der Zauberberg*, Berlin: Fischer, 1928

Marmier, Xavier, *Lettres sur L'Adriatique et le Monténégro*, tome deuxième, Paris: Imprimerie Ch. Lahure, Société de Géographie, 1853

Milčinski, Fran, *Dnevnik 1914–1920*, Ljubljana: Slovenska matica, 2000

Missaelidis, Kostas, *En Bithynie: Par le fer et par le feu*, Athens: Le Bureau de la Presse du Ministère des Affaires Etrangères, 1922

Montpéreux, Frédéric Dubois de, *Voyage autour du Caucase, chez les Tcherkesses, et les Abkhases, en Colchide, en Géorgie, en Arménie et en Crimée*, Paris: Librarie de Gide, 1839

Morel, Edmund Dene, *The Black Man's Burden*, London: National Labour Press, 1920

Morgenthau, Henry, *Ambassador Morgenthau's Story*, London: Hodder & Stoughton, 1918

Morse, John T., Jr, 'The Dreyfus and Zola Trials', *Atlantic Monthly*, vol. 81, no. 487, May 1898.

Nansen, Fridtjof, *Armenia and the Near East*, London: Allen & Unwin, 1928

Newman, John Henry, *Historical Sketches, 1. The Turks in Their Relation to Europe, Marcus Tullius Cicero, Apollonius of Tyana, Primitive Christianity*, London: Longman Green, 1889, p. 113

Niepage, Martin, *The Horrors of Aleppo, Seen by a German Eyewitness*, London: T. Fisher Unwin, 1916

Njegoš, Petar Petrović, *Gorski Vijenac*, Sarajevo: Svjetlost, 1990

Orwell, Sonia and Ian Angus (eds), *The Collected Essays, Journalism and Letters of George Orwell*, Harmondsworth: Penguin, 1971

Paléologue, Maurice, *Journal de l'affaire Dreyfus, 1894–1899: L'Affaire Dreyfus et le Quai d'Orsay*, Paris: Librarie Plon, 1955

Pittard, Eugène, *A travers l'Asie-Mineure: Le Visage nouveau de la Turquie*, Paris: Société d'Editions Géographiques Maritimes et Coloniales, 1931

Pobyedonostseff, Konstantin P., *Reflections of a Russian Statesman*, London: Grant Richards, 1898

Popa, Vasko, *Pesme: Izbor*, Belgrade: Rad, 1985

Popović, Vladeta (ed.), *The Mountain Wreath of P. P. Nyegosh, Prince Bishop of Montenegro, 1830–1851*, trans. James William Wyles, London: George Allen & Unwin, 1930

Pranaïtis, Iustinus Bonaventura, *Das Christenthum im Talmud der Juden*, Vienna: Verlag des Sendboten des Hl. Joseph, 1894

Preobrazhensky, Evgenii and Nikolai Bukharin, with an introduction by Edward Hallett Carr, *The ABC of Communism*, Harmondsworth: Penguin, 1969

Price, Morgan Philips, *War and Revolution in Asiatic Russia*, London: George Allen & Unwin, 1918

Price, Walter Harrington Crawfurd, *The Balkan Cockpit: The Political and Military Story of the Balkan Wars in Macedonia*, London: T. Werner Laurie, 1914

Puaux, René, *La Déportation et le rapatriement des Grecs en Turquie*, Paris: Editions du Bulletin Hellénique, 1919

Reed, John, *War in Eastern Europe. Travels through the Balkans in 1915*, London: Orion, 1999

Reeves, William Pember, *The Great Powers and the Eastern Christians: Christiani ad Leones! A Protest*, London: Anglo-Hellenic League, 1922

Reitlinger, Gerald, *A Tower of Skulls*, London: Duckworth, 1932

Richardson, James, *Travels in Morocco*, London: Charles Skeet, 1860, Vol. 2

Rohrbach, Paul, *Die Bagdadbahn*, Berlin: Verlag von Wiegandt und Grieben, 1902

———— *Vom Kaukasus zum Mittelmeer. Eine Hochzeits- und Studienreise durch Armenien*, Leipzig and Berlin: B. G. Teubner, 1903

———— *Deutsche Kolonialwirtschaft 1*, Berlin and Schöneberg: Hilfe Verlag, 1907

———— *Der Deutsche Gedanke in der Welt*, Düsseldorf and Leipzig: Karl Robert Langewiesche Verlag, 1912

———— *Um des Teufels Handschrift. Zwei Menschenalter erlebter Weltgeschichte*, Hamburg: Hans Dulk, 1953

Rosen, Georg, *Die Balkan-Haiduken*, Leipzig: F. A. Brockhaus, 1878

Sanders, Liman von, *Fünf Jahre Türkei*, Berlin: Scherl, 1920

Sandwith, Humphrey, 'From Belgrade to Constantinople Overland', *Living Age*, vol. 130, no. 1684, 16 September 1876.

Serge, Victor, 'The Writer's Conscience', in David Craig (ed.), *Marxists on Literature*, Harmondsworth: Penguin, 1977, pp. 435–44

Seton-Watson, Robert W., *The Problem of Small Nations and the European Anarchy*, Nottingham: Nottingham University, Montague Burton International Relations Series, 1939

Smith, Munroe, 'German Land Hunger', *Political Science Quarterly*, vol. 32, no. 3, September 1917, pp. 459–79

Stritar, Josip, *Zbrano Delo, Šesta knjiga, Pogovori 1870–1879*, Ljubljana: Državna založba Slovenije, 1955

Suetonius Tranquillus, Gaius, *The Twelve Caesars*, trans. Robert Graves, Harmondsworth: Penguin, 1957

Sukhanov, Nikolaï Nikolaievich, *Zapiski o revoliutsii*, Mosocw: Izdatel'stvo politicheskoï literatury, 1991–2, Vols 1–3

Tacitus, Cornelius, *The Annals of Imperial Rome*, trans. with an introduction by Michael Grant, Harmondsworth: Penguin, revised edn, 1996

Le Tellier, Robert Ignatius, *The Diaries of Giacomo Meyerbeer*, Cranbury, NJ: Associated University Presses, 1999

Tennyson, Alfred Lord, *Poetical Works*, London: Macmillan, 1926

Thomson, Harry Craufuird, *The Outgoing Turk: Impressions of a Journey through the Western Balkans*, New York: D. Appleton, 1897

Titmarsh M. A. (William Makepeace Thackeray), *Notes of a Journey from Cornhill to Grand Cairo, by Way of Lisbon, Athens, Constantinople and Jerusalem*, London: Chapman & Hall, 1846

Tolstoy, Leo, *War and Peace*, London: Pan, 1972

Torrès, Henry, *Accusés hors série*, Paris: Gallimard, 1957

Townsend, A. F., *A Military Consul in Turkey. The Experience and Impression of a British Representative in Asia Minor*, London: Seeley, 1910

Toynbee, Arnold Joseph, *Turkey: A Past and a Future*, New York: George H. Doran, 1917

Trotsky, Leon, *The History of the Russian Revolution*, trans. Max Eastman, Chicago: University of Michigan Press, 1957

————— *1905*, Harmondsworth: Penguin, 1973

————— *My Life. An Attempt at an Autobiography*, Harmondsworth: Penguin, 1975

————— *The Balkan Wars 1912–13*, New York: Monad Press, 1980

————— *How the Revolution Armed. The Military Writings and Speeches of Leon Trotsky*, Vol. 5, 1921–3, trans. Brian Pearse, London: New Park, 1981

Turgenev, Ivan, *The Jew and Other Stories*, London: Heinemann, 1899

Die Türkische Nachbarländer an der Südostgrenze Österreichs: Serbien, Bosnien, Türkisch-Kroatien, Herzegovina und Montenegro, Pest, Vienna and Leipzig: Hartleben's Verlag-Expedition, 1854

Twain, Mark, *King Leopold's Soliloquy. A Defense of his Congo Rule*, Boston, MA: P. R. Warren, 1905

————— 'Life on the Mississippi', in idem, *Mississippi Writings*, New York: Library of America, 1982, pp. 217–616

Vereschagine, Basile, *Voyage dans les provinces du Caucase (1864–65). Le Tour du Monde*, Vol. 17, 1868, pp. 161–208

Villari, Luigi, *Fire and Sword in the Caucasus*, London: Unwin, 1906

Villiers de l'Isle-Adam, Auguste, *Nouveaux contes cruels*, Paris: Calmann Lévy, 1893

Virgil, *The Eclogues translated by Wrangham, the Georgics by Sotheby and the Aenied by Dryden*, Vol. 2, London: Henry Colburn and Richard Bentley, 1830

Voltaire (François-Marie Arouet), *Essai surs les moeurs et l'esprit des nations*, Paris: chez Werdet et LeQuien fils, 1829

Ward, Mark H., *The Deportations in Asia Minor 1921–1922*, London: Anglo-Hellenic League & British Armenia Committee, 1922

Watson, J. S. and Henry Dale (eds), *Xenophon's Cyropaedia or the Institution of Cyrus and the Hellenics or Grecian Historys*, London: Henry G. Bohn, 1855

Wegner, Armin T., *Der Prozess Talaat Pascha: Stenographischer Prozessbericht*, Berlin: Verlag für Politik und Geschichte, 1921

Weininger, Otto, *Geschlecht und Charakter: Eine prinzipielle Untersuchung*, Vienna: Braumüller, 1908

Werda, Joel, *The Flickering Light of Asia or The Assyrian Nation and Church*, New York: published by the author, 1924

Werfel, Franz, *Die vierzig Tage des Musa Dagh*, Berlin: P. Zsolnay, 1933

West, Rebecca, *Black Lamb and Grey Falcon. A Journey through Yugoslavia*, New York: Viking Press, 1941

Wiesel, Elie, *All Rivers Run to the Sea. Memoirs. Volume 1: 1928–1969*, London: HarperCollins, 1995

Wingfield, William Frederick, *A Tour in Dalmatia, Albania and Montenegro, with a Historical Sketch of the Republic of Ragusa*, London: Richard Bentle, 1859

Wyon, Reginald, *The Balkans from Within*, London: J. Finch, 1904

Yriarte, Charles, *Bosnie et Herzégovine: Souvenirs de voyage pendant l'insurrection*, Paris: Plon, 1876

Secondary Sources

Aberbach, David, 'The Poetry of Nationalism', *Nations and Nationalism*, vol. 9, no. 2, 2003, 255–75

Abramson, Henry, *A Prayer for the Government: Ukrainians and Jews in Revolutionary Times, 1917–1920*, Cambridge, MA: Harvard University Press, 1999

Akbar, Ahmed, 'Ethnic Cleansing: A Metaphor for Our Time?', *Ethnic and Racial Studies*, vol. 18, no. 1, 1995, pp. 2–25

Akçam, Taner, *Armenien und der Völkermord: Die Istanbuler Prozesse und die Türkische Nationalbewegung*, Hamburg: Hamburger Edition, 1996

Allcock, John B., *Explaining Yugoslavia*, London: Hurst, 2000

Allen, Warren Dwight, 'Music in Russia and the West', *Russian Review*, vol. 8, no. 2, 1949, p. 108

Aly, Götz and Susanne Heim, *Architects of Annihilation. Auschwitz and the Logic of Destruction*, London: Phoenix, 2002

Ambler, Effie, *Russian Journalism and Politics, 1861–1881: The Career of Aleksei S. Suvorin*, Detroit: Wayne State University Press, 1972

Anderson, Benedict, *Imagined Communities: Reflections on the Origin and Spread of Nationalism*, New York: Verso, 1991

Anderson, Margaret Lavinia, ' "Down in Turkey, Far Away": Human Rights, the Armenian Massacres, and Orientalism in Wilhelmine Germany', *Journal of Modern History*, vol. 79, no. 1, 2007, pp. 80–111

Angress, Werner T, 'The German Army's "Judenzählung" of 1916: Genesis – Consequences – Significance', *Leo Baeck Institute Year Book*, vol. 23, 1978, pp. 117–35

Anzulović, Branimir, *Heavenly Serbia: From Myth to Genocide*, London: Hurst, 1999

Appadurai, Arjun, 'Dead Certainty: Ethnic Violence in the Era of Globalization', *Development and Change*, vol. 29, no. 4, 1998, pp. 905–25

————— 'New Logics of Violence': http://www.india-seminar.com/2001/503/503%20 arjun%20apadurai.htm

Arblaster, Anthony, *Viva la libertà! Politics in Opera*, London and New York: Verso, 1992

Arendt, Hannah, *The Origins of Totalitarianism*, London: Andre Deutsch, 1986

————— *Eichmann in Jerusalem: A Report on the Banality of Evil*, London: Penguin, 2002

Arfi, Badredine, 'Ethnic Fear: The Social Construction of Insecurity', *Security Studies*, vol. 8, no. 1, 1998, 151–203

Aronson, Michael I., 'The Attitudes of Russian Officials in the 1880s Towards Jewish Assimilation and Emigration', *Slavic Review*, vol. 34, no. 1, 1975, pp. 1–18

Ascher, Abraham, *The Revolution of 1905: A Short History*, Stanford, CA: Stanford University Press, 2004

Astourian, Stephan, 'The Armenian Genocide: An Interpretation', *History Teacher*, vol. 23, no. 2, 1990, pp. 111–60

Auron, Yair, 'The Forty Days of Musa Dagh. Its Impact on Jewish Youth in Palestine and Europe', in Richard G. Hovannisian (ed.), *Remembrance and Denial: The Case of the Armenian Genocide*, Detroit, MI: Wayne State University Press, 1999, pp. 147–64

Badinter, Robert, 'Une victoire de l'humanité sur elle-même', http://www.ecpm.org/ french/getinformed_featurednews_badinter_interview_fr.shtml

Bakhtin, Mikhail, *The Dialogic Imagination: Four Essays*, ed. Michael Holquist and trans. Caryl Emerson, Austin: University of Texas Press, 1981

Bakić-Hayden, Milica, 'National Memory as Narrative Memory: The Case of Kosovo', in Maria Todorova (ed.), *Balkan Identities: Nation and Memory*, London: Hurst, 2004, pp. 25–40

Balakian, Peter, *Black Dog of Fate: A Memoir*, New York: Broadway Books, 1998

Ballinger, Pamela, *History in Exile. Memory and Identity at the Borders of the Balkans*, Princeton, NJ: Princeton University Press, 2003

Banac, Ivo, *The National Question in Yugoslavia: Origins, History, Politics*, Ithaca, NY: Cornell University Press, 1984

Band, Arnold J., 'Kafka and the Beiliss Affair', *Comparative Literature*, vol. 32, no. 2, 1980, pp. 168–83

Bandžović, Safet, 'Koncepcije Srpskog kulturnog kluba o preuredenju Jugoslavije 1937–1941', *Prilozi*, vol. 30, Sarajevo, 2001, pp. 163–93

———— 'Ratovi i demografska deosmanizacija Balkana (1912.–1941.)', *Prilozi*, vol. 32, Sarajevo, 2003, pp. 179–229

Bajohr, Frank, '*Unser Hotel ist judenfrei'. Bäder-Antisemitismus im 19. und 20. Jahrhundert*, Frankfurt am Main: Fischer Verlag, 2003

Barsoumian Hagop, 'Economic Role of the Armenian Amira Class in the Ottoman Empire', *Armenian Review*, vol. 31, March 1979, pp. 310–16

Bartov, Omer, 'Defining Enemies, Making Victims: Germans, Jews, and the Holocaust', *American Historical Review*, vol. 103, no. 3, 1998, pp. 771–816

Basil, John D., 'Konstantin Petrovich Pobedonostsev: An Argument for a Russian State Church', *Church History*, vol. 64, no. 1, 1995, pp. 44–61

Bauer, Yehuda, *Rethinking the Holocaust*, New Haven, CT: Yale University Press, 2002

Bauman, Zygmunt, *Modernity and the Holocaust*, Cambridge: Polity Press, 1991

Baylen, Joseph O. and Jane G. Weyant, 'Vasili Vereshchagin in the United States', *Russian Review*, vol. 30, no. 3, 1971, pp. 250–9

Begić, Miron Krešimir, *Ustaški Pokret 1929–1941: pregled njegove poviesti*, Buenos Aires: Naklada Smotre Ustaša, 1986

Beiderwell, Bruce, *Power and Punishment in Scott's Novels*, Athens, GA: University of Georgia Press, 1992

Beller, Steven, *Vienna and the Jews, 1867–1938: A Cultural History*, Cambridge: Cambridge University Press, 1989

Ben-Amos, Avner, 'La "Panthéonisation" de Jean Jaurès. Rituel et politique pendant la IIIe République', *Terrain: Revue d'ethnologie de l'Europe*, no. 15, 1990, pp. 49–64

Ben-Amos, Batsheva, 'A Tourist in 'Ir ha-Haregah (A Tourist in the City of Slaughter) – Kishinev 1903', *Jewish Quarterly Review*, vol. 96, no. 3, summer 2006, pp. 359–84

Benbassa, Esther, *Juifs des Balkans: Espaces judéo-ibériques, XIVe-XXe siècles*, Paris: La Découverte, 1993

Benjamin, Walter, *Understanding Brecht*, London: New Left Books, 1977

Benz, Wolfgang, 'The November Pogrom of 1938: Participation, Applause, Disapproval', in Christian Hoffmann, Werner Bergmann and Helmut Walser Smith (eds), *Exclusionary Violence. Antisemitic Riots in Modern German History*, Ann Arbor: University of Michigan Press, 2002, pp. 141–59

Berghe, Pierre, van den, *The Ethnic Phenomenon*, New York: Elsevier, 1981

Bergman, Werner, 'Exclusionary Riots. Some Theoretical Considerations', in Christian Hoffmann, Werner Bergmann and Helmut Walser Smith (eds), *Exclusionary Violence. Antisemitic Riots in Modern German History*, Ann Arbor: University of Michigan Press, 2002, pp. 161–84

Berkhoff, Karel, *Harvest of Despair. Life and Death in Ukraine under Nazi Rule*, Cambridge, MA: Belknap/Harvard University Press, 2004

Berkowitz, Joel, 'The "Mendel Beilis Epidemic" on the Yiddish stage', *Jewish Social Studies*, vol. 8, no. 1, 2001, pp. 199–225

Berman, Marshall, *All That Is Solid Melts Into Air: The Experience of Modernity*, Harmondsworth: Penguin, 1988

Biagio D'Angelo, 'Epique et parodie dans *Taras Boulba* de Gogol en rapport avec le roman historique de son temps', *Interlitteraria*, vol. 6, 2001, pp. 272–83

Bieber, Florian, 'Muslim Identity in the Balkans before the Establishment of Nation States', *Nationalities Papers*, vol. 28, no. 1, March 2000, pp. 13–28

Bieber, Hans-Joachim, 'Anti-Semitism as a Reflection of Social, Economic and Political Tension in Germany 1880–1933', in David Bronsen (ed.), *Jews and Germans from 1860–1933: The Problematic Symbiosis*, Heidelberg: Carl Winter Universitätsverlag, 1979, pp. 33–77

Billig, Michael, *Laughter and Ridicule: Towards a Social Critique of Humour*, London: Sage, 2005

Biondich, Marc, *Stjepan Radić, the Croat Peasant Party and the Politics of Mass Mobilization, 1904–1928*, Toronto: University of Toronto Press, 2000

Bley, Helmut, 'Continuities and German Colonialism: Colonial Experience and Metropolitan Developments 1890–1955', paper presented at the Nineteenth International Conference of the Vereinigung von Afrikanisten in Deutschland, Hannover University, 2–5 June 2004

Blobaum, Robert, *Antisemitism and its Opponents in Modern Poland*, Ithaca, NY: Cornell University Press, 2005

Bloxham, Donald, 'Three Imperialisms and a Turkish Nationalism: International Stresses, Imperial Disintegration and the Armenian Genocide', *Patterns of Prejudice*, vol. 36, no. 4, 2002, pp. 37–58

————— 'The Armenian Genocide of 1915–16: Cumulative Radicalisation and the Development of a Destruction Policy', *Past and Present*, vol. 181, no. 1, 2003, pp. 141–91

————— 'Determinants of the Armenian Genocide', in Richard Hovannisian (ed.), *Looking Backward, Moving Forward: Confronting the Armenian Genocide*, New Brunswick, NJ: Transaction Publishers, 2003, pp. 23–50

————— *The Great Game of Genocide*, Oxford: Oxford University Press, 2005

Blumenkranz, Bernhard, et al., *Histoire des juifs en France*, Toulouse: Edouard Privat, 1972

Boehm, Christopher, *Montenegrin Social Organization and Values: Political Ethnography of a Refuge Area Tribal Adaptation*, New York: AMS Press, 1983

Boime, Albert, *The Art of the Macchia and the Risorgimento: Representing Culture and Nationalism in Nineteenth-Century Italy*, Chicago: University of Chicago Press, 1993

Borowsky, Peter, 'Paul Rohrbach und die Ukraine: Ein Beitrag zum Kontinuitätsproblem', in Imanuel Geiss and Bernd Jürgen Wendt (eds), *Deutschland in der Weltpolitik des 19. und 20. Jahrhunderts. Fritz Fischer zum 65. Geburtstag*, Düsseldorf: Bertelsmann, 1973, pp. 437–62

Bourdieu, Pierre, *Outline of a Theory of Practice*, Cambridge: Cambridge University Press, 1977

Bourke, Joanna, *An Intimate History of Killing. Face-to-Face Killing in Twentieth Century Europe*, London: Granta, 1999

Braber, Ben, 'The Trial of Oscar Slater (1909) and Anti-Jewish Prejudices in Edwardian Glasgow', *History*, vol. 88, no. 290, 2003, pp. 262–79

Bradshaw, David and Kevin J. H. Dettmar, *A Companion to Modernist Literature and Culture*, Oxford: Blackwell, 2006

Bringa, Tone, *Being Muslim the Bosnian Way*, Princeton, NJ: Princeton University Press, 1995

Brown, Keith, ' "The King is Dead, Long live the Balkans!" Watching the Marseilles Murders of 1934', Paper presented at the Sixth Annual Convention of the Association for the Study of Nationalities, New York, April 2001

Brown, Michael E., 'The Causes of Internal Conflict: An Overview', Michael E. Brown, Owen R. Cote Jr, Sean M. Lynn-Jones and Steven E. Miller (eds), *Nationalism and Ethnic Conflict*: revised edn, Cambridge, MA: MIT Press, 2001, pp. 3–25

Browning, Christopher R., *Ordinary Men. Reserve Police Battalion 101 and the Final Solution in Poland*, Harmondsworth: Penguin, 2001

———— with contributions by Jürgen Matthäus, *The Origins of the Final Solution*, Lincoln, NE: University of Nebraska Press, 2004

Brubaker, Rogers, *Nationalism Reframed. Nationhood and the National Question in Europe*, Cambridge: Cambridge University Press, 1996

Brustein, William I. and Ryan D. King, 'Balkan Anti-Semitism: The Cases of Bulgaria and Romania before the Holocaust', *East European Politics and Society*, vol. 18, no. 3, 2004, pp. 430–54

Burleigh, Michael and Wolfgang Wippermann, *The Racial State: Germany 1933–1945*, Cambridge: Cambridge University Press, 1991

Byrnes, Robert F., 'Russia and the West: The Views of Pobedonostsev', *Journal of Modern History*, vol. 40, no. 2, 1968, pp. 234–56

Carlson, Paul R., *Christianity after Auschwitz: Evangelicals Encounter Judaism in the New Millenium*, Philadelphia, PA: Xlibris, 2000

Carmichael, Cathie, ' "A People Exists and That People Has Its Language". Language and Nationalism in the Balkans', in Stephen Barbour and Cathie Carmichael (eds), *Language and Nationalism in Europe*, Oxford: Oxford University Press, 2000, pp. 221–39

———— *Ethnic Cleansing in the Balkans: Nationalism and the Destruction of Tradition*, London: Routledge, 2002

———— 'The Violent Destruction of Community during the "Century of Genocide" ', *European History Quarterly*, vol. 35, no. 3, 2005, pp. 395–403

———— 'Violence and Ethnic Boundary Maintenance in Bosnia since 1992', *Journal of Genocide Research*, vol. 8, no. 3, 2006, pp. 283–93

———— 'Was Religion Important in the Destruction of Ancient Communities in the Balkans, Anatolia and Black Sea Regions c. 1870–1923?, *Journal of South Eastern Europe and Black Sea Studies*, vol. 7, no. 3, 2007, pp. 357–72

Carter, F. W. and H. T. Norris (eds), *The Changing Shape of the Balkans*, London: UCL Press, 1996

Cartledge, Paul, *Thermopylae. The Battle that Changed the World*, London: Pan/Macmillan, 2006

Cerović, Ljubivoje, *Srbi u Rumuniji od ranog srednjeg veka do današnjeg vremena*, Novi Sad: Matica srpska, 1997

Cervinka, František, 'The Hilsner Affair', *Leo Baeck Institute Year Book*, vol. 13, 1968, pp. 142–157

Charlesworth, Andrew, 'The Topography of Genocide', in Dan Stone (ed.), *The Historiography of the Holocaust*, London: Palgrave, 2004, pp. 216–52

Chase, Bob, 'Walter Scott: A New Historical Paradigm', in Bill Schwarz (ed.), *The Expansion of England*, London: Routledge, 1996, pp. 92–129

Chasiotes, Ioannes K. et al. (eds), *The Jewish Communities of Southeastern Europe: From the Fifteenth Century to the End of World War II*, Thessalonica: Institute for Balkan Studies, 1997

Cohen, Stanley, *States of Denial. Knowing about Atrocities and Suffering*, Cambridge: Polity Press, 2001

Cohn, Norman, *Warrant for Genocide: The Myth of the Jewish World-Conspiracy and the Protocols of the Elders of Zion*, Harmondsworth: Penguin 1967

Cole, Laurence, *Für Gott, Kaiser und Vaterland: Nationale Identität der deutschsprachigen Bevölkerung Tirols, 1860–1914*, Frankfurt: Campus Verlag, 2000

Čolović, Ivan, *Dubina: članci i intervjui, 1991–2001*, Belgrade: Samizdat B92, 2001

Conklin Akbari, Suzanne, 'The Jews in Late Medieval Literature', in Ivan Davidson Klamar and Derek J. Penslar (eds), *Orientalism and the Jews*, Waltham, MA: Brandeis University Press, 2005, pp. 32–50

Connor, Maureen P. O., 'The Vision of Soldiers: Britain, France, Germany and the United States Observe the Russo-Turkish Wars', *War in History*, vol. 4, no. 3, 1997, pp. 264–95

Conversi, Daniele, 'Violence as an Ethnic Border: The Consequences of a Lack of Distinctive Elements in Croatian, Kurdish and Basque Nationalism', in Justo G. Beramendi, Ramón Máiz and Xosé M. Núñez (eds), *Nationalism in Europe Past and Present*, Vol. 1, Santiago de Compostela: Universidade de Santiago de Compostela, 1994, pp. 167–98

————— 'Nationalism, Boundaries and Violence', *Millennium: Journal of International Studies*, vol. 28, no. 3, 1999, pp. 553–84

Cox, John K., *The History of Serbia*, Westport, CT: Greenwood Press, 2002

Cropper, Corry, 'Prosper Merimée and the Subversive "Historical" Short Story', *Nineteenth Century French Studies*, vol. 33, nos 1–2, 2004–5, pp. 57–74

Curp, T. David, ' "Roman Dmowski Understood": Ethnic Cleansing as Permanent Revolution', *European History Quarterly*, vol. 35, no. 3, 2005, pp. 405–27

Curtin, Philip D., 'Epidemiology and the Slave Trade', in Gad J. Heuman and James Walvin (eds.), *The Slavery Reader*, London: Routledge, 2003, pp. 11–29

Curtis, Michael, *Verdict on Vichy: Power and Prejudice in the Vichy France Regime*, London: Weidenfeld & Nicolson, 2002.

Czerny, Boris, 'Paroles et silences. L'Affaire Schwatzbard et la presse juive parisienne (1926–27), *Archives Juives*, vol. 34, 2001–2, pp. 57–71

Dabrowski, Patrice M., *Commemorations and the Shaping of Modern Poland*, Bloomington: Indiana University Press, 2004

Dadrian, Vahakn N. 'The Secret Young Turk-Ittihadist Conference and the Decision for the World War I Genocide of the Armenians', *Holocaust and Genocide Studies*, vol. 7, no. 2, 1993, pp. 173–201

————— *The History of the Armenian Genocide. Ethnic Conflict from the Balkans to Anatolia to the Caucasus*, Providence, RI and Oxford: Berghahn, 1995

————— 'The Armenian Genocide: An Interpretation', in Jay Winter (ed.), *America and the Armenian Genocide*, Cambridge: Cambridge University Press, 2003, pp. 52–100

————— 'Comparative Aspects of Armenian and Jewish Cases of Genocide: a Sociohistorical Perspective', in Alan S. Rosenbaum, (ed.), *Is the Holocaust Unique? Perspectives on Comparative Genocide*, Boulder, CO: Westview Press, 1996, pp. 101–35

Daniel, Valentine E., *Charred Lullabies: Chapters in an Anthropography of Violence*, Princeton, NJ: Princeton University Press, 1996

Daskalov, Roumen, 'Ideas About, and Reactions To, Modernization in the Balkans', *East European Quarterly*, vol. 31, no. 2, June 1997, pp. 141–80

Dedijer, Vladimir, *The Road to Sarajevo*, London: MacGibbon and Kee, 1967

————— *The Yugoslav Auschwitz and the Vatican: The Croatian Massacre of Serbs during World War II*, Buffalo, NY: Prometheus Books, 1992

Delbrück, Hansgerd, 'Antiker und moderner Helden-Mythos in Dürrenmatts "ungeschichtlicher historischer Komödie" Romulus der Große', *German Quarterly*, vol. 66, no. 3, 1993, pp. 291–317

Deringil, Selim, 'The Invention of Tradition as Public Image in the Late Ottoman Empire, 1808 to 1908', *Comparative Studies in Society and History*, vol. 35, no. 1, 1993, pp. 3–29

————— ' "There Is No Compulsion in Religion": On Conversion and Apostasy in the Late Ottoman Empire: 1839–1856', *Comparative Studies in Society and History*, vol. 42, no. 3, 2000, pp. 547–75

Derogy, Jacques, *Resistance and Revenge: The Armenian Assassination of the Turkish Leaders Responsible for the 1915 Massacres and Deportations*, New Brunswick, NJ: Transaction, 1990

Dijtink, Gertjan, 'Geopolitics as a Social Movement?', *Geopolitics*, vol. 9, no. 2, 2004, pp. 460–75

Dinkel, Christoph, 'German Officers and the Armenian Genocide', *Armenian Review*, vol. 44, no. 1, 1991, pp. 77–133

Djilas, Aleksa, *The Contested Country: Yugoslav Unity and Communist Revolution, 1919–1953*, Cambridge, MA: Harvard University Press, 1991

Dobrivojević, Ivana, 'Policija i žandarmerija u doba šestosiječanjskog režima kralja Aleksandra (1929.–1935.), *Časopis za suvremenu povijest*, vol. 38, no. 1, 2006, pp. 99–137

Douglas, Mary, *Purity and Danger: An Analysis of the Concepts of Pollution and Taboo*, London: Routledge & Kegan Paul, 1966

Dulić, Tomislav, *Utopias of Nation: Local Mass Killing in Bosnia and Herzegovina, 1941–42*, Uppsala: Acta Universitatis Upsaliensis, Studia Historica Upsaliensia, 2005

———— 'Mass Killing in the Independent State of Croatia, 1941–1945: A Case for Comparative Research', *Journal of Genocide Research*, vol. 8, no. 3, 2006, pp. 225–81

Dwork, Deborah and Robert Jan van Pelt, *Holocaust: A History*, London: John Murray, 2003

El Kenz, David, 'La Naissance de la tolérance au 16e siècle: L' "Invention" du massacre', *Revue sens publique*, September 2006, pp. 1–18

Elazar, Daniel et al. (eds), *The Balkan Jewish Communities: Yugoslavia, Bulgaria, Greece and Turkey*, Lanham, MD: University Press of America, 1984

Eley, Geoff, 'Reviewing the Socialist Tradition', in Christina Lemke and Gary Marks (eds), *The Crisis of Socialism in Europe*, Durham, NC: Duke University Press, 1992, pp. 21–60

Elfering, Raimund 'Die "Bejlis-Affäre" im Spiegel der liberalen russischen Tageszeitung Reč', *Digitale Osteuropa-Bibliothek Geschichte*, no. 7, 2004, www.vifaost.de

Elwert, Georg, 'Nationalizmus und Ethnizität. Über die Bildung von Wir-Gruppen', *Kölner Zeitschrift für Sociologie und Sozialpyschologie*, vol. 3, 1989, pp. 440–64

Engel, David, 'Being Lawful in a Lawless World: The Trial of Scholem Schwarzbard and the Defense of East European Jews', *Jahrbuch des Simon-Dubnow-Instituts*, vol. 5, 2006, pp. 83–97

Fearon, James D., 'Rationalist Explanations for War', *International Organization*, vol. 49, no. 3, 1995, pp. 379–414

———— and David D. Laitin, 'Explaining Interethnic Cooperation', *American Political Science Review*, vol. 90, no. 4, 1996, pp. 715–35

Fein, Helen, 'A Formula for Genocide: Comparison of the Turkish Genocide (1915) and the German Holocaust (1939–1945)', *Comparative Studies in Sociology*, vol. 1, 1978, pp. 271–93

Feinstein, Sara, *Sunshine, Blossoms and Blood: H. N. Bialik in His Time, a Literary Biography*, Lanham, MD: University Press of America, 2005

Ferguson, Niall, *The Pity of War. Explaining World War I*, London: Basic Books 1999

Ferro, Marc, *Nicolas II*, Paris: Payot, 1991

Fiedler, Lutz, 'From the Minority Question to the Genocide Convention. The Case of Raphael Lemkin', Paper presented at Bern University, Switzerland. Workshop on Genocide Denial in Theory and Practice, June 2007

Figes, Orlando, *Natasha's Dance. A Cultural History of Russia*, Harmondsworth: Penguin, 2002

Figes, Orlando and Boris Kolonitskii, *Interpreting the Russian Revolution. The Language and Symbols of 1917*, New Haven, CT: Yale University Press, 1999

Fink, Carole, 'The Murder of Walter Rathenau', *Judaism*, vol. 44, no. 175, 1995, pp. 259–71

Finnin, Rory, 'Mountains, Masks, Metre, Meaning: Taras Shevchenko's "Kavkaz" ', *Slavonic and East European Review*, vol. 83, no. 3, July 2005, pp. 396–439

Fisher, Michael, *Counterflows to Colonialism: Indian Travellers and Settlers in Britain, 1600–1857*, Delhi: Permanent Black, 2004

Frankel, Jonathan, *The Damascus Affair: 'Ritual Murder', Politics, and the Jews in 1840*, Cambridge: Cambridge University Press, 1997

Freeborn Richard, *The Russian Revolutionary Novel: Turgenev to Pasternak*, Cambridge: Cambridge University Press, 1982

Friedman, Saul S., *Pogromchik. The Assassination of Simon Petlura*, York: Hart, 1976

Fussell, Paul, *The Great War and Modern Memory*, Oxford: Oxford University Press, 1975

Gellately, Robert, *Lenin, Stalin and Hitler: The Age of Social Catastrophe*, New York: Alfred A. Knopf/London: Jonathan Cape, 2007

Gellner, Ernest, *Nations and Nationalism*, Ithaca, NY: Cornell University Press, 1983
———— 'Nationalism and Politics in Eastern Europe', *New Left Review I*, vol. 189, September–October 1991, pp. 127–34

Geraci, Robert P., *Window on the East: National and Imperial Identities in Late Tsarist Russia*, Ithaca, NY and London: Cornell University Press, 2001

Gerlach, Christian, 'The Wannsee Conference, the Fate of the German Jews, and Hitler's Decision in Principle to Exterminate All European Jews', *Journal of Modern History*, vol. 70, no. 4, 1998, pp. 759–812

Gerschenkron, Alexander, *Economic Backwardness in Historical Perspective*, Cambridge, MA: Harvard University Press, 1962

Getzler, Israël, *Martov. A Political Biography of a Russian Social Democrat*, Cambridge: Cambridge University Press, 2003

Geyer, Martin H., 'Munich in Turmoil. Social Protest and the Revolutionary Movement 1918–19', in Chris Wrigley (ed.), *The Challenges of Labour: Central and Western Europe, 1917–1920*, London: Routledge, 1993, pp. 51–71

Gilbert, Martin, *First World War*, London: Weidenfeld & Nicolson, 1994

Glenny, Misha, *The Balkans 1804–1999. Nationalism, War and the Great Powers*, London: Granta, 1999.

Glover, Jonathan, *A Moral History of the 20th Century*, London: Jonathan Cape, 2000

Godelier, Maurice, 'Infrastructures, Societies and History', *Current Anthropology*, vol. 19, no. 4, 1978, pp. 763–71

Goldhagen Daniel Jonah, *Hitler's Willing Executioners. Ordinary Germans and the Holocaust*, London: Little, Brown, 1996

Goldstein, David I., *Dostoïevski et les juifs*, Paris: Gallimard, 1976

Goldstein, Ivo, *Croatia: A History*, London: Hurst, 1999

Goldsworthy, Simon, 'English Non-Conformity and the Pioneering of the Modern Newspaper Campaign, Including the Strange Case of W. T. Stead and the Bulgarian Horrors', *Journalism Studies*, vol. 7, no. 3, June 2006 pp. 387–402

Goldsworthy, Vesna, *Inventing Ruritania: The Imperialism of the Imagination*, New Haven, CT/London: Yale University Press, 1998

Gordon, Sarah, *Hitler, Germans and the Jewish Question*, Princeton, NJ: Princeton University Press, 1984

Gottlieb, Julie V., ' "Motherly Hate": Gendering Anti-Semitism in the British Union of Fascists', in *Gender and History*, vol. 14, no. 2, 2002, pp. 294–320

Green, Linda, *Fear As a Way of Life: Mayan Widows in Rural Guatemala*, New York: Columbia University Press, 1999

Greengrass, Mark, 'Hidden Transcripts: Secret Histories and Personal Testimonies of Religious Violence in the French Wars of Religion', in Mark Levene and Penny Roberts (eds), *The Massacre in History*, New York and Oxford: Berghahn Books, 1999, pp. 69–88

Gruber, Ruth Ellen, *Virtually Jewish: Reinventing Jewish Culture in Europe*, Berkeley, CA: University of California Press, 2002

Gunnemann, Karin Verena, *Heinrich Mann's Novels and Essays: The Artist as Political Educator*, Rochester, NY/Woodbridge, Suffolk: Boydell & Brewer, 2002

Hagen, Gottfried, 'German Heralds of Holy War: Orientalists and Applied Oriental Studies', *Comparative Studies of South Asia, Africa and the Middle East*, vol. 24, no. 2, 2004, pp. 145–62

Hagen, Rainer and Rose-Marie Hagen, *What the Great Paintings Say*, Vol. 1, Cologne: Taschen, 2003

Hall, John A., 'Towards a Theory of Social Evolution: On State Systems and Ideological Shells', in Daniel Miller, Michael Rowlands and Christopher Y. Tilley (eds), *Domination and Resistance*, London: Routledge, 1989, pp. 96–107

Hall, Murray G., *Der Fall Bettauer*, Vienna: Löcker, 1978

Hall, Richard C., *The Balkan Wars 1912–13. Prelude to the First World War*, London: Routledge, 2000

Hansen, Miriam, *Babel and Babylon: Spectatorship in American Silent Film*, Cambridge, MA: Harvard University Press, 1994

Hawkins, Mike, *Social Darwinism in European and American Thought, 1860–1945*, Cambridge: Cambridge University Press, 1997

Hayes, Carlton J. H., 'The Challenge of Totalitarianism', *Public Opinion Quarterly*, vol. 2, no. 1, 1938, pp. 21–6

Heine Teixeira, Christa, 'Lion Feuchtwanger: *Der falsche Nero* Zeitgenössische Kritik im Gewand des historischen Romans: Erwägungen zur Entstehung und Rezeption', *Amsterdamer Beiträge zur neueren Germanistik*, vol. 51, 2001, pp. 79–89

Henry, Patrick, 'Banishing the Coercion of Despair: Le Chambon-sur-Lignon and the Holocaust Today', *Shofar: An Interdisciplinary Journal of Jewish Studies*, vol. 20, no. 2, 2002, pp. 69–84

Hilberg, Raul, *The Destruction of the European Jews*, New Haven, CT/London: Yale University Press, vol. 1, 3rd edn.

Hirschon, Renée, *Heirs of the Greek Catastrophe: The Social Life of Asia Minor Refugees in Piraeus*, Oxford: Oxford University Press, 1989

———— *Crossing the Aegean: The Consequences of the 1923 Greek–Turkish Population Exchange*, New York: Berghahn, 2003

Hoenicke Moore, Michael E., 'Reading Livy Against Livy: The Dream and Nightmare of (American) Empire', *European Legacy. Toward New Paradigms*, vol. 10, no. 3, 2005, pp. 149–59

Hofmann, Tessa, *Verfolgung, Vertreibung und Vernichtung der Christen im Osmanischen Reich 1912–1922*, Münster: Lit, 2004

Holquist, Peter, 'To Count, to Extract, to Exterminate: Population Statistics and Population Politics in Late Imperial and Soviet Russia', in Ronald Grigor Suny and Terry Martin (eds), *A State of Nations: Empire and Nation-Making in the Age of Lenin and Stalin*, New York and Oxford: Oxford University Press, 2001, pp. 111–44

———— *Making War, Forging Revolution. Russia's Continuum of Crisis, 1914–1921*, Cambridge, MA: Harvard University Press, 2002

Horvat, Branko, *Kosovsko Pitanje*, Zagreb: Globus, 1989

Hosfeld, Rolf, *Operation Nemesis: Die Türkei, Deutschland und der Völkermord an den Armeniern*, Cologne: Kiepenheuer und Witsch, 2005

Housepian, Marjorie, *Smyrna 1922: The Destruction of a City*, London: Faber, 1972

Hovannisian, Richard G. 'Bitter-Sweet Memories. The Last Generation of Ottoman Armenians', in Richard Hovannisian (ed.), *Looking Backward, Moving Forward: Confronting the Armenian Genocide*, New Brunswick, NJ: Transaction Publishers, 2003, pp. 113–24

Hroch, Miroslav, 'Nationalism and National Movements: Comparing the Past and the Present of Central and Eastern Europe', *Nations and Nationalism*, vol. 2, no. 1, 1996, pp. 35–44

Hunt, Lynn, *Inventing Human Rights: A History*, New York: W. W. Norton, 2007

Ibrahimagić, Omer, *Srpsko osporavanje Bosne i Bošnjaka*, Sarajevo: Magistrat, 2001

Iliev, Chavdar Lynbenov, 'The Bulgarian Nation Through the Centuries', *Journal of Muslim Minority Affairs*, vol. 10, no. 1, 1989, pp. 9–10

Ireton, Sean, 'Heinrich Manns Auseinandersetzung mit dem Haβ: Eine Analyse der Henri Quatre-Romane im Rahmen der exilbedingten Haβliteratur', *Orbis litterarum: International Review of Literary Studies*, vol. 57, no. 3, 2002, pp. 204–21

Jacobs, Steven L., 'Raphael Lemkin and the Armenian Genocide', in Richard Hovannisian (ed.), *Looking Backward, Moving Forward: Confronting the Armenian Genocide*, New Brunswick, NJ: Transaction Publishers, 2003, pp. 125–36

Jäschke, Gotthard, 'Der Turanismus der Jungtürken. Zur osmanischen Auβenpolitik im Weltkriege', *Die Welt des Islams*, vol. 23, nos 1 & 2, 1941, pp. 1–54

Jelavich, Barbara, *History of the Balkans*, Vols 1–2, Cambridge: Cambridge University Press, 1983

Jelić-Butić, Fikreta, *Četnici u Hrvatskoj 1941–1945*, Zagreb: Globus, 1986

Jennings, Jeremy, 'Of Treason, Blindness and Silence. Dilemmas of the Intellectual in Modern France', in Jeremy Jennings and Anthony Kemp-Welch (eds), *Intellectuals in Politics*, London: Routledge, 1997, pp. 65–85

Jensen, Ronald J., 'Eugene Schuyler and the Balkan Crisis', *Diplomatic History*, vol. 5, no. 1, 1981, pp. 23–37

Jezernik, Božidar, *Dežela, kjer je vse narobe: Prispevki k etnologiji Balkana*, Ljubljana: Znanstveno in publicistično središče, 1998

Johnson, Sam, ' "Confronting the East". Darkest Russia, British Opinion and Tsarism's "Jewish question" ', *East European Jewish Affairs*, vol. 36, no. 2, 2006, pp. 119–211

Jonca, Karol, *Noc kryształowa i casus Herschela Grynszpana*, Wrocław: Wydawn, 1998

Jones, W. R., 'The Image of the Barbarian in Medieval Europe (in Perception of Ethnic and Cultural Differences)', *Comparative Studies in Society and History*, vol. 13, no. 4, 1971, pp. 376–407

Judah, Tim, *The Serbs. History, Myth and Destruction of Yugoslavia*, New Haven, CT and London: Yale University Press, 1997

Judge, Edward H., *Easter in Kishinev: Anatomy of a Pogrom*, New York: New York University Press, 1992

Kahn, Victoria Ann, and Hutson, Lorna, *Rhetoric and Law in the Early Modern Europe*, New Haven, CT and London: Yale University Press, 2001

Kaiser, Hilmar, 'The Baghdad Railway 1915–1916: A Case Study in German Resistance and Complicity', in Richard Hovannisian (ed.), *Remembrance and Denial: The Case of the Armenian Genocide*, Detroit, MI.: Wayne State University Press, 1999, pp. 67–112

Kallis, Aristotle A., 'The Jewish Community of Salonica Under Siege: The Antisemitic Violence of the Summer of 1931', *Holocaust and Genocide Studies*, vol. 20, no. 1, spring 2006, pp. 34–56

Kappeler, Andreas, 'Ukrainian History from a German Perspective', *Slavic Review*, vol. 54, no. 3, 1995, pp. 691–701

Karakasidou, Anastasia N., *Fields of Wheat, Hills of Blood: Passages to Nationhood in Greek Macedonia 1870–1990*, Chicago: University of Chicago Press, 1997

Karlinsky, Simon (ed), *Anton Chekhov's Life and Thought: Selected Letters and Commentary*, trans. Michael Henry Heim, Evanston, IL: Northwestern University Press, 1997

Karsten, Stefan, *Der Völkermord an den Armeniern in Romanen von Werfel, Hilsenrath, Mangelsen und Balakian*. Munich/Ravensburg: Grin Verlag, 2007

Kasaba, Reşat, 'İzmir 1922; A Port City Unravels', in Leila Fawaz and C. A. Bayly, with the collaboration of Robert Ilbert (eds), *Modernity and Culture from the Mediterranean to the Indian Ocean, 1890–1920*, New York: Columbia University Press, 2002, pp. 204–29

Kassimeris, George, *Warrior's Dishonour: Barbarity, Morality and Torture in Modern Warfare*, Dartmouth: Ashgate, 2006

Kellogg, Michael, *The Russian Roots of Nazism: White Emigrés and the Making of National Socialism*, Cambridge: Cambridge University Press, 2005

Kershaw, Ian, *Popular Opinion and Political Dissent in the Third Reich: Bavaria 1933–1945*, Oxford: Oxford University Press, 2002

Kévorkian, Raymond, *Le Génocide des Arméniens*, Paris: Odile Jacob, 2006

Khiterer, Victoria, 'Arnold Davidovich Margolin: Ukrainian–Jewish Jurist, Statesman and Diplomat', *Revolutionary Russia*, vol. 18, no. 2, 2005, pp. 145–67

Khodarkovsky, Michael, 'Of Christianity, Enlightenment, and Colonialism: Russia in the North Caucasus, 1550–1800', *Journal of Modern History*, vol. 71, no. 2, 1999, pp. 394–430

Kiernan, Ben, *Blood and Soil. A World History of Genocide and Extermination from Sparta to Darfur*, New Haven, CT: Yale University Press, 2007

Kieval, Hillel J., 'Antisémitisme ou savoir social? Sur la genèse du procès moderne pour meurtre rituel', *Annales: Histoire, Sciences Sociales*, vol. 49, no. 5, 1994, pp. 1,091–1,105

———— 'Death and the Nation: Jewish Ritual Murder as Political Discourse in the Czech Lands', *Jewish History*, vol. 10, no. 1, 1996, pp. 75–91

Kirli, Biray Kolluoğlu, 'Forgetting the Smyrna Fire', *History Workshop Journal*, vol. 60, autumn 2005, pp. 25–44

Kitromilides, Paschalis, ' "Balkan mentality": History, Legend, Imagination', *Nations and Nationalism*, vol. 2, no. 2, 1996, pp. 163–91

Klier, John, 'The Pogrom Paradigm in Russian History', in John Klier and Shlomo Lambroza, (eds), *Pogroms: Anti-Jewish Violence in Modern Russian History*, Cambridge: Cambridge University Press, 1991, pp. 13–38

———— 'Russian Jewry on the Eve of the Pogroms', in John Klier and Shlomo Lambroza, (eds), *Pogroms: Anti-Jewish Violence in Modern Russian History*, Cambridge: Cambridge University Press, 1991, pp. 3–12

———— 'Soviet Jewry on the Eve of the Holocaust', *Slavonic and East European Review*, vol. 81, no. 2, 2003, pp. 368–9

———— 'Cry Bloody Murder', *East European Jewish Affairs*, vol. 36, no. 2, December 2006, pp. 213–29

Klotz, Martin B., 'Poetry of the Present: Isaak Babel's Red Cavalry', *Slavic and East European Journal*, vol. 18, no. 2, 1974, pp. 160–9

Klugkist, Thomas, *Der pessimistische Humanismus: Thomas Manns lebensphilosophische Adaption der Schopenhauerschen Mitleidsethik*, Würzburg: Verlag Königshausen und Neumann, 2002

Knepper, Paul, 'British Jews and the Racialisation of Crime in the Age of Empire', *British Journal of Criminology*, vol. 47, no. 1, 2007, pp. 61–79

Köhler Thomas and Christian Mertens (eds), *Justizpalast in Flammen. Ein brennender Dornbusch. Das Werk von Manès Sperber, Heimito von Doderer und Elias Canetti angesichts des 15. Juli 1927*, Vienna/Munich: Verlag für Geschichte und Politik/Oldenbourg Wissenschaftsverlag, 2006

Kohut, Zenon E., 'The Khmelnytsky Uprising, the Image of Jews, and the Shaping of Ukrainian Historical Memory', *Jewish History*, vol. 17, no. 2, May 2003, pp. 141–63

Kolb-Seletski, Natalia M., 'Elements of Light in the Fiction of Korolenko', *Slavic and East European Journal*, vol. 16, no. 2, 1972, pp. 173–83

Kolluoğlu Kirli, Biray, 'Forgetting the Smyrna Fire', *History Workshop Journal*, vol. 60, no. 1, 2005, pp. 25–44

Kössler, Gottfried, Angelika Rieber and Feli Gürsching (eds), . . . *dass wir nicht erwünscht waren: Novemberpogrom 1938 in Frankfurt am Main. Berichte und Dokumente*, Frankfurt: Dipa-Verlag, 1993

Kramer, Alan, *Dynamic of Destruction: Culture and Mass Killing in the First World War*, Oxford: Oxford University Press, 2007

Kuper, Leo, *Genocide: Its Political Use in the Twentieth Century*, New Haven, CT: Yale University Press, 1982

Kuraev, Oleksyj, 'Der Verband "Freie Ukraine" im Kontext der deutschen Ukraine-Politik des Ersten Weltkriegs', *Osteuropa-Institut Muenchen: Mitteilungen*, no. 35, August 2000, pp. 1–47

Lahiri, Shompa, *Indians in Britain: Anglo-Indian Encounters, Race and Identity, 1880–1930*, London: Frank Cass, 1999

Lambroza, Shlomo, 'The Pogroms of 1903–1906', in John Klier and Shlomo Lambroza, (eds), *Pogroms: Anti-Jewish Violence in Modern Russian History*, Cambridge: Cambridge University Press, 1991, pp. 195–247

LaVaque-Manty, Mika, 'Dueling for Equality: Masculine Honor and the Modern Politics of Dignity', *Political Theory*, vol. 34, no. 6, 2006, pp. 715–40

Le Rider, Jacques, *Modernité viennoise et crises de l'identité*, Paris: Presses Universitaires de France, 1990

Levene, Mark, 'The Changing Face of Mass Murder: Massacre, Genocide and Post-Genocide', *International Social Science Journal*, vol. 54, no. 174, 2002, pp. 443–52

———— 'The Experience of Genocide: Armenia 1915–1916 and Romania 1941–1942', in Hans-Lukas Kieser and Dominik J. Schaller (eds), *Der Völkermord an den Armenien und die Shoah*, Zürich: Chronos Verlag, 2002, pp. 423–62

———— *Genocide in the Age of the Nation State: The Rise of the West and the Coming of Genocide*, Vols 1–2, London: I. B. Tauris, 2005

Levin, Vladimir, 'The Jewish Socialist Parties in Russia in the Period of Reaction', in Stefani Hoffman and Ezra Mendelsohn (eds), *The Revolution of 1905 and Russia's Jews*, University Park, PA: Penn State Press, 2008, pp. 111–27

Lieberman, Benjamin, 'Ethnic Cleansing in the Greek and Turkish Conflicts from the Balkan Wars through the Treaty of Lausanne: Identifying and Defining Ethnic Cleansing', in Steven Vardy and Hunt Tooley (eds), *Ethnic Cleansing in Twentieth Century Europe*, New York: Columbia University Press, 2003, pp 181–97

———— 'Nationalist Narratives, Violence between Neighbours and Ethnic Cleansing in Bosnia-Hercegovina: A Case of Cognitive Dissonance?', *Journal of Genocide Research*, vol. 8, no. 3, 2006, pp. 295–10

———— *Terrible Fate: Ethnic Cleansing in the Making of Modern Europe*, Chicago: Ivan R. Dee, 2006

Lih, Lars T. 'The Mystery of the ABC', *Slavic Review*, vol. 56, no. 1, 1997, pp. 50–72

Lindemann, Albert S., *The Jew Accused: Three Anti-Semitic Affairs (Dreyfus, Beilis, Frank) 1894–1915*, Cambridge: Cambridge University Press, 1991

Liulevicius, Vejas Gabriel, *War Land on the Eastern Front. Culture, National Identity and German Occupation in World War I*, Cambridge: Cambridge University Press, 2000

Lohr, Eric, 'The Russian Army and the Jews: Mass Deportation, Hostages, and Violence during World War I', *Russian Review*, vol. 60, no. 3, 2001, pp. 404–19

Loughlin, Michael B., 'Gustave Herve's Transition from Socialism to National Socialism: Continuity and Ambivalence', *Journal of Contemporary History*, vol. 38, no. 4, 2003, pp. 515–38

Lower, Wendy, 'Anticipatory Obedience and the Nazi Implementation of the Holocaust in the Ukraine: A Case Study of Central and Peripheral Forces in the Generalbezirk Zhytomyr, 1941–1944', *Holocaust and Genocide Studies*, vol. 16, no. 1, 2002, pp. 1–22

Löwith, Karl, *Von Hegel zu Nietzsche. Der revolutionäre Bruch im Denken des 19. Jahrhunderts*, Hamburg: Meiner Verlag, 1995

Luz, Ehud, 'The Moral Price of Sovereignty. The Dispute about the Use of Military Power within Zionism', *Judaism*, vol. 7, no. 1, February 1987, pp. 51–98

McCarthy, Justin, *Death and Exile: The Ethnic Cleansing of Ottoman Muslims 1821–1922*, Princeton, NJ: Darwin Press, 1996

Madley, Benjamin, 'From Africa to Auschwitz: How German South West Africa Incubated Ideas and Methods Adopted and Developed by the Nazis in Eastern Europe', *European History Quarterly*, vol. 35, no. 3, 2005, pp. 429–64

Magocsi, Paul, *A History of Ukraine*, Toronto: University of Toronto Press, 1996

Malcolm, Noel, *Kosovo. A Short History*, London: Macmillan, 1998

Mamedov, Mikhail, ' "Going Native" in the Caucasus: The Impact of the Region on Russian Identity in the First Half of the Nineteenth Century', Paper delivered at the American Association for the Advancement of Slavonic Studies, Pittsburgh, 21–24 November 2002

Mandel, Maud, *In the Aftermath of Genocide: Armenians and Jews in Twentieth-Century France*, Durham, NC: Duke University Press, 2003

Mango, Andrew, *Atatürk*, London: John Murray, 1999

Mann, Michael, *The Dark Side of Democracy. Explaining Ethnic Cleansing*, Cambridge: Cambridge University Press, 2005

Marks, Steven G., *How Russia Shaped the Modern World: From Art to Anti-Semitism, Ballet to Bolshevism*, Princeton, NJ: Princeton University Press, 2004

Marriott, John A. R., *The Eastern Question: An Historical Study in European Diplomacy*, Oxford: Clarendon Press, 1940

Marrus, Michael R., 'The History of the Holocaust: A Survey of Recent Literature', *Journal of Modern History*, vol. 59, no. 1, 1987, pp. 114–60

———— 'Hannah Arendt and the Dreyfus Affair', *New German Critique*, no. 66, Special Issue on the Nineteenth Century, 1995, pp. 147–63

Matković, Hrvoje, *Povijest Nezavisne Države Hrvatske*, Zagreb: Nakalda Pavičić, 1994

Mazower, Mark, *The Balkans*, London: Weidenfeld & Nicolson, 2000

———— 'The G-Word', *London Review of Books*, vol. 23, no. 3, 8 February 2001, pp. 1–5

———— *Inside Hitler's Greece*, New Haven, CT: Yale University Press, 2001

———— *Salonica, City of Ghosts: Christians, Muslims and Jews*, London: HarperCollins, 2005

Melson, Robert F., *Revolution and Genocide: On the Origins of the Armenian Genocide and the Holocaust*, Chicago: University of Chicago Press, 1992

Mentzer, Raymond A. and Andrew Spicer, *Society and Culture in the Huguenot World, 1559–1685*, Cambridge: Cambridge University Press, 2002

Merlino, Joseph P., Marilyn S. Jacobs, Judy Ann Kaplan and K. Lynne Moritz (eds), *Freud at 150: 21st-Century Essays on a Man of Genius*, Plymouth: Rowman & Littlefield, 2008

Meyer, Henry C., 'Rohrbach and his Osteuropa', *Russian Review*, vol. 2, no. 1, 1942, pp. 60–9

De Michelis, Cesare G., *Il manoscritto inesistente: I 'Protocolli dei Savi di Sion': Un apocrifo del XX secolo*, Venice: Marsilio, 1998

Michlic, Joanna Beata, *Poland's Threatening Other. The Image of the Jew from 1880 to the Present*, Lincoln, NE: University of Nebraska Press, 2006

Milazzo, Matteo, *The Chetnik Movement and Yugoslav Resistance*, Baltimore and London: Johns Hopkins University Press, 1975

Milich, Zorka, *A Stranger's Supper: An Oral History of Centegenarian Women in Montenegro*, New York: Twayne Publishers, London: Prentice Hall International, 1995

Miller, Donald E. and Lorna Touryan Miller, 'The Armenian and Rwandan Genocides: Some Preliminary Reflections on Two Oral History Projects with Survivors', *Journal of Genocide Research*, vol. 6, no. 1, 2004, pp. 135–40

Miller, Nick, *The Non-Conformists: Culture, Politics and Nationalism in a Serbian Intellectual Circle, 1944–1991*, Budapest: Central European Press, 2007

Mirnić, Josip, *Nemci u Bačkoj u drugom svetskom ratu*, Novi Sad: Institut za izućavanje istorije Vojvodine, 1974

Mitrović, Andrej, *Prodor na Balkan. Srbija u planovima Austro-Ugarske i Nemačke 1908–1918*, Belgrade: Nolit, 1981

———— *Srbija u prvom svetskom ratu*, Belgrade: Srpska književna zadruga, 1984

———— *Serbia's Great War 1914–1918*, London: Hurst, 2007

Moeller-Sally, Stephen, 'Parallel Lives: Gogol's Biography and Mass Readership in Late Imperial Russia', *Slavic Review*, vol. 54, no. 1, 1995, pp. 62–79

Mondry, Henrietta, *Pisateli-narodniki i evrei. G. I. Uspenskiĭ i V. G. Korolenko*, St Petersburg: Akademicheskiĭ proekt, 2005

Moore, Gregory, 'From Buddhism to Bolshevism: Some Orientalist themes in German Thought', *German Life and Letters*, vol. 56, no. 1, 2003, pp. 20–42

Moranian, Suzanne E., 'The Armenian Genocide and American Missionary Relief Efforts', in Jay Winter (ed.), *America and the Armenian Genocide*, Cambridge: Cambridge University Press, 2003, pp. 185–213

Mosse, Werner E. and Arnold Paucker (eds.), *Deutsches Judentum in Krieg und Revolution 1916–1923*, Tübingen: Schriftenreihewissenschaftlicher Abhandlungen des Leo Baeck Instituts 25, 1971

Murav, Harriet, 'The Beilis Ritual Murder Trial and the Culture of Apocalypse', *Cardozo Studies in Law and Literature*, vol. 12, no. 2, 2000, pp. 243–63

———— *Identity Theft: The Jew in Imperial Russia and the Case of Avraam Uri Kovner*, Palo Alto, CA: Stanford University Press, 2003

Mutafchieva, Vera, 'The Notion of the "Other" in Bulgaria: The Turks. A Historical Study', *Anthropological Journal on European Cultures*, vol. 4, no. 2, 1995, pp. 53–74

Myhill, John, *Language, Religion and National Identity in Europe and the Middle East: A Historical Study*, Philadelphia, PA: J. Benjamins, 2006

Naimark, Norman M., *Fires of Hatred: Ethnic Cleansing in Twentieth Century Europe*, Cambridge, MA: Harvard University Press, 2001

Nassibian, Akaby, *Britain and the Armenian Question 1915–1923*, Beckenham: Croom Helm, 1984

Nicault, Catherine, 'Le Procès des "Protocoles des Sages de Sion": Une tentative de riposte juive à l'antisémitisme dans les années 1930', *Vingtième Siècle. Revue d'histoire*, no. 53, January–March, 1997, pp. 68–84

Noveck, Beth, 'Hugo Bettauer and the Political Culture of the First Republic', in Günter Bischof, Anton Pelinka and Rolf Steininger (eds), *Austria in the Nineteen Fifties*, Edison, NJ: Transaction Publishers, 1995, pp. 138–70

Olson, Robert W., 'The Remains of Talat: A Dialectic between Republic and Empire', *Die Welt des Islams*, New Series, vol. 26, nos 1–2, 1986, pp. 46–56

Orbach, Alexander, *New Voices of Russian Jewry: A Study of the Russian–Jewish Press of Odessa*, Leiden: Brill, 1980

Owen, Thomas C., *The Corporation Under Russian Law, 1800–1917: A Study in Tsarist Economic Policy*, Cambridge: Cambridge University Press, 2002

Palmier, Jean-Michel, *Weimar in Exile: The Antifascist Emigration in Europe and America*, London: Verso, 2006

Paris, Edmond, *Genocide in Satellite Croatia, 1941–45*, Chicago: American Institute for Balkan Affairs, 1961

Passmore, John, 'The Treatment of Animals', *Journal of the History of Ideas*, vol. 36, no. 2, 1975, pp. 195–218

Pauley, Bruce F., *From Prejudice to Persecution. A History of Austrian Anti-Semitism*, Chapel Hill, NC: University of North Carolina Press, 1998

Pavlović, Srdja, 'Understanding Balkan Nationalism: The Wrong People, in the Wrong Place, at the Wrong Time', *Southeast European Politics*, vol. 1, no. 2, 2000, pp. 115–24

Pavlowitch, Stevan K., *A History of the Balkans 1804–1945*, London: Longman, 1999

Pegalow, Thomas, ' "German Jews", "National Jews", "Jewish Volk" or "Racial Jews"? The Constitution and Contestation of "Jewishness" in Newspapers of Nazi Germany, 1933–1938', *Central European History*, vol. 35, no. 2, 2002, pp. 195–221

Penkower, Monty Naum, 'The Kishinev Pogrom of 1903: A Turning Point in Jewish History', *Modern Judaism*, vol. 24, no. 3, 2004, pp. 187–225

Pérez, Joseph, *The Spanish Inquisition: A History*, New Haven, CT: Yale University Press, 2005.

Peristiany, Jean G., (ed.), *Honour and Shame: The Values of Mediterranean Society*, Chicago: University of Chicago Press, 1966

Peto, Artan, 'La Communauté juive en Albanie avant et durant la seconde guerre mondiale', in Ioannes K. Chasiotes et al. (eds), *The Jewish Communities of Southeastern Europe: From the Fifteenth Century to the End of World War II*, Thessalonica: Institute for Balkan Studies, 1997, pp. 427–31

Platt, Kevin M. F., *History in a Grotesque Key: Russian Literature and the Idea of Revolution*, Stanford, CA: Stanford University Press, 1997

Poliakov, Léon, *The History of Anti-Semitism*, Philadelphia, PA: University of Pennsylvania Press, Vol. 4, 2003

Posen, Barry R., 'The Security Dilemma and Ethnic Conflict', *International Security*, vol. 35, no. 1, 1993, pp. 27–47

Power, Samantha, '*A Problem from Hell*. America and the Age of Genocide*, New York: Perennial, 2003

Prein, Philipp, 'Guns and Top Hats: African Resistance in German South West Africa 1907–1915', *Journal of South African Studies*, vol. 20, no. 1, 1992, pp. 99–121

Proffer, Carl R., 'Gogol's *Taras Bulba* and the *Iliad*', *Comparative Literature*, vol. 17, no. 2, 1965, pp. 142–50

Quartaert, Donald, 'Machine Breaking and the Changing Carpet Industry of Western Anatolia, 1860–1908', *Journal of Social History*, vol. 19, no. 3, 1986, pp. 473–500

Quasimodo, Salvatore, *Il falso e vero verde: Con un discorso sulla poesia*, Milan: Mondadori, 1956

Rabinowitch, Alexander, 'The Shchastny File: Trotsky and the Case of the Hero of the Baltic Fleet', *Russian Review*, vol. 58, no. 4, 1999, pp. 615–34

Rae, Heather, *State Identities and the Homogenisation of Peoples*, Cambridge: Cambridge University Press, 2002

Ragni, Stefano, 'Les Huguenots di Meyerbeer, tra George Sand e Mazzini', *Annali dell'Università per Stranieri di Perugia*, N.S.I. 1993, pp. 165–81

Redfield, Robert, *Peasant Culture and Society*, Chicago: University of Chicago Press, 1965

Reeves, William Pember, *The Great Powers and the Eastern Christians: Christiani ad Leones! A Protest*, London: Anglo-Hellenic League, 1922

Reid, James, 'Batak 1876: A Massacre and Its Significance', *Journal of Genocide Research*, vol. 2, no. 3, 2000, pp. 375–409

Richards, Michael, *A Time of Silence: Civil War and the Culture of Repression in Franco's Spain 1936–1945*, Cambridge: Cambridge University Press, 1998

Riha, Thomas, 'Riech: A Portrait of a Russian Newspaper', *Slavic Review*, vol. 22, no. 4, 1963, pp. 663–82

Robb, Graham, *Victor Hugo*, London: Macmillan, 1997

Rogger, Hans, 'The Beilis Case: Anti-Semitism and Politics in the Reign of Nicholas II', *American Slavic and East European Review*, vol. 25, no. 4 1964, pp. 615–29

———— *Russia in the Age of Modernisation and Revolution, 1881–1917*, London: Longman, 1983

Roizen, Ron, 'Herschel Grynszpan: The Fate of a Forgotten Assassin', *Holocaust and Genocide Studies*, vol. 1, no. 2, 1986, pp. 217–28

Rorty, Richard, 'Human Rights, Rationality and Sentimentality', in idem, *Truth and Progress. Philosophical Papers*, Cambridge: Cambridge University Press, 1998, pp. 167–85

Rosen, Georg, *Die Balkan-Haiduken*, Leipzig: F. A. Brockhaus, 1878

Roshwald, Aviel, 'Jewish Cultural Identity in Eastern and Central Europe during the Great War', in Aviel Roshwald and Richard Stites (eds), *European Culture in the Great War: The Arts, Entertainment and Propaganda, 1914–1918*, Cambridge: Cambridge University Press, 1999, pp. 89–125

———— *Ethnic Nationalism and the Fall of Empires: Central Europe, Russia and the Middle East, 1914–1923*, New York: Routledge, 2001

Rothkirchen, Livia, *The Jews of Bohemia and Moravia: Facing the Holocaust*, Lincoln, NE: University of Nebraska Press, 2005

Rothschild, Joseph, *Ethnopolitics: A Conceptual Framework*, New York: Columbia University Press, 1981

Rousso, Henry, 'The Dreyfus Affair in Vichy France: Past and Present in French Political Culture', in Jonathan Frankel (ed.), *The Fate of the European Jews, 1939–1945. Continuity or Contingency?*, Oxford: Oxford University Press 1997, pp. 153–69

Rubinstein, William D., *Genocide*, London: Longman, 2004

Rugg, Dean S., *Eastern Europe*, London: Longman, 1985

Rummel, Rudi. J., *Death by Government: Genocide and Mass Murder since 1900*, New Brunswick, NJ: Transaction Publishers, 1994

Said, Edward, *Orientalism. Western Conceptions of the Orient*, 2nd edn, London: Penguin, 1995

Samper, Rudolf, *Die neuen Jakobiner: Der Aufbruch der Radikalen*, Munich: Herbig Verlag, 1981

Sanna, Vittoria, *I Romanzi Gotici di Ann Radcliffe*, Pisa: ETS Editrice, 1985

Sava, George, *The Chetniks*, London: Regular Publication, 1955

Schabas, William A., *Genocide in International Law: The Crimes of Crimes*, Cambridge: Cambridge University Press, 2000

Schaller, Dominik, 'Die Rezeption des Völkermordes an den Armeniern in Deutschland', in Hans-Lukas Kieser and Dominik J. Schaller (eds), *Der Völkermord an den Armeniern und die Shoah*, Zürich: Chronos Verlag, 2002, pp. 517–55

Schindler, John R., 'Yugoslavia's First Ethnic Cleansing. The Expulsion of the Danubian Germans 1944–46', in Steven Béla Várdy and T. Hunt Tooley (eds), *Ethnic Cleansing in 20th-Century Europe*, Boulder, CO: Social Science Monographs, Columbia University Press, 2003, pp. 359–72

———— 'Defeating Balkan Insurgency: The Austro-Hungarian Army in Bosnia–Hercegovina, 1878–82, *Journal of Strategic Studies*, vol. 27, no. 3, 2004, pp. 528–52

Schlee Günther (ed.), *Imagined Differences: Hatred and the Construction of Identity*, New York: Palgrave, 2004

Schmaltz, Eric J. and Samuel D. Sinner, 'The Nazi Ethnographic Research of Georg Leibbrandt and Karl Stumpp in Ukraine, and its North American Legacy', in Ingo Haar and Michael Fahlbusch (eds), *German Scholars and Ethnic Cleansing, 1920–1945*, New York and Oxford: Berghahn, 2005, pp. 51–85

Schnöring, Kurt, *Auschwitz begann in Wuppertal: Jüdisches Schicksal unter dem Hakenkreuz*, Wuppertal: Hammer Verlag, 1981

Schröter, Klaus, *Heinrich Mann*, Hamburg: Rewohlt, 1967

Schwandner-Sievers, Stephanie, 'The Enactment of "Tradition". Albanian Constructions of Identity, Violence and Power in Times of Crisis', in Bettina E. Schmidt and Ingo W. Schröder (eds), *Anthropology of Violence and Conflict*, London: Routledge, 2001, pp. 97–120

Scott, James C., *Weapons of the Weak: Everyday Forms of Peasant Resistance*, New Haven, CT: Yale University Press, 1985

Šehić, Nusret, *Četništvo u Bosni i Hercegovini (1918–1941). Politička uloga i oblici djelatnosti Četničkih udruženja*, Sarajevo: Akademija nauka i umjetnosti Bosne i Hercegovine, 1971

Sekelj, Laslo, 'Anti-Semitism in Yugoslavia, 1918–1945', *East European Quarterly*, vol. 22, no. 2, 1988, pp. 159–72

Sells, Michael, *The Bridge Betrayed: Religion and Genocide in Bosnia*, Berkeley: University of California Press, 1998

Sfikas, Thanasis D., 'National Movements and Nation Building in the Balkans, 1804–1922: Historic Origins, Contemporary Misunderstandings', in Thanasis D. Sfikas and Christopher Williams (eds), *Ethnicity and Nationalism in East Central Europe and the Balkans*, Ashgate: Aldershot, 1999, pp. 13–44

Shapira, Anita, ' "In the City of Slaughter" versus "He Told Her" ', *Prooftexts*, vol. 25, 2005, pp. 86–102

Shaw, Martin, *What Is Genocide?*, Cambridge: Polity, 2007

Sheffi, Na'ama, 'The Jewish Expulsion from Spain and the Rise of National Socialism on the Hebrew Stage', *Jewish Social Studies*, vol. 5, no. 3, 1999, pp. 82–103

Shenfield, Stephen, 'The Circassians: A Forgotten Genocide?', in Mark Levene and Penny Roberts (eds), *The Massacre in History*, Oxford: Berghahn, 1999, pp. 149–62

Shepherd, Ben, *War in the Wild East: The German Army and Soviet Partisans*, Cambridge, MA: Harvard University Press, 2004

Sicher, Efraim, ' "The Jewish Cossack". Isaac Babel in the First Red Calvary', in Jonathan Framkel (ed.), *The Jews and the European Crisis, 1914–1921*, Studies in Contemporary Jewry IV, Oxford: Oxford University Press, 1988, pp. 113–34

Simić, Andrei, 'Nationalism as Folk Ideology. The Case of the Former Yugoslavia', in Joel M. Halpern and David A. Kideckel (eds), *Neighbors at War. Anthropological Perspectives on Yugoslav Ethnicity, Culture and History*, Pennsylvania: Penn State Press, 2000, pp. 103–15

Skendi, Stavro, 'Crypto-Christianity in the Balkan Area under the Ottomans', *Slavic Review*, vol. 26, no. 2, 1967, pp. 227–46

Skinner, Barbara, 'Borderlands of Faith: Reconsidering the Origins of a Ukrainian Tragedy', *Slavic Review*, vol. 64, no. 1, 2005, pp. 88–116

Slezkine, Yuri, *The Jewish Century*, Princeton, NJ: Princeton University Press, 2004

Slijepčević, Djoko M., *Pitanje Bosne i Hercegovine u XIX veku*, Keln: Iskra, 1981

Sluga, Glenda, *The Problem of Trieste and the Italo-Yugoslav Border. Difference, Identity and Sovereignty in Twentieth Century Europe*, New York: SUNY, 2000

Sohrabi, Nader, 'Global Waves, Local Actors: What the Young Turks Knew about Other Revolutions and Why It Mattered', *Comparative Studies in Society and History*, vol. 44, 2002, pp. 45–79

Spector, Scott, 'Modernism Without Jews: A Counter-Historical Argument', *Modernism/ Modernity*, vol. 13, no. 4, 2006, pp. 615–34

Spence, Richard B., 'General Stephan Freiherr Sarkotić von Lovćen and Croatian Nationalism', *Croatian Review of Studies in Nationalism*, vol. 17, nos 1–2, 1990, pp. 147–55

Spoerri, Theophil, 'Mérimée and the Short Story', *Yale French Studies*, no. 4, *Literature and Ideas*, 1949, pp. 3–11

Staub, Ervin, *The Roots of Evil. The Origins of Genocide and other Group Violence*, Cambridge: Cambridge University Press, 1989

Stefanović, Djordje, 'Seeing the Albanians through Serbian Eyes: The Inventors of the Tradition of Intolerance and their Critics 1804–1939', *European History Quarterly*, vol. 35, no. 3, 2005, pp. 465–92

Stieg, Gerald, *Frucht des Feuers: Canetti, Doderer, Kraus und der Justizpalastbrand*, Vienna: Edition Falter, ÖBV, 1990

Stoianovich, Traian, *Balkan Worlds: The First and Last Europe*, New York and London: Sharpe, 1994

Stolleis, Michael, *A History of Public Law in Germany, 1914–1945*, Oxford: Oxford University Press, 2004

Stone, Dan, 'Genocide as Transgression', *European Journal of Social Theory*, vol. 7, no. 1, 2004, pp. 45–65

———— 'The Historiography of Genocide: Beyond "Uniqueness" and Ethnic Competition', *Rethinking History*, vol. 8. no. 1, 2004, pp. 127–42

Strom, Adam and Dan Eshet, *Totally Unofficial: Raphael Lemkin and the Genocide Convention*, Facing History and Ourselves Foundation, 2007, online at http://www.facinghistory.org

Subtelny, Orest, *A History of the Ukraine*, Toronto: University of Toronto Press, 2000

Tanner, Marcus, *Croatia. A Nation Forged in War*, New Haven, CT: Yale University Press, 1997

Tasić, Dragan, 'Gerilski rat u planovima vojska kraljevine Jugoslavije 1938–1941. godine', *Istorija 20. Veka*, vol. 13, no. 2, 1995, pp. 91–102

Taylor, Christopher C., *Sacrifice as Terror. The Rwandan Genocide of 1994*, Oxford: Berg, 1999

Todorova, Maria, *Imagining the Balkans*, New York/Oxford: Oxford University Press, 1997

Tolstoy, Nikolai, 'The Klagenfurt Conspiracy: War Crimes and Diplomatic Secrets', *Encounter*, vol. 60, no. 5, 1983, pp. 24–37

Tomasevich, Jozo, *War and Revolution in Yugoslavia*, Stanford, CA: Stanford University Press, 1975

Tomašić, Dinko, *Personality and Culture in East European Politics*, New York: Stewart, 1948

Torgovnick, Marianna, *The War Complex: World War II in Our Time*, Chicago: University of Chicago Press, 2005

Trachtenberg, Barry, 'Di Algemeyne Entsiklopedye, the Holocaust and the Changing Mission of Yiddish Scholarship', *Journal of Modern Jewish Studies*, vol. 5, no. 3, 2006, pp. 285–300

Trifković, Srdja, 'Rivalry between Germany and Italy in Croatia', *Historical Journal*, vol. 36, no. 4, 1993, pp. 879–904

Troyat, Henri, *Tolstoy*, Harmonsdsworth: Penguin, 1970

Trudgill, Peter, 'Greece and European Turkey: From Religious to Linguistic Identity', in Stephen Barbour and Cathie Carmichael (eds), *Language and Nationalism in Europe*, Oxford: Oxford University Press, 2000, pp. 240–63

Vahakn N., Dadrian, 'The Comparative Aspects of the Armenian and Jewish Cases of Genocide: A Sociohistorical Perspective', in Alan S. Rosenbaum (ed.), *Is the Holocaust Unique? Perspectives on Comparative Genocide*, Boulder, CO: Westview Press, 1996, pp. 101–35

Valentino, Benjamin A., *Final Solutions: Mass Killing and Genocide in the Twentieth Century*, Ithaca, NY: Cornell University Press, 2004

Vardy, Steven and Hunt Tooley (eds), *Ethnic Cleansing in Twentieth Century Europe*, New York: Columbia University Press, 2003

Verkaaik, Oskar, 'Fun and Violence: Ethnocide and the Effervescence of Collective Aggression', *Social Anthropology*, vol. 11, no. 1, 2003, pp. 3–22

———— *Migrants and Militants: Fun and Urban Violence in Pakistan*, Princeton, NJ: Princeton University Press, 2004

Voigt, Vilmos, '*Primus inter pares*. Why Was Vuk Karadžić the Most Influential Folk Lore Scholar in South Eastern Europe in the Nineteenth Century?', in Michael Branch and Celia Hawkesworth (eds), *The Uses of Tradition: A Comparative Enquiry into the Nature, Uses and Functions of Oral Poetry in the Balkans, the Baltic and Africa*, London: School of Slavonic and East European Studies, 1994, pp. 179–93

Vucinich, Wayne S., *The First Serbian Uprising 1804–1813*, New York: Columbia University Press, 1982

Vyleta, Daniel, 'Jewish Crimes and Misdemeanours: In Search of Jewish Criminality (Germany and Austria, 1890–1914)', *European History Quarterly*, vol. 35, no. 2, 2005, pp. 299–325

Wachtel, Andrew B., 'How to Use a Classic. Petar Petrović Njegoš in the Twentieth century', in John R. Lampe and Mark Mazower (eds). *Ideologies and National Identities: The Case of Twentieth Century Southeastern Europe*, Budapest: Central European University Press, 2004, pp. 131–53

Walker, Christopher J., *Armenia – The Survival of a Nation*, New York: St Martin's Press, 1980

Walser Smith, Helmut, *The Butcher's Tale. Murder and Anti-Semitism in a German Town*, New York and London: Norton 2002

———— *The Continuities of German History. Nation, Religion and Race across the Long Nineteenth Century*, Cambridge: Cambridge University Press, 2008

Ward, David, *T. S. Eliot Between Two Worlds: A Reading of T. S. Eliot's Poetry and Plays*, London: Routledge, 1973

Waxman, Meyer, *A History of Jewish Literature*, Vol. 4, part 1, New York: Thomas Yoseloff, 1960

Weaver, Gordon, *Conan Doyle and the Parson's Son: The George Edalji Case*, Cambridge: Vanguard, 2006

Weber, Thomas, 'Anti-Semitism and Philo-Semitism among the British and German Elites: Oxford and Heidelberg before the First World War', *English Historical Review*, vol. 118, no. 475, February 2003, pp. 86–119

Weinberg, Robert, 'Workers, Pogroms and the 1905 Revolution in Odessa', *Russian Review*, vol. 46, no. 1, 1987, pp. 53–75

Wiener, Jon, interviewer, 'Mike Davis Talks about "Heroes of Hell" ', *Radical History Review*, no. 85, winter 2003, pp. 227–37

Williams, Brian Glyn, 'Hijra and Forced Migration from Nineteenth-Century Russia to the Ottoman Empire', *Cahiers du monde russe*, vol. 41, no. 1, 2000, pp. 79–108

———— *The Crimean Tatars: The Diaspora Experience and the Forging of a Nation*, Leiden: Brill, 2001

———— 'Hidden Ethnocide in the Soviet–Muslim borderlands: The Ethnic Cleansing of the Crimean Tatars', *Journal of Genocide Research*, vol. 4, no. 3, 2002, pp. 357–73

Wilson, Andrew, *The Ukrainians: Unexpected Nation*, New Haven, CT and London: Yale University Press, 2000

Wilson, Stephen, *Ideology and Experience: Antisemitism in France at the Time of the Dreyfus Affair*, Rutherford, NJ: Fairleigh Dickinson University Press, 1982

Wimmer, Andreas, *Nationalist Exclusion and Ethnic Conflict: Shadows of Modernity*, Cambridge: Cambridge University Press, 2002

Wistrich, Robert S., *Laboratory for World Destruction. Germans and Jews in Central Europe*, Lincoln: Nebraska University Press/Vidal Sassoon International Center for the Study of Antisemitism, 2007

Woodhouse, C. M., *The Greek War of Independence: Its Historical Setting*, London: Hutchinson, 1952

Wysling, Hans W. (ed.), *Letters of Heinrich and Thomas Mann, 1900–1949*, Berkeley: University of California Press, 1998

Yeomans, Rory, 'Of "Yugoslav Barbarians" and Croatian Gentlemen Scholars: Nationalist Ideology and Racial Anthropology in Interwar Yugoslavia', in Marius Turda and Paul Weindling (eds), '*Blood And Homeland*': *Eugenics and Racial Nationalism in Central and Southeast Europe, 1900–1940*, Budapest: Central European University Press, 2006, pp. 83–122

Yokota-Murakami, Takayuki, 'Attila, Tolstoi, Edison: The Triangular Construction of a "Peace-Loving" Russian Identity across Borders', *Slavic and East European Journal*, vol. 45, no. 2, 2001, pp. 217–29

Young, Robert, *White Mythologies. Writing History and the West*, London: Routledge, 1990

Zamir, Israel, *Journey to My Father, Isaac Bashevis Singer*, New York: Arcade Publishing, 1995

Zayas, Alfred de, *A Terrible Revenge. The Ethnic Cleansing of the East European Germans*, London: Palgrave Macmillan, 2nd edn, 2006

Zenner, Walter, 'Middlemen Minorities', in John Hutchinson and Anthony Smith (eds), *Ethnicity*, Oxford: Oxford University Press, 1996, pp. 179–86

Zimmerer, Jürgen, 'Geburt des "Ostlandes" aus dem Geiste des Kolonialismus, Die national-sozialistische Eroberungs- und Beherrschungspolitik in (post-)kolonialer Perspektive', *Sozial Geschichte*, vol. 19, no. 1, 2004, pp. 10–43

———— 'Colonialism and the Holocaust. Towards an Archaeology of Genocide', in A. Dirk Moses (ed), *Genocide and Settler Society: Frontier Violence and Stolen Indigenous Children in Australian History*, New York/Oxford: Berghahn Books, 2004, pp. 49–76

———— *Von Windhuk nach Auschwitz. Beiträge zum Verhältnis von Kolonialismus und Holocaust*, Münster: LIT Verlag, 2007

Index